Fashion Design Course:
Accessories

Fashion Design Course:
Accessories

WITHDRAWN

Jane Schaffer & Sue Saunders

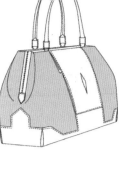

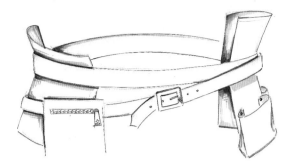

A QUARTO BOOK

First edition for North America published in 2012 by Barron's
Educational Series, Inc.
Copyright © 2012 Quarto Inc.
All rights reserved. No part of this publication may be
reproduced or distributed in any form or by any means without
the written permission of the copyright owner.

*All inquiries should
be addressed to:*
Barron's Educational Series, Inc.
250 Wireless Boulevard
Hauppauge, NY 11788
www.barronseduc.com

ISBN: 978-0-7641-4754-8

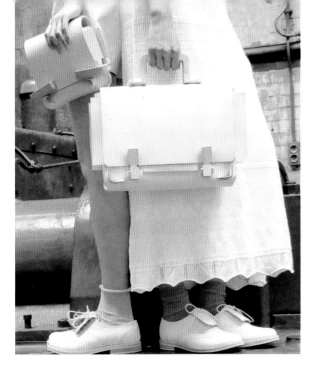

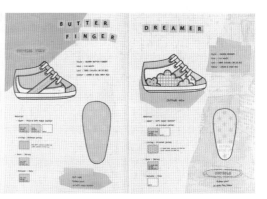

Library of Congress Control Number: 2011941528
QUAR:FGAD

Conceived, designed, and produced by
Quarto Publishing plc
The Old Brewery
6 Blundell Street
London N7 9BH

Editor: Lily de Gatacre
Art editor: Jo Bettles
Designers: Elizabeth Healey and Karin Skånberg
Design assistant: Rohit Arora
Art director: Caroline Guest
Copy editor: Ruth Patrick
Proofreader: Claudia Martin
Indexer: Ann Barrett
Picture researcher: Sarah Bell

Creative director: Moira Clinch
Publisher: Paul Carslake

Color separation in China by Pica International Pte Ltd
Printed in China by 1010 Printing International Ltd

9 8 7 6 5 4 3 2 1

ABOUT THIS BOOK

This book will introduce you to the genre of accessory design. The three main chapters—handbags, footwear, and millinery—are structured in a similar way, each chapter covering parallel areas as they relate to the particular discipline under discussion. This structure is described in the panel below.

SECTION 1 • THE CREATIVE PROCESS
(PAGES 10–73)

From researching the brief and consumer research to initial design ideas, design development, materials selection, and presentation, this chapter introduces the creative process.

SECTION 2 • HANDBAGS
(PAGES 74–119)

Get to grips with the process of bag making: understand what a handbag designer puts into a spec sheet; evaluate and select the appropriate skin; learn about handbag "furniture" and how to design with a target customer in mind. See how many individual components make up a simple shoulder bag and how different bags are constructed.

SECTION 3 • FOOTWEAR
(PAGES 120–159)

An introduction to footwear design, including studying the key designers and looking over the shoulder of an experienced shoemaker as a shoe is assembled. Shoe designers must

HOW THE CHAPTERS ARE STRUCTURED

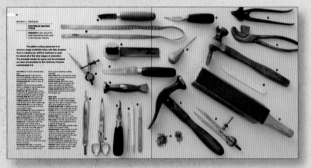

TOOLS OF THE TRADE
Looks at the key tools used in the craft.

Objective
A summary of the main teaching points and the skills you will acquire.

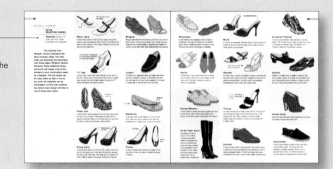

STYLE SELECTOR
Key styles are illustrated here, vintage and contemporary. An understanding of different styles helps designers build their own creations.

KEY DESIGNERS
Discusses leading designers, their signature looks, and iconic pieces.

ANATOMY
Here a bag, shoe, or hat is deconstructed to show its individual components.

Deconstructed examples
Samples are shown deconstructed, so sense can be made of what happens during their construction.

balance comfort with desirability, and these design considerations are discussed in full, along with illustrations showing the development of designs for all kinds of shoes, from the vertiginous high heel to the flat pump.

SECTION 4 • MILLINERY
(PAGES 160–203)

Discover the technical skills for blocking and shaping felt and straw hats and learn to make basic patterns for fabric hats. Materials and trims are discussed in depth and there's a collection of specialist millinery stitches explained with how-to instructions.

SECTION 5 • SMALL LEATHER GOODS
(PAGES 204–213)

As a category, small leather goods include gloves, belts, purses, wallets, key fobs, credit card holders, and other small items. Many of the construction methods and materials are similar to those described in the Handbags chapter, so this chapter is shorter than others, with the focus on gloves and belts.

SECTION 6 • RESOURCES AND PROFESSIONAL PRACTICE
(PAGES 214–251)

A resources section that looks at places to study and how to build a convincing résumé and portfolio to impress potential employers. Also included are the types of jobs you can expect to find in the industry, as well as a list of trade fairs, a further reading list, and detailed glossaries.

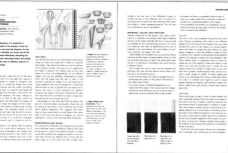

DESIGN CONSIDERATIONS
Lists, discusses, and illustrates the design elements that contribute to the creation of the perfect accessory.

Sidebars

Tips, checklists, and exercises that help you build a portfolio.

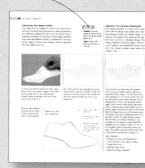

Glossary

Technical words and phrases are explained on the page that they are used (and also summarized at the back of the book).

TECHNICAL HOW-TOS
The basic construction methods for each of the three disciplines are explored using step-by-step photography and instructional captions, including pattern making, pattern cutting, and assembly.

Step-by-step sequences

Look over the shoulder of a professional at work.

MATERIALS
While leather is discussed in general in the opening chapter, here is an opportunity to look in detail at a range of specific materials, depending on the discipline you are designing for: appropriateness, relative cost, aesthetic appeal.

Visual examples

Packed with inspiring visual examples from initial brainstorming sketches to finessed designs, maquettes, and made-up samples.

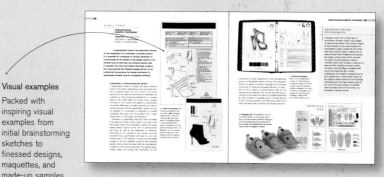

SPEC SHEETS
Specification sheets give all the vital instructions for the manufacture of a design. It is an essential tool for communication with your factory—the blueprint for your design. How to build a fail-safe spec for each of the categories is explained in full.

My interest in fashion started at an early age—my father worked in children's clothing and twice-yearly huge boxes of samples would arrive. I awaited them with great excitement, dove into the boxes, and helped him hang the garments up, making comments about the styles, colors, and fabrications, and—of course—which ones I wanted. At college I tried fashion design but garment construction held no interest for me, as the garment needed a body frame to make it three dimensional. I went on to study 3D design and my obsession with accessories started there, albeit in a very experimental way. Hats became my focus, and an apprenticeship with one of the Queen's milliners ensued. I fell into teaching by accident really, after a request from the Royal College of Art in London to help support a millinery project they had embarked upon with the womenswear students. More teaching followed, but I eventually gave up all other teaching and focused on developing the accessories courses at the London College of Fashion, firstly at degree level and then post-graduate. Responding to the market, the accessories courses focused on leather goods, and my enthusiasm and involvement with leather and bags grew. Teaching stimulates, invigorates, and astonishes; students never fail to amaze with their creativity and commitment. The area of accessory design is relatively niche, but it has had massive impact on the market in the last decade. It is a flourishing area of the fashion industry and there are many opportunities within it, so go for it.

J. Schaffer

JANE SCHAFFER

My first "I want those shoes" moment was at the age of four when a little girl walked by in a pair of bright red Mary Janes. I stared at them in delight, then envy when my mother said NO. My love affair with footwear began there and then, developed into a career as a designer, and more recently a lecturer. Through my work I have traveled the world, met many inspiring and talented people on the way, and seen excellence in shoemaking in the most unexpected places. Teaching has introduced me to some of the brightest and best young shoe designers, who learn, then challenge, the rules; question the constructions, materials, and techniques; and develop revolutionary ideas. I love the fact that just when I think I've seen everything, a student will come up with something completely surprising and new. Even after so many years in the industry, I am still learning; that is why I still do what I do. My aim in writing this book is to introduce you to the exciting world of shoe design and inspire you to think about a career in footwear. It will take you wherever you want to go. There is room for anyone with passion for the subject: be it in traditional shoes, performance footwear, or extreme fashion, you can find a place that fits your talents, and I hope you do.

Sue Saunders

SUE SAUNDERS

The creative process

This section will introduce you to the creative process that is used by all designers working in the industry, regardless of the product area or market level. The step-by-step process is used to gather inspiration and information, and to synthesize ideas and develop them into exciting yet realistic design solutions.

Learning the basic design process is the first stage for any designer and it is essential to master this through constant practice. Only then can you begin to experiment and develop your own personal style that will distinguish you from others in this highly competitive industry.

Being a designer in the fashion world is not for the faint-hearted. You must be absolutely passionate about your chosen career and about what you need to learn. There are so many factors that contribute to the realization of a product and you must understand and appreciate the importance of each one. It is a demanding and often exhausting job but when a collection finally comes together the exhilaration you will feel is an experience not to be missed. Learning about the processes you need to be in control of, and the many different aspects of the industry, will give you an idea of what the job entails.

SECTION 1 | THE CREATIVE PROCESS

WHAT MAKES A DESIGNER?

Objective Assess whether you have what it takes to become a designer.

On its own, the tried and tested methodology discussed in this chapter will not turn you into a successful designer. You must also have talent, ambition, the tenacity to overcome whatever problems you encounter, and be prepared to take risks. The more you put in, the more you will achieve.

▲ **Studying Egypt** This shoe is based on a study of ancient Egypt. The monumental statues, precise lines of paintings, and the reverence of cats have influenced this design. A good example of an abstraction from the original source material.

▼ **African influences** Here we see two pages from a sketchbook based on the textiles, weaving, beading, carving, sculpture, and colors of Africa. They demonstrate the wealth of source material available when you research different aspects of a particular culture.

Following the steps outlined in this chapter will introduce you to a logical way of working that produces results. Whether you are involved in a course of study, employed as a designer, or creating your own label, results are crucial. Responding to a brief in the right way is not just about exploring aesthetics. The consumer, the price points, the mood of the season, and the technical considerations relating to production must all be taken into consideration—a multifaceted task. Your ability to be proactive and reactive to the breadth of issues will determine your success.

RESPONDING TO A BRIEF

As you work through different briefs, you will develop your own way of approaching the process, adapting the method to suit you as an individual and discovering fast-track solutions to meet deadlines. At the same time, your confidence will build, and your personal style will develop. As a student, testing yourself against a variety of briefs will allow you to discover your strengths and weaknesses and where you might fit into the fashion world. If you are working for a well-known brand, your particular style will be important as that is the added value you can bring to a company. In developing your own collection, your signature look is crucial; this is what a consumer buys from a designer label.

In addition to the research you conduct for each individual brief, you need to familiarize yourself with a range of influences and background knowledge that will support your work. The stronger this knowledge is, the better your work will be—often you will already have some of the answers to a design brief in your repertoire, saving time in the initial stages and allowing you to focus on development at an earlier stage. It also means you can react positively to a last-minute request and deliver what is needed quickly and efficiently.

FASHION AND CULTURE

Cultural, social, and ethical influences are the fabric of our society and fashion is a reflection of this. Some cultures can be identified by their dress code, others reveal a wealth of traditional craft skills, while many

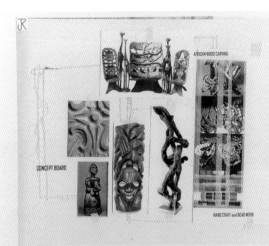

focus on new technology and what can be created now. Social influences are studied extensively by marketing experts to ensure consumers' needs are being addressed and new products created to increase demand. People-watching is a very good way for a designer to learn more about consumer lifestyles and fashion direction.

In recent years, ethical considerations, such as improving working conditions for people in the developing world, have become increasingly important. Reducing the carbon footprint of a product is being taken seriously by many companies, and creating products from sustainable materials is another focus. Our global society is becoming more responsible and serious in the way it approaches these issues, and that is apparent in the fashion industry today.

BE AWARE OF NEW DEVELOPMENTS

Contemporary fashion brands and new own-label designers have tremendous influence on the direction of fashion and the consumer. You need to keep up with what is happening in the world of fashion at all times to understand the prevailing mood and discover what is new. The same is true of retail: you need to know where the cool area is in each fashion capital and explore the newest shops. What product mix is being offered, and is it different from last year or the year before? Knowing what is going from season to season will help you to develop a sense of what is to come. This is true of e-tailing too. Keeping an eye on the latest fashion blogs will also help you to understand what the wider world is thinking.

Technology develops at an ever-increasing pace and, with it, new possibilities for the designer. It is essential to know what is available within your specialist area to support production. Having in-depth knowledge of all the techniques that can be used will extend your visual vocabulary as a designer. Beyond the creative process, there is a whole area of product development, quality control, sample monitoring, and sales that you could become involved in. Clear communication with manufacturers is vital to ensure you arrive at the end product you envisaged. Learning the correct terminology is the best way to achieve this. As it can vary from country to country, you must be alert to these differences.

EXERCISE: EXPLORING CULTURES

Identify a culture you have never delved into and research its textiles, painting, sculpture, music, dance, fashion, and customs. Create a sketchbook full of imagery from as many different sources as possible to enrich your experience and your visual resources. Understand the materials local to your chosen culture and how they have influenced that society's creations. Consider their production methods and how they compare with the world you are accustomed to. In using this research to create ideas, make sure you think about the context of the market you are designing for. A reproduction of the original will not work for today's consumer.

Being openly curious about the world around you will put you in tune with the spirit of the times, enabling you to develop a sense of what people will want next. You need to look forward, create your own unique blend of these influences, and have confidence in your vision. Study the history of fashion in general and in depth for your chosen specialist area. How often do you read in the fashion press about a return to the 1920s or the '60s? Reworking and renewing ideas from past decades is common practice. If you already know enough about the look of an era, you can immediately start to develop it in a new way for a different generation. When you revisit the past, it is important to create a look for today that refers to the past but does not replicate it.

THE DESIGN PROCESS

Key stages
- Brief
- Research
- Initial design ideas
- Analysis
- Design development 2D and 3D
- Analysis
- Design selection
- 2D presentation and communication
- Prototype production
- Presentation

Key elements
- Form
- Line
- Proportion and scale
- Texture(s) and materiality
- Color(s)
- Details
- Function
- Ergonomics

GLOSSARY

E-tailers: Online retailers.

▶ **Finding inspiration** This is an example of a simple indoor shoe decorated with the traditional embroidery of Estonia. The quality of the product does not match the high level of craftsmanship seen in the embroidery. A designer could be inspired to use these skills in a fashion context and create a quality product for a discerning consumer.

SECTION 1 | THE CREATIVE PROCESS

THE PROJECT BRIEF

Objective Learn how to understand, interpret, and scope out the brief.

The project brief is formulated to give you a clear set of guidelines regarding the project you are asked to undertake. The brief will state the requirements and the timescale in which you must complete the work. It is vital that you understand the importance of research planning and hone your project management skills.

▼ **Project brief** The brief describes the market level for which the designs are to be made. The inspirational context is outlined together with the line requirements and the work to be produced. Enough information is given to create a framework for project planning without inhibiting the designer's creativity.

Whether at college or already working in industry, all designers work to a brief, whether this is of their own creation or given by the creative director, project manager, or lecturer. Working in fashion industry design is about solving problems to create original products for an identified market. Industry briefs always state the season and market level you are working on, and they may include materials or color focus and any other technical constraints to consider.

It is key to remember that however well researched, designed, and constructed your ideas are, they will only be successful if they meet the requirements and conditions stated in the brief. In industry, you will need to work within the given constraints, whatever level of the market you are working for. Whether it is producing a collection of shoes that can be retailed at a certain price point, or a range of bag designs that can be produced using the manufacturing resources of a specified overseas factory, you must understand what your constraints are and work creatively within them.

In answering a brief, research is the essential ingredient informing successful design. Without in-depth research into a variety of areas, your work at college or in industry will lack true innovation.

INTERPRETING THE BRIEF

It is vital that you read the brief carefully and understand clearly what it asks of you. It is essential that this information is interpreted correctly to reach appropriate creative solutions. Check anything you do not understand before you start the project.

A brainstorm or concept map is often used at the start of the process to help extend and push your thinking—these will help you explore your initial thoughts and make connections. To start your concept map, write down your central idea, then think of new and connective ideas that radiate from this central initial idea. By focusing and connecting your thoughts, you are mapping your creative thinking and extending your ideas.

KEY STAGES
- What are you being asked to design? Is it specific or can you determine the outcome?
- Who are you designing for? Is the market level or market type stated?

PROJECT BRIEF

The new definition of luxury in today's fashion market means special and unique as opposed to mass production and limitless availability of products that can be seen across all market levels. Luxury can be about owning a product that very few people have, doing something that others have not, or simply having time and space to relax.

The consumer's growing interest in the different and the authentic can be seen in the re-emergence of handmade products, craft skills clubs, and searching for vintage pieces and secondhand products.

Consumers have also become more interested in the provenance and quality of the products they purchase. The rise in sales of locally produced or sourced goods is also an indicator that the consumer is concerned with how the products are grown or made and how many miles they have traveled to reach the store.

This project provides a valuable opportunity to integrate consumers' needs and desires into your design work and ultimately the end product. You will need to consider the creative, technical, and practical developments of ideas from concept to end product. It will encourage you to consider consumer lifestyles, aspirations, and consumer demands. It should show the development of a complete body of work that demonstrates the journey from research to realization with an understanding of how your products can target a specific consumer.

You are asked to create a Spring/Summer line of 12 designs for the luxury market incorporating and inspired by the traditional craft skills of a country/culture of your choice. Research into the market level and consumer is essential to create a focus for your creative thinking.

You are required to produce the following elements:
- A research sketchbook
- A concept board and a consumer board
- A written overview of the luxury market
- Initial design ideas
- Design development in 2D and 3D
- A design sheet for each of the 12 pieces
- A line plan
- A single prototype of one of the pieces in the line

PLANNING YOUR PROJECT

In order to ensure you are tracking all areas of the brief and will hit the deadline requirements, a plan of action is required. You need to consider: The What, The How, and The Why. By establishing and answering these, you can then prioritize the order they need to be completed in.

What... are you being asked to do?
are the deliverables?
information do you need?
research will be required?
are the constraints of the brief?
are your deadlines?

How... will you research this project?
will you communicate your findings?
will you manage your time?

Why... to identify the consumer.
to consider the level of need/desire.
to establish suppliers of materials/components/fittings.
to establish timelines for delivery of materials/fittings.
to establish market level.
to identify competitors.

EXERCISE

Part one
Write yourself a personal project brief, ensuring you have all the instructions needed. Decide upon a brand/label that you would like to work for. Then, assign a concept or theme that you feel would be brand appropriate and would give you a rich source of inspiration to explore.
• Brand
• Season
• Concept
• Product type and range
• Deliverables
• Deadline

Part two
Having written yourself a brief, formulate a concept map, placing your concept at the center. Connect your ideas to push your creative thinking and extend your links and branches as far as possible.

Part three
Write up a research plan considering where you will gather inspiration and information. Consider:
What?
Where?
Why?

• What are you actually being asked to produce? What are the deliverables?
• What is the deadline for the work's completion?

PLANNING YOUR RESEARCH

Research is essential to stir your creative juices. From your brainstorm/concept map, you can plan where to begin your research. Remember, it is an organic journey, and discoveries will lead on to things you had not previously considered.

Once you have established answers to The What, The How, and The Why, make an action plan with mini-deadlines built in to help you achieve your goals within the given time frame. A Gantt chart is a useful project management tool that can help you do this. In industry they are also used for resource planning, for managing costs, and for tracking such areas of project progress as marketing and promotion, designing, sampling, and delivery to the warehouse.

GLOSSARY

Brainstorm: A freethinking exercise where jotting down the first word that comes into your head leads to a connection to another thought or word, which connects to another, and so on.

Brief: A set of instructions for a project outlining the required deliverables within a given context.

Concept map: A visual plan taking the words from a brainstorming exercise and linking them logically in groups or paths.

Gantt chart: A visual project management tool creating a linear schedule, in the correct sequence, for each activity that must be undertaken to deliver the requirements of a project brief on time.

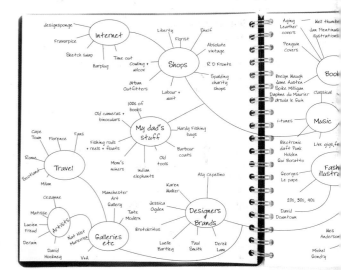

▲ **Concept map** In this mind map, a single word has been used as the starting point for a project. New ideas branch out from the original word as a note is made of every thought. Every new word has produced its own cluster of new ideas, and the map has to travel across to the facing page to express everything in the designer's mind.

DESIGN TOOLS

Objective Build a tool kit
of art materials.

Design materials are essential to
any designer because they are the tools of
our trade. Our visual communication needs to
have clarity, a level of professionalism, and the
means to convey our design message clearly to
our viewers. Leathers, fabrics, and materials need
to be rendered to give an accurate impression
of the surface quality and finish. Quality materials
and tools are key to creating a body of work
that will help you achieve your first step on the
career ladder.

◄ **Just doodling!**
Rough doodles and
back-of-the-envelope-
style sketches can be
done in the tool that's
closest to hand. This
sketch uses biro and
fine fibertip.

◄ **Thumbnail sketches** A middle-grade pencil is good for thumbanail drawings where precise lines and shading are both called for.

► **Line weights** Pencils come in a range of weights, reflecting the different marks they make.

GRAPHITE PENCILS

Graphite pencils of various grades are essential tools for all stages of the design process, from sketching out initial design ideas through penciling out development sheets. H denotes hardness—the higher the grade, the harder the lead and the more precise and faint the drawn line. B denotes blackness—the higher the number, the softer the lead, the more graphite is deposited on the paper and the blacker and softer the line is. Grades are typically 6B–B, HB, H–6H. HB is a middle-grade pencil such as a No. 2 pencil and is good for design work. Artists are more likely to use the softer B grades for rich lines, whereas architects need the clean, precise lines of the H-grade pencils.

Buying guide: Collect a range of grades from 2H to 6B. They are cheap to buy.

Paper: Can be used with all types of paper.

Strengths: Cheap and easy to buy, easy to carry with you, the line is erasable, and layouts can be mapped out prior to inking up.

Drawbacks: Lack of blackness to line and over time the line can fade.

Ease of use: Easy.

RETRACTABLE MECHANICAL PENCILS AND LEADS

Some designers prefer mechanical pencils to the traditional graphite pencils. A variety of leads can be purchased for these pencils, giving a range of hardness and blackness to the quality of your line drawing. They are similar in most ways to the more traditional pencil. Finding what works well for you is important. It is generally a matter of personal preference, so explore to discover.

Buying guide: Lead size will be your first consideration, followed by the shape of the pencil sleeve and the type of grip.

Strengths: The lead is often retractable, ensuring that it doesn't get broken in transport.

Drawbacks: The leads have to be sharpened by a blade.

Ease of use: Easy.

Note: Charcoal is rarely used in a design portfolio, since it can be rather dirty to use and tends to leave the crisp, white page gray and smudged.

INKING PENS

These pens are easy to use once confidence in drawing has been established. You may choose to draw directly using these pens for design development drawings. The thinner-line pens are used to ink in stitch lines and topstitch details. Try a variety of brands to see which you prefer, but you need a pen that has smooth, flowing ink, is water resistant, and won't fade.

Buying guide: Pens come in a variety of line thicknesses—it is worth purchasing a range: 0.05 mm, 0.1 mm, 0.2 mm, 0.3 mm, 0.4 mm, 0.5 mm, and 0.8 mm.

Paper: Can be used with all types of paper.

Strengths: Pen lines are excellent for showing details. Contour lines are sharp, the black ink line does not smear once dry, and it will not fade. They are cheap, easy to purchase, and very portable.

Drawbacks: Can dry up quickly.

Ease of use: Moderately difficult.

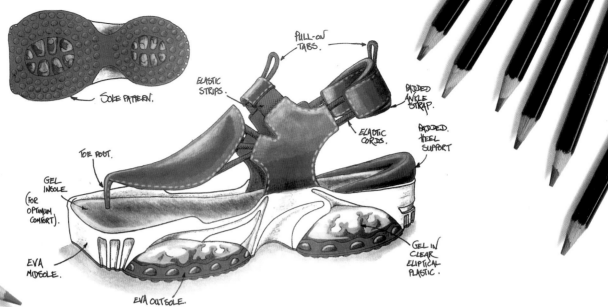

▶ **Wet and dry** The dual function of watercolor pencils as a wet and dry medium allows for loose washes and tight detail, both of which are shown to good effect in this example.

PULL-ON TABS.

ELASTIC STRIPS.

PADDED ANKLE STRAP.

ELASTIC CORDS.

PADDED HEEL SUPPORT.

SOLE PATTERN.

TOE ROOT.

GEL INSOLE (FOR OPTIMUM COMFORT).

EVA MIDSOLE.

EVA OUTSOLE.

GEL IN CLEAR ELLIPTICAL PLASTIC.

▲ **Lots of lovely colors** These pencils come in a huge range of shades. The softer the pencil, the easier it is to apply pigment to paper.

WATERCOLOR PENCILS

Watercolor pencils can be used with a brush and water or used dry as a pencil. They can be used alone or combined with other media, they are great for details and surface texture rendering, and Adobe Illustrator work can be worked into/over with colored pencils to add definition and surface details. Mixing media by applying a layer of marker or watercolors followed by colored pencils for details is a technique that works well. Colored pencils are often used on finished presentation drawings and on design sheets.

Buying guide: Watercolor pencils are available in a wide variety of colors. Buy a set and add to this by purchasing additional colors as you need them.

Paper: All types of paper work well with colored pencils; you can use them on any color or weight of paper. Watercolor pencils work better with a thicker paper or thick watercolor paper.

Strengths: Combined usage negates the need to buy colored pencils and watercolor pencils. Pencils can be used dry or wet. Pencil lines are excellent for showing details. Contour lines are sharp, and colored pencils come in a wide variety of colors.

Drawbacks: A few colored pencils are not enough to make a difference to your illustration—you'll need to buy a set. Pencils don't erase and are very waxy if applied too thickly.

Ease of use: Easy. A layered approach—using colored pencils to add details over a base layer of watercolor or marker—is a technique you will often use.

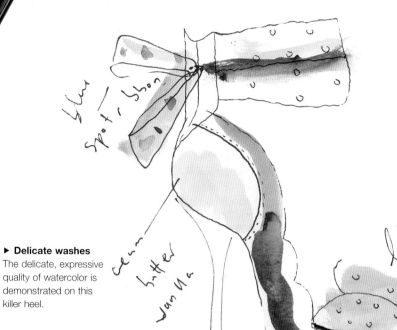

▶ **Delicate washes**
The delicate, expressive quality of watercolor is demonstrated on this killer heel.

▼ **Watercolor pans** Half pans are more readily available than pans.

WATERCOLOR

Watercolor is excellent for blended color, achieved by applying colors over clear water. Or aim for a looser application with paint drips, spatters, and surprise effects.

Buying guide: The choice is between tubes or pan colors that come in a set. For ease of use, pan colors are more workable. For better-quality color and pigment, or for mixing quantities of paint, choose tubes.

Paper: White paper is recommended: you will want to take advantage of the luminous quality of the paint by building up transparent layers. Thick watercolor paper is best, since the water causes thinner paper to buckle.

Strengths: Excellent for creating a vibrant and luminous surface appearance that can then be worked in to create detail.

Drawbacks: Watercolor paint is transparent, so it's hard to rectify a mistake by painting over it.

Ease of use: Moderately easy.

UNPREDICTABLE EFFECTS

Care needs to be taken because watercolor can drip and run; however, this can be part of the appeal of this media. By using wet-in-wet or dry-brush techniques, you can get a great many textures and effects. Watercolor paint is not permanent and will dissolve with water even after it is dry, so care in handling the finished illustration is necessary. When applying layers, care is needed to avoid muddy color effects and over-blended areas of paint. It is best used in combination with colored pencils.

▶ **Brushes** The larger the brush head, the more paint it will hold, so have a choice of sizes for different applications.

▶ **Watercolor tubes**
Always look for the label "artists' watercolor" and don't be tempted to buy the less expensive paints, known as students' colors.

GOUACHE: RECOMMENDED COLOR PALETTE

- Alizarin Crimson
- Spectrum Red
- Grenadine
- Bengal Rose
- Orange Lake Light
- Naples Yellow
- Spectrum Yellow
- Yellow Ocher
- Permanent Green Middle
- Olive Green
- Cobalt Blue
- Turquoise Blue
- Ultramarine Blue
- Prussian Blue
- Spectrum Violet
- Burnt Sienna
- Burnt Umber
- Van Dyke Brown
- Zinc White
- Jet or Lamp Black

▲ **Adaptable** Gouache is a wonderful paint: it has the properties and color brilliance of watercolor but it is opaque and becomes transparent when mixed with water.

GOUACHE

Gouache's color brilliance and opacity make it a popular choice among designers.

Buying guide: Buying a few paints in order to mix a full color range requires a selection of key colors. A basic palette would include: Permanent White, Ivory Black, Flame Red (warm), Bengal Rose (cool), Turquoise Blue (warm), Ultramarine Blue (cool), Cadmium Yellow Pale (warm), and Lemon Yellow (cool). From these basic colors, you can mix all the colors you will need. A fuller palette is recommended in the panel above.

Paper: Gouache paint can work on small format paper. A variety of surfaces are also possible, including the following paper types: white drawing paper, watercolor paper, and colored paper.

Strengths: Gouache paints are opaque and vibrant, or dilute them with water and they become transparent. From eight tubes, all color variations can be mixed. They produce a richly colored rendering with an attractive, velvety surface to the dried paint.

Drawbacks: Gouache does not dry permanent and a single drop of water on a finished piece can ruin the painted surface.

Ease of use: Moderate.

LIGHT-OVER-DARK LAYERING

Gouache paint is a valuable tool although it is not used widely in modern presentation techniques. It is rarely used alone and more often used with a mix of media. A light-colored gouache paint will easily cover a darker background paper surface or rendering. Care needs to be taken upon completion of the rendering to avoid ruining the paint surface, since gouache paint does not dry permanently.

▼ **Put a lid on it** Vibrant and in an unbelievable range of colors, markers' one drawback is that they dry out quickly.

◄ **Marker magic** Markers quickly cover large areas in saturated color.

MARKERS

These come in many guises—often markers are double ended, offering a thick line and a thin one. They can also be purchased with brush nibs that replicate a paintbrush stroke. They have lots of applications, including surface rendering, body rendering, and small-format illustrations. Colored markers will give you an immediate effect that can be layered and combined with pencils for maximum color and textural surface effects. To use markers well, you need a selection of color and value effects. Markers can be blended with a marker blender, which looks like a clear, colorless marker. When mastered, you will use markers frequently in your presentation work, as they give quick, reliable results.

Buying guide: The initial outlay for a wide selection of colors and a marker case is likely to be high. You can overlay colors to get more range from a set that has a minimal number of markers.

Paper: White paper of any weight works well for marker pens. However, textured paper can make rendering certain textures (such as shine) more difficult. Special marker paper is available for use with this medium and makes applying and blending the colors easier.

Strengths: Markers are a quick-to-apply, layered technique. Although classified as a wet medium, they dry rapidly and can be applied with one layer over another in a matter of minutes.

Drawbacks: Markers dry up easily, and you have to use them quickly.

Ease of use: Need practice, otherwise an even coloration will be hard to achieve.

OTHER MATERIALS

Explore format and decide what works for you. Portrait or landscape—the choice is yours—but landscape is usually the preferred format for the development of design ideas.

Sketchpads: An 11 in. x 14 in. (28 cm x 35 cm) sketchpad for research and initial ideas. Ensure you buy a brand that has good-quality paper that will take wet and dry media. Avoid sketchbooks where paper can tear out easily.

Layout pads: You may want to use a layout pad as you begin to develop and find confidence in your drawing style. The benefit of using layout pads is that you can draw the outline of your accessory design and trace through the thin paper, varying the details and exploring options for placement, while the outline remains constant. Development is always presented on separate sheets.

Eraser: White plastic erasers give a very clean erase, while kneaded erasers (commonly used in fine arts) can also be used when sketching.

Pencil sharpener: No comment needed.

White tack: For exploring layouts—concept boards, consumer boards, etc.

Masking tape: Masking off areas of boards and for exploring layouts.

Spray adhesive: Gluing images to boards.

SECTION 1 | THE CREATIVE PROCESS

CAD: COMPUTER-AIDED DESIGN

Objective Learn about computer-aided design work within the accessories and footwear industry.

▶ **Combining software** A combination of Adobe programs, Illustrator and Photoshop, has been used to tell the story of this design. The technical aspects, text, and brand logo utilize the clean lines of Illustrator. The texture of the materials and the 3D effect of the colored illustration are created with Photoshop.

Major change has swept through the creative industries in the past two decades—change in the form of technology that previously could only have been dreamed about. The arrival of computer-aided design or "CAD" programs in the early 1990s has revolutionized the way designers work and increased the speed and productivity of many companies.

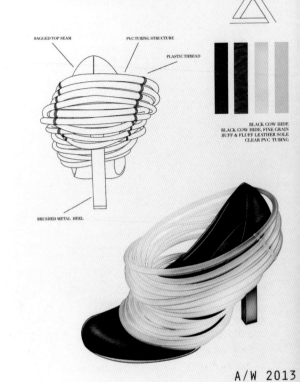

IZAR

BAGGED TOP SEAM   PVC TUBING STRUCTURE

PLASTIC THREAD

BLACK COW HIDE
BLACK COW HIDE, FINE GRAIN
BUFF & FLUFF LEATHER SOLE
CLEAR PVC TUBING

BRUSHED METAL HEEL

A/W 2013

RESOURCES

For additional information on software packages, you could visit:

• Adobe.com

• support.romans-cad.com

TECHNOLOGICAL ADVANCES

Where previously "coloring up" a line would take weeks of laborious application of color rendering with suitable media such as Pantone markers, now coloring up can take a matter of days or hours, with each rendering being saved or changed at the click of a mouse. Huge swathes of work that previously would have been cut and pasted onto mount boards for presentation are now manipulated and set into digital presentations. These are easily edited, re-ordered, and saved without the need for printing out and wasting valuable resources or ink. They can be sent to the other side of the world at the click of a button, saving companies precious work hours and expensive logistics bills. Designers now have more digitally developed creative freedom than ever before.

The obvious benefits to designer and business alone have been enough to drive the industry forward and continue to evolve it at an amazing pace. CAD skills have become one of the most important factors in a designer's toolbox today, and most companies cite CAD skills as a requirement on a potential employee's résumé as much as proof of ability to draw proportionally and well. The evolution of CAD products has taken design to another level, one where nothing is impossible and visualization has no boundaries. If you can imagine it, you can realize it with CAD. Standards of presentation of work have never been more enhanced, and everywhere you look, IT and CAD are being used to present and enhance the work, lives, and learning of billions of people.

FASHION AND SOFTWARE

Within the accessories and footwear industry, many relevant CAD programs have been developed over the past decades. Art-based packages such as Adobe Photoshop, Adobe Illustrator, Adobe InDesign, Sketchbook Pro, and Lectra Romans CAD 2D Bag are invaluable, along with 3D programs developed for manufacturing, such as Shoemaster and Lectra Romans CAD 3D Design.

The original 3D programs for shoe manufacturing taught designers to work from 3D lasts digitized onto the screen that were transformable into 2D flat patterns for sample making and manufacturing. This gave

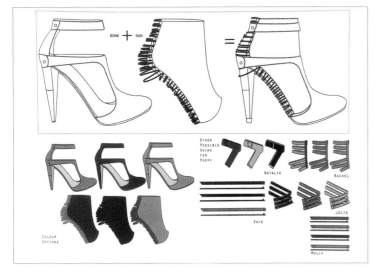

◄ **Using CAD to present work** The designer has used Illustrator with its flat diagramatic style to create this explanatory sheet. The top half of the page shows the basic shoe and how one of the interchangeable pieces works. The lower half shows the shoe and all of the alternative pieces available in every color option.

▲ **Technical drawings** CAD program Illustrator has been used to draw a bag. This technical style of drawing is used on specification sheets.

▶ **Chart (next page)** This chart demonstrates the extensive use of CAD in the industrial design and sampling process. This example shows how the system works in a corporate environment and how important it is for the designer to master a range of software programs to communicate with others involved in the process.

designers a unique insight into the shape and form of new designs instantly. Alternating between the 2D and 3D form gave the ability to instantly alter design details and solve problems that may previously have remained undiscovered until sample making. It also gave pattern cutters the ability to manipulate and recut patterns with speed, saving time and cost.

Equally, the art-based programs such as Adobe Photoshop and Adobe Illustrator have revolutionized the way that we approach the more time-consuming tasks within our remit. Coloring up photocopies of original designs to create alternative colorways has now been replaced by digitally mastering layers of work and changing the colors onscreen, with millions of new color and texture opportunities being available at the click of a button. Where previously representing a particular texture or leather would have been impossible and only communicated by providing swatches, now we are able to fully represent these by digitally scanning and applying them to our artwork within these software packages. These packages have become so advanced that they are now able to transform drawings and rough sketches into line art that can be manipulated into clear technical drawings ready for specification in a sample room or factory. They are a valuable asset for any designer who may struggle with technical drawing. Artwork is fully exportable to other programs, such as PowerPoint, to digitally present and communicate ideas to peers and employers alike. Using these programs has become a standard requirement for most industry partners, and most designers leave education with some or good knowledge of these.

CAD IN PRACTICE

In order to fully explain the process of footwear design and the use of CAD within the process, an example is given on the next page of the life of a design within a large corporate company from concept to realized sample. This will give you a very good idea of all the different uses of CAD-based programs and how they may be applied. This is a very detailed process that you may simplify according to the kind of company you are employed by, and it may also be adapted for use within the scope of project work within college or university.

It should be noted that the process described on the next page is purely to demonstrate the use of CAD within the product development process, and many of the integral steps of line planning and marketing have been purposely left out.

KEY STAGES
• Examine the different uses of CAD and the application of the different types of software programs that are available to us as users.
• Learn about what CAD means to designers and its effect on industry.
• Identify the different software packages available and the application of these software packages.
• Explore the possibilities of new technology.

STAGE OF DESIGN	DEPARTMENT	SOFTWARE PACKAGE USED	METHODS EMPLOYED
Research and concept development	Design and trends and innovations team	PowerPoint/Photoshop/ Sketchbook Pro	Collation of all research from travel and retail visits and consumer profiling.
Trend presentation and concept presentations	Design and trends and innovations team	PowerPoint/Photoshop	Presentation of storyboards created in PowerPoint and Photoshop. Storyboards to include mood/concept boards/consumer profile boards/innovations/materials and color boards.
Sketch work for first-round meetings	Design team	Hand drawings and Sketchbook Pro	Draw up first ideas and develop conceptual work.
Present back to product team	Design and technical support team	Hand drawings and Sketchbook Pro/PowerPoint where needed. Romans CAD and Pro Engineer	Present sketchwork in an informal setting with backup of original PowerPoint presentation work and original storyboards to reinforce new concepts and ideas. Present back any new initial ideas that may have been 3D rapid prototyped to show team in greater detail. This could be small components like eyelets or larger components such as sole units or heels.
Rework sketches	Design team	Hand drawings and Sketchbook Pro	Reworking designs and changing them to suit all the feedback given at presentations from product team.
Present back to product team	Design and technical support team	Hand drawings and Sketchbook Pro. Also now showing Illustrator drawings and Photoshop color renderings.	Presenting back again with more advanced and detailed artwork. Showing reworked 3D prototypes and color drawings.
Specification to source or sample room	Design team	Illustrator/Photoshop with some use of other suitable programs for making technical specs, which could even be Word, Excel, or PowerPoint, depending on the individual company. It may be at this stage that technical and 3D teams will create spec packages for first molds on items like sole units, heels, and lasts.	Originating all the first design specification sheets for request of first samples. Depending on the company, this may be a sample room locally or a factory sample room in another country. Whichever the case, it is vital that you select the most appropriate method of conveying that information in the clearest way possible.

STAGE OF DESIGN	DEPARTMENT	SOFTWARE PACKAGE USED	METHODS EMPLOYED
Receipt of first samples from source or sample room	Design and technical team	Digital photos/Photoshop/Illustrator	Evaluating the samples received and photographing them for correction purposes. This may be done in Illustrator and Photoshop, and samples are then prepared for presentation to the product team.
Presentation of samples to product team	Design and technical team	Most software packages that have contributed to the origination of this range will be present in this stage as work is reevaluated and represented.	Presenting back all the work done so far with the presence of 3D samples and first prototypes.
First amendments to samples and color up of line	Design and technical team	Photoshop/Illustrator/Romans CAD/Pro Engineer/digital photos	All amendment specs are collated and re-sent to the source or sample room for second-round samples to be made, according to the changes that need to be made to those samples that have made it through the selection process. At this point, the design team begin to work on coloring up the line according to the color palette defined in the original presentation meetings. This work is done in Illustrator and Photoshop. Designers all work differently, but it is generally accepted that most designs will be either hand drawn and scanned into Photoshop to be colored up or drawn in Illustrator and imported into Photoshop for coloring up. Some designers do color up in Illustrator.
Color meetings with second-round samples	Design and product team	Illustrator drawings, Photoshop color renderings, and PowerPoint	Colorways of chosen styles will be presented at this meeting and the presentation may be made digitally in PowerPoint or on more traditional mount boards. It would not be unusual for this process to be completed by the pinning of the selected colorways to a wall or suitable presentation board.
Final sample request (sealed samples)	Design and technical team	Illustrator/Photoshop with some use of other suitable programs for making technical specs, which could even be Word, Excel, or PowerPoint, depending on the individual company. At this stage technical and 3D teams will create FINAL spec packages for molds on items like sole units, heels, and lasts.	Originating all the FINAL design specification sheets for the request of FINAL (sealed) samples. The samples will be requested in more than one colorway and it is likely that all the specs will be requested in Word format to enable the manufacturers to load onto their factory systems.

COLOR THEORY AND DESIGN

Objective Learn about the principles of color theory.

Knowing the basic principles of color theory will help you to use color effectively in your work and understand how to mix colors for your illustrations and designs.

An accessories designer will always be working toward a particular season or a specific line, and the color palette will be influenced by this. In spring, light neutrals and pastels prevail, strong brights and nautical colors are summer favorites, warm earthy colors are introduced in fall, and dark, somber colors prevail during the winter season. Given our emotional attachment to color, it's no surprise that even fashion follows the rhythm of the natural world. The pastel shades of spring bulbs, strong colors of exotic summer flowers, rich colors of dying leaves in fall, and dark silhouettes of bare winter trees inform the fashion world.

This gives you an initial guide to selecting your colors, but within each category, there are a thousand shades of every color and choosing the right one at the right time is your challenge.

SELECTING YOUR COLOR PALETTE

Color is the first thing a consumer notices when shopping. You must consider your target market when selecting a color palette to avoid any negative cultural connotations. Consider lifestyle too: a city dweller working in banking will buy and wear different colors from someone living in a rural environment.

You will also use trend information (see page 34) and investigate what is on offer from materials suppliers to support this process. Having gathered all this information, you must analyze your needs and select your

palette. A range of neutrals will form the basis of your range to which you will add a choice of seasonal colors. Use your instinct and think about how the colors will look together. Are you planning to use contrast colors, tone on tone, multicolor, or small accents? Even if all of your products will be made in a single color, they will be seen together when the full range is shown to a buyer. A useful tool for any creative process is a color wheel: it helps you select colors that work together.

▲ **Color board: brights** The designer has chosen magazine tears and has manipulated her own photographs using Photoshop to achieve tonal color balance. Images are butted together before a color palette is teased out and placed at the side of each image.

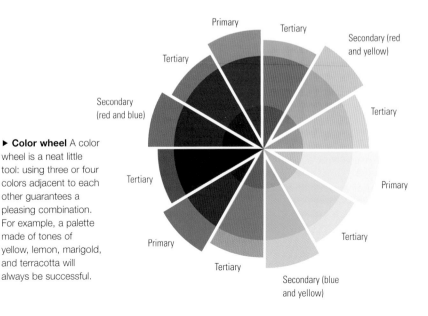

▶ **Color wheel** A color wheel is a neat little tool: using three or four colors adjacent to each other guarantees a pleasing combination. For example, a palette made of tones of yellow, lemon, marigold, and terracotta will always be successful.

Primary

Tertiary

Secondary (red and yellow)

Tertiary

Tertiary

Secondary (red and blue)

Tertiary

Tertiary

Primary

Tertiary

Primary

Tertiary

Primary

Secondary (blue and yellow)

◀ Ferrous color choices Black and brown are the best-selling colors for all accessories. In this color board, the designer has taken one single image to inspire the ferrous color palette.

▼ Different references Here, the designer draws on a wide range of different visual references to build a color board.

My colour palette for this season/range honey browns, rich burgundy reds an

I wanted to keep my colour palette quite refined and The palette is not too loud and is designed so that the different outfits, this was something that I found in my Development) I also wanted my customers to be able seasons as my brand is not trend led the sh mix with new seasonal clothing

CONSIDER COLOR CAREFULLY

If you are using more than one color in any design, you must consider the proportions of each color very carefully; too much of a sharp accent color can reduce its impact, while just the right amount will enhance the product significantly.

A brief that demands single-color products need not limit your use of color. Using a contrasting lining will make the design more exciting, the color of metal fittings on a bag adds interest, a colored sole on a shoe can create a signature style, and a shoelace in a different color will make a difference. The possibilities are endless; the choices you make will give your designs an individual style.

Whatever your color choices, it is important to recognize that black and brown are always the best-selling color for all accessories, with navy, white, and natural beige or tan taking a leading role during the shorter summer season. You must always include these basics in your palette, but you should make most of the samples in the new colors of the season to attract the attention of buyers. As well as creating visual impact, sales could be increased as buyers might be tempted to order more than one color of a design. Never underestimate the power of color.

GLOSSARY

Complementary colors: Colors opposite each other on the color wheel.

Contrast colors: On the color wheel, colors separated from each other by other colors.

Primary color: Pure colors that can be mixed to create secondaries.

Secondary color: Purple, turquoise, orange, and lime.

Tertiary color: Combination of primary and secondary colors.

Tone: Graduating shades of one color.

EXERCISE: UNDERSTAND THE POWER OF COLOR

Complementary colors can create strange sensations when juxtaposed. Try painting a large red square, leaving a small square in the center. Paint the small square green and stare at it, then look at a piece of white paper. Now paint alternating stripes of equal width next to each other in blue and orange. The stripes will appear to move.

RESEARCH AND INSPIRATION

Objective Learn how to collect research and information to fuel your creative thinking. What is inspirational research, and where can your inspirational trigger be found?

▲▶ Layout reflects inspiration
The top example is laid out in a linear style, reflecting images hanging in a gallery. A less rigid layout (right) explores bird motifs.

Research is crucial to the design process—without deep, rich, varied research sources, innovation cannot exist. Your creative thought processes need fuel to ignite the spark. The more in depth your research is, the greater the potential is for idea generation. The next few pages examine research, exploring what it can be and examining research methods used by designers to generate ideas and inform design solutions.

CONDUCTING RESEARCH

There are two very different research types—primary and secondary—and both are needed for a successful project outcome.

Primary research is the collecting of data that does not already exist. It is research material that you generate; therefore it can be described as proactive. There are two forms of primary research:
- Inspirational primary research—includes photographs, drawings, and practical exploration and experimentation.
- Information and data primary research—this takes the form of questionnaires, focus groups, and interviews.

Primary research can be further broken down into qualitative and quantitative methods.

Qualitative research is a technique in which data is obtained from a relatively small case study, observations, or focus group.

Quantitative research is the gathering and analyzing of measurable data obtained from questionnaires or surveys. It is a type of research that supports your decisions with numbers, percentages, assumptions, opinions, or behavior.

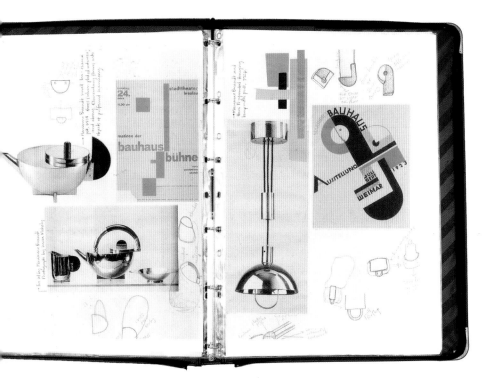

◀ Art movement Bauhaus research informs the designer's initial shape exploration. The block layout reflects the use of color in the images selected. Annotations are written vertically down the page, following the lines in the images.

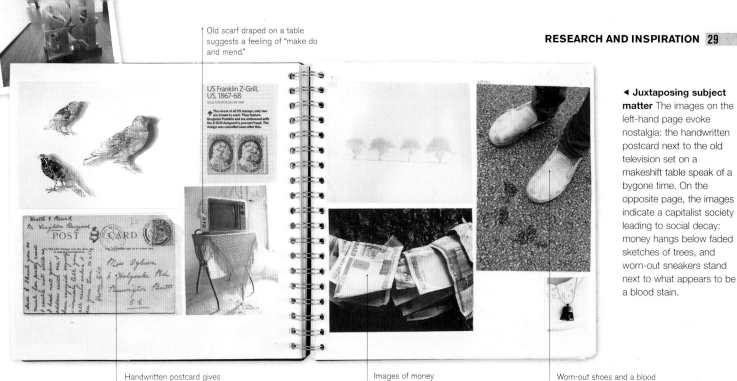

Old scarf draped on a table suggests a feeling of "make do and mend."

US Franklin Z-Grill, US, 1867-68

SOLD FOR $935,000 IN 1998

The rarest of all US stamps, only two are known to exist. They feature Benjamin Franklin and are embossed with the Z-Grill designed to prevent fraud. The design was cancelled soon after this.

POST CARD

◀ **Juxtaposing subject matter** The images on the left-hand page evoke nostalgia: the handwritten postcard next to the old television set on a makeshift table speak of a bygone time. On the opposite page, the images indicate a capitalist society leading to social decay: money hangs below faded sketches of trees, and worn-out sneakers stand next to what appears to be a blood stain.

Handwritten postcard gives a nostalgic feel.

Images of money indicate capitalism.

Worn-out shoes and a blood stain on the road point to urban decay.

Secondary research is research that has been carried out by another and already exists. It is published material. It can be described as reactive:

- Internet
- Newspapers
- Books
- Films
- Magazines
- Trade journals
- Trend information
- Existing market research

A rich mix of the above methodologies and sources is recommended when starting your design project.

FINDING INSPIRATION

Inspiration is crucial to the design process. Without inspirational research, we regurgitate designs and versions of products that have already been seen, even if we do so unknowingly.

Inspiration is very broad, diverse, and personal. Inspiration can come from absolutely anywhere and anything. A fold in a piece of material, a detail on a piece of baroque furniture that triggers an idea for a design detail, an image or scene from a movie that speaks to you of a rich vibrant color palette, a piece of music that evokes an emotional response, a crack in a pavement, the curves of a wrought-iron gate, the color of a door that you pass every morning, a building with strong vertical lines, or a reflection in a puddle—the list is endless.

Inspiration should be leading you to ideas for:
- Concept
- Shape
- Color
- Texture
- Detail
- Function
- Materials/fittings
- Construction
- Proportion/scale
- Silhouette
- Balance
- Surface

▼ **Sculptural contours** Through a series of line drawings, sculptures are evaluated, exploring the body of the shoe in relation to the body contours of sculptural forms.

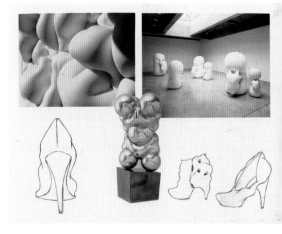

INSPIRATIONAL RESEARCH

Your inspirational research should be from a diverse array of methodologies and sources. Keep your eyes open and see the world around you as a valuable source of visual stimulation every day. To capture these images, you should carry a camera and a pocket-sized sketchbook wherever you go. Things that attract your attention may mean nothing to others. That personal reaction to your surroundings is what creates a designer's individual style.

When working on a particular project brief, you should be disciplined and focused in your research. Too many sources of inspiration can result in a spread of ideas that will not hang together as a collection. A carefully chosen selection of sources will result in research with depth that you can integrate to create a strong look. Don't forget to go back through your personal sketchbooks to see what you already have that is relevant to the project you are working on.

Put together a mind/concept map to create potential avenues to explore and link together (see page 15 and below).

CREATING YOUR RESEARCH PLAN

It is a good idea to put together a research plan to be used in conjunction with your mind/concept map. This will help you start to investigate and explore, plan visits and field research, and collect visual information to help develop and support your emerging concept.

To create your inspirational research plan, consider the research sources you will use:

Libraries are a great place to kick-start your research: magazines, journals, and books.

Online sources and e-journals. Lots of information and inspiration can be found on the Internet, but ensure this is not the only resource you use.

Visits to museums, galleries, specialist markets, etc. to sketch or photograph exhibits, artifacts, products, or details.

Trips to the theater, movies, clubs, or concerts—all of these can be used as triggers to start off your creative thinking. Music is a key emotional stimulus, often evoking strong reactions; think about how you can express those feelings visually. Film and theater can provide historical information, evoke the zeitgeist of another era, and show an insight into another culture, as well as providing visual inspiration. Events such as Mardi Gras, the arrival of celebrities at a movie premiere, impromptu street dancing, and street performers can all enrich your imagination.

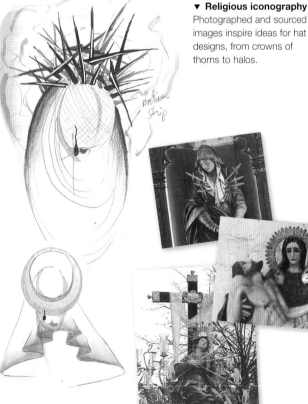

▼ **Religious iconography** Photographed and sourced images inspire ideas for hat designs, from crowns of thorns to halos.

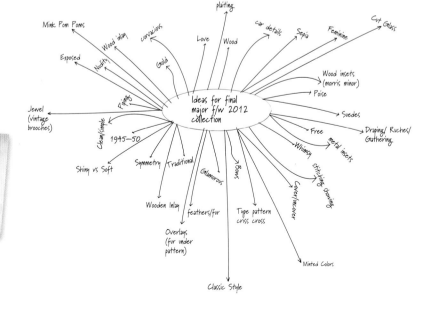

▼ **Exploring ideas** This mind map shows the initial thoughts of a designer exploring concepts and possibilities for her Fall/Winter 2012 collection. This is the very first stage of scoping out ideas.

▶ **Runway images**
Seasonal observations from the runway inform us of past bag shapes prevalent in the new collections. Analysis of how the shapes can be developed for next season is undertaken and initial ideas for color combinations are noted.

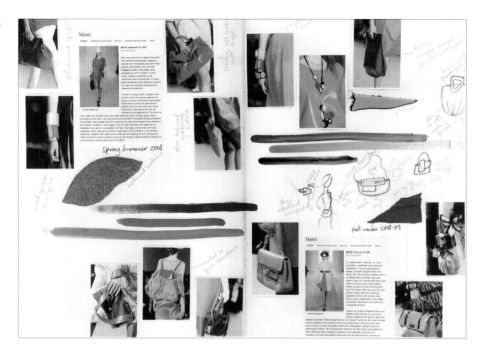

OTHER FORMS OF INSPIRATION

Do not leave out the impact that the written word has: lyrics can often be a key stimulus, as can poems and prose. It's not only the meaning of the words: the layout, the font, the texture and color of the paper, and the design of the book cover can also act as visual stimuli. Old books are a great source of information, giving contemporary voice to a specific era, and you can often be inspired by the way they are illustrated.

Issues can also inspire, be they ethical, social, cultural, or political. All of these are encompassed in current growing concerns for the sustainability of our world. As a designer, this is an area you will be expected to consider.

Image selection is key, and your image sources in your research should be varied and wide—take care not to only have magazine tears. Supplement your research with photographs, postcard images, and drawings. The greater the variety, the richer the research, and the more likely it will be to fuel your creative thinking.

Materials can also be very inspirational, and their research is crucial to the design process. Visits to specialist material/hardware/component stores and suppliers, and trade fairs are essential to look at what is seasonal and to view the new developments and technological advancements for the coming season. When researching materials/fabrics, you need to find out availability of colors, performance/function, size of skins if leather, minimum quantity for order, lead times, and price points.

Creativity is like a raging fire. Unless you add fuel to the fire, the fire diminishes and goes out. If your research isn't working for you, you need to change it, alter it, diversify it, or deepen it—or evaluate and respond to it at a deeper level.

As you start to collect your research, set up separate files to keep your information and inspiration organized prior to editing and setting up your sketchbook.

KEY STAGES

- Mind/concept map.
- Research planning.
- Visits—photograph and draw.
- Collection of inspiration.
- Collection of data/information.
- Explore and source materials.
- Order swatches if necessary.

SECTION 1 | THE CREATIVE PROCESS

UNDERSTANDING THE MARKET

Objective Learn about the fashion accessories/ footwear market.

Understanding the market levels and identifying current trends is absolutely fundamental to the designer. With regular visits to identified shops, independent boutiques, and department stores to look at the products, you will be able to gain a bigger picture of the accessories and footwear market. Visits and analysis will help you determine potential competitors and establish what will set your product apart from your competitors by building in your competitive edge. This will enable you to establish if there is a potential market for your idea/product.

MARKET LEVELS

In order to fully understand the market, you need to know the market levels that exist and what defines them. The market can generally be divided into four sectors:
• Luxury
• Designer
• Main street
• Value

Defining the market levels involves first having an understanding of how companies market themselves, through their brand. Brands market themselves through their external visual communication with the public:
• Store windows
• Advertisements
• Editorials in magazines
• Point-of-sale material—shopping bags, boxes, wrapping, look books, etc.

Companies use advertising to tempt us into buying, or make us long to buy their products. Their advertisements speak to us of lavish lifestyles, power, seduction,

▶ **Prada** The outline of the name Prada on the window and the Italian heritage suggested by the word "Milano" are very subtle ways of immediately telling the consumer that this is a luxury brand. The display is limited to a few key pieces that epitomize the label.

Complicated upper is carefully constructed from soft calf leather with fine stitching requiring a high level of skill.

Simple pump made from suede split with a synthetic lining in a seasonal color. A minimal amount of stitching required to construct the upper.

Fine and delicate heel with subtle curves that complement the whole shoe.

Sole is made from the finest-quality Italian soling leather finished with a contrasting edge color.

Platform and heel are covered in contrasting synthetic reptile print, and the sole is made from synthetic resin.

▲ **Market comparison** These two shoes were created for the opposite extremes of the market. The luxury shoe (left) has been thoughtfully designed to achieve a rhythmic quality; the last shape, heel, and lines of the upper all blend together perfectly. The soft, tactile quality of the upper leather can be seen even in the photograph. The value shoe (right) is simple and does not require the same level of skill of production. There is no subtlety in the lines, and the upper is rigid and less comfortable. The shoe is well made from lower-quality materials, and the color and material choices are fashionable for the season.

and money. We want to be the people in the advertisements; we want to look like them, belong to their tribe. The brands define their offer through these advertisements, store windows, and point-of-sale material.

WHAT IS A BRAND?

A brand is a name or trademark associated with a product type, or is a designer or manufacturer who offers a particular type of product. The product and the brand sometimes become synonymous, for example Gucci—bag. Although Gucci offers many product types, menswear and womenswear, when someone mentions Gucci, the first thing we think of is a bag. Similarly, if someone says Jimmy Choo, we instantly picture high heel shoes. When we hear the name Philip Treacy, we see delicate, sculptural, statement hats.

A brand is recognizable by its:
• Name
• Sign
• Symbol
• Design/handwriting

A combination of all of the above elements can be employed by a brand to identify the products and/or

services they offer that differentiate them from their competitors.

Luxury brands are the top-market level. Luxury does not necessarily mean custom-made, and therefore the products are not made for individual customers; however, the consumer needs to have enough disposable income to be able to purchase one of these products. Great care is taken in the design, choice, and cut of the materials and fabric. Accessories and footwear are sometimes made in small quantities to guarantee exclusivity, so they are expensive. The number of products released at a time is often limited to build up a buying frenzy, which often results in waiting lists adding to the exclusive status of the brand. Unlike designer brands, luxury brands rarely reinvent their complete range every season. The iconic pieces that epitomize the brand will run through several seasons with new colors and materials selected to update the products.

▶ **Marc Jacobs**
The luxury detail of the Marc Jacobs runway collection can be seen in the clean finish of the geometric element of this bodice, the color-toned accessories of the right scale to balance the outfit, and the rope effect repeated around the neck and on the shoes.

BRANDS AND TRENDS ACROSS MARKET LEVELS

Here we list a few well-known brands for each market level, and look at four bags
of similar style to explore how design, materials, and production values vary across the market.

Luxury brands

Alexander McQueen, Balenciaga, Bottega Veneta, Chanel, Christian Dior, Gina, Hermès, Jil Sander, Lanvin, Louis Vuitton, Manolo Blahnik, Marc Jacobs, Prada, Sergio Rossi, Vivienne Westwood, YSL, and Zagliani.

Designer brands

Alexander Wang, Ally Capellino, Anya Hindmarch, Bill Amberg, Chloé, Christian Louboutin, Comme des Garçons, Costume National, Donna Karan, Fleet Ilya, Georgina Goodman, Giuseppe Zanotti, Jimmy Choo, Marchesa, Michael Kors, Miu Miu, Mulberry, Natalie Brill, Nicholas Kirkwood, Pierre Hardy, Ralph Lauren, and Stuart Weitzman.

Main street brands

Abercrombie & Fitch, Ann Taylor, Anthropologie, Banana Republic, Express, French Connection, J. Crew, Karen Millen, Nine West, Reiss, The Gap, The Limited, Topshop, Urban Outfitters, and Zara.

Value brands

Charlotte Russe, Forever 21, H&M, Old Navy, Strawberry, and Uniqlo.

▲ **Luxury** This handcrafted Hermès Birkin bag uses the highest-quality leather and fittings. The crocodile Birkin shown here has a pricetag of $34,000 and will not be found in any Hermès store. There is a waiting list for this iconic piece; it is the holy grail of handbags.

▲ **Designer** Anya Hindmarch's Carker bag is from the core collection so is produced in the colors and materials of every season. Manufactured in small numbers in Europe from quality materials, the bag's price varies from around $900 to $1150. Here it is shown in quality patent leather mock croc with the Anya Hindmarch signature lock.

▲ **Main street** The French Connection Twinkle bag is made from faux-python leather embossed with a python textured grain. The bag is made in Asia in quantity as French Connection has 1,000 stockists worldwide and an online store. The retro 70s feel was on-trend for F/W 2011. It ran for one season and retailed at around $300.

▲ **Value** This Forever 21 bag is made from suedette and synthetic imitation crocodile leather, with cheap metal-alloy fittings. Forever 21 has stores worldwide and mass manufactures their products in Asia in order to meet competitive price points; this bag retailed at approximately $30. The bag was on-trend for F/W 2011 and ran for only one season.

The characteristics of a luxury brand include:
• Quality of materials
• Attention to detail
• Craftsmanship
• Level of design
• Status
• Longevity
• Heritage
• Where and how the products are manufactured
• How the product is retailed

Designer brands target specific consumers, and they do not often have mass appeal. Designer brands are often categorized as ready-to-wear collections. They are usually presented by fashion brands each season during a period known as Fashion Week. This is the major event in the world fashion calendar, and shows take place in the world's fashion capitals—New York, London, Milan, and Paris—twice a year.

Designer brands share many of the same qualities as the luxury brands; however, they do not have the status, prestige, or heritage of a luxury brand. Innovation and creativity are the key features of a designer brand. These companies invest heavily in the research and development of new products inspired by new materials and techniques. The competition to stage the most press-worthy fashion show each season is immense, allowing the design team to indulge in extreme ideas supported by quality manufacturing.
• Quality and diversity of materials used
• Attention to detail
• Craftsmanship
• Design innovation
• Status
• Where and how the products are manufactured
• How the product is retailed

Main street brands aim for mass appeal to a targeted consumer. Often fashion forward, they follow trends and update their stock regularly to keep consumers interested.
• On-trend design
• Often made off-shore
• Material quality medium to low
• Relatively easy to manufacture
• Value for money

EXERCISE: **COMPARING MARKET LEVELS**

Conduct research focused by visiting stores and researching brands to gain an overview of the market.

From your visits and additional research of the market levels, establish the size of each market level and who the market leaders are. Which are the most important brands in each market level?

Select one brand from each market level and explore:
• Look at how materials vary between levels.
• Compare the quality of manufacture across levels.
• Look at the color palettes and how color is used in each market level.
• How do the fittings and design details relate to the price bracket?
• What age group does each level appeal to and why?

Value brands aim for volume, mass-market sales. This is the fastest growing sector of the fashion market. The value brands cater to a wide range of consumers, producing ready-to-wear clothes, footwear, and accessories in large quantities and standard sizes. Cheap materials, creatively used, produce affordable fashion. Value brand designers generally adapt the trends set by the famous names in fashion. They often wait around to make sure a style is going to catch on before producing their own versions of the original look. In order to save money and time, they use cheaper fabrics and simpler production techniques. The end product can therefore be sold more cheaply. Their characteristics include:
• Use of cheaper materials
• Cheaply manufactured
• Mass manufactured
• Often manufactured in developing countries
• Trend-driven designs (versions of designer/ luxury brands)
• Constantly updating stock
• Value for money
• Philosophy—stack them high and sell them cheap

Concern is growing about the impact of producing cheap, disposable fashion products. Cheap production, child labor, unethical practices, and the increase in products and materials being dumped in landfills are all issues that have been recently highlighted.

GLOSSARY

Brand: Products of a particular make or trademark.

Fashion forward: Trendsetting, up to date with the latest trends.

Heritage: Long-established reputation and history.

Off-shore: Production in other countries, often Asia and the Pacific Rim.

SECTION 1 | THE CREATIVE PROCESS

STORE REPORTS

Objective Understand how and why designers carry out store reports, and learn how to conduct them yourself.

A store report is a summary of what is happening in retail at any given point. Having collected information and analyzed data gathered from visits to stores, boutiques, and online retailers, a report is constructed. The report identifies current trends, consumers, and competition, along with other specific findings.

As a designer it is imperative to be informed on what is happening out there in the retail market-place. Visiting the stores regularly will help you:
* Analyze current trends
* Assess what is selling and what is not
* Understand the importance of the retail environment
* Identify who the consumers are for particular brands
* Investigate possible competition

WHY STORE REPORTS ARE USEFUL

As a student or as a professional, compiling store reports will help update your knowledge of what is happening at retail, keeping you abreast of new developments and able to speculate where trends are heading. Be aware of the impact of e-tailing—a separate e-tail report may be necessary, particularly with the purchase of accessories that are not impacted by fit issues.

Conducting store reports enables you to compare styles offered and identify current trends. In conducting a visual and commercial summary of the product offering from targeted brands and boutiques, you will be able to identify key styles for the season, since every brand will carry its own version of them. Identify new players in the market and assess the health of the brands and their retail operations. Two to three visits per season is an average—at the start of the season and toward the end of the season are good times to visit.

On the first visit, observe and analyze the new lines and identify who is buying what. Predict what you feel will be the best-selling items and consider whether your selection matches those being pushed/promoted by the merchandisers (those styles/products that are featured in windows and displayed in prominent places within the store). Mid-season visits can show you what is selling and what is not—look at what has been reduced already. On the final visit of the season, assess whether your predictions were correct and if the key pieces favored by the merchandisers have been bought by the consumers. It's also interesting to see if the consumer segment noticeably changes when the prices are slashed and the sales are on.

EXERCISE: CONDUCT A FORMAL STORE REPORT

- Focusing on a specific area of the accessories market, choose a quality department store, an independent boutique, and a flagship store of a well-known fashion accessories brand.
- Check if they have an online presence and note the brands/labels they sell.
- Choose a selection of brands and labels to focus on from the department store.
- All the relevant product area brands for the independent boutique should be explored.
- Take note of how they market themselves through use of visuals, text presentation, and layout of their Web site.
- Make a list of criteria/questions you want to find answers to from the visit.
- Map out a route and undertake visits to the stores taking with you a notebook and a camera. Remember you will need to gather the same information for each of the stores and brands/labels you chose to investigate. Care will be needed if you try to take photographs of products/layout in store—a cell phone with a camera could be useful.
- Window display shots are useful, since key pieces being promoted are usually showcased in the windows.
- During your visits, engage retail assistants— they can have valuable information on consumers, best-sellers, etc. Ask for look books and any other point-of-sale material.
- Note ambience and store layout.
- Try on the accessories and scrutinize construction methods, materials, fittings and trims, and fit and comfort. Note where the products are made, prices, and number of products in the collections.
- Consider the overall design aesthetic of the brand for the season and mood of the collection.
- Observe the consumers. If there is a cafe nearby with a clear view of the store, have a coffee and make notes about the customers entering the store.
- Analyze your findings—if you feel information is lacking, conduct another set of visits and/or supplement information with research from brand/store Web sites.

CHOOSING THE RIGHT STORES

Choosing the stores and areas to visit should be done with due consideration. Often brands that attract the same type of consumer can be found in the same or connecting locations. It is useful to note also when visiting department stores like Barneys, Macy's, Neiman Marcus, Bloomingdale's, Nordstrom, and Saks Fifth Avenue, competing brands are often grouped together—this makes it easier for the targeted consumer to compare products and make an informed choice without leaving the store. The customer is also able to discover different brands with similar aesthetics and prices simply by moving into the adjacent brand's area.

Add a selection of independent boutiques into the mix so you can keep up with young emerging designers and new brands—they could be key players in the future.

Brands' own stores are also essential to visit, since here you can really gain an understanding of the retail experience and the service they offer their consumers, which should reflect the brand philosophy.

KEY STAGES

The key elements to observe and identify in the store report are as follows:

1. Summary of the merchandise
- Product offer
- Brands stocked (if a department store, boutique, or independent boutique)
- Key styles of each brand
- Color palette for the season of each brand
- Material and fittings used for each brand offering
- Moods/themes/trends

2. Commercial summary
- Line structure—number of items, styles in the line, and colors offered
- Where the product was manufactured
- Entry, core, and high price points
- What is not selling

3. Brand image
- Window display
- Retail space and ambience
- Advertising
- Point-of-sale material
- E-tail presence/online store
- Service offered
- Staff

4. Competing brands
- Image and style
- Price points
- Line offer
- Consumer

5. Consumer
- Who are they? Who is the actual customer buying these products, as opposed to the aspirational customer depicted in ads?
- Lifestyle
- Fashion characteristics
- Buying habits
- Expectations

Do not expect to gain all this information in one visit—you may need to conduct this research over a few days.

PRESENTING A STORE REPORT

How the information gathered is analyzed and the store report is presented depends very much on its audience and purpose. If it's merely for personal insight, it may remain in note format. If it is for a formal presentation, a formal report-style format supported by visuals is recommended. If you are presenting the findings to a team of designers, creative director, or other creative staff, a more visual approach is usually taken that includes a summary of the brands, which usually results in a table comparing the brands against each other under appropriate criteria.

GLOSSARY

E-tailing: Harnessing the power of the Internet to contact customers globally to sell products.

Look book: A brochure produced to showcase the product line for the season.

Point-of-sale material: Printed matter given away when a purchase is made, e.g. bags, postcards, invitations to special events.

Store report: A summary of what is happening in retail at a given time.

SECTION 1 | THE CREATIVE PROCESS

TREND FORECASTING AND INFORMATION

Objective Understand the fashion cycle and the importance of trend forecasting.

Designers of accessories and footwear constantly strive to have their fingers on the pulse of social, cultural, economic, and political climate, to second-guess what consumer desires will be for the forthcoming season. Obviously, as designers, we need to derive our own conclusions from our multifaceted research—a mix of observation and conjecture informs our design solutions.

SEASONAL TRENDS

Fashion design, and therefore accessories and footwear design, is categorized by the season for which the products are designed—fashion requirements in hot, sunny climates are very different than those in cold, wet climates. Styles of footwear change significantly in the winter months, requiring insulating and waterproofing properties, in comparison with the open sandals and pumps of the summer season.

Materials also change: lightweight, breathable fabrics and materials for summer give way to warm and waterproof materials in the winter. Colors also have an important role, since they have seasonal significance and can herald the arrival of spring and also the oncoming darkness of winter. So when researching and designing, be mindful of the season you are directing your collections toward—fall/winter or spring/summer.

EXERCISE: IDENTIFY TRENDS

Visit the stores and identify three prominent trends that are prevalent this season. Note which brands and labels have been inspired by these trends. Research and collect visuals that you feel represent these trends and put together a concept board for each of these trends—ensure you reference color, details, and key inspirational visuals.

TREND FORECASTING AND INFORMATION

Trend forecasting has become a very lucrative business, and there are many companies that sell trend packages to fashion businesses. The areas they cover are varied and far reaching:
- Sports footwear: toe shapes, key last shapes (the shoe form), sole units, materials, and colors
- Seasonal color palettes
- Fabrics, materials, and fittings
- Retail marketing
- Consumer trends
- Social and cultural trends

Research is conducted and a forecast is given two years in advance of the season. Often trend companies have offices in many global locations, collecting and digesting a wide variety of information, from noting shifting consumer behavior patterns to monitoring the retail environment. This research is analyzed and predictions are then produced as to the next season's key silhouettes, styles, materials, fittings, and colors.

TREND AGENCIES AND INFORMATION SERVICES

WGSN Worth Global Style Network was launched in 1998 and is a global, Web-based trends information site; it offers a massive range of information. WGSN offers each client its own unique experience, governed by how the client searches and interacts with the site. The site includes a 12-year archive with more than 5 million images and thousands of pages of information. It is the market leader using this platform.

Trend Union is essentially Lidewij Edelkoort—she is one of the most revered trend forecasters. Li and her team travel, search, and shop around the world "gathering information, emotions, studying the fabric of society and picking up materials, words, figures and flowers like global beachcombers." This rich mass of inspiration and information is analyzed and presented via the Trend Union trend books that Li Edelkoort and her creative team produce each year, and perhaps more inspiringly, through her 20-minute audiovisual presentations, which have viewings in Paris, London, Stockholm, New York, Tokyo, Seoul, and Amsterdam. Books are produced in September for the Spring/Summer trends and in

▲▶ Pantone's Fall fashion color report
Each season, key color themes are identified
by Pantone. In this catalog, leading fashion
designers are invited to choose one of the
color themes and use it in a design (from left,
Peter Som, Tommy Hilfiger, and Ella Moss).

February for the Fall/Winter trends. *The General Trend Book* is the main publication and forecasts trends two years in advance.

Viewpoint is a journal and is very different than the other forms of trend information described previously. Founded by David Shah in 1997, *Viewpoint* focuses primarily on consumer and market trends and is produced biannually. The publication reports on medium- and long-term trends, focusing on developments of future markets, target consumer groups, buying habits, and drivers, informed by deep analysis of socioeconomic developments, cultural trends, and lifestyles.

Pantone View Color Planner is a cross-industry color forecast information service, producing color ranges and inspiration for fashion, interiors, cosmetics, and product design industries. It is published 18 months in advance of the season. Its content is inspiring and includes comprehensive imagery, which builds concepts/moods, materials, patterns, and structures. It usually has eight color themes for each season made up of at least 50 colors, showing possible applications and combinations. It is a very user-friendly publication that is used widely within the design field.

USING THE INFORMATION

Leather tanners and fabric manufacturers work closely with trend information, creating materials and fabrics in the right color, tone, and finish for the next season. Materials are presented to the industry in a series of trade fairs showing developments for the coming seasons. Trade fairs are held twice a year: in September/October to present for Spring/Summer and in February/March to present for Fall/Winter. Lineapelle in Bologna, Italy, is the biggest and most important trade fair, and suppliers and tanneries show their leather, materials, and components for the accessories and footwear industries. Première Vision Pluriel brings together six related trade fairs: Expofil for fiber, Première Vision for fabrics, Indigo for textile design and creation, Le Cuir à Paris for leather and fur, ModAmont for trimmings and hardware, and Zoom by Fatex for fashion manufacturing. See pages 234–236 for more information on trade fairs.

GLOSSARY

Key last shape: The shape of the mold on which the shoe is made.

Leather tanners: Stabilize, color, and finish leather.

Pantone: Color referencing system acknowledged globally.

Trend forecast: Prediction of consumer desires for the upcoming season.

SECTION 1 | THE CREATIVE PROCESS

CONSUMER RESEARCH

Objective Learn how to research and identify your target consumer.

Researching your target consumer is essential in order to gain diverse information about your potential consumers and get a general insight into their lifestyles, buying habits, level of aesthetic, fashionability, disposable income, marital status, family lifecycle, education, etc. In order for your design to be relevant, desirable, fit for purpose, and price sensitive, you need to ensure that a variety of information has been gathered, evaluated, and analyzed, so you can more accurately specify your products to meet your target consumer's needs and desires.

▲ **Study your customer** Get out and about and start people-watching in stores and coffeeshops, wherever your idealized customers might congregate.

CONSUMER BEHAVIOR

By researching how our consumers behave, we gain an insight into their buying decisions, taste, style, purchasing power, and buying habits. Studying the characteristics of individual consumer groups such as demographics, psychographics, and behavioral variables gives an indication of people's wants and needs. You can also assess influences on the consumer from groups such as family, friends, groups, and society in general. The choices we make define us in many ways:
• How we shop and where we shop.
• What we wear and how we wear it.
• Where we socialize, how often we socialize, and who we socialize with.
• Are we body conscious and do we exercise regularly. Do we belong to a gym.
• Do we pamper ourselves with massages, manicures, and facials.
• Where do we vacation, with whom, and how often.

The list of considerations is as long as our personal preferences, but insight and conclusions can be reached by determining those of your consumer.

WHO IS YOUR CUSTOMER?

The project brief will usually give you an indication about your target customer—or at least a clue about where to start researching them. If you are designing for a particular brand or label, the easiest way to study its consumers is to go to one of the stores and observe the clientele.

Much can be learned from observing your target consumer group. First of all, think about what you want to find out about them. For instance, what is their fashion style? What brands are they wearing? What is their approximate age? What shopping bags are they carrying? In order to observe customers at your leisure, try to find a cafe nearby and make notes/sketches on the people you see.

If you are feeling brave, you could also approach them and ask if they mind having their photograph taken since they look fabulous—flattery often works in this situation. You could ask them a few questions at the same time to find out: how they travel, what brands they are wearing, and how they describe their fashion style.

IN-DEPTH CONSUMER ANALYSIS
GEOGRAPHICAL

Focus on where the target consumer lives. You should consider the country, city, or region. Is it urban, suburban, or rural? What is the climate? What is the population density? Where people live says a lot about them and their needs and desires. A consumer in the tropics would have no use for a pair of sheepskin boots.

DEMOGRAPHICS

This is a statistical view of a population, generally including age, gender, education, and occupation. All of these factors affect how we engage with products, and also how and what we buy. For example, a 24-year-old woman has very different taste, style, desires, needs, and spending ability than a 55-year-old woman. You can decide whether age is an issue you need to consider. People are living a lot longer and are much more vital and active way into old age. The traditional precepts are being broken down in this area.

OCCUPATION AND INCOME

What we do for a living can define us to a certain extent. However, people tend to have a very prescriptive view of a doctor or lawyer, for example, so we need to be aware of these. Also, social status is beginning to be blurred and harder to define by occupation. However, occupation can give us an insight into earning capabilities and ultimately salary, which helps to establish your target consumer's DPI.

DPI (disposable personal income) needs to be considered in relation to the consumer's expenses to gain a view of their spending capabilities. Are they single? Are they the main money earner? What expenses do they have? Do they have children? All of these things have implications for limitations on spending. A single person earning $75K–100K would have very different DPI to someone in the same life stage earning $25K–35K. So, in essence, money matters. However most of us have credit facilities, and we can be swayed at times. We can also be aspirational purchasers and save for that very special pair of shoes, or bag, if they are the must-have objects of desire.

PSYCHOGRAPHICS

Attributes relating to personality, values, attitudes, interests, and lifestyles are also called IAO variables (interests, activities, and opinions). IAOs have a huge impact on style, taste, and needs. If we participate in a sport, for instance, we will need to buy the relevant equipment and clothing. Cultural values and references also impact on our taste and purchases.

Your findings should be based on actual information and also some considered conjecture. Constructing a questionnaire is a tried and tested method of gathering consumer information (more on this later), but it is worth backing up your primary research with secondary research that can be gathered from a variety of sources. Web sites that focus on consumers from a style point of view, such as www.streetpeeper.com, www.thesartorialist.com, and stylebubble.typepad.com (among others) are worth investigating. Spend some time surfing the Web and you will discover just how many of these sites there are.

Consumer or market research information providers are also often used within industry. One of the more popular is Mintel, which publishes reports on consumer preferences and buying habits. The information is extensive and ranges from how often we vacation to what we consider when buying bags. Mintel also contains other useful demographic and statistical information and is continually updated.

ACORN CLASSIFICATION SYSTEM

This is a method of consumer profiling devised by CACI, a U.K.-based company offering market intelligence, solutions, and information systems. ACORN stands for A Classification Of Residential Neighborhoods. These classifications segment small neighborhoods into five categories, 17 groups, and 56 types. These classifications are a commonly used benchmark in industry, although some people believe they are outdated as ACORN groupings assume that all people in a particular neighborhood behave in the same way.

To really identify and distinguish your consumer, visual and written profiling should be undertaken to put flesh on the bones of your target consumers and help you to gain a clearer understanding of them and their needs.

EXERCISE: YOU AS A CONSUMER

You know yourself better than anyone else. Answer the following questions. Be descriptive but concise.
• At what stage are you in your career? What is your job?
• Where, and with whom, do you live?
• Where do you shop, and what brands do you favor?
• What is your disposable personal income (DPI)?
• How would you describe your fashion style?
• Who is your fashion icon?
• Where, and with whom, do you socialize?
• What music do you listen to?
• What is your favorite movie?
• Are you health conscious? Are you a member of a gym?
From answering these questions, you can start to evaluate your personal lifestyle, fashion style, aspirations, spending power, shopping habits, favorite brands, etc. What conclusions can you reach? By undertaking this exercise, you can see how this information would be very useful to designers if you were part of their target group. By reading your profile, a designer could start to target designs specifically toward you in terms of style, price sensitivity, and product appropriateness. Right product + right price + right place = success.

SECTION 1 | THE CREATIVE PROCESS

CONSUMER QUESTIONNAIRES

Objective Learn how to compile a consumer questionnaire.

When researching the potential consumer, questionnaires can be a useful tool—they can help gather more specific information about your consumer group and help to shape your solutions. They are generally used to find out people's opinions on products that exist or proposed products or services. Results are then analyzed to determine the buying behavior of customers, attitudes, awareness, desires, and demand.

12.5%
Don't know

62.5%
YES

25%
NO

▲ Presenting results
Questionnaires were filled in by 40 target customers. To a specific question: 25 responded YES, 10 responded NO, and 5 responded DON'T KNOW. So, in percent terms: 100% would be 40 respondents, 62.5% said YES, 25% said NO, and 12.5% said DON'T KNOW.

Questionnaires are commonly used in industry. They allow the company to find out answers to questions that specifically deal with a product or service—the consumer reaction to its price, quality, practicality, or desirability. Questionnaires allow you to gather original information—your questionnaire will be unique, and you will be gathering fresh information and insight.

Before constructing your questionnaire, careful thought is needed: what are your research aims and what information do you want to gather? Possible focus areas include the following:
• Lifestyle
• Spending habits
• Stimulus for purchasing
• Favored designers/brands
• Favorite styles

CONSTRUCTING YOUR QUESTIONNAIRE
Careful construction of questions is essential, since some questions/answers can give you more depth of information than just an answer to the question asked. For example, the answer to a question such as "favorite brands purchased" could help you to establish a ballpark figure for this person's spending habits. You will need a balance of open and closed questions within your questionnaire in order to get an adequate depth of information to analyze.

Open questions usually ask for opinion and require short or multiple-choice answers:
• What is your opinion on the new collection?
The multiple choice answers for this question could be something like: Fantastic, I would buy more than one piece; Innovative; Good use of color and/or materials; Some good pieces; Disappointing.
• How do you think it could be improved?
This question could be left without multiple choice options for the consumer's own comments.

Closed questions require yes or no answers:
• Do you often shop here?
To gain more information, you could follow this with:
• How many times have you shopped here?
• Do you buy this brand frequently?
• How many products of this brand do you purchase per year?

SIMPLE RULES FOR CONSTRUCTING QUESTIONNAIRES
• Never ask more than 10 questions.
• Write questions that are short, succinct, and numbered.
• Avoid leading questions.
• Group similar questions for ease and flow.
• Limit the number of open questions. Use mainly multiple choice questions to ensure you produce reliable results and gain a consensus of opinion.
• Use the check-box system for responses, but give many choices of answer. Cover all possibilities within reason.
• Always offer "other" as a possible answer and a space to write a response.
• Give clear instructions in italics, e.g. please check one relevant box.
• Use a clear font and make good use of bold and underline.
• Stick to landscape or portrait formats—never mix the two.
• Make sure the questionnaire is easy to navigate.
• Use visuals where necessary.
• Do not overfill the page.

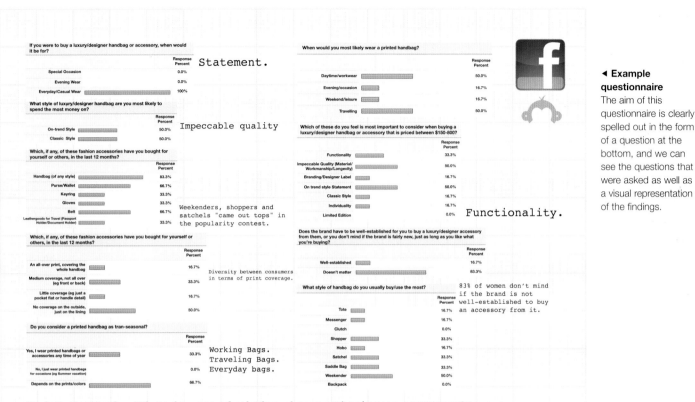

If you were to buy a luxury/designer handbag or accessory, when would it be for?

	Response Percent
Special Occasion	0.0%
Evening Wear	0.0%
Everyday/Casual Wear	100%

Statement.

What style of luxury/designer handbag are you most likely to spend the most money on?

	Response Percent
On-trend Style	50.0%
Classic Style	50.0%

Impeccable quality

Which, if any, of these fashion accessories have you bought for yourself or others, in the last 12 months?

	Response Percent
Handbag (of any style)	83.3%
Purse/Wallet	66.7%
Keyring	33.3%
Gloves	33.3%
Belt	66.7%
Leathergoods for Travel (Passport Holder/Document Holder)	33.3%

Weekenders, shoppers and satchels "came out tops" in the popularity contest.

Which, if any, of these fashion accessories have you bought for yourself or others, in the last 12 months?

	Response Percent
An all-over print, covering the whole handbag	16.7%
Medium coverage, not all over (eg front or back)	33.3%
Little coverage (eg just a pocket flat or handle detail)	16.7%
No coverage on the outside, just on the lining	50.0%

Diversity between consumers in terms of print coverage.

Do you consider a printed handbag as tran-seasonal?

	Response Percent
Yes, I wear printed handbags or accessories any time of year	33.3%
No, I just wear printed handbags for occasions (eg Summer vacation)	0.0%
Depends on the prints/colors	66.7%

Working Bags.
Traveling Bags.
Everyday bags.

When would you most likely wear a printed handbag?

	Response Percent
Daytime/workwear	50.0%
Evening/occasion	16.7%
Weekend/leisure	16.7%
Travelling	50.0%

Which of these do you feel is most important to consider when buying a luxury/designer handbag or accessory that is priced between $150–800?

	Response Percent
Functionality	33.3%
Impeccable Quality (Material/Workmanship/Longevity)	50.0%
Branding/Designer Label	16.7%
On trend style Statement	50.0%
Classic Style	16.7%
Individuality	16.7%
Limited Edition	0.0%

Functionality.

Does the brand have to be well-established for you to buy a luxury/designer accessory from them, or you don't mind if the brand is fairly new, just as long as you like what you're buying?

	Response Percent
Well-established	16.7%
Doesn't matter	83.3%

What style of handbag do you usually buy/use the most?

	Response Percent
Tote	16.7%
Messenger	16.7%
Clutch	0.0%
Shopper	33.3%
Hobo	16.7%
Satchel	33.3%
Saddle Bag	33.3%
Weekender	50.0%
Backpack	0.0%

83% of women don't mind if the brand is not well-established to buy an accessory from it.

Market Research: "What do women look for when purchasing an accessory?"

In order to define what women look for in an accessory, a survey was taken on networking website Facebook. The survey was targeted at 25 females that varied in family life status and age, but who all work in a professional working context of a global fashion company, Hugo Boss. The reasoning behind this decision was that the women all have something in common. Personal experience of working alongside them at the company gave me knowledge that they spend a reasonably high amount of money on high-end accessories and are well-informed in terms of what to look for when purchasing a luxury handbag.

◄ **Example questionnaire**
The aim of this questionnaire is clearly spelled out in the form of a question at the bottom, and we can see the questions that were asked as well as a visual representation of the findings.

CONDUCTING YOUR QUESTIONNAIRE

Initially, the best way to conduct your questionnaire would be a face-to-face street survey. Careful consideration needs to be given when determining the area where you are going to do your questionnaires. You could go to more than one area or street to get a more mixed sample. Briefly explain what the aim of the questionnaire is to your respondent before starting and always thank them at the end. Dress smartly and smile; a sense of humor is also a useful tool. You should aim to get a minimum of 50 responses.

Industry questionnaires are delivered in a variety of ways—by phone, by mail, in person, or via the Internet. There are specific Web sites set up for this very purpose, such as www.surveymonkey.com.

KEY STAGES
- What do you want to find out?
- Develop questions to get those specific answers.
- Ensure your choice of answer is broad enough.
- Consider the design layout of the questionnaire.
- Consider where you will ask the questionnaires— where is your target consumer likely to be found?
- Decide what time of day you will do your questionnaires.
- Analyze data by counting up the responses to the questions. This should be collated and communicated using bar charts or pie charts.

GLOSSARY

Closed questions: Questions that require yes or no answers.

Open questions: Questions that usually ask for opinion and require short or multiple-choice answers.

Sample: A number of respondents.

CONSUMER ANALYSIS

Objective Learn how to analyze your consumer research to create a consumer profile and consumer board and set up a focus group.

Having researched information about your consumer, you need to edit your findings and present them in a written consumer profile and visually through a consumer board.

WRITE A CONSUMER PROFILE

This serves as a written narrative of your consumer, an informed analysis based on findings from primary research observations and questionnaires, and secondary research and data. It contains basic personal information about them and their lifestyle choices. By researching your consumer and their lifestyle needs and preferences, you can better target your designs to fulfill these, ensuring your designs are appropriate, desirable, and hit the right price points.

You can decide on the categories depending on the focus of your research, but a combination of personal information and personal preferences make for a good descriptive narrative. Be specific in your detail to create maximum effect. Include information such as:

PERSONAL INFORMATION
• Age group
• Occupation
• Where they live—area/zip code?
• How they live—alone, with partner, or with friends?
• Rent or own?
• Married, single, or with partner?
• Family situation—children: no/yes; how many?
• Education—college, university?

◄ **Consumer board** The consumer board shows the visual triggers that represent your key customer—the person you are designing for: her lifestyle and passions. This idealized customer is a hip young thing into planet-saving-eco stuff, arty, and drawn to vintage glamour.

▲ Filling the page Images on this consumer board are given a similar weighting in terms of size and importance. A city dweller with a good lifestyle indicated by a beautiful apartment and soft-top car for weekends away. This person is into music and technology, and her style icon is Maggie Gyllenhaal.

PREFERENCES

- How they would describe their fashion style
- Favored brands/labels
- Where and how they shop
- Where and how they socialize
- Where and how they relax
- Where they vacation
- Media habits
- What is their favorite movie, book, or band?
- What is their perfume?
- Who is their icon?

KEY STAGES

- Decide on the categories of personal information and preferences you want to include in your profile.
- Plan and write your profile.

CREATE A CONSUMER BOARD

A consumer board is the summary of your consumer research in visuals. The board will provide the visual stimulus to give the viewer an at-a-glance overview of your core consumer, conveying their lifestyle, needs, desires, influences on their life, role models, and priorities. The visuals you select and how you present them will be key to giving the right impression and feel of your consumer and her or his lifestyle.

Throughout the research stage of your project you will have been collecting information and visuals that will have been informing and developing your core target consumer. You should have a variety of information to draw upon:

- Primary consumer observations—photographs, sketches, and notes.
- Analysis from your questionnaire, if you have conducted one.
- Your customer profile.
- Consumer trend information, if you have access to it.
- A selection of collected visuals.

From all of this information, a clear visual should be emerging of who he or she is, what they look like, and their attitude. You have outlined their preferences and personal details in your consumer profile. So do you have the visuals to back that up?

Presentation of your board There are different types of consumer boards, and it really depends how much detail you want to go into. The amount of visuals you select to convey the consumer is very much up to the individual. Have more images than you need and try a variety of combinations and layouts before choosing the best. Layout of and scale of images is key here, and you need to work on placement and grouping of the visuals to gain maximum visual impact. Keep in mind the attitude and feeling you want to convey. The color of the board selected is of paramount importance, so consideration and careful selection is required here. Try a layout, photograph it, and then refine—you will find you do this many times before you reach the best solution. To help with decision making, it can be useful to get others' opinions on which board communicates with most clarity your consumer profile. You may use text if you feel this is relevant.

If you have a scanner available, images can be scanned and manipulated using Photoshop—this will give you opportunity to recolor if necessary and augment images to make them more appropriate.

If you are using the traditional method, once placement of images has been decided upon, ensure you have reference points for where each image needs to be attached, and then use a ruler or set square to ensure images are perpendicular to the edge of the

Consumer profile

The Look: Curve-enhancing dresses and print mixing

"Curvy, cheeky, and full of attitude."

Occupation: Junior Stylist

Favorite Designers: Louis Vuitton, Miu Miu, and Victoria's Secret.

Style Icon: Beth Ditto and Brigitte Bardot.

Aspirations: To fall in love with the man of her dreams, learn the French language, and open a cupcake café/lifestyle boutique in the heart of Paris.

Favorite Cupcake Flavor: Carrot Cake or Red Velvet.

Shops Mostly At: Vintage and thrift stores for most of her clothing, but treats herself occasionally to mid-market/high-end footwear and accessories.

▲ Diagonal layout These images have been augmented using Photoshop. Use of overlaying images cleverly suggests travel between New York and London. This guy is stylish and creative, indicated by the SLR camera, books, and music. He cares deeply about how he dresses, and technology is also important.

board. Use spray glue for best results and color photocopy the board for a more professional finish. The consumer board sits in your final portfolio and portrays your consumer focus for the project.

In-depth visual consumer analysis If you want to explore your consumer in more depth, you can divide the boards up to communicate particular preferences or attributes of your consumer. Where and how she lives and what she surrounds herself with can define her lifestyle choices and preferences in more depth.

A board focusing on her fashion style and attitude is often created to give further depth to your analysis. You need to judge what is required for each particular project.

KEY STAGES

- Select more images than needed (directed by your profile).
- Research more images if necessary.
- Decide on digital or traditional approach.
- Scan in images and save, augment, and recolor images, if necessary.
- Explore color of board, if you are working traditionally,

or tone of background, if working digitally.
- Assemble images to visually communicate your profile.
- Explore a series of options, recording/saving outcomes to help with making the final decision.
- Review the series of boards developed to make a final decision.
- Create your final consumer board.

ORGANIZE A FOCUS GROUP

Once you have established your core consumer group, you may feel the need for a greater level of investigation into their attitudes, preferences, and buying habits. The more you know about your consumer, the greater the possibility of designing successful products that will satisfy their needs or stimulate a need or desire. Further consumer analysis is often undertaken in the form of focus groups. A focus group is an ideal way to gather in-depth information you can then use to ensure that your designs are targeted, market appropriate, and desirable to the core consumer group.

What are focus groups? Focus groups are made up of a small number of your core target consumer group, usually between five and 10 people. They are essentially multiple interviews.

How do they work? You prepare a series of questions. Questions are asked, and a discussion ensues. You facilitate discussion and make notes or record responses. These sessions can be extremely useful, particularly to find out specific, detailed information, such as how consumers use/interact with various products, what people carry in their daily-use handbags, or reactions to visual images, designs, or color combinations. This information feeds into your research findings or product development, depending on the stage at which you conduct the focus group.

PLANNING FOR YOUR FOCUS GROUP

- Identify your objective—what do you want to find out?
- Plan your questions; five or six should be sufficient. Send these to your focus group members before the session, so they can prepare.
- Plan your session to be no longer than 1.5 hours.
- Plan the location for the meeting.
- Identify and invite your focus group members.

Loves to have little plants in her apartment.

Simple and comfortable living space with wooden and white elements.

Likes to put things in order and knows how to use the sources around her to make her apartment decorative and functional.

D a y

t i m e

l i f e

s t y l e

Poivre Tapioca Chicorée Vermicelle

Eats healthily and will sometimes bake at home.

Loves natural/ wooden furniture and has a bike which she often rides.

Loves to put clothes in color order, which becomes the color palette of her closet.

Has one dog. Loves to spend time with him and take him to the park on sunny weekends.

15

◀ **Visuals and text** Here, the designer uses visuals of interiors to give us an insight into how this consumer lives, eats, commutes, and dresses. This is supplemented by the use of boxed text giving further details.

FINDING PARTICIPANTS

- If you are planning a focus group post-questionnaire, you could enlist participants while you conduct your questionnaire.
- Ask people who you think fit your target profile.
- Call on friends of friends or family members who might fit your profile, or put a call out on Facebook or other social networking sites.

DURING THE FOCUS GROUP

- Stay focused.
- Keep the flow of discussion going.
- Make sure your questions are answered.

AFTER THE FOCUS GROUP

- Circulate your findings to the focus group members. (This is a good way of staying in touch in case you want to do a follow-up session as the product develops.)

- Always record the session, since you will not be able to take notes and facilitate at the same time—do not rely on your memory alone.
- Analyze your findings—findings from these sessions will inform your decision making. Analyze these in the same way as questionnaire results, looking at group responses and opinions. What percentage agreed or disagreed? Was there a consensus of opinion? Where did opinion differ? How did it differ?

KEY STAGES

- Plan focus group questions.
- Plan location.
- Identify and invite members.
- Run session.
- Analyze findings.

GLOSSARY

Agenda: Outline of how the session will run and what questions will be asked.

Consumer board: An at-a-glance visual representation of your target consumer's personal style and lifestyle.

Consumer profile: A written narrative of your consumer.

SECTION 1 | THE CREATIVE PROCESS

COMPILING A SKETCHBOOK

Objective Learn how to compile a sketchbook and respond effectively to your research.

A sketchbook is a vital tool in the designer's arsenal. It contains edited research and shows the journey the research has taken. The sketchbook allows you space to conceptualize and formulate your design ideas, develop color palettes, consider techniques you could use, and explore possible material combinations.

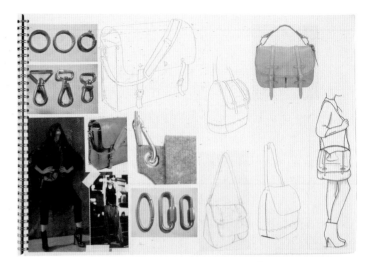

PLAN YOUR FORMAT
The format of your sketchbook is very much up to you but professional designers use 11 in. x 14 in. (28 cm x 35 cm) sketchpads. Quality of paper is crucial and should be able to sustain both wet and dry media. Some designers work on loose sheets that they compile at a later stage—the sketchbook can be reordered if necessary and this gives the designer more freedom when working. Try both methods and see which one works for you.

▼ Cutouts and line drawings Bird motifs have been cut from a map and stuck on the opposite page while birds cut from similar colored patterns are stuck on the map. Magazine tears are cut away, leaving space for line drawings.

▲ Fittings and classic bags Researched visuals of bags, magazine tears, and sourced fittings are pasted in this sketchbook. Visuals inform the sketches, which explore the construction and scale of a bag and possible usage of fittings.

Having researched and gathered a variety of inspiration and information, it is now time to edit and analyze your research findings. The amount of images used on the page is very much up to you—but careful consideration of page layout contributes to the success of the sketchbook and ultimately its usefulness. A sketchbook that is not used as a tool is just a collection of images.

Behind every item in your sketchbook, there should be a thoughtful and reasoned explanation for why you have selected and included it. Since you selected the image, it must have suggested something to you: a texture, a form, a style line? Plan your page considering layout—negative space is as important as positive.

At this stage, your sketchbook now contains the analysis of your research—you have developed your concept, organized your information, and the next stage is to evaluate your research.

BINDING
Spiral binding is the best method of binding your sketchbook pages together, as it allows the pages to be turned easily. The spiral can be made of metal or plastic and comes in various sizes. Most schools and colleges have the necessary equipment. Alternatively, you could

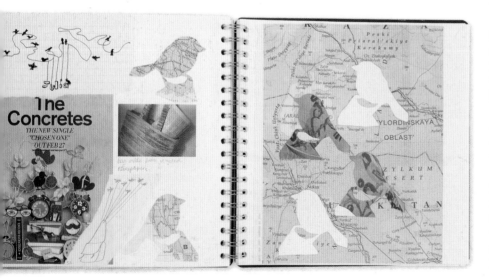

SKETCHBOOK PRESENTATION TIPS

- Use white paper for a more professional finish.
- Always stick to a format—choose between landscape and portrait and never mix the two.
- Draw or sketch directly onto the pages in your sketchbook—never cut and paste, since it wastes time and energy, and looks unprofessional.
- Do not over-decorate your pages—complex, cluttered backgrounds will detract from the inspiration.
- If using loose pages, explore and plan which method of binding you are going to use—this will affect the margin of clearance needed. Ensure you incorporate this into your page layout.
- Everything included in your sketchbook needs to be secured to the page. Care needs to be taken when securing images, swatches, and experimentation in your sketchbook. Use a spray glue for images and paper-based research—this will not buckle the paper as other glues do. Explore the best method for including samples and swatches. See page 50 for some advice on this.
- Never stick dense photocopied pages of information into the sketchbook—summarize data before adding. Retype/write out quotes, lyrics, prose, or poems if these are part of your inspirational research, considering type, font, and scale.
- Ensure you have annotations in your sketchbook to help clarify and show your analysis.

▼ **Sketchbook** Images of wooden sculptures and constructed forms explore how wood can be used to create headpieces. The ideas are expanded through sketches and written notes.

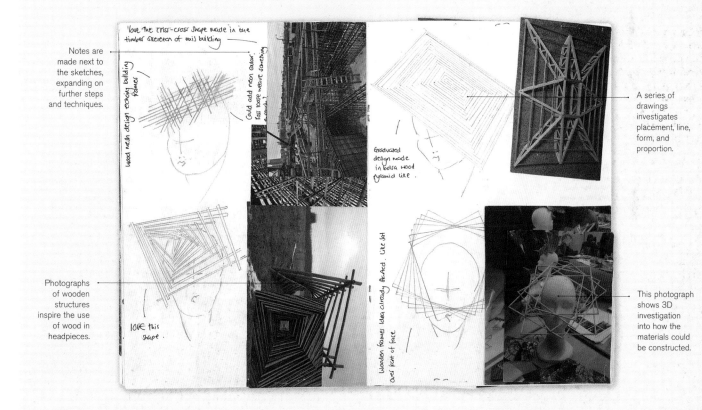

Notes are made next to the sketches, expanding on further steps and techniques.

A series of drawings investigates placement, line, form, and proportion.

Photographs of wooden structures inspire the use of wood in headpieces.

This photograph shows 3D investigation into how the materials could be constructed.

▶ **2D and 3D research** The designer explores joinings, slots, and flatpack technology through a combination of researched visuals, cutouts, and graphics.

stick or stitch the pages together along the left-hand edge. Don't forget that you will need front and back covers to protect your work. These can be made from card, heavyweight paper, or clear plastic. It is always a good idea to put a title on the cover and your name and contact details inside either the front or back cover so that your book can be returned to you should you lose it.

INSERTING SAMPLES AND SWATCHES

Swatches can be stapled, stuck in with double-sided tape along the top edge, or stitched to the page. Samples might be thicker than other items in the sketchbook and can be stuck or stitched to the page. If your samples are very thick, it can be better to attach

them to a piece of card with notes about the materials/ techniques involved and keep them in a separate box for current and future reference. This way you can build up a library of techniques and finishes that will become a 3D sketchbook. These samples are also invaluable when you come to draw up your design ideas as you have something in front of you that is exact in every detail. This will result in greater accuracy in your drawings and therefore clearer communication.

KEY STAGES
• Edit research and start to group and collate images.
• Decide on closed sketchbook or loose-sheet method.
• Put your sketchbook together.

▶ **2D sampling and tears** The designer has combined both tears and sampling on this page, leathers have been coated in resins to explore the effect, while the visuals show objects that appear to be resin-coated or melted.

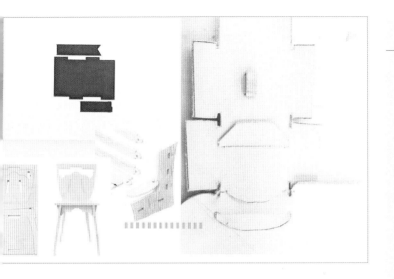

Choose any one of the titles below that inspires you or use one of your own.

Soft and hard
Diaghilev
Reflections
Japan
Heritage
Camouflage
Architecture
Art Nouveau
Film Noir

Write your chosen title in the center of your sketchbook. Create a mind map around your chosen title. Find the areas in your mind map that will provide inspiring imagery for your sketchbook. Write a list of places to visit; find things to examine, sketch, or photograph based on your mind map.

Carefully plan a route to ensure you can visit all the places you have identified—you should set aside a whole day for this. Don't forget your tools: sketchbook, pencil, and camera. At each stop on your route, get as much imagery into your sketchbook and camera as possible. If anything attracts your attention while traveling around, record that too. Make notes as you go; it's important that you know exactly where each image came from. If you're visiting museums or art galleries, you may not be allowed to take photographs or have time to sketch everything you wish to record. You could buy a few postcards to add to your collection of images. Once you have completed your tour, stick all your images into your sketchbook. Add notes explaining where each image is from, why you collected it, and any other notes you have gathered.

If anything else springs to mind while you are compiling your sketchbook—a piece of music, a poem, a quote from a book, an editorial in a magazine—add notes about this too; it will create a fuller picture of your thoughts. To test your success, ask a friend to look through your sketchbook (but do not show them your mind map) and see if they can guess the title you chose as a starting point.

SECTION 1 | THE CREATIVE PROCESS

EVALUATING YOUR RESEARCH

Objective Learn how to interrogate and evaluate your research.

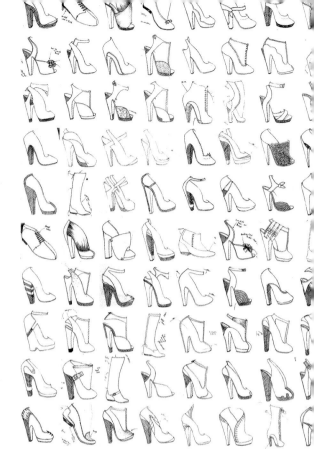

In this section we will look at how to evaluate research effectively. This process is fundamental to the creation of design ideas. Evaluation must include interrogation, investigation, interpretation, exploration, and experimentation.

> *Evaluation is creation: hear it, you creators! Evaluating is itself the most valuable treasure of all that we value. It is only through evaluation that value exists: and without evaluation the nut of existence would be hollow.*
>
> *Friedrich Nietzsche*

Through careful and thoughtful editing, everything you have collected and collated within your sketchbooks will have a purpose and a reason to be included. Evaluating your material—analyzing it and formulating conclusions—should inspire you and will ultimately inform your:

- Aesthetic, concept/mood, and color palette.
- Product shape, line, proportion, volume, and scale.
- Fabrication, material, drape, finish, texture, and surface detail.
- Construction and technical detailing.
- Component parts, details, hardware, and fittings.
- Target consumer group, needs, desire, and lifestyle.
- Potential competitors in the market.

THE EVALUATION PROCESS

Evaluation starts by posing a series of questions. Why have you selected this piece of research, and what are you going to use it for/what is it inspiring or informing? For example, an image might be inspiring a particular type of color palette, so in evaluating it, you would be asking yourself a variety of questions:

- What would the dominant color be?
- What would the accent colors be?
- What proportion of each color will I use in developing my color palette?
- Are these colors on trend and season relevant?
- Are they appropriate to my target consumer group?
- How will these colors relate to the material considerations, availability, and sourcing?

Practical exploration is often needed in order to answer these types of questions. In this case, it would result in some color experimentation being undertaken in your sketchbook.

METHODS OF EVALUATION INCLUDE:

- Creative thinking aided by probing critical analysis.
- Joined-up thinking to link ideas.
- Drawing from your research in order to flesh out and explore your ideas.
- Annotate to aid clear communication.
- Investigate and interrogate to explore a wide variety of options.
- Consider functionality and fit for purpose.
- Experiment to come up with possible new solutions and formulate ideas.
- 3D exploration to further investigate and inform initial design ideas.
- Sample and test techniques and possible methods of construction.

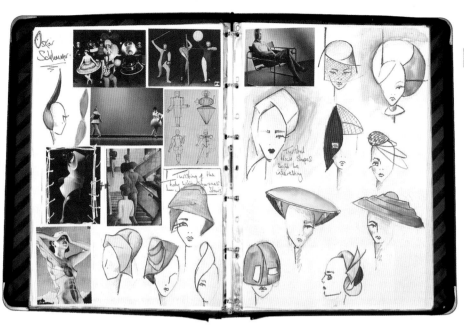

◄► Thumbnails The designer explores a variety of initial design ideas very quickly through thumbnail sketches. It is a rapid way of getting what is in your head down on paper. Some designers choose to do this next to visuals in their sketchbook while others do so on loose paper. Explore and see what works for you.

• Interpreting and conceptualizing ideas.
• Thumbnail sketches (small sketches created quickly to get an idea from your mind on to the paper) to explore initial design ideas.

EVALUATION OUTCOMES
The objective of your evaluation is to identify areas for further consideration and development.

INITIAL DESIGN IDEAS
Thumbnail sketches show your initial thoughts and design direction. They explore a variety of ideas, product categories, form, scale, line, balance, types of construction, and design details.

The next stage is to create your concept boards to communicate your findings and focus your decision making (see page 54), finalize your consumer profile, and begin to develop your design ideas in much more detail.

KEY STAGES
• Evaluate research material.
• Begin to formulate initial design ideas.

EXERCISE: ANALYZING RESEARCH IMAGERY

From your collection of research images, choose the two you find the most interesting. Analyze them by looking at them in different ways.

Color: What do they tell you about color? Reproduce the colors exactly using any media you wish.
Texture: What do they tell you about texture? What materials might be used to create that texture in your design work? Write a list.
Line: What are the predominant lines in the image? How could these be used to inform your design? Try them out in different ways through quick pencil sketches.
Shape: What shapes can you find within the images? How could these be used to influence your designs? Do some thumbnail sketches to test these ideas.
Proportion: Are there any unusual proportions within the images? How can you use this information in your design work? Do thumbnail sketches to test this too.
Details: Can you find anything that would create an interesting detail or trim? Would this be in metal, fabric, or leather? Make notes or do sketches of ideas.

Now you should have several pages of sketches and notes. Selecting at random, mix these ideas together, and draw four pages of thumbnail sketches. Create as many different looks as possible. If this comes easily, then you have selected and analyzed your research imagery well. If you find this difficult, then you may need to select other images or go back over each area to see if you have missed anything.

SECTION 1 | THE CREATIVE PROCESS

CREATING A CONCEPT BOARD

Objective Learn how to impart a mood through the visual message of the concept board.

The concept or mood board defines the aesthetic for the product, line, or collection.

A concept board is produced at the research evaluation stage and should summarize your findings. The board's primary function is to help focus the designer on the aesthetic and style direction, and it also communicates or hints at the color story and design area and gives visual information about the research influences.

The concept board is produced before any serious design development begins. The success of a board is down to the image selection, editing, and layout; this must be sympathetic to the mood or concept the board is trying to convey. The amount of information needed to convey the mood/concept is decided by the designer and can vary tremendously. Images are selected from your research and can be from both primary and secondary sources. Some designers use a pin board on the wall of their studio and photograph it as the mood/concept for the collection develops and changes throughout the research-gathering process.

▼ Limited imagery Three strong images are used here to show the fragility of the component parts and the strength of the whole. This board shows that the technique of weaving is central to the concept.

PUTTING YOUR BOARD TOGETHER

Below is a list of points to consider when putting your concept board together:

- Be focused and evaluate: what is the message and mood you want to convey?
- Do you have enough visuals that hang together? Review images from your research.
- Add to the images if necessary.
- Do your images need augmenting/changes to the color/changes in tone or intensity/cropping? All of these things can be done with a scanner and Photoshop, of which most aspiring designers have a working knowledge.
- Consider paper choices: weight, texture, finish, color, and quality all help to communicate your message and should be selected carefully.
- The board needs to go through a development stage of experimentation and analysis. Try a layout, photograph it or save it if using a computer, evaluate, and then refine—you will find you do this many times before you reach the best solution.
- Consider juxtaposition of images—try overlapping them and grouping them in a variety of ways before evaluating what gives you the best results.

◀ **Delivering the concept**
Combining similar images
can help to make your
concept clear, as in the
flatpack construction
methods successfully
conveyed here. Minimalism is
shown through the choice of
color and the simple layout.

Negative space: Blank space
in between visuals.

Positive space: Space that is
filled by a visual.

▲ **Solid block color** Blocks of color are central to this concept, as is the
angular architecture of Mexico. In this concept board, the layout enhances and
exaggerates the rectangular, colored planes of the images.

- Remember negative space can be as important
  as positive space. Consider this—it can help add
  clarity to your communication, focus the eye, or
  diffuse intensity.
- Before you make your final decision as to layout,
  image selection, and placement, it is worth asking
  the opinion of others—what do they feel the board
  represents, and what does it communicate to them?
  How strongly does it communicate the message you
  want to convey?

FINALIZING YOUR BOARD

Traditional method: Once you have decided on the
image placement, ensure you have reference points for
where each image needs to be attached. It is essential
to use a ruler or set square to ensure images are perpendicular to the edge of the board. Use spray glue for
best results and color photocopy the board for a more
professional finish.

Digital method: If you have a scanner available, images
can be scanned, manipulated, and augmented using
Photoshop. This allows you to recolor, resize, merge, and
overlay images exactly how you want them.

KEY STAGES
- Analyze images collected.
- Research more if necessary.
- Determine the message/mood you want to convey.
- Decide on traditional or digital approach.
- Research paper options.
- Explore, develop, and refine layout and images.
- Evaluate development and select the best solution.
- Print or compile your board.

RESEARCH BOARDS

Research is evaluated, summarized,
and presented via a series of
boards which sit in your portfolio.
They help tell the story of your
project focus and findings,
presenting the viewer with a
professional overview of your
research findings.

Consumer board: Visually profiles
your target consumer, conveying
their lifestyle, needs, desires,
influences on their life, role models,
and priorities. It should identify their
fashionability, outlining where they
shop and what brands they buy
(see page 45).

Color board: Communicates the
main colors and the accent colors,
the proportion, and color mix. It
should follow the aesthetic of your
concept board.

Materials board: Shows your
materials direction and will include
swatches of the material/fabric/
hardware/fittings/components you
intend to use. Sometimes color and
material boards are amalgamated to
reinforce the message.

Details board: Depicts the key
design details you will use
throughout your designs. The
images used may be photographs
taken from sampling/
experimentation you have
undertaken, magazine tears showing
similar details used by others in their
products, images of techniques
taken from technical books, scans
of hardware, or fittings and trims
you have sourced.

SECTION 1 | THE CREATIVE PROCESS

INITIAL IDEAS

Objective Learn how to start designing your products.

▶ **Sculptural inspiration**
The sculptures of Barbara Hepworth and 1970s fiber art have inspired this designer. Initial ideas in pencil and ink explore tension between line and form.

Putting your initial ideas down on paper is the next stage in the design process; this can be both exciting and daunting. It will test the value of your research and your ability to create. The purpose is to note all of your thinking to provide an extensive range of ideas from which you can develop a line to fit the brief you have been given.

▲ **Exploring details** The designer explores her ideas through a series of pencil drawings and experimental sampling of detail to help test a variety of possibilities and finalize her decisions in a more informed way.

USE YOUR RESEARCH AND EVALUATION

You will have jotted some ideas down as they pop into your head while conducting your research. Now you have a solid body of inspiration and information, it's time to start designing in earnest. This initial investigation is important, since it avoids the temptation to work with your very first ideas rather than use everything you have discovered to inspire your designs. Is your research informative enough to enable you to create design ideas without thinking too much?

THUMBNAIL YOUR DESIGN IDEAS

You can work either in your sketchbook or on separate sheets of paper. If you choose the former, all of your work is contained in one place. The advantage of separate sheets is that you can spread them out and see all your ideas at a glance. Try both methods for different projects and see which works for you.

Don't worry too much about the quality of your sketches at this stage. Using a soft pencil, draw intensively and instinctively. Getting your ideas down quickly is vital: small sketches, known as thumbnails, will help you to work at speed. Keep your work flowing; these drawings are not for presentation to an audience, but they are simply to interpret your thoughts and collate your ideas. If color or materials options come into your mind, make a note of them next to the idea they refer to or add actual color and materials swatches. Anything else that springs to mind should be annotated next to the design as a reminder of your thinking.

Once you have produced several pages of thumbnails and the ideas stop flowing quickly, take a break. Look through your research again to make sure you have used everything you collected. Draw up the ideas that emerge from this overview.

The next stage is to edit and focus on the more successful designs. Examine your thumbnails and choose the best to develop further. Scan or copy your selection onto one or two sheets of paper, grouping similar ideas together. You are now ready to develop your initial ideas into considered designs.

KEY STAGES

- Draw up initial thumbnail sketches.
- Review your research.
- Annotate where necessary.
- Add to your thumbnails.
- Analyze and edit your ideas.
- Copy selected successful ideas on to one or two sheets of paper.

SAMUEL
SHEPHERD

◀ **Quick ideas** Here, the designer is thinking on the page and communicating with himself without relating to an audience. He is trying to make sense of his research in relation to his product area and tease out ideas. The ideas are the important thing here, not how they are communicated; the designer understands them.

GLOSSARY

Materials swatches: Small pieces of material to show color, texture, and handle.

Thumbnail: A quick pencil sketch communicating a design idea.

EXERCISE: THE EMOTION OF LINE

Sit in a quiet, comfortable space with a large blank sheet of paper in front of you and a sharp pencil in your hand.

Think about a time when you were extremely sad. Concentrate on re-creating that feeling. Once you are completely enveloped by the emotion, draw lines on the paper without thinking about what you are drawing. Keep your focus on the feeling.

Now repeat the process, feeling…
• Confident
• Angry
• Happy
• Envious
• Calm

Now you have a set of lines that will convey emotional energy and feelings in your designs. Ask friends to do the same exercise and compare the results.

EXERCISE: GENERATION OF IDEAS

It is important to devise strategies that will enable you to perform consistently in the commercial world. A designer without ideas is of little value to an employer.

If ideas are not flowing, go back to your research to refresh your memory. Are you using everything you've discovered? Ask yourself what excited you about each visual and how it could be used to inform your designs.

Still having difficulty? Re-examine your research under the headings: shape, proportion, detail, and function. What is your research not telling you? Analyze the missing elements and research further into those areas immediately.

Consider your consumer—what would he or she want and need in their wardrobe? Make a list of the types of product you should consider and start creating thumbnails related to this list.

SECTION 1 | THE CREATIVE PROCESS

DESIGN DEVELOPMENT

Objective Learn how to develop your initial ideas into realistic design solutions.

For a design to be successful, serious investigation has to take place. You will be examining an edited range of ideas, layer by layer, in detail, to discover what will be successful from all aspects. Working in 2D and 3D will give you the answers you need. First and foremost, you must ensure that your design is visually desirable and will appeal to your identified consumer. The selected materials must be tested for suitability, and the techniques used need to be compatible with the manufacturing process.

▼ 3D development
Sampling is undertaken at development stage to investigate ideas. Here the designer explores design details and methods of lacing a shoe.

DEVELOP YOUR INITIAL IDEAS
Starting with your selected initial ideas, choose one of the groups and examine it in different ways. You should work on a larger scale now and draw more carefully. Try different shapes, lines, proportions, and scale, vary the position of the details and examine any fittings that might be used. Use separate sheets of paper for each group of ideas and keep exploring them until you have exhausted the possibilities. At this stage, try mixing two or more ideas together, creating links between the different groups you have explored. Once you have done

that, your designs on paper should begin to look considered and finished. Review your work and check that you have covered all the types of product that the brief and your consumer require; add to the mix if necessary. Choose the designs you feel are the most successful and draw them accurately from all angles, examining every area. Next you should start refining the color and materials. Redraw these designs and experiment with different color and materials combinations until you are satisfied with one or two versions of each design.

Now you are ready to take these designs forward and start experimenting in 3D. This is the next level of research that a designer should undertake to satisfy practical concerns and ensure that the 2D image can be translated into a real product. You must find out if the materials you plan to use are suitable and the mix of color or texture works. Details, fittings, and trimmings need to be considered in 3D to ensure they create the effect you have drawn.

EXERCISE: **UNDERSTANDING HOW COLOR AFFECTS DESIGN**

Choose three designs you have created that are constructed from at least two pieces. Draw each one 30 times. Select a range of no more than six colors. Color each drawing differently using a single color, single color with a highlight, combinations of two or three contrasting colors, and, finally, tones of one color. Now analyze the results:

Which designs are suited to formal wear?
Which are the most extreme?
Which would be good occasion wear?
Which attracts the most attention?
Which designs look fresh and new?
Which designs don't work? Why?
Which do you think would sell well? Why?
Which one would you choose to advertise your designs if you had your own label going into production? Why?

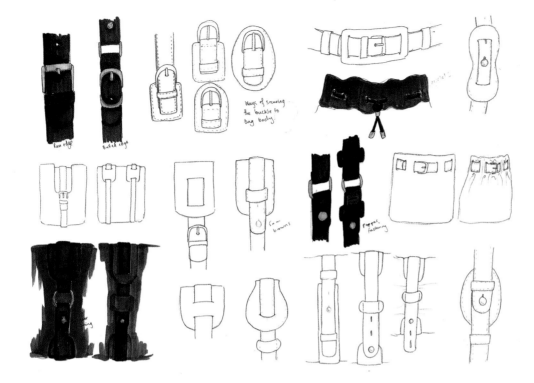

◀ **Development of straps, buckles, and closures**
Drawings exploring component parts and fittings are undertaken through the development phase. A variety of possibilities are drawn before decisions are made, and 3D sampling is conducted to test suitability.

GLOSSARY

Mock up: A 3D representation of the design.

Sample: A test piece.

CREATE A SERIES OF SAMPLES

These small samples should examine all relevant aspects of the design:

Seams: Will they work with the material selected?

Stitching: Will you use matching thread or contrasting thread as a feature? Is the stitching for practical purposes or for decoration? Are you using standard thread or a heavier one as a feature?

Edge finishes: Will they work with the material? If you are using binding or piping, what size will this be? Will it be a matching or contrasting color or texture?

Details: Experiment with the scale of details to discover the best solution.

Fittings: How are they going to be attached? Consider different methods before deciding.

Trimmings: Try two or three options before making the final choice.

These 3D experiments will help you to explain your final design decisions on paper and ensure that many potential problems have been ironed out. You are now ready to make the first mock up. Details of this process can be found in each specific product section.

KEY STAGES

- Select from the groups of initial ideas and look at them in depth from every angle.
- Examine line, proportion, scale, detail, trimmings, and fittings in 2D.
- Experiment with color and materials.
- Mix and remix your ideas.
- Reread the brief.
- Check that you have the correct range of products.
- Check that you have addressed the needs of your consumer.
- Experiment in 3D to test and problem solve before finalizing the designs in 2D.

▼ **2D exploration** 2D and 3D development are combined here, showing a thorough investigation of initial ideas. The drawings are backed up by annotation outlining possible material choices and technical detailing.

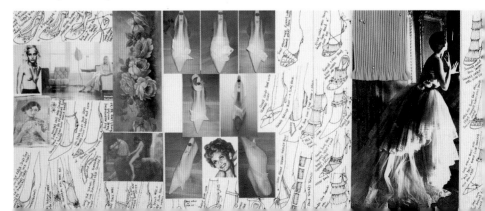

SECTION 1 | THE CREATIVE PROCESS

DESIGN PRESENTATION SPREADS

Objective Learn how to present and communicate your designs.

Expressing your designs in an appealing way that can be understood clearly by others is a crucial skill for a designer. Lecturers, employers, manufacturers, and buyers are the people you will need to communicate with. Visual accuracy is important, leaving no room for misinterpretation. Without this ability, your designs may not be selected by your creative director to be part of a line, and manufacturers could make samples that are not true to your idea and consequently don't appeal to buyers. As a student, inadequate information will lead to poor communication and a lower level of achievement.

CREATING A DESIGN PRESENTATION SHEET
A design presentation sheet is a close examination of a design idea from as many angles as necessary to understand it thoroughly, communicate it clearly, and show every detail.

Size: Use an 11 in. x 14 in. (28 cm x 35 cm) sketchpad. You do not want to produce either empty or overcrowded sheets. If, at any time, you might need to change the size of your work, you should scan it into your computer and resize as required. Alternatively, the work could be enlarged on a color copier. Use good-quality paper appropriate for the media you are using.

Layout: Decide on landscape or portrait and stick to that format. Make your sheets interesting by varying the position of your drawings; just reversing the layout can be enough. Consider the position of materials swatches; do not put them in the same position on every sheet because this will create thickness in one area when the work is filed in a portfolio and the paper will bend. You may be required to include a logo or some form of branding depending on the brief you are working to. Do not let this take over from the content; communication of the design is paramount.

Drawings: Do not do too many drawings, just enough to explain everything. Only you as the designer can decide what is important. A three-quarter view of a product will usually convey more information than any other. One drawing should be in full color; others can be simple, clean outline drawings that show all the technical details. The main drawing can be in a more illustrative style to convey the mood while the others should be accurate representations of the product. To add interest, you might use a different scale for the drawings that communicate the technical details. Your design sheets can be created entirely by hand, entirely using CAD (see page 22), or a mix of the two. Use the method that gives you the best results.

Color: You need to ensure that the colors are accurate. Often, the use of CAD results in a mismatched color; check this, since it is important to get it right. If you are working with the internationally recognized Pantone color-matching system, quoting the number of the color you are using will ensure a match.

Swatches: Add real materials, swatches wherever possible. These should be attached so that they can be touched to communicate the handle in addition to the color and texture. If you are using a combination of materials, textures, and colors, you should attach a small sample to your sheet to show exactly what this combination will look like. This also applies to edge finishes, details, and trimmings.

Technical annotation: This helps your audience to understand the construction of your design and shows that you have considered every aspect. Make sure you explain everything that is not apparent visually.

▶ **Condensed views** The designer has condensed the other views by just drawing components (base, top view) and also focusing on the detail of the leather stud panels, giving us all the information we need.

STYLE: MALACHUS BAG

DESIGN SHEET

MATERIALS

DISSECTION

LUCY ROWLAND

Brand logo and season indication.

Shoe parts are listed by number, relating to figures on the design drawing which shows color placement.

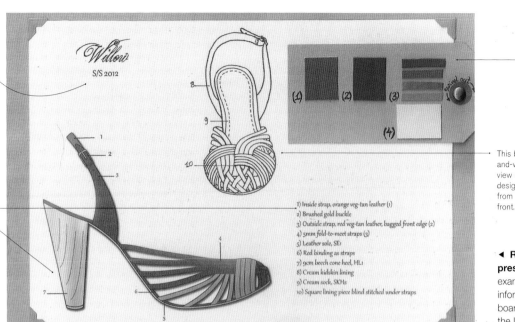

Willow

S/S 2012

1) Inside strap, orange veg-tan leather (1)
2) Brushed gold buckle
3) Outside strap, red veg-tan leather, bagged front edge (2)
4) 5mm fold-to-meet straps (3)
5) Leather sole, SE1
6) Red binding as straps
7) 9cm beech cone heel, HL1
8) Cream kidskin lining
9) Cream sock, SKH1
10) Square lining piece blind stitched under straps

Fabric choices and color options are shown in swatches.

This black-and-white view shows design detail from the front.

◀ **Requirements of a presentation board** This example will show the vital information that all presentation boards must include; however the layout varies.

When complete, your design sheets should show your design in full detail, be interesting; and, if you are a student, demonstrate your skills. Your design sheets, together with a specification sheet, should enable a manufacturer to create your product exactly as you envisage it without any other communication. For information on specification sheets, see pages 118–119 and 156–159.

KEY STAGES
- Decide on size and format. This should match the other boards for this project.
- Explore and plan the layout of the presentation board, drawings, material swatches, and text.
- Decide on media, hand drawn, CAD or both.
- How many views are needed to clearly communicate your design?
- What text is required—season, brand/project.
- Add technical annotation to fully communicate design.
- Nomenclature of materials used. What font and size?

EXERCISE: COMMUNICATING IDEAS

Communicating your ideas is a fundamental design skill, and creating the right layout is an important part of the process. You should use the standard 11 in. x 14 in. (28 cm x 35 cm) size sketchpad for this exercise. Start by drawing your design from as many angles as necessary to show all the details. Do two or three of each drawing in different sizes, as the change in scale will often help you to create a more interesting design sheet. Now, using a layout pad, place your original drawings under the page and trace them. Sketch the outlines, grouping them carefully to create a clear vision of the design. Do this several times, changing the layout and scale of the drawings.

Consider all the drawings on the page. Do you need all of them to explain the design completely? If not, eliminate the unnecessary drawings at this stage and revise your sheets. Conversely, if you are communicating a very complicated bag design or a shoe with an intricate sole unit, you will need two pages to describe the idea clearly. Place all the sheets you have created side by side and select the two that show the design most clearly. Draw these two again, paying attention to every detail; add color to the largest main drawing and a fine black outline to the rest of your drawings. Now choose the one that works best for you.

DESIGNING WITH LEATHER

Objective Learn about the opportunities and complexities of designing with leather.

▶ **Frog skin** These tanned frog skins are sometimes mistaken for reptile leathers. They are lightweight and incredibly strong.

Leather is a very beautiful, unique material to work with. Before you start to design with leather, you need to know some basic facts. This will enable you to make informed choices about selecting leather that is fit for purpose and cost effective.

▼ **Wolffish leather** These pieces of leather are easily identifiable as wolffish because of their large, black spots.

Leather is very simply the core of an animal skin that has been chemically treated to preserve its natural qualities and cured in order to prevent decay; it is rendered pliable by using fats, oils, tannic acid, and an assortment of other chemical agents. Leather is essentially a by-product of the meat industry. There is a vast array of tanning methods and materials, and the choice primarily depends on the raw material and properties required in the finished leather.

Leather is sold by the skin—each one is unique, and its size depends on which animal the skin has been taken from. Leather is measured by either the square foot or square meter, and a skin will be sold according to size, e.g. $65 per sq. ft., so if the skin was 10 sq. ft., it would cost $650.

TYPES OF HIDES AND SKINS
- **Hides**: Skins from large animals.
- **Sides**: Half hides where the hide is cut down the backbone.
- **Skins**: Skins from smaller animals.
- **Kips**: Skins from medium-sized bovine animals.

Hides and skins differ in their structure, depending on where and how they were raised/farmed, season of year, age of animal, sex, and breed. Each hide is unique, as the skins of no two animals are exactly the same. Animals with less hair or wool produce tougher, stronger-grained skins/hides. Younger animals give thinner, smaller skins and finer, smoother-grained structures. This is because they are less likely to have been exposed to skin damage caused by sores, insect bites, mites, and scratches. Every mark made on the skin of an animal from barbed wire, insect bites, ticks, brand marks, or disease leaves a trace on the actual leather, so this impacts on the quality and type of processing the skin/hide needs and ultimately affects price.

Leather can be obtained from many sources which are detailed over these six pages. Skins and hides of different animals have a variety of characteristics and properties, and their leathers are suitable for many different product types.

DOMESTIC MAMMALS
These are mammals that we rear primarily for meat, such as cattle for beef and sheep for lamb. The skins are essentially waste products that are sold on for the making of leather.

COMMONLY USED DOMESTIC MAMMALS
Calf Leather produced from the skin of a juvenile cow/bullock. It is usually tanned with chromium salts or vegetable tanned.
Size: Varies widely 5–18 sq. ft. (0.5–1.7 sq. m.).
Structure: Has a close fibrous structure with little variation across the skin.
Grain: Should not crack when folded. The grain surface formed by sweat glands and hair follicles is small and fine with no definite pattern.
Substance: Little variation across the skin but thicker in the butt.
Feel: Slightly rubbery.
Color: Good, even dye absorption.
Surface finishes: Smooth, boarded, suede, patent.

Cattle The terms "bull" and "cow" denote full-grown male and female animals; "ox" and "steer" denote castrated males. The skins from cattle are haired and relatively dense in structure. The fiber of the skin is heavier in the back area compared to the belly. The best hides are from breeds bred especially for beef, e.g. Aberdeen Angus—they are tougher, more uniform in thickness, and more square in shape. In comparison, dairy breeds generally give a looser-textured hide, are less square in shape, and are looser or thinner in the belly area. These hides are often sold in sides. They can be chrome, semi-chrome, or vegetable tanned.

Size: 11–35 sq. ft. (1–3.3 sq. m.).

Structure: Strong but fibrous, structure varies across the whole skin.

Grain: Similar in nature to calf skin (see above) but coarser in texture.

Substance: Wide variation, looser and thinner in the belly and flank areas, the butt area is much tighter and thicker.

Feel: Coarser and heavier than calf and without the rubbery feel of calf skin.

Color: Dye absorption rate varies due to varying fibrous structure producing color variation across the side.

Surface finishes: Smooth, boarded, or printed grain; coarse suedes. If sides are extra thick, flesh splits may be taken off and processed separately as suede.

Sheep The skin of the sheep supports the growth of wool so it's not a protective organ in itself. Sheepskin is very porous, and it contains very little structural fiber. Hair sheep typically come from Ethiopia and warmer climes. The skin of these animals is fine with a tight, strong grain—ideal for fine gloves. The leather is of a higher quality than a normal (wool) sheep. Normally both these skins are vegetable tanned, with a wide variety of grains printed on to the sheepskins.

Size: 2–9 sq. ft. (0.2–0.8 sq. m.).

Structure: Loose, fibrous structure.

Grain: Surface is loose but with a pattern of sweat glands and hair follicles, which is similar to goat grain (see below) but much coarser.

Substance: Light to medium.

Feel: Soft with little resilience.

Color: Even dye absorption produces even color.

Surface finish: Suede, smooth.

Goat and kid Goatskin is produced from fully grown animals and kid skin from younger animals, with

the best-quality skins coming from countries with hot, dry climates. Usually chrome tanned but can be vegetable tanned.

Size: 4–9 sq. ft. (0.4–0.8 sq. m.).

Structure: Not as dense and fibrous as calf skin but is still strong. It has a noticeable variation between the butt and belly.

Grain: Tight grain with a regular pattern of sweat glands and follicles.

Substance: Light to medium with little variation across the skin, but heavier in the butt.

Feel: Papery.

Color: Dye absorption rate varies because of varying fibrous structure, producing color variation in shank and belly.

Surface finishes: Glazed, suede, crushed, Morocco.

LESS COMMON DOMESTIC MAMMALS

Pig skin is very easy to identify by the marks the hair follicles leave on the skin. The pig has very little hair and is protected by a layer of fat just below the surface of the skin. The skin is relatively tough with a tight, weave-structured grain. The skin is porous due to the hair follicles running through the skin. Pigskin is soft, supple, and durable.

Horse hides are seldom of uniform quality. The back portion of the hide—the rump—contains a much thicker, less porous, and tougher area known as the crup, which is traditionally where Cordovan leather is taken from. The fore part of the hide is known as the horse front and is used for heavy gloving leather and for the uppers of shoes.

Buffalo hides are strong, tough, and have an interesting texture with a rubbery feel and a pebbly look. These hides tend to be thick, badly wrinkled over the shoulders, and of a coarser, looser texture than ox. These hides can usually be split two or three times.

SPECIALIST LEATHERS

Other, non-domestic mammals, birds, fish, amphibians, and reptiles are also used to produce leather, although in smaller quantities than those described above. Using rare and exotic skins is the subject of debate as there are concerns about the impact

1 Butt
2 Shoulder   Backbone
3 Neck
4 Belly
5a Fore shank
5b Hind shank
6 Offal

▲ **Leather map** The diagram above shows the different sections and quality variations of a skin, 1 being the best-quality area.

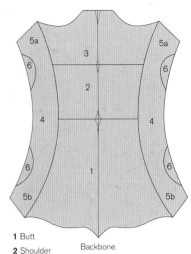

▼ **Ostrich leather** This unusually shaped skin is recognizable as ostrich because of the raised hair follicles on the central section of the skin.

ETHICAL
CONSIDERATIONS

CITES (Convention on International Trade in Endangered Species) was set up in 1973, and this agreement enforces strict policies for capturing and processing crocodile, alligator, snake, and lizard skins, and the fur of any fauna that appear on the endangered list.

There are also restrictions on importing and exporting the skins of crocodiles, alligators, snakes, lizards, seals, and other exotics.

this has on fragile species. A CITES certificate (see panel) ensures that the skin comes from a farmed source or is harvested under a strict quota system.

REPTILES

Reptile skins are devoid of hair and fat glands. The scales have similar functions as, and are chemically related to, the hair of warm-blooded animals, and as with hair, the scales are removed before tanning. The weave of the fiber is different, being much more horizontal and dense, so the skin tends to be tough and thin.

Alligator and crocodile skins are thick and scaly, but the belly and the back have very differing characteristics. The belly is supple with a uniform thickness, and the back is stiff with scaly plates. The fiber structure varies in each section of the skin. Tough, pliable, and durable, these skins are warm to the touch. In terms of leather, these skins command the highest prices, with saltwater crocodiles being the most expensive. Crocodile skins are generally much higher in price than alligator. The skins vary in size depending on the age and type of animal and can be anything from 3–16 ft. (1–5 m.) in length. Unlike other skins and hides, they are usually sold by the square inch.

Snake skins vary greatly in size depending on the type of snake, e.g., the skin of a whip snake could measure 20 in. (50 cm) while a boa constrictor or a python could measure up to 13 ft. (4 m.) in length. The scales make for bold distinctive patterns, and the larger the snake, the larger the scales. Snake skin is lightweight but strong and can have a papery feel to it.

Lizards vary in size according to type. A lizard skin can be between 8–20 in. (20–50 cm) in width (we don't measure the length as the tail is usually lost in the process). The skins have distinctive, small diamond scale markings. Like snake skin, lizard skin is light in weight but strong and can feel papery.

AMPHIBIANS

Frog and toad skins are very similar to lizard skins, and share many of the same characteristics and properties. They are exotic in appearance and vary in the size and surface depending on the species.

Frog skins generally have a smoother finish than toad skins. The leather is light in weight but strong. The size of these skins varies, from 3–5 in. (7.5–13 cm) in width and 4–6 in. (10–15 cm) in length.

Toad skin shares many of the same characteristics as frog skin but varies more greatly in size due to variations across species. The cane toad can grow up to 10 in. (25 cm) long and has recently become popular for tanning due to its status as vermin in countries such as Australia. The leather of the cane toad is strong, tough, and durable. It has an almost plated surface in its center and is often confused by the uninitiated for crocodile leather. The skins vary in length between 5 and 10 in. (13 and 25 cm).

OTHER MAMMALS

This refers to any mammal that is not necessarily farmed for its meat, but a free, wild animal. Kangaroo, elk/moose, peccary, and seal are included in this category. Deer is sometimes included, but it is sometimes categorized as a domestic mammal as it is farmed for its meat.

▲ **Croc bag** A vintage bag made of crocodile leather. The raised, plated surface on the back of the skin is the most highly prized and expensive section of the skin.

◄ **Crocodile leather** The belly side of the crocodile skin is soft and supple without the raised plate of the back. This skin is from a very young crocodile.

► **Lizard skin** This is the leather of a ring lizard, usually sourced from Indonesia. The skins range from 5 to16 in. (15–40 cm) at their widest point. This one is missing a hind leg.

Kangaroo skin is stronger than cow hide, and lightweight. It has a very uniform fiber structure and a skin of relatively even thickness. It can be split thinly and still retain strength. It is produced from free-ranging animals under strict Australian government regulation.

Deer skin is soft and supple to the touch. It has a tight grain structure and is very strong. It is washable and abrasion resistant. The skin is thicker in the butt and looser and thinner in the belly area. The skin generally is very stretchy, so care needs to be taken when selecting this leather. The size of the skins varies: 7–12 sq. ft. (0.7–1.1 sq. m.).

Elk/moose skin produces a very heavy leather with similar properties to deerskin, except the hides are much thicker and require splitting. Sizes vary: 9–16 sq. ft. (0.8–1.5 sq. m.).

Peccary produces a fine leather with unique properties—it is extremely soft, pliable, stretchy, porous, and opaque. It is similar to pig skin, which has triangular clustered hair follicle markings. On the peccary these are slightly larger, since the animal has coarser hair. It is hunted under conservation regulations determined by the Peruvian government. It has a limited availability and strict export restrictions, which makes this leather very expensive and luxurious.

Seal skin makes strong, soft, flexible leather. Pin seal has a minute, pebbly grain and may have a dull or glazed finish. This type of skin is usually vegetable tanned and not as durable as calf skin. Seal skin can also come with fur on. The outer fur is removed to reveal a soft, short under-fur.

Antelope leather is very difficult to find. It is virtually nonexistent in the U.K. and Europe. However, both kudu and springbok are available for purchase on the Internet. This leather has a velvety feel and is usually sueded on the flesh side.

BIRDS

Very few birds are used for leather. Ostrich, emu, and chicken are all farmed for their meat and their skin is a by-product which is then tanned to make leather.

Chicken feet are the only parts of the bird that are tanned. They look slightly scaly and reptilian but are smooth to the touch. Chicken gives a thin, papery leather that is used mainly for small leather goods and is often patchworked.

Ostrich is referred to as an exotic leather. It is easily recognizable by the raised bumps on the surface of the leather pattern caused by its quill sockets. These bumps are localized in the center of the skin and only one-third of the skin has these bumps—the area known as the crown. The leather is flexible, pliable, durable, and soft to the touch. It has a tight grain structure and is very strong. The average size of a skin is 16 sq. ft. (1.5 sq. m.). Ostrich legs are also tanned and have become popular for their exotic, reptilian appearance. The shins have platelets down the front of them and the legs often have the claws left on, sometimes used as a design feature. The legs measure approximately 20 in. (50 cm) in length and 5 in. (12.5 cm) in width.

Emu leather is very similar to ostrich leather but the skin is completely covered in raised imprints left from the feather follicle structure, which makes it easily identifiable. The average size of an emu skin is 6–7 sq. ft. (0.6–0.7 sq m.).

FISH

Fish skins are very durable and lightweight. They are a waste product of the food industry and are reasonably environmentally friendly—neither limes nor acids are required in pre-tanning, since there is no hair to remove. The skins carry the characteristics and colorings of their species and have unique patterns caused by the removal of the scales. If the scales are large this will be reflected on the leather. Fish that are commonly tanned include eel, wolffish, perch, cod, and salmon.

Eel skins are lightweight, supple, and incredibly strong; 2–3 times stronger than cowhide of the same thickness. The skin has a unique appearance and is instantly recognizable by the wrinkles that run down the center of the skin from top to bottom. Eel skin is very narrow—a single skin measures 15 in. (37 cm) in length and

▲ **Quill markings** A close-up of this ostrich skin shows the raised quill socket markings on the crown (the central part).

▼ **Perch** This skin has come from the Nile perch. The perch is easily recongizable by the rough surface created by its coarse scales.

PRE-TANNING PROCESSES USED IN LEATHER MANUFACTURE

Flaying: Removing the skin from the animal.

Curing: Preserving skins for transport or storage.

Washing: Wetting or soaking salted skins/hides, then drying them to restore them to a natural raw condition.

Liming: Loosening hair, fat, flesh etc., and plumping up the skin ready for tanning.

Unhairing: Removal of hair.

Fleshing: Cutting away fat and flesh.

Deliming: Neutralization of alkaline content from the liming process.

Bating: Making the skin softer and clearer.

Pickling: (drenching or souring). Brings the skin to the acidic state necessary for the chemical reaction of tanning to take place. It also preserves the skins prior to tanning.

▶ **Python skin** Pythons can produce very large skins—approximately 56 in. (1.6 m) long and 6 in. (15 cm) wide.

2½ in. (6 cm) in width—and is often sold stitched together in plates of 60 x 23 in. (1.5 x 0.6 m.). The eel skins are placed side by side and sewn together down the whole length.

Wolffish skin has a unique character thanks to the dark spots on the skin. Wolffish leather can be dyed any number of colors and tones, and the back dots will show through. Leather is smooth, as wolffish do not have scales. The skins are on average 1 sq. ft. (0.1 sq. m.).

Nile perch skin is characterized by a rough surface of scales. Perch leather is much thicker than other types of fish leather (such as salmon) and can be dyed easily to create a variety of tones. It is available in two finishes: open scaling, which gives a coarse finish, and closed scaling, which gives a finer finish. Sizes vary: from 6–20 in. (15–50 cm) in length. The average size is approximately 1 sq. ft. (0.1 sq. m.).

Cod gives a leather that is an unusual mix of coarse and fine textures. The scales are slightly finer than that of salmon, but the texture is more varied—mostly smooth but with coarse patches. Likewise, the palette of cod leather is nuanced, with delicate gradations of hue. It can be dyed any color or tone. Like perch, cod is available in open scaling or closed scaling, the latter producing a finer finish. The length of a cod skin is 15–20 in. (40–50 cm), and the shape is unique: the hides are triangular, 5–6 in. (12–15 cm) at the neck, which is the widest point, and tapering back toward the tail.

Salmon leather is pliable and quite strong compared to other skins of similar thickness, and can be dyed a variety of colors. The scales follow a delicate, repeated pattern, and it is available in open scaling (which creates a coarse finish) or closed scaling (which creates a smooth finish) finishes. The most noticeable feature is the narrow band that runs along the center of salmon skin. The skins are on average 24 in. (60 cm) long and 5 in. (12 cm) at the widest point.

Stingray skin is unique—it is covered in thousands of tiny pearl-like scales that run through the grain of the skin. It is one of the toughest leathers—it is incredibly strong and does not bend easily. It is difficult to cut with a knife and will not tear. It often has an eye-like white marking "star" located on the widest part of the skin that has a shell-like feel. Stingray is extremely difficult to stitch as the scales are very hard and can break the machine needle.

LEATHER TANNING

The process of tanning stabilizes the preserved skin/hide, converting the perishable into the beautiful. The tanning process converts the raw hide into a material that will not putrify, while making it softer, more pliable, and durable. Tanning takes place in large wooden or metal drums. Tannages are unique to the tannery, and all tanners have their own, often closely guarded, recipes that may have been developed and refined over many years.

Chrome tanning uses chromium sulphates or chlorides. The reaction with the chromium salts gives a very stable hide fiber that is resistant to bacterial attack and high temperatures. Without further processing, however, chrome-tanned leather does not have many of the properties or qualities desired for useful products. Chrome tanning must be used in conjunction with additional processes of dyeing, fat liquoring, and perhaps vegetable re-tannage to produce useable leathers. The main advantages of chrome tanning are high speed and low cost, producing supple, pliable leather with an extensive range of color capabilities.

Vegetable tanning uses water extracts of barks, woods, leaves, roots, and fruit matter. This tannage gives a pale, uniform biscuit shade, which will dye and fix any color easily. The leather will have the correct degree of flexibility, and the appearance of the grain will be enhanced. Vegetable tan gives a firm finish to the leather, which means it keeps structure well. It also gives a clean, attractive cut edge and retains embossed patterns particularly well. It has little water resistance unless specifically treated. One of the characteristics of vegetable-tanned leather is that the color will deepen with age.

Semi-chrome tanning is a vegetable tanning process followed by a chrome tannage. This type of tannage ensures the leather has the best properties of each tanning process. The main characteristics of the leather will be of vegetable-tanned leather, but it will have some benefits of chrome-tanned leather: a more pliable handle, a better resistance to water, fade resistance, and better coloration.

Aldehyde tanning uses glutaraldehyde, and originally formaldehyde, mixed with water to create a chemical solution called formalin. It produces a leather that is referred to as "wet white" because of its color. Deerskins are most commonly tanned using this method—the property it imparts to the leather is washability. The leather often has a slightly distressed or cracked appearance but an incredibly soft handle.

SORTING AND SPLITTING

After tanning, the leathers are sorted and, if required, split by machine. The leather is rolled between a rotating drum blade that cuts/splits the skin into the required thickness. The layers are called splits, the best and most valuable of which is the top grain split (the outer skin of the animal's body). This is easy to identify, since it has one rough and one smooth surface. The top grain skins/splits are then checked for marks—if the skin has a small amount of or no skin defects/scars, it will be processed into a full grain leather, which requires no surface correction. If it is scarred, the surface will be semicorrected by buffing or even fully embossed to correct or add to the grain. The lower split can either be processed as it is into suede leather or be further processed to become coated split leather. Coated split are less durable and much stiffer than top grain leather; they need further processes and are often processed into patent leathers with high-gloss finished surfaces.

COLORING AND FINISHING LEATHER

After the leather has been tanned and split to the required thickness for the intended product, it requires finishing. Finishes determine the properties of the leather as well as the feel, surface detail, and the color. Finishing processes may include dyeing, embossing, fat

liquoring, spraying, lacquering, glazing, waxing, buffing, antiquing, milling, waterproofing, flame proofing, and stain proofing. Leather can be fully struck—dyed through all layers—or partially struck, where only the flesh and grain surface are penetrated with color. Color can also be applied by coating the surface. Pigments are usually sprayed or coated on to the skin/hide and require a finish to be applied to ensure the color fastness.

After the leather is dyed/colored, a sealant is often applied to provide a level of protection against abrasion and staining and to enhance the color. Depending on the number of coats applied, the leather can become stiffened and may require softening. The leather is then dried to remove all moisture.

The final stage of the operation is called plating, where the leather is pressed under 300 tons of pressure per square inch. This smoothes the surface prior to the final checking and grading processes.

GRADING

Leather is sold by grade. The grading system refers to the amount of scarring or skin imperfections. Most tanneries use the following grading system but some do have their own systems:

A/1 Grade: No imperfection/marks or scars
B/2 Grade: 5–10 percent imperfections
C/3 Grade: 10–20 percent imperfections
D/4 Grade: 20–30 percent imperfections
E/5 Grade: 30–40 percent imperfections
F/6 Grade: Factory reject

BUYING LEATHER

Leather is usually sold by leather merchants or by tanneries directly; a search on the Internet will reveal many. Tannery numbers are dwindling, but they still exist—usually near to sources of water, since water is one of the key components in the tanning process. In Italy there are many tanneries lining the River Arno in Tuscany. Started in 1981, Lineapelle is the most important leather and component trade fair worldwide. It is held twice a year, in Bologna, Italy, and has more than 1,000 exhibitors from all areas of the sector, including more than 550 tanneries from all over the world, so it is a great place to source and research leather. See pages 234–236 for more on trade fairs.

See pages 234–236 for more on trade fairs.

GLOSSARY

Butt: Thickest, strongest part of the hide.

Crushed: Leather that has had its grain pattern accentuated by rolling or plating.

Glaze: Kid leather, usually chrome-tanned, with a highly polished surface.

Grading: Quality control for leather, skins, and hides.

Hides: The complete covering of a larger animal.

Kips: Small type of cattle hide from India and Pakistan.

Morocco: Vegetable-tanned goat skin with a distinctive pebble grain.

Sides: Half a hide, cut down the backbone.

Skins: General term for the outer covering of a smaller animal.

Tanning: Converting raw hides into a stable material that will not decay.

▲ **Sizing leather** The underside of a glazed kid skin has its square footage stamped onto it to enable accurate pricing.

SECTION 1 | THE CREATIVE PROCESS

COMMUNICATION AND PRESENTATION

Objective Understand the importance of communication and presentation in creating a successful product line.

In your research, you have identified your target consumer and position in the marketplace. Now you need to determine the price architecture and how many products will go into each category. You will communicate this information in a line plan or lineup.

▶ **Line planning** The designer is re-examining the initial line proposal and revising the balance after design development. After analyzing the line in relation to the design work, she has decided to add an ankle boot to the high level and to add another product to the core level, reducing the number of pieces in the entry level by one to accommodate this.

LINE BUILDING

A line can be of any size—from half a dozen products to hundreds—but the principles remain the same. Your target consumer's lifestyle will help you to make decisions about your line. Everyone needs different products for different purposes. At times, your consumer may want to appear extremely fashion aware while on other occasions a more conservative or comfortable look will be appropriate. What we wear during the week is often ruled by the culture of the organization we work for. On vacation and in our personal time, we may dress quite differently, often in a more relaxed style. In addition to everyday needs, there are occasions that demand a special outfit: weddings, formal dinners, etc. Responding to all these lifestyle aspects will create a line that can tempt the consumer to buy several products.

LINE LEVELS

The next step is to define the price points and the types of products that will go into each level. You also need to consider how many designs and colorways will be offered at the different levels. It is usual to offer more products at the entry and middle levels. The purpose of this is to attract your secondary consumer through offering a more affordable part of the line as well as appealing to the target consumer to purchase more than one item. At the top end of the line, the specials show the designer's signature style without compromise. These products are more fashion forward and would usually be purchased for a special occasion. They are also used for marketing the season's line.

DESIGNER- OR MARKETING-LED?

Using this framework, you will work in one of two ways to produce a balanced range of products. If the collection is designer-led, it will develop organically with the designer in control, but if marketing-led, it will be constructed to a predetermined plan.

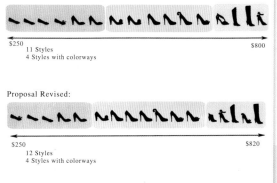

LINE PLANNING

Concept Development Proposal:

$250 $800
11 Styles
4 Styles with colorways

Proposal Revised:

$250 $820
12 Styles
4 Styles with colorways

I have added an extra style which is a boot because I felt that the line was missing an ankle boot. I have also added a few more colorways to allow the customers to have more choice. This is a good way of giving the customer choice without having to buy new kits or get more patterns graded adding to extra costs.

Entry Level

Core Level

High Level

Each shoe/boot silhouette represents a shoe in the collection. If it is the same symbol its the same style in a different colorway.

Most of the boots need to be in the high level because of the amount of leather used to create them and the additional kit I would need to buy.

PRICE POINTS

Entry level: Simpler products that can be produced for a lower price, creating an opportunity for a wider range of consumers to buy into a brand.

Core level: The main section of any line, where the products all have the recognizable design signature of the brand and attract the loyal consumer season after season.

High level: More extreme fashion leads at this level, and it can also include products that are costly to manufacture. Pieces are usually selected from this group to advertise the brand.

1. The designer will develop ideas, then apply them to different types of products to create a line that is balanced, addresses the consumer group needs for the season, and fits within the levels.

2. The marketing department will produce a plan based on sales figures from previous seasons and knowledge of future buying and fashion trends. The number of styles and colorways for each type of product will be set out in a chart that the design team will work to. If a design has sold extremely well, it might be carried over to the next season. The colors and materials will be updated, but the product will remain the same. This is known as a "cash cow" because all of the development costs of the product were recovered in the previous season. In producing the design again, profit will be increased as materials, manufacturing, and delivery are the only costs involved.

LINE OVERVIEW

Once all the designs are selected, a lineup will be drawn so that the whole collection can be seen at a glance. At this stage, the materials and colors will be re-examined to ensure they work as a complete line. Changes will be made until the line hangs together and tells a story. Then second, and sometimes more, color and materials options will be decided; these are often referred to as "skus."

The line will be examined once again to check that each product appears to be good value at the level it sits in. Alterations will be made if an item is too complicated or simple for the price position. The objective is to create enough options to satisfy the target consumer without creating so many choices that the customer is confused.

It is also important to consider the implications for the production process at this stage. Planning, purchasing, and product development departments will be involved in this area.

If too many materials and colors are selected, purchasing materials for production will be more complicated, and quantities will be diluted, reducing the scope for negotiating prices.

Too many different constructions will also be detrimental, since production may have to be distributed across a wide range of manufacturers, again reducing opportunities for negotiation on quantity and, consequently, reducing profit margins. Once the color/materials options have been agreed for each design, a line plan can be drawn up.

▼ **Line board** This designer has created a well-organized line board that communicates all the essential information about each product while giving an overview of the whole line at a glance. Season, style name, dimensions, price, materials, color, and the purpose of each bag are all stated.

▼ **Finished bag** The "Selina" bag from the line to the right is a general-purpose day bag that is beautifully crafted and has a specific design signature.

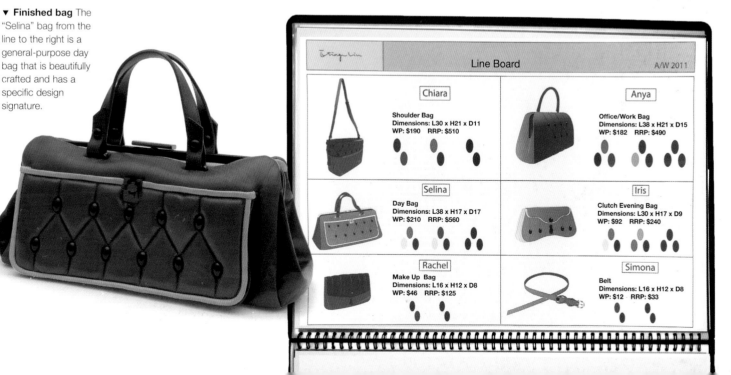

| Line Board | A/W 2011 |

Chiara
Shoulder Bag
Dimensions: L30 x H21 x D11
WP: $190   RRP: $510

Anya
Office/Work Bag
Dimensions: L38 x H21 x D15
WP: $182   RRP: $490

Selina
Day Bag
Dimensions: L38 x H17 x D17
WP: $210   RRP: $560

Iris
Clutch Evening Bag
Dimensions: L30 x H17 x D9
WP: $92   RRP: $240

Rachel
Make Up Bag
Dimensions: L16 x H12 x D8
WP: $46   RRP: $125

Simona
Belt
Dimensions: L16 x H12 x D8
WP: $12   RRP: $33

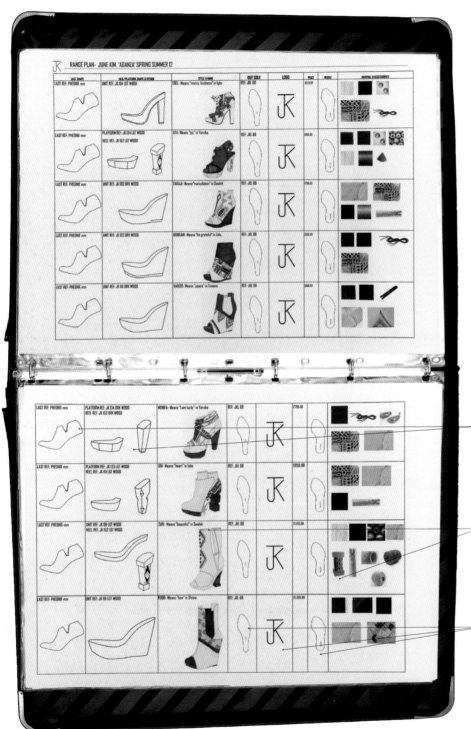

LINE PLAN

The line plan for the season should be organized in a logical way to show each design, with its name or reference number, in every colorway with materials swatches and prices. Other details should be included depending on the products in question. The lasts and heels should be shown for a line of footwear and dimensions included for a line of bags.

The line plan acts as an at-a-glance outline of the products on offer for the season. It creates a guide for the marketing department, the buyer, the retailer, and the designer. Once the season is over, it can be used to show the quantities sold of each item in each colorway, creating a body of information to support the next line.

SPECIFICATION SHEETS AND SAMPLE PRODUCTION

The next stage is sample production. Each item in the line will be made up in the first color/material combination for approval. A specification sheet must be created for each design, giving clear and comprehensive instructions to the sample manufacturer. The specification sheet, together with the design presentation sheet and accurate technical drawings, should communicate

The first two columns identify the last and the components that make up the bottom of the shoe by name and shape.

An illustration of the design shows the placement of the materials, which are shown along with all the trims and fittings.

The branding logo is included, and its positions on both the sole and sock are highlighted.

◄ **Complex line plan** A lot of thought has gone into creating a plan that communicates all the necessary details in this complicated line of footwear. The grid formation with similar information in each column works well. This type of line plan would only be used internally by a company, as there is too much information on it to present to a buyer. A simpler version or a look book would be created for customers.

all elements of the design clearly and concisely. An essential tool in the global market, it is used to communicate with the sample room, which may be at the other side of the world. To overcome language barriers and possible misunderstanding, it is important to include as much visual information as possible and to use tools such as the international Pantone color referencing system. Every company has its own style, but the information required is the same. The more detail the specification sheet contains, the less chance there is of error. Examples of specification sheets can be found elsewhere in this book (see pages 118–119 and 156–159).

The specification also acts as a record of the sample created for future reference for both the company that created the design and the sample manufacturer. Every specification will have its own unique number to enable clear communication between all parties when discussing a particular sample. When a design is sampled in more than one colorway, each color will have its own dedicated reference number to avoid confusion.

Once the first samples have been delivered, the design and marketing team will check them thoroughly and try them on the body to ensure the proportions, fit, and look are right. Anything that needs to be corrected will be noted, and a request for a second sample will be made, and so on, until the product is perfect. Once the sample has been approved it will be "sealed," that is, it will be marked in some way that cannot be removed. The most common method of sealing is to make a small hole in the sample and thread a fine, strong cord through it. The ends of the cord are then trapped in plastic or a metal tag and heat sealed. The seal cannot be removed without cutting the cord. The sealed sample acts as the approved model that must be matched exactly by the manufacturer when producing the accessory collection.

When the line has been shown to buyers, and orders received, further testing will take place to ensure every aspect of the product is suitable for production, and a final specification will be written for the manufacturer to follow.

GLOSSARY

Line plan: A detailed outline of every product in every color and material combination with associated season, names/reference numbers, and prices.

Lineup: A drawing of every item in a line or collection, in color. Used as a check by the designer and sometimes marketing to ensure that the right balance has been achieved throughout.

▼ **Lineup** This is an example of the type of lineup that would be shown to a buyer. The complete collection is shown and it identifies the style, price, colors, and materials of each piece. The measurements show how each product compares in size to other pieces in the collection, giving an accurate picture of the line.

EXERCISE: A DIFFERENT VIEWPOINT

As a designer it is useful to understand the fashion business from another perspective. Think about the concerns of the marketing department and what influences them when they put together a line plan for the coming season.

- What is the price range?
- How many items should be at each price level?
- Are there any items that should be carried over from the previous season?
- What type of products will be at each level?
- How many color/material options will there be for each item?
- Answer these questions and then put them in a line plan together using a grid. You should attempt to give enough detail to guide the design team but not so much that you compromise their creativity.

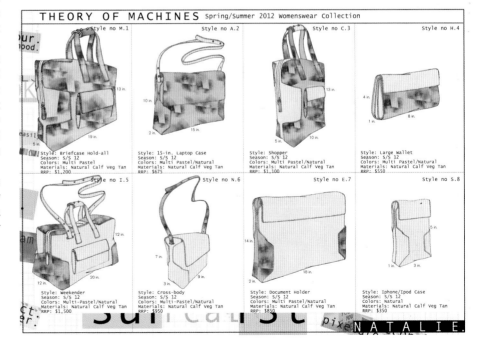

THEORY OF MACHINES Spring/Summer 2012 Womenswear Collection

Style no M.1
Style: Briefcase Hold-all
Season: S/S 12
Colors: Multi Pastel
Materials: Natural Calf Veg Tan
RRP: $1,200

Style no A.2
Style: 15-in. Laptop Case
Season: S/S 12
Colors: Multi Pastel/Natural
Materials: Natural Calf Veg Tan
RRP: $675

Style no C.3
Style: Shopper
Season: S/S 12
Colors: Multi Pastel/Natural
Materials: Natural Calf Veg Tan
RRP: $1,100

Style no H.4
Style: Large Wallet
Season: S/S 12
Colors: Multi Pastel/Natural
Materials: Natural Calf Veg Tan
RRP: $550

Style no I.5
Style: Weekender
Season: S/S 12
Colors: Multi-Pastel/Natural
Materials: Natural Calf Veg Tan
RRP: $1,500

Style no N.6
Style: Cross-body
Season: S/S 12
Colors: Multi-Pastel/Natural
Materials: Natural Calf Veg Tan
RRP: $950

Style no E.7
Style: Document Holder
Season: S/S 12
Colors: Multi Pastel/Natural
Materials: Natural Calf Veg Tan
RRP: $850

Style no S.8
Style: Iphone/Ipod Case
Season: S/S 12
Colors: Natural
Materials: Natural Calf Veg Tan
RRP: $350

ADVANCED TECHNOLOGIES

Objective Learn about advanced technologies used in the accessories industries.

Advances in technology have changed the world and created a whole new range of creative opportunities for designers. CAD (see page 22) in all its forms allows communication across the globe at the touch of a button. The design studio might be in London, the head office in New York, and the manufacturer in Hong Kong. Everything can be realized without the people involved ever meeting.

The four most commonly used technological systems are outlined here. Being familiar with what is new is crucial in the field of design. Knowing the possibilities will enable you to explore things in different ways and reach solutions with greater accuracy and speed. Even if you don't have access to all of these technologies, understanding their potential is vital.

RAPID PROTOTYPING

This process uses virtual designs from CAD systems and transforms them into solid objects that are built up layer by layer, gradually creating the required shape. Any shape that can be created in the CAD program can be built in 3D. Although the process is called "rapid" prototyping, a large, complicated structure will take a long time to build. Different machines use different materials, from thermoplastics to paper to titanium alloys.

The advantage of this process in the accessories industries is that components and fittings can be realized in 3D in minute detail before making final decisions to progress a design. Anything can be made, from a complicated sports footwear sole to the smallest rivet for a purse or bag. The whole appearance of a design can be tested before committing to mold making or tooling, which can cost many thousands of dollars.

LASER CUTTING

Laser cutting is exactly what it says—cutting a material with a laser. Computer software is used to create the shape or pattern to be cut. The material is then cut automatically by the machine with complete accuracy. It creates a perfectly vertical cut and can be used to create complicated patterns that would be impossible to cut by any other means. This process works with a wide range of materials from paper and plywood to Perspex, leather, and metal, almost all of which are used in accessories. The opportunities this has opened up for the designer are endless. The only drawback is that, with some materials, the cut edge is burnt in the process, creating a dark edge, or even worse, it can leave a sooty residue with an unpleasant smell. Sophisticated

▶ **Rapid prototyping** This process was used to create the sculptural form of this fashion shoe. It is finished with high-gloss paint and the soft leather interior was added afterward—the opposite of traditional shoemaking.

▲ **Cameos** Rapid prototyping was used to create this "cameo," designed as a subtle type of branding for the waist area of the sole of a shoe. Once the designer approved the final sample, a mold was made and the cameo was cast in metal.

◀ **Laser-etched leather** Deep-etched lines can affect leather like scoring and cause it to fold. The technique is used to great effect on this collar to enhance fit and comfort.

◀ **Laser-cutting technology** This shoe is constructed from a series of interlocking pieces that form a rigid, wearable structure. Laser cutting was used to achieve absolute accuracy, and the transparent, reflective qualities of Perspex highlight the construction.

▶ **Digital prints** This bag shows the use of digitally printed leather. In this case, the leather hide was printed prior to the cutting of the pattern pieces. The same person designed the print and the bag.

computer-operated laser-cutting machines have been developed for use in the accessories industry. The machine scans the skin of leather, highlighting any defects, then projects a layout of all the pieces that can be cut from the skin, avoiding all the blemishes. Once this has been approved by an operator, the machine cuts the pieces. Although these machines are costly, the savings are considerable. No knives are needed, which saves both time and money, and the manpower required is reduced significantly.

DIGITAL PRINTING

A digital image is created for a print by the designer, and the printing machine, using specially modified inkjet technology, re-creates the design on fabric. Although, area for area, this process is more costly than traditional printing methods, it is a fast and efficient way of testing out a new print, allowing more flexibility for the designer, who can try out several versions and colorways before deciding on the final look. It is commonly used for small runs as well as sampling, since it is cheaper than other methods when working with small quantities. The technology involved produces extremely accurate results and can be used with a wide range of fabrics and leather.

BODY AND FOOT SCANNING

This process is used to create a digital image of the form of a body or foot. It is used by designers to achieve an exact fit for a pair of shoes or test out the shape of a bag to ensure it is ergonomically correct. It is this equipment that is used in some stores to check your body shape and advise you on the best cut and fit of, for instance, a pair of jeans. Specialty shoe stores also use this method to determine the best size and last shape for a customer. The images created by moving the body or foot during this process can be very interesting, and designers have been known to use the resulting visuals as inspiration for their work.

▲ **Rhino 3D software** This screen shot shows the development of a design using 3D software. Once the designer is satisfied with the look, the file is sent to the rapid prototyping machine, which will print an exact replica.

GLOSSARY

CAD: Computer-aided design.

Digital printing: A method of printing using digitally created images whereby the images are sent directly to the printer.

Ergonomics: The science of refining a design to optimize it for human use.

Laser cutting: Digital images are sent to the laser cutter, and it reproduces the design exactly.

Laser etching: Digital images are sent to the laser cutter, and the design is etched on to the material.

Rapid prototyping: Virtual designs created using software are printed in 3D, layer by layer, to produce a solid object.

SECTION 2
Handbags

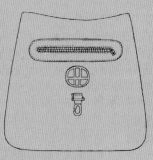

In this section we will show you how to move your bag design ideas from your sketchbook into a realizable design entity. In order to design effectively and efficiently, a basic level of introductory technical knowledge is essential, so we introduce you to specialist processes. The anatomy of a bag breaks a handbag down into its component parts, while an overview of specialist materials, reinforcements, and fittings further clarifies usage of the all-important structural reinforcement.

You will learn about the specialist construction methods for leather goods, explore the different construction styles for bags, and how these can be assembled using a variety of seam types. Basic pattern cutting principles for pattern shapes common to many styles of handbag are introduced to you through a series of step-by-step exercises and easy-to-follow diagrams.

Aesthetics, practicalities, ergonomics, and usage are all key factors that need to be addressed when creating a bag, and so we investigate the process of design development; evolving your embryonic design ideas into considered design solutions. You will gain an understanding of the importance of materials testing, 3D exploration, and evaluation through the process of mocking up, and learn how to communicate to the manufacturer vital instructions for the production of your design using a specification sheet.

BAG MAKING TOOLS

Objective Learn about the tools used in bag making.

The tools shown on these pages are used by leather workers and in particular bag designers, makers, and students. Using these tools will help you to understand the processes involved in making a bag or small leather goods. Once in industry, you will find machinery is used for almost all of the other stages of production.

Strap cutter (1): Used for cutting leather into accurate strips. The width setting is adjustable.

Edge bevelers (2, 16): For edging thick vegetable-tanned leather. These shave away the straight edge, leaving a rounded or beveled edge, depending on the blade shape of the beveler.

Awl (3): A pointed tool used for piercing patterns or materials to create location points as a guide for cutting or stitching.

Clicking knife with a straight blade (4): Used for cutting materials other than leather, such as paper and card. A curved blade is used for cutting leather. The clicking knife is a handle with interchangeable blades.

Hole-punch set (5): For creating holes in material used for decorative purposes and for eyelets.

Small scissors or thread snip (6): Used for trimming thread ends. You could also use a cigarette lighter for this purpose.

Creasing irons (7, 15): Tools used for making creases in thick vegetable-tanned leather so it will fold more easily and cleanly. **7** is a double-headed creasing iron.

Crew hole punch (8): For punching oval-shaped holes in leather, particularly used with buckles. The buckle prong is inserted through the crew hole, and the leather is folded over prior to stitching.

Bone folder (9): Originally made from bone, now more commonly made from plastic, used to assist the turning over and/or pleating of a folded edge.

Dividers (10): Measuring tools that can be opened to any required width and used to create a parallel line along an edge as a guide for cutting. Used extensively in pattern cutting for adding seam/folding allowances.

Steel ruler (11): A ruler made from steel that is strong enough to retain a perfect straight edge even when used as a guide for cutting with a sharp scalpel. 12 in. (30 cm) and 3 ft. (1 m.) in length.

Cutting weight (12): Used for holding down pattern card and material while cutting.

Glue brush (13): Used for pasting adhesives.

Pencils (14): 2H or 3H pencils are used for technical processes; they should be sharpened to a fine point.

Rotating hole punch (17): A hole punch with various sized cutters for punching holes.

Mallet (18): Used with the hole-punch set.

Folding hammer (19): A small handheld, round-ended hammer used to flatten a folded edge. The rounded end prevents the surface of the leather from being bruised or damaged. The flattened end is used for folding.

Double-sided tape (20): An adhesive tape used to hold pieces of leather together prior to machine stitching.

Other tools

Silver marking pen: A pen with silver ink that is used to mark guidelines on leather pattern pieces (see page 122).

Pattern knife: A specialist pattern-cutting tool that has a blade on one end and an awl-like point on the other (see page 122).

Scalpel: A cutting knife with a very sharp blade, used for pattern cutting (see page 122).

Clicking knife with a curved blade: Used for leather, the curve reduces the drag on the blade when cutting leather (see page 122).

Masking tape: An adhesive tape with slight stretch. 1 in. (2.5 cm) or 1¼ in. (3 cm) in width.

Paring knife: For hand skiving and trimming leather.

Glue knife: A spatula used for applying glue.

Cutting mat: A self-healing synthetic cutting surface used for pattern cutting.

Clicking board: A smooth board on which to hand cut the pattern and leather or material pieces. Traditionally, clicking boards were made of blocks of wood glued together with the grain vertical, similar to a butcher's block. Nylon or plastic boards are more common now.

Pattern cutting card: Any very thin, hard card. Good-quality firm cartridge paper can be used as a substitute but will not be as strong.

Adhesives: Rubber solution is used in the manufacture of bags. Neoprene is a very strong glue used mainly for molded constructions.

SECTION 2 | HANDBAGS

HANDBAG DESIGNERS AND BRANDS

Objective Learn about key handbag designers and brands.

The following is a list of must-know designers of handbags. Some names are in every fashion magazine. These names usually belong to esteemed families that have a long lineage of creating extremely well-made luxury products. Some of the following names are up-and-coming designers, making a reputation for themselves as innovative style setters.

▲ **Hands-free** Anya Hindmarch's contemporary bag in a supple, caramel color has leather strips stitched onto suede. It can be carried in the hand or across the body.

ANYA HINDMARCH
(contemporary)
BRITISH

At the age of 18, while traveling in Italy, Anya Hindmarch was struck by the ease and usefulness of leather workman's bags that she saw being used. Hindmarch went back to London and re-created the bag for Harpers and Queen. Hindmarch currently specializes in custom-made bags from her store in London, such as the "Be a Bag" in which any image can be placed on any bag for a truly personal touch.

Signature style: Hindmarch's style is largely unadorned with one significant feature. Her customers appreciate the unstuffy yet stylish qualities of the bags.

Iconic piece: The Maud clutch has a traditional frame and clasp closure and can be any color in satin. The inside displays any personalized picture.

BALENCIAGA
(early 20th century–contemporary)
FRENCH

Cristobal Balenciaga was an innovative and highly respected couturier. Balenciaga created several hats to accompany his dresses but did not invest time or resources in expanding licensees or alternative product lines. In our contemporary fashion culture, it is essential for a designer to create all product categories. Nicolas Ghesquière joined Balenciaga as creative director in 1997 at the age of only 25 and has since reinvigorated the House of Balenciaga back to a position of style and trendsetting innovation.

Signature style: The Lariat bag in several variations has been the staple of the Balenciaga bag collection.

Iconic piece: The Lariat shoulder bag was introduced in 2001. The tote has many tassel zipper pulls, buckles, and metal rivets that suggest a chic-yet-hard motorcycle jacket aesthetic. Ghesquière ensured the bag's success by passing it to his stylish friends such as Kate Moss, Sienna Miller, and Charlotte Gainsbourg before its release, starting a trend buzz.

BILL AMBERG
(contemporary)
BRITISH

Bill Amberg began his leather goods company in 1994 and concentrates on creating practical, well-made, unisex bags for a city dweller. Amberg has focused his company on socially and environmentally friendly production practices, using vegetable-based dyes on his leather and keeping all production in his home city of London. Bill Amberg cites Tokyo, London, Steve McQueen, Peter Blake, and Clarke Gable as his main style inspirations.

Signature style: Clean and unadorned in rich, natural colors, Bill Amberg bags are perfect for men and, at the same time, beautiful and chic for women.

Iconic piece: Amberg often uses historical references of well-used bags and reinterprets them for the luxury market. Two examples are the reinterpretation of the Gladstone medicine bag and the "Truffle Bag" originally made in canvas with leather trim.

BOTTEGA VENETA
(mid-20th century–contemporary)
ITALIAN

Bottega Veneta, which means "Venetian atelier," was founded in 1966 by Michele Taddei and Renzo Zengiaro as an artisanal leather goods company. The company had initial success for its understated elegance and discreet logo. The two founders left the company in the early 1970s, and the new management floundered in continuing the success of the company. In 2001, Gucci Group bought the brand. In 2005, German Tomas Maier became the creative director of the company, returning the brand to understated luxury.

Signature style: Like Tomas Maier's collections, Bottega Veneta bags are understated yet have subtle twists in the construction and materials to make them interesting and provocative.

Iconic piece: The intrecciato technique of interweaving fine pieces of leather in recent collections has pushed the bags into style watchers "must have" lists.

CHANEL
(early 20th century–contemporary)
FRENCH

The legendary Gabrielle "Coco" Chanel opened her business in 1909, first as a milliner's, but it quickly became the couture house that is so well known today. After World War II, in the 1950s, Chanel staged a comeback, sensing that her brand of practical and wearable clothing would become popular again. She was correct, of course, and was reintroduced to the American market, guaranteeing international success. In 1983 Karl Lagerfeld became creative director of Chanel. He has done much to reinterpret and carry on the traditions of Chanel.

Signature style: Chanel favored clean and simple decoration and focused on pieces that were useful yet stylish. Karl Lagerfeld has done a great deal to use the signatures of the House of Chanel, such as the white gardenia, the interlocking Cs, and the quilted leather that Coco preferred.

Iconic piece: In February 1955, Chanel launched her signature handbag, which she simply referred to as "2-55." The bag features quilted leather and the iconic gold chain strap.

COACH
(mid-20th century–contemporary)
AMERICAN

The company that started out as Gail Manufacturing Inc. was bought by Miles Cahn and his wife, Lillian, in 1946 and began working under the name Coach in 1957. The company was very small and operating out of a loft in New York City. In 1962, Miles Cahn hired already established fashion designer Bonnie Cashin to design bags, which she did until 1974. Cashin's contribution was extremely successful and helped to ensure the company's success.

Signature style: Bonnie Cashin used bright colors and began creating pockets specifically for items that people often carried, such as keys or pens. While this seems mundane now, at the time it had never been considered.

Iconic piece: Coach continues the silver toggle introduced by Cashin, based on the ease of using her car convertible top. The satchel, bucket, and shoulder bag with long overleaf are all well-known Coach bags.

▲ **Instantly recognizable Chanel** With its quilted fabric, gold chain strap, and interlocking Cs clasp, there is no mistaking this classic Chanel bag. Each bag is issued with an individual serial number and the carte registration, which proves that the bag is authentic, rather than a fake.

DELVAUX
(early 19th century–contemporary)
BELGIAN

Charles Delvaux founded his namesake company in 1829, making it the oldest luxury leather establishment in the world. In 1933 Edmond Schwennicke bought the company, and it is still run by the family. Delvaux boasts a craftsman-focused construction process that never uses an assembly line.

Signature style: Clean, largely unadorned, and classic.

Iconic piece: The Grand Bonheur bag was created for Belgian princess Paola for a wedding gift. It was an alligator top-envelope purse with silver hardware at the base and sides.

DIOR
(mid-20th century–contemporary)
FRENCH

In 1947, Christian Dior became a household name when he introduced his Corolle collection, otherwise known as "The New Look." It was not until 1989 that accessories began to be made at the Dior fashion house under the leadership of the creative director Gianfranco Ferrè. In 1996, John Galliano replaced Ferrè, having a great impact on all products of the House of Dior. He left the company in 2011.

Signature style: Throughout Dior's history, the bags have always matched the aesthetic of the designer's vision.

Iconic piece: In 2000, Galliano for Dior launched the Saddle Bag and in 2006 the Gaucho. Both have an interesting shape, detail, and the Dior medallion from 1947. Both bags are regularly featured on trendsetting lists of influential luxury bags.

FENDI
(early 20th century–contemporary)
ITALIAN

Edoardo and Adele Fendi opened a fur and leather goods store in Rome in 1925. The couple had five daughters who worked to expand the business into different categories. In 1972, Karl Lagerfeld began to freelance for the sisters, helping them with furs, clothing, and accessories. In the 1970s, the Fendi sisters began to apply the untraditional approach of using soft leather to achieve an unstructured bag. In 2004, the company was acquired by LVMH.

Signature style: Fendi bags always display the interlocking FF, but come in an amazing array of colors, materials, and styles.

Iconic piece: In 1997, Silvia Venturini Fendi created the Fendi Baguette that was immensely popular and introduced a new shape of handbag. There are more than 600 versions that have been made by Fendi.

GUCCI
(early 20th century–contemporary)
ITALIAN

Guccio Gucci opened a small leather goods company in 1921 in his native Florence. His aim was to combine the gentrified English aesthetic with the craft and leatherworking skills of Italy. The store carried actual and fashion-inspired equestrian products. Due to leather shortages in World War II, Gucci began experimenting with alternative materials such as hemp, linen, jute, and bamboo for handles, which is still a common feature. In the 1950s, the company began using the trademark green-and-red stripe, which is derived from traditional saddle girths.

Signature style: The luxury Gucci brand uses several identifiers such as the intersecting GG, particular oval-shaped buckles, green-and-red striped canvas, and printed canvas.

Iconic piece: The bamboo-handled Boxcar bag and the Constance slouch shoulder bag are classic Gucci bags often found with hardware meant to resemble a horse's bit.

HERMÈS
(19th century–contemporary)
FRENCH

Thierry Hermès established his luxury bridle and harness business in Paris in 1837 and quickly expanded to saddles and other equestrian products. In 1922, the first bag was created and in 1924 the Hermès family began to open stores that sold these bags in European resort destinations, cementing the image of luxury. The Hermès family expanded to include the famous Hermès scarves and a clothing collection in 1929.

Signature style: Hermès bags are always delivered in the signature orange box with the Duc carriage and horse suggesting the company's origins. All Hermès bags are unique because of the painstaking labor required by only one craftsman. The result of this endeavor is clean and dramatic elegance and superior craftsmanship.

Iconic piece: In 1935, the Sac à Dépêches was introduced, but it was not until Grace Kelly was photographed using it that Hermès began to call it the Kelly bag in 1956. In 1981, actress and singer Jane Birkin met Jean Louis Dumas, Hermès chief executive, on a plane. After hearing her complaining about aspects of her Kelly bag, Dumas created a new bag called the Birkin. The Kelly and the Birkin bags are extremely successful and very expensive.

▶ **Big bag** Dior sent this deep olive green bag down the runway during its Fall/Winter collection 2011/2012.

JUDITH LEIBER
(early 20th century–contemporary)
HUNGARIAN/AMERICAN

During World War II, Judith Peto narrowly escaped with her family to Switzerland to escape Nazi persecution. After meeting and marrying an American soldier, Gerson Leiber, she immigrated to the United States in 1948. She came with skills learned in her native Hungary and worked for several handbag companies before opening her own business in 1963. Leiber's work became popular with socialites, celebrities, and First Ladies. In 1994, the CFDA gave her a Lifetime Achievement Award, and she is in the permanent collection of the Metropolitan Museum, the Victoria and Albert Museum in London, and the Smithsonian Museum in Washington, D.C.
Signature style: Judith Leiber had an extensive offering of bags under her name and throughout her career, but her name is synonymous with the jeweled minaudière.
Iconic piece: Judith Leiber's minaudières were often inspired by the natural world. Fruit, animals, eggs, sea shells, and other objects could be found richly bedecked in the signature colorful crystals of an opulently dressed woman.

KATE SPADE
(contemporary)
AMERICAN

Kate Brosnahan was a *Mademoiselle* magazine accessories editor but felt there was a distinct absence of particular types of bags in the market. Brosnahan began making a simple bag

Iconic piece: Le Pliage is a foldable travel bag that was introduced in 1993 with incredible success. The body is of a nylon that comes in a rainbow of colors with leather handles and flap closure.

LOUIS VUITTON
(19th century–contemporary)
FRENCH

Louis Vuitton opened his first store in 1854 in Paris, based on the positive response that he had to his flat, lightweight, and airtight gray trianon canvas steamer trunks. The use of the canvas was an innovative technical breakthrough and has become a staple of the house's primary material. The 19th and 20th centuries saw the development of bags and the trademark logos that have become staples of the present company. In 1998, Marc Jacobs became the artistic director and has excelled in expanding the trendsetting notoriety of the brand.

Signature style: In 1888, the company created the checkerboard pattern and in 1896, the monogram that is now so identifiable. The bag shapes are true to their origins of duffles, sacks, and trunks that are just as recognizable as the logos.

Iconic piece: Marc Jacobs has collaborated with several different designers each season to create new interpretations of the venerable Vuitton bag. In 2000, Steven Sprouse created a graffiti version, and in 2009 Japanese artist Takashi Murakami created an anime-inspired version. Vuitton bags called Speedy, Never Full, and the Keep All attest to the ultimate functionality of the product, despite the attention to aesthetic innovation.

▲**Classic LV** With the classic LV logo, this Louis Vuitton handbag has sturdy metal bag feet, strap buckles, and a clasp in the same finish.

in 1993 with resounding success. She married Andy Spade in 1994 and expanded to include men's accessories that were conceived and designed by her husband. In 1996, Kate Spade opened her first store in New York's SoHo and in the same year was honored by the CFDA for New Fashion Talent in Accessories. In 1998 she was CFDA's Accessory Designer of the Year. In 2007 Kate Spade sold her company to Liz Claiborne, Inc.

Signature style: A Kate Spade bag has little if any exterior decoration or embellishments. The bags have a great deal of bright graphic color with the Kate Spade name printed in lowercase letters.

Iconic piece: While Kate Spade bags now feature color, the original bag that got her noticed was a simple black canvas tote with woven straps. That first tote matched the desire for understated luxury so prevalent in the 1990s.

LONGCHAMP
(mid-20th century–contemporary)
FRENCH

Longchamp was founded in 1948, employing craftsmen throughout the Loire Valley to make small leather goods. In the 1970s, the company's lightweight travel bags became extremely popular, and they were able to compete in the luxury market in the United States. In 2010, Kate Moss designed a collection for Longchamp.

Signature style: The company is experimenting with trying to compete in a luxury market, but the backbone of the company is usable leather goods.

LULU GUINNESS
(contemporary)
BRITISH

In 1989, Guinness quit her job in video production and started a business in the basement of her London home. Today Guinness has a thriving international handbag empire and several pieces in fashion museum collections such as the Victoria and Albert Museum in London and the Metropolitan Museum of Art in New York, as well as being shown in several exhibitions. She was awarded the OBE (Officer of the Order of the British Empire) in 2006 and in 2009 was awarded a Lifetime Achievement Award in Handbag Design by the Independent Handbag Designers Awards ICONOCLAST.

Signature style: Lulu Guinness is known for her 1950s high glamour, and absolutely feminine and coquettish style with a lovely sense of eccentric British humor.

Iconic piece: The "lips clutch" is often seen in the hands of actresses and style makers and is easily associated with Guinness. The clutch comes in a wide variety of colors, textures, materials, and has even been made to look like the Union Jack or American flag.

MATT MURPHY
(contemporary)
AMERICAN

Matt Murphy graduated in 1996 from the Art Center College of Design in California with a degree in environmental design. While architecture is clearly an important source of inspiration, Murphy began working on a handbag collection before he had even graduated. In 2002 Murphy began a private label division of his company.

Signature style: Matt Murphy uses a lot of color with the refinement of fine Italian leather and sterling silver hardware.

Iconic piece: The Metro Tote is versatile and practical due to its size and handles, allowing a woman to hold the bag in several ways and carry a wide variety of her day-to-day items.

MULBERRY
(contemporary)
BRITISH

Roger Saul and his mother, Jean, began the luxury bag company Mulberry in 1971 at Biba. Mulberry was an early example of a British luxury brand and has since expanded to become an international brand. The company has always focused on creating its entire product line in England and in 2006 started a successful training program to keep leather work and bag production alive. In 2008, Emma Hill was appointed creative director and subsequently won a Best Accessory Designer of the Year Award in 2010 and then 2011.

Signature style: Mulberry bags have a mix of rough-hewn practicality and sophistication. The bags often feature multiple straps for versatility and outside buckle pockets.

Iconic piece: The Alexa is an extremely popular bag named for British fashion icon and model Alexa Chung. Emma Hill combined two traditional Mulberry bags—the Bayswater and Elkington—to create the Alexa bag in 2010.

PRADA/MIU MIU
(early 20th century–contemporary)
ITALIAN

In 1979, Miuccia Prada began experimenting with the black Pocone nylon fabric that had been used to cover her grandfather's steamer trunks. It was not until 1985 that the idea became a success in the form of a small backpack. The label that Prada used was a sedate inverted triangle.

Signature style: While Prada received initial success with a type of anti-luxury fashion statement, the shifts of style have changed to demand obvious luxury. Today Miuccia Prada matches her accessories with her critically acclaimed and wildly popular clothing collections. The results are colorful, innovative, and easily recognizable.

Iconic piece: The black nylon backpack that started it all remains a classic with several variations and styles.

ROBERTA DI CAMERINO
(early 20th century–contemporary)
ITALIAN

Giuliana Coen trained in her grandfather's pigment factory before World War II, which had a direct effect on her use of color and materials when designing her bags. Forced to flee Italy with her husband due to the persecution of Jews, Giuliana di Camerino fled to Switzerland. In 1945, she began her own company, the name Roberta borrowed from a Ginger Rogers and Fred Astaire movie. During her innovative career, she made a great deal of advancements in bag design and was subsequently often copied by her competitors. Di Camerino's work has been exhibited at the Whitney Museum of Art and the Fashion Institute of Technology (FIT) Museum, both in New York.

Signature style: The bags of Roberta di Camerino had a richly colored palette with fabrics that were traditionally reserved for apparel. Many bags also featured clever use of trompe l'oeil.

Iconic piece: Many women loved the brightly colored velvet-top clasp clutch or envelope clutch because they were both luxurious and elegant.

STYLE SELECTOR: BAGS

Objective Learn about several styles of bags.

The basic design of any bag is functional but the many forms and silhouettes are beautiful and stylish. On these pages all the major types of bags are listed and examined. The fundamental functional ideas in these bags are the platform for materials, color, detail, silhouette, finishing hardware, and endless variations of style.

Gladstone/Doctor bag

The contemporary version of a 19th- and early 20th-century doctor bag. The bag has a short handle, rigid clasp or buckle opening, and a soft but durable pouch bag often reinforced with flaps.

Bucket

The name of the bag suggests the shape. The bucket is a hand or shoulder bag that features a round bottom and an open top that either ties, buckles, or snaps.

Backpack

A bag that is worn on the back with two shoulder straps. The backpack can be utilitarian, used for hiking (also called a frame pack) or decorative, as in the Prada bag mentioned on page 83. The backpack is a ubiquitous bag for college students.

Top opening closes with a zipper or drawstring.

Shopper

A large, rectangular double-handled bag that has an open top and a large main compartment, perfect for shopping.

Tote

The tote is meant to be an easy-to-use bag that is worn on the shoulder, handheld, or worn on the forearm. A tote usually has minimal opening hardware for easy access into the large compartments inside.

Sewn straps for visual durability.

Zippered opening for security and ease.

Fanny pack

Despite the negative connotations of the 1980s version of the fanny pack, the bag is popularly worn by athletes and travelers. The fanny pack is a small bag that fits around the waist.

Kelly bag

In 1956 Hermès began to call one of its bags a Kelly bag after the Princess of Monaco and Hollywood legend Grace Kelly. It now describes any version that has the distinctive shape, one top handle and the front clasp, even if not made by Hermès.

Shoulder bag

Any bag that hangs from the shoulder under the arm. Shoulder bags are usually small.

Reinforced "x" stitching for durability.

Laptop bag

The bag is similar to a briefcase and is sometimes used interchangeably. A laptop bag is used to carry a laptop computer and has a handle, a shoulder strap, and a place for the battery charger and any other computer attachments.

Messenger bag

The bag is worn flat across the back and is used by bicycle messengers in major metropolitan areas because it does not interfere with movement. In fashion, messenger bags are used for much the same reason.

Clutch

The clutch is a small rectangular bag with no straps that is meant to be held in the hand or held under the arm against the body. The clutch is often considered an evening bag.

Frame clutch

A bag that has a metal opening frame with a clasp. The bag portion can be made from a variety of materials and is meant to be held in the hand, usually for evening use.

Boston/Hold-all/Weekender bag

A rectangular purse with two straps that is meant to be worn on the forearm or held in the hand. Some Boston bags have a slightly wider bottom than top, and the opening is usually zippered between the straps. Weekenders are larger versions of the same bag.

Toaster

This bag has a flat bottom and a curved top. Very similar to a bowling bag, it hangs off the forearm or can be worn on the shoulder. The bag usually has a zipper opening between the straps running the length of the bag.

Satchel

Akin to a briefcase, satchels have a short handle and a flat rigid bottom but with a top opening, sometimes with a flap and buckles. Satchels are casual and can also be interchangeable with an overnight bag.

Duffle bag

Originally from the armed services, the duffle bag is round on both ends and shaped like a tube with two straps that can create a backpack.

Front pocket for commonly used essentials.

Hobo

A hobo bag is usually slouchy with a scooped center and one strap that can be worn on the shoulder or across the back. The name has stuck regardless of the negative connotations of the term "hobo."

Frame bag

A small, hard decorative bag used for eveningwear that is held in the hand and meant only for your keys and some lipstick.

Barrel bag

The bag is the same shape as a duffle bag but is a smaller piece of luggage or a handbag.

Straps continue around the bag for a balanced look.

Bowling bag

A rigid bag that is wide at the bottom and has a large arc opening at the top with two rigid straps. The bowling bag gets its name from the sport but is now used as a fashionable handbag.

ANATOMY OF A BAG

Objective Identify individual handbag components and see how they fit together.

Dozens of individual components go into making even the simplest bag. Handbags are much more complex than first viewing suggests. Component parts differ from style to style. The number and type of components depends on style, complexity of design, design details, material, fittings and hardware (and their application), construction, and reinforcements.

REINFORCEMENTS

There are a various types of reinforcement for bags: iron-on, woven, and nonwoven fabrics as well as paper and card, in many different finishes and weights (see pages 97–99).

Reinforcements are added to areas of the bag that need more structure, depending on the firmness of the leather used. Often there is reinforcement in the base of bags; around the collar (top edge of the bag); in the gusset to give added rigidity; and usually behind heavy hardware that rivets onto the body of the bag, such as twist-lock plates (commonly used by Mulberry and Hermès), to support the body of the bag from collapsing under the weight of the hardware.

PIPING

Piping has a core that is usually made out of plastic or twisted paper (see pages 98–99). This is covered with material before being sewn into the seam and or gusset. It is usually used on turned construction bags, holdalls, some totes, and weekenders. The main function of piping used on turned construction bags is to help retain the bag shape, but it can also be used as a design detail on any bag.

EXERCISE: FIND OUT MORE FOR YOURSELF

To gain more knowledge of what parts make up a bag, deconstruct one to its basic components.

1. Ensure you photograph or draw it from all angles, including the interior, in order to record what it looked like before deconstruction.
2. Take a set of measurements, noting location of handles, pockets, and so on.
3. Using a scalpel and/or seam ripper, disassemble the bag, unpicking the stitches. Leave any eyelets, rivets, or duradots; trying to disassemble these is difficult. Strip away the layers, taking off any external features, such as pockets.
4. Photograph to record the stages and number the pattern pieces, noting what was attached where.

1 Front and back body pieces (two of) Stitched together at the sides using the turned construction method.

2 Base Stitched to the body once the front and back slip pockets have been attached.

3 Flap and flap lining (two of) Covers the front part of the bag, forming the closure.

4 Flap-closure strap lining Two layers of leather are used for the strap for strength and aesthetic purposes.

5 Flap-closure strap outer Stitched onto the middle of the flap, with eyelets feeding into the buckle to close the bag.

6 Buckle tab pieces (three of) Tabs attach the buckle to the body of the bag. The tab has a crew hole in the midsection for the buckle pin to be inserted through.

7 Buckle The metal fitting that the strap feeds through in order to attach the two straps together. It also acts as the closure mechanism for the satchel.

8 Buckle-strap keeper (three of) Strap that retains the end of the flap-closure strap once it is threaded through the buckle.

9 Shoulder strap (four of) Strap of leather worn over the shoulder to carry the bag. The strap is made in two sections of two layers (for strength and appearance), hence the four components.

10 D-ring (two of) Metal ring used for both aesthetic purposes on the shoulder strap and practical purposes on the back slip pocket, acting as a tag to open the pocket.

11 D-ring tabs (two of) Thin strap that is threaded through the D-ring to allow for attachment of the D-ring to the shoulder strap and back slip pocket.

12 Side pocket body pieces (two of) These make up the front of the side pockets.

13 Side pocket flaps (two of) The top piece that makes it a closed pocket.

14 Side pocket gusset (two of) The strip of material that is stitched along one edge to the front pocket body to give volume to the pocket, and on the opposite edge to attach it to the side of the bag.

15 Eyelets Metal inserts that protect and reinforce the holes for the buckle pin.

16 Zipper For the internal pocket.

17 Front and back body tops (two of) The top section of the front and back of the body which is attached to the top edge of the lining collar, and the bottom edge of the front and back slip pocket linings.

18 Front and back lining collars (two of) The inner collars of the bag lining.

19 Bag lining (two of) Canvas lining pieces stitched together as a T-base style with an additional base seam.

20 Slip pocket lining (two of) For front and back pockets.

21 Interior zipped pocket lining The drop-in zippered pocket is attached to the back lining.

COMPONENTS

In this example, a satchel with front, back, and side pockets is used to demonstrate the component pieces of a bag. All bags will differ to a degree in their construction, but the satchel is a good example to start with.

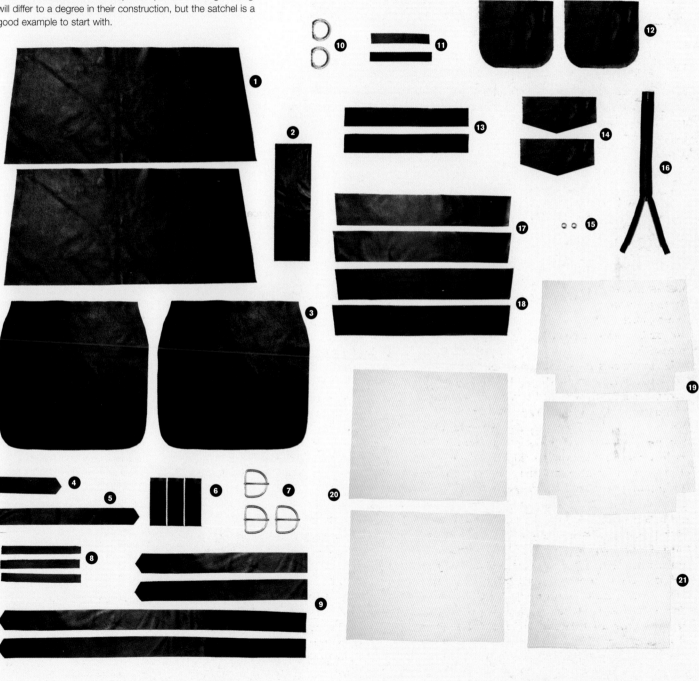

SECTION 2 | HANDBAGS

DESIGN CONSIDERATIONS: BAGS

Objective Learn the key considerations when designing a bag.

Having an understanding of the considerations when designing a bag or a line of bags is extremely important. The product ultimately needs to be desired by the consumer, fit for purpose, and designed within the constraints of the brief.

▲ **Handle positioning** Here the designer is examining the positioning of the handle and how the bag could be carried. The weight of the bag and its contents are considered so that the product will balance and be comfortable to carry.

CRITERIA FOR CONSIDERATION

Designs need to be informed by research—from analysis of information and inspiration, there will have been initial ideas generated in the form of thumbnail drawings (see pages 56–57). Color palettes are explored and finalized (see pages 26–27), and materials, reinforcements, and hardware are researched and selected (see pages 96–101). When designing, there is a series of criteria that it is useful to examine your initial ideas against. Bag design is really about marrying aesthetics and

practicality. Each design consideration listed below needs to be explored from both standpoints, finding often a happy compromise between the two.

FUNCTION AND PRACTICALITY

What is the bag to be used for? This dictates to a certain extent the size of the product and style type. You must consider what your consumer would be carrying in the bag. A good way to establish size is to pile up the items you think your consumer would be carrying in the bag and take a photograph of them and measure the space they occupy (height, width, and depth). When you are designing, you will have these loose measurements in mind.

The size of the bag will also affect the way the bag is carried/held and what type of handle or strap system could be used. Ergonomics (comfort of wear) is also a factor: Is the handle comfortable; does the strap need to be adjustable? Where will she/he be wearing the bag? This will also need to be considered: it could affect the material choice and color palette, along with the practical details.

MATERIALS AND FABRICATION

Materials need to be researched, sourced, and determined before the design process begins (see pages 96–99). A designer needs to know what the characteristics of the materials they are designing with are: For instance, are the leathers soft and supple, drapey and buttery, slightly rubbery, tumbled and plump, stiff with a high shine, or have the ability to hold a curve? What are the required practicalities of the materials? Do they need to be waterproof, hardwearing, breathable, or portray luxury or quirkiness? Bag constructions are material-sensitive and cannot be achieved if the wrong type of material is used. A stiff

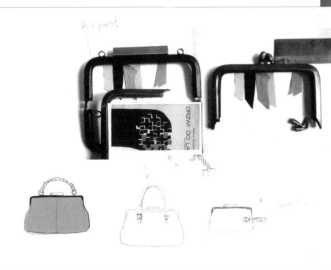

▶ **Frames** In this line development exercise, the basic ideas have been selected, and the designer is now looking closely at frames to decide the size, shape, proportion, color, and finish for this part of the bag.

patent leather cannot be turned, so any construction that requires turned seams is not possible in this material. Soft, buttery napa leather drapes exquisitely, so you should never try to reinforce this leather in order to make a structural bag from it. Contemplate the feel and even the sound of the material. Investigate and ponder the mix of materials, outers, and linings. Material choice is extremely important and can add to the success or ultimate failure of a product. Never force materials to do what they do not do naturally. Select the materials for their natural characteristics and qualities.

FORM

Exploring the form and refining the shape of the bag is an absolute essential. Gussets, insets, gathers, or pleats could be used to add volume. The bag could have a structured or unstructured body, or a combination of the two. The bag could be rounded or angular. All these possibilities should be explored.

To start exploring form, draw a series of body shapes for the bags. Examine and vary the shape: square, rectangular, ellipsed circles, triangles, rounded edges, and asymmetric shapes. Once these have been explored, favorites can be selected and forms developed further into actual bag designs.

CONSTRUCTIONS

Having a detailed understanding of bag constructions and seam types provides you with the necessary design vocabulary

EXERCISE: **EXPLORE AND INVESTIGATE THE DIFFERENCES CONSTRUCTION METHODS MAKE TO DESIGN AESTHETIC**

Using your research (see pages 28–47), start to develop body form and shape—do not use preconceived ideas of traditional bag designs. Evaluate your research and respond by doing thumbnail sketches. Once you have at least twenty initial shapes drawn, select at least five for further investigation and development. Draw each body shape from a three-quarter view on to a piece of 11 in. x 14 in. (28 cm x 35 cm) paper, using a different sheet for each shape. Apply and draw at least three different construction methods for each shape, then explore and vary gussets and methods of creating volume within each further drawing—continue on another sheet of paper if necessary.

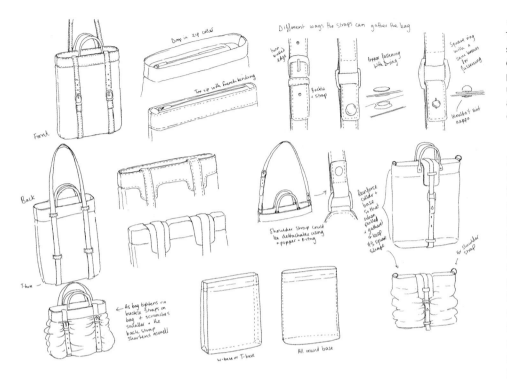

Front

Back

T-base

Drop in zip collar

Top zip with French binding

Different ways the straps can gather the bag

Turn under edge

Buckle + strap

Popper fastening with D-ring

Square ring with a scun button for fastening

Wouldn't suit nappa

Shoulder strap could be detachable using a popper + D-ring

Reinforce collar + base so that when pulled + gathered it keeps it's square shape

For shoulder strap

As bag tightens via buckle straps on bag it scrunches smaller + the back strap shortens aswell

W-base or T-base

All round base

◄ Selecting straps
The designer explores straps and handles, considering the position and type to use, and assessing the adjustability of a variety of fittings.

you need when exploring the possibilities for bags. Changing the construction and seam types of a basic bag form can give the design a very different feel. This knowledge is fundamental when designing bags and essential for a successful transition from 2D design to 3D realization. Choose a selection of bag forms—explore these body forms using a variety of construction types, varying gusset types if appropriate. You will observe subtly differing aesthetics between the emerging bag forms.

COMPONENTS AND DETAILS
Once the basic body shapes have been selected and constructions considered, the handbag designer expands the design by exploring component options through the drawn medium. These need to be explored for both aesthetic and

practical purposes, and sometimes adjustments made to compromise one for the other.

Closure: The means of how a bag closes and opens has a massive bearing on design from an aesthetic point of view and also a constructional one. Zipper, drawstring, flap, and frame are a few traditional closures worth exploring.

Handles: How will the bag be carried/worn? What type of handle or strap will it have? Functional or decorative? Adjustable? Detachable? How could the handles/straps be attached to the bag and where? How will this affect the balance of the bag? All of these issues need to be explored and resolved from both a visual and functional position.

Pockets: Pocket detailing can be used for both the visual impact, to break an area of the bag, and also for practical

reasons. There are many types of pocket construction, giving a variety of capacities from a practical perspective, but also offering great diversity of aesthetic. Pocket detailing can completely change the form, volume, and line of the bag. Placement of pockets is a huge consideration not only from a visual viewpoint, since balance also needs to be maintained. If you have a large pocket on only one side of the bag, will it cause the bag to tilt when being carried if filled to capacity? Closures come into play here too—how will the pockets close? Remember that interiors of bags also need to be considered when designing—a bag rarely sells if it does not have at least one internal pocket. Security is one of the buying determinates of the average consumer.

Detail: Detail contributes to the whole design and is central to the success of the bag/product. Accessory design is all about consideration of and attention to detail. It is essential that you explore and experiment with your chosen details. Consider scale and placement of the details; hardware/fittings; the color and type/thickness of thread; and whether you want to use bound, piped, or topstitched seams. Is there a surface detail, e.g. accents of snakeskin on a smooth grain leather? Explore the positioning and amount of detail. If a surface print or a motif is being used, look at the placement and try varying the scale. If you are designing a line, consider the usage across the collection, build intensities, and vary the amount of print/detail used.

LINE, BALANCE, AND PROPORTION

Line and silhouette, balance, and proportion are all key ingredients to consider when designing a handbag. The proportion of the bag in relation to the body is crucial. Where and how the bag is to be worn is a vital element to explore and resolve.

Draw the bag on a body form and analyze, then cut the front body of the bag out of card, attach card/tape/ribbon handles and get a model to hold it, then you can evaluate and develop further if necessary. Proportion and balance of design detailing is also an area that needs exploration and experimentation. Vary positioning and proportion of detail to explore and evaluate the possibilities.

Balance is about the harmony or discord of the design detailing, but it is also about the hang of the bag when being worn. Bags are affected by the pull of gravity and the form is often altered when the bag is filled. Both elements are vital to resolve at the 3D design development stage.

FITTINGS AND HARDWARE

Types, finishes, and sizes of fittings and hardware need to be researched and sourced. If you are planning to design your own fittings, build this in to your time management plan and budget for it. Placement of fittings needs exploration and resolution—here again you must be mindful of weight, balance, and harmony of line.

COLOR

Your color palette will be established through your research, but how you apply and position your color and accent colors needs experimentation

and investigation. Color has a major role to play in bag design so always try a variety of options. Color can influence your mood: for example, a brightly colored leather bag could lift your spirits on a gloomy winter morning. Color contrasts and tones can add a level of sophistication or fun depending on the combinations and proportions. For example, black and white can have a strong 1960s vibe but can also speak to us of classic sophistication. Scan your drawings into Adobe Photoshop and apply different colors. Observe the differences, considering which are the best options for the project in hand.

SEASON

This will have been determined by your brief, but does need to be considered throughout your design development. The season will affect color palette, material choice, and also appropriateness of motif if you are using one.

KEY STAGES

- Reread the brief.
- Select initial ideas to develop.
- Explore line, form, proportion, scale, balance, and details.
- Experiment with color and materials.
- Draw from every angle.
- Consider construction options, seam type, and edge finishes.
- Examine use and position of handles, straps, fastenings, closures, and fittings.
- Consider pockets and lining.
- Consider functionality and practicality of the handbag. Are you satisfying the target consumer?

EXERCISE: **EXPLORE THE EFFECT OF PRINT AND COLOR**

Evaluate your research (see pages 52–53) to develop a motif or simple print, and explore and investigate two different color palettes. Using this print design, develop a line of three bags. Explore and experiment with print scale and placement variations across the line, building intensity and subtlety of usage. Apply the two print colorways and observe the differences created by the change in color palette.

GLOSSARY

Colorway: One of several different color combinations offered.

Construction: The methods used in the variety of ways a bag/product can be assembled.

Gusset: Component of a bag used to hold the back and front together and add depth/volume.

Hardware: Usually indicates metal fittings.

Inset-gusset: Where the front body and back body are cut in one piece and the side gussets are separate.

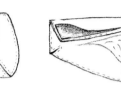

DESIGN DEVELOPMENT: BAGS

Objective Learn to develop bag designs to meet your brief.

The process of design development is fundamental, since it ensures that the most successful design is created rather than the very first idea that came to you. It enables you to explore and refine your initial design ideas in 2D, experiment, investigate, and test materials, and refine the form through 3D exploration. It is essential to balance and maintain an appropriate level of creativity and commercial knowledge throughout the design development process. Answering the brief is the most important element—giving the client what they want is essential and can mean the difference between maintaining your freelance work or not. If your designs do not measure up to expectation at design presentation, you may find yourself reworking your ideas with a very tight deadline.

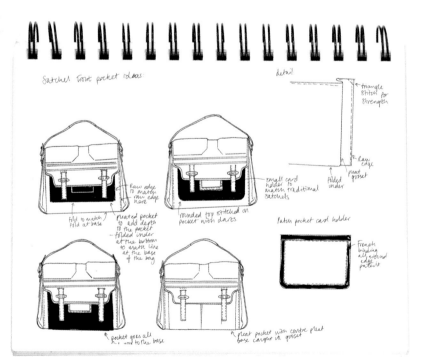

▲ **Placing fastenings** The designer is considering the placement of design details and the position of fastenings in these sketches.

DEVELOPING INITIAL DESIGN IDEAS IN 2D

Design development is evaluation of initial design ideas through considered examination.

From your sketchbook (see pages 48–49), select the most exciting ideas. Individually copy these ideas onto a white sheet of 11 in. x 14 in. (28 cm x 35 cm) paper. Using clear line drawings, increase the scale of your initial design idea so you can evaluate the design more easily (see pages 58–59).

The line drawings should communicate coherently—front, side, back, top, and bottom views are essential for all 3D products. If the base of your bag is detailed, you also need to draw the bottom view. You must also design the interior lining, pocket requirements and placement, and closure of pockets.

Development may be thought of as a one-sided conversation. Ask questions of your designs and then respond with a drawing:
"How would you look if…
…I changed your construction from butted to turned?
…I altered how I can carry you?
…I attached the handles differently?
…I changed your proportion slightly?"

◄ **Added details** While exploring pocket detailing, this designer tests the inclusion of luggage tag details.

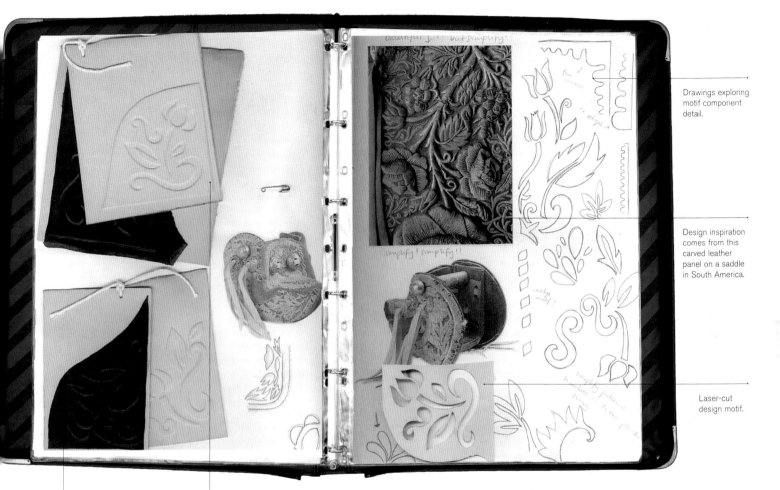

Drawings exploring motif component detail.

Design inspiration comes from this carved leather panel on a saddle in South America.

Laser-cut design motif.

Testing embossing a design motif on pieces of different colored leathers.

Testing de-bossed/plugged design motifs on different color leathers.

Be aware that one change may impact on another part or component of the design, so you may need to make further revisions. Zoom in and enlarge smaller areas with a separate drawing that allows you to explore this area for design detail—remember the design is in the detail with accessories. Consider top-stitching and color of threads, too.

The questions you asked yourself before you began your design, your key considerations (see pages 88–91), need to remain at the forefront of your mind

▲ **Explore many options** In this portfolio we can see how the designer has tested design motif detailing in actual leather, using a variety of methods and two colors of leather before choosing one for use on the bag.

EXERCISE: **DEVELOPMENT SHEETS**

From a completed sketchbook (see pages 48–51), select four very different designs and, following the instructions in this section, produce eight design development sheets.

From each initial design, develop the following two designs:

• A day bag—you specify the consumer.
• An occasional bag—you determine the occasion and consumer.

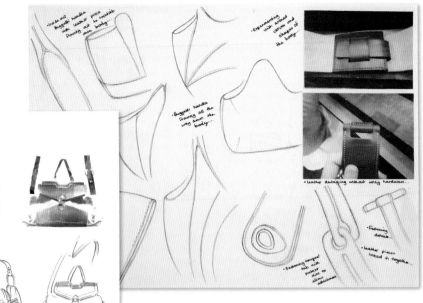

AW11 - DESIGN DEVELOPMENT

▶ Consider the whole line The designer in this example explores the design detailing across a breadth of styles for inclusion in the line.

Aquascutum

▲ Think 3D 3D sampling is undertaken to further develop and resolve the design.

as you develop your designs. You need to evaluate the following design elements through your drawings:
• Scale
• Proportion
• Placement of details, both functional and decorative
• Handles and straps
• Balance
• Construction
• Edge finishes
• Seam types and panels

▼ Consider the tiny details Design details are tested in a variety of leathers. Application techniques for the details and studding are also explored.

• Attachment and placement of any hardware and fittings
• Surface detailing
• Practicality issues
• Closure methods and size of openings
• Color and materials

Your design development should flow, but do not overcrowd the page—allow space for the designs to communicate clearly.

DEVELOPING YOUR DESIGNS IN 3D
Once you have come up with a variety of designs you are satisfied with in 2D, it is time to move on to 3D sampling and testing. A series of samples must be made to test your material choices in relation to constructions and seam types, and to test your details and edge finishes.

Ask yourself:
• Are the materials you have chosen suitable—are they fit for purpose?
• Can you recreate the design?
• Do the texture and color choice work together?

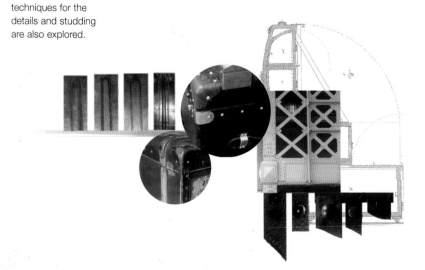

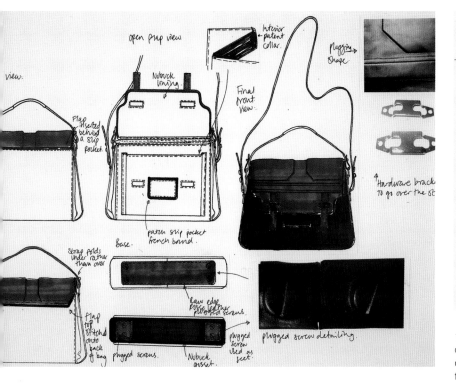

MAKING FINAL DESIGN DEVELOPMENT SHEETS

- To make your sheets interesting, vary the position of the design drawings.
- On 11 in. x 14 in. (28 cm x 35 cm) paper, draw back view, side view, three-quarter view, interior view, and base view if necessary.
- Use landscape or portrait format (never mix the two).
- Do line drawings (hand, CAD, or mixed).
- Ensure you have one drawing in full, accurate color.
- Zoom in to show details.
- Add swatches but do not put swatches in the same position on each page, since this will add bulk and create issues within your portfolio.
- Annotate your designs to ensure you explain everything that is not apparent visually, such as scale and dimensions.

▼ **Color choices** A variety of color combinations are explored by the designer before the use of color is finally selected. See how the different color combinations dramatically alter the look of the bag.

You should explore options through sampling and then evaluate which works the best and gives you the desired effect. Flaws in designs are edited out at this sampling stage, and designs are often revised or adjusted. It is often necessary to go back and do a final design sheet from these findings.

KEY STAGES
- Select the best styles that you have developed.
- Further examine the design detailing across the line.
- Refine and test detailing in actual material.
- Draw out and color up designs to assess the best possible options.
- Have you balanced the product categories within the collection?
- Experiment in 3D to test and problem solve before finalizing designs.

▲ **Comparing options** Here the designer shows the bag from all angles. There are two choices for the back and base views of the bag.

GLOSSARY

Design development: Evaluation of initial design ideas through considered examination.

Swatch: Small sample of material/fabric.

Technical annotation: Notes on technical information.

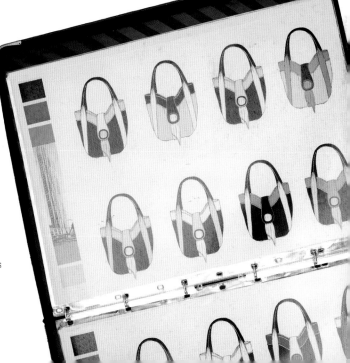

MATERIALS AND REINFORCEMENTS: BAGS

Objective Learn about the materials and reinforcements used in bag manufacturing.

Materials for bags are not easily purchased at retail, so sourcing suppliers and researching tanneries and leather merchants is essential. The next four pages give an overview of the materials you will be working with.

MATERIALS FOR BAGS

Visiting specialist trade fairs like Le Cuir and Modamont in Paris and Lineapelle in Italy gives a great overview of what materials and fittings are available globally. See pages 234–236 for more details on trade fairs.

A high percentage of bags are designed in leather. The best leathers used for leather goods, with the exception of exotics, are usually full-grain, aniline-finished calfskin. The different types of leather are discussed in more detail on pages 62–67. Bags are rarely made up from one material alone, so we will look at other body materials, reinforcements, and linings in this section.

Faux leather: Synthetics can imitate any grain surface, such as this faux snake skin in vinyl.

SYNTHETICS

PVC (polyvinylchloride) and PU (polyurethane) imitation leather has been growing in popularity over the last few years, being championed by the

Ballistic nylon: Hard-wearing fabric, often used for sports bags and backpacks.

likes of Stella McCartney and Matt & Nat on ethical grounds. Imitation leathers have improved recently with advances in technology. Most leather can now be imitated to some degree of success. Grains are embossed/imprinted onto the surface, and the materials are available in a variety of weights. These materials do not have the superior handle of leather and often have a chemical smell. However, they are sold by the yard, so there is little or no wastage.

PVC and PU-coated fabrics are common in sporty accessories. When coated, these materials become enhanced by being waterproof and durable. Fabrics that are often coated are nylon, ripstop, polyester, canvas, and acrylic. Synthetic fabrics tend to dye well and are available in a large range of color options.

PERFORMANCE FABRICS AND NYLON

Cordura/ballistic nylon fabrics are available in various weights, from ultra-light to heavy weight. Ballistic fabric is constructed with high-tenacity yarns that are woven 2 x 2 for enhanced durability and tear abrasion, originally made for the military. The fabrics are available in a variety of constructions and textures. Cordura/ballistic fabrics are mainly used for more sporty products such as backpacks and hybrid bags using a mix of leather and ballistic. (Cordura is a brand name like Goretex). Kevlar can also be used, but this is a very specialist fabric used by the military for its protective bulletproof quality, and as a high-performance material, it carries a hefty price tag.

PU-coated nylon: Used at the value end of the market, and for sports bags.

STRAW CLOTH AND WOVEN STRAWS

These fabrics come in a variety of fibers, weaves, patterns, and colors. They are sold by the yard in an assortment of widths. They are also sold woven into basic shopper shapes that only require handles to be added. Beach bags and informal bags are the usual result of using these materials. They are not particularly durable and will probably only last one season.

DUCK CANVAS, OXFORD, AND DRILL COTTONS

Canvases are used extensively for casual/informal and sporty bags. Canvases, Oxfords, and drills are available in a variety of weights and finishes, such as lightly waxed, heavily waxed, and antiqued. They are strong and durable but often come in limited colors.

Canvas totes and shoppers are increasingly seen in summer season lines by Ally Capellino and Bill Amberg. They use waxed canvas as a material of choice with vegetable-tanned leather straps and trims to give a traditional old-school feel.

DENIM, CORDUROY, CAVALRY TWILL, AND WOOL TWEED

These fabrics are all suitable for bag making, used alone, or in conjunction with leather. All come in a variety of colors. The tweeds come in a variety of weaves that create their own unique patterns, e.g. dog's tooth, window pane, and Prince of Wales, or all-check patterns,

Straw cloth: Often included in summer and cruise collections across market levels.

Silk grosgrain: Used, with a backer, for evening bags and purses.

Tea bag and swansdown backer: Both are iron-on, fusible backers.

High-density foam: Used for adding substance to the bag outer material.

and herringbone is created with a twill weave structure. It is usually necessary to iron on a fabric backer to tweed to help prevent fraying while the bag is in production.

WOOL FELT AND BOILED WOOL

Wool felt is a nonwoven fabric and as such is good for bag making, since it is the only material other than leather that can be used on raw-edge designs. The wool fibers that make up the felt are matted together by heat, steam, and pressure, and as a result, felt has a slightly hairy brushed surface. Color availability is often limited. Note that lightweight craft felt is not suitable.

Boiled wool is very similar to felt, but it is made in a totally different way. Boiled wool is a knitted jersey which is boiled and shrunk by 25–30 times.

DUCHESSE SATIN, TAFFETA, SILK DUPION, SLUB SILK, MOIRE, AND VELVET

These lustrous dress fabrics are often used for evening bags because they hold a drape and some pleat well. Bag companies often buy these fabrics ready backed with an iron-on reinforcement fabric so they are ready to

use. When reinforced these fabrics are often referred to as laminated.

REINFORCEMENTS FOR BAGS

A reinforcements is a material of a different thickness and stiffness used to give the outer material more structure or add support to fittings, components, or bases of bags. There are many types of materials used as reinforcements, and they come in differing weights and thicknesses. There are many different softer ones, and the selection of these is sometimes more important that stiffer ones. Selection depends on the type of leather/material, the use of fittings and hardware, style of the bag, and the construction method. The reinforcement is usually glued onto the area that requires strengthening prior to construction of the bag. Iron-on backers usually completely cover the leather and are stitched into the seam; they are also attached to the full face of the component part. Others are attached only to the area that requires the additional reinforcement.

PAPERS AND CARDS

A variety of papers and cards is used. They vary in weight, texture, and range from sugar

Lining silks: Light, hardwearing, and available in a variety of colors. Can be laminated for strengthening.

REINFORCEMENTS

Popular reinforcements include:
• Papers and cards
• Boards
• Fabrics
• Reprocessed leather
• Foam and padding
• Plastics
• Handle and piping cores
• Leather
• Wood
• Metal

Canvas: Used extensively as an outer material. Available in many weights, colors, and finishes.

paper to ⅛ in. (3 mm) -thick card. They are primarily used in all qualities of small leather goods (SLGs) and lower-quality bags. Paper and card is not highly durable, so does not have longevity, but it is light and has a degree of strength and flexibility.

BOARDS AND FIBERBOARDS

Paper board and fiberboard are used for bag bases and for molded work. Varying in weight and thickness, fiberboard generally has better flexibility and is longer lasting than paper board. Aqualine is a good example of a medium-weight fiberboard which is strong and durable.

WOVEN AND NONWOVEN FABRICS

Fabric backers are available with or without iron-on adhesives; both are used in the industry. Often thought of as interlinings, fabric backers are subtle reinforcement and can be used to enhance substance, add strength, and add structure to components and areas of the bag that require it. The backers are available in a variety of weights. Woven backers offer good flexibility, tending not to crack.

Aqualine: Medium-weight fiberboard reinforcement.

Swansdown: A woven iron-on, light- to medium-weight fabric, with a slightly plumped/brushed surface.
Tea bag: Iron-on, nonwoven, light-weight backer, with a slightly waffled surface.
Linen: Iron-on woven backer that adds a slight crispness to the material.
Nonwoven: By their very nature these are less flexible and stiffer, and used to strengthen the areas where fittings are attached and when a thin rigidity is needed.

REPROCESSED LEATHER

Made from scraps of waste leather that are compressed together with a binder, reprocessed leather is sold by the roll and comes in different thicknesses. It is a good alternative to card and boards, giving a more natural handle to the material and adding durability to the product.

FOAM

Foam is used to add a padded finish to the product. It can be quilted, that is, stitched all over in a pattern, as with Chanel's classic quilted handbag, or just attached to the body of the bag to add a soft, spongy appearance to the material.

Foams come in a variety of thicknesses and different types:
• Open-cell foam does not hold its depth but squashes down when put under pressure.
• Denser foam offers a more robust padding that only yields slightly to pressure, and

Laminated fabric: Fusible backer is added to the fabric prior to sale to add strength, enabling more fabrics to be used for bag construction.

these foams can come with an adhesive backer on them for ease of attachment.
• Another type of padding that is used is ice wool or wadding. This gives a different, looser, less regimented padding.

PLASTICS: WOVEN AND SHEET

Plastic reinforcements are used primarily for base boards; they are added to the base of bags like hold-alls/weekenders to give rigidity. These boards are sandwiched between the bag body and the lining. Occasionally they are removable: they are covered in lining fabric and are placed into the bottom of the handbag on completion. Woven plastic sheet has more flexibility and is used mainly for the bases of smaller bags.

HANDLE AND PIPING CORES

A very different type of reinforcement is used for both piping cores and handle cores. These come in a variety of widths and are made from paper, extruded plastic, and compressed fiber covered with cotton netting. These are used as fillers for rounded handles and for piping. Both add structure and density to these components.

Webbing: Used for handles and straps, and available in various fibers, widths, and colors. Patterns and logos can be woven in.

Synthetics: Can create cheaper imitations of expensive fabric, such as woven leather.

Synthetic quilted fabric: Used for fashion bags and hold-alls.

LININGS FOR BAGS

The lining fabric is usually the cheapest material used in the bag, but obviously exceptions occur: some luxury brands line their bags with leather or suede. Fabrics used primarily for linings include faux suede, light cotton drill, polyesters, rayon, and cotton mixes. Linings need to be reasonably strong and have a tight weave structure so threads don't pull. Some linings are reinforced with a light iron-on backer to add extra structure to the bag.

KEY STAGES

Many materials and fabrics are appropriate for use, but when selecting the materials, thought needs to be given to the following:
- Style of bag and construction
- Brief: What are you being asked to do?
- Season
- Trends: Colors, textures, and patterns
- Practicality: What is the end usage?
- Market level: Luxury, designer, main street, or value?
- Consumer: Who are you targeting?

Oxford weave: A modification of plain weave in which two warp yarns are woven together as one.

◀ **Faux leather** This pre-prepared faux leather piping is often used for sports bags and fashion bags.

▼ **Handles and piping cores**
1, 2, 3, and 4 are made of compressed fiber covered with braided cotton and loose cotton netting. 5 is an example of an extruded plastic core used for piping.

SUSTAINABILITY

Anya Hindmarch had huge success with her "I'm not a plastic bag" canvas shopper, highlighting the amount of resources used and waste created by the plastic bag. As environmental concern grows, ethical issues are increasingly beginning to inform the consumer's choices. Fabric developers and tanneries are very attuned to this growing awareness, and technical developments on fiber processing and leather tanning are under way to find cleaner ways of developing materials, and reducing waste and harmful by-products that result from the processing. Although in their infancy, both fabric and leather are available that have been more responsibly sourced and processed; at present they come at a cost, but as developments and practices become more mainstream, sustainable materials will become more affordable.

RESEARCH LEATHERS AND MATERIALS

It is a good idea to visit the nearest local leather merchant to see and feel the variety of leathers and finishes offered. Only by handling the leather will you begin to understand the properties and characteristics of the hides and skins. Understanding the characteristics and handle of materials is essential to an accessories designer. We always design with a selected/given material, so prior to selection, we need to analyze the properties of the material to ascertain what it will and won't do.

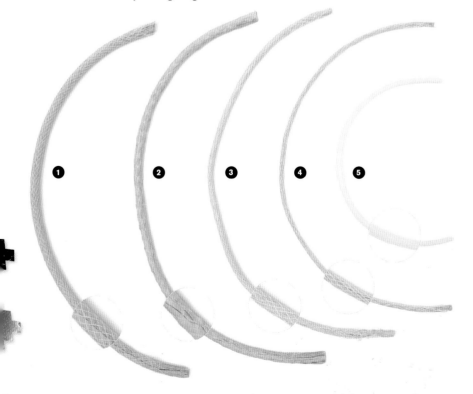

① ② ③ ④ ⑤

SECTION 2 | HANDBAGS

HARDWARE: BAGS

Objective Learn about the different types of hardware used in bag making.

Hardware covers the variety of fittings used on all leather goods. Fittings are both functional and decorative, and as a designer, knowledge of usage and sourcing is essential.

Hardware is often designed and specified by the accessory designer, working with hardware/fitting companies. Fittings are mocked up for sampling and only put into production proper when orders have been secured. With the advanced technologies of rapid prototyping, this can be achieved reasonably swiftly. Hardware is usually featured on most types of leather goods; however, it is not essential. As a designer you determine the amount and type of hardware.

MATERIALS, COLORS, FINISHES

Fittings come in many different metals. Brass, nickel, zinc alloy, pewter, and copper are available in a range of finishes—brushed, burnished, antiqued, chromed, lacquered, enameled, and coated. The spectrum of colors available is also extensive—brass, chrome, silver, dull silver, rose silver, nickel, gold, rose gold, gun metal, ruthenium, and titanium. With enamels and coatings, the whole spectrum of colors is available. Plastics, resins, nylons, and woods are also used.

BAG CLOSURES

Security is often of the greatest concern to consumers, so we need to consider this when we design or choose hardware for bags.

Dog clips: Come in various sizes, push release and trigger release styles for attaching occasionally used straps.

Strap locks: Nylon side-release strap fasteners, seen here in a variety of sizes and styles.

Eyelets: Available in a variety of sizes, and as one- or two-part fittings, such as these large sail eyelets (left) and small, tubular eyelets (above).

Decorative studs: Purely for decorative purposes.

Two-part plate locks: These locks consist of a front piece and a back plate. Here we see a top-loaded spring-release lock (top) and a traditional briefcase lock (below).

Turn lock: A four-part fitting shown here in a brushed nickel finish.

Dots: Magnetic dots (top) are often used for closures and are invisible from the outside. The dura dot (below) is a four-part press stud with a visible dome.

Cord locks: A selection of cord locks that are used to secure drawstrings on sports bags.

Zipper pullers: The choice of size and finish is extensive: resin, nickel, acrylic, ball-and-chain, novelty.

Strap attachments: Square, O-ring and D-ring, and decorative chain mail attachments shown in brushed silver, brass, nickel, and pewter.

Buckles: These come in a huge range of styles and sizes.

▲ **Zipper** These come in a variety of chain type and size, tape color and fabrication, and slider and puller designs.

▲▼ **Prefabricated handles** These handles are often used in pairs and are made from many different materials, from wood, to resin, to plastic.

ZIPPERS

Zippers are used for securing pockets and as closures for bags. They are present in many types of leather goods, even belts and gloves. They are available in a great variety of styles and colors—the more commonly used are:

- Closed end—often seen in bowling bags and used in the interiors for pockets.
- Open ended—e.g., totes and weekenders.
- Two-way closed—common in hold-alls.

When ordering zippers you need to specify zipper type, length from top stop to bottom stop, tape color and fabrication, chain and tooth type, size and fabrication, and the type of slider and puller required.

Zippers can be purchased on the roll and cut to the required length, for sampling and production. Top and bottom stops, sliders, and pullers then need to be added before use.

FRAMES

Frames are popular closures for bags, and there are a variety of types and designs. Frames may have plated or raw metal finishes (raw-metal frames need covering with material). Wooden and plastic/acrylic resin frames are available too. The more commonly used frames are upright section frames and side section frames, but there is also an inverted section frame. All frames are hinged, and they usually close by a twist-knob or spring-catch fastener. Usually the material of the bag is placed in between the metal of the frame, and the frame is then crimped flat with special framing pliers. When using a frame, the frame dimensions dictate the pattern.

BUCKLES

Buckles come in all shapes and sizes and are used as closures for flaps and also as attachments for straps. Often they are dummy buckles and don't actually operate—the buckle strap has a discreet magnetic dot behind it making it a quicker and more convenient method of fastening. Sew-in magnets are

used too and these are sewn in-between the materials and are not visible, giving the material a clean surface. Velcro is also a popular choice of fastening for more sporty bags, as are press studs and Sam Browne's (also known as mushroom rivets).

DRAWSTRINGS

Drawstrings require the use of eyelets to help strengthen and protect the hole and guide the thong/braid through. Eyelets come in many sizes, colors, and finishes.

LOCKS

Many different types are available—turn locks, key locks, and chain locks in traditional and nontraditional styles.

ATTACHMENTS

These are decorative and functional fittings that connect the handle or straps to the bag, available in a wide variety of materials, sizes, and finishes. When purchasing attachments you need to measure the width of the strap or handle to ensure you buy the right size fitting. Attachments include D-rings, O-rings, H-rings, and square rings. Adjustable attachments include dog clips and nylon side-release clips, which are often used on straps of backpacks and messenger bags. Detachable dog clips are used on straps that need to be removed.

DECORATIVE FITTINGS

Decorative fittings are varied and extensive in style and fabrication. Studs, motif studs, plates, diamante rivets, and tubular rivets can all be used. Some decorative fittings also

perform a secondary function; for example, rivets can add strength to a seam or a joining, and studs can protect the base of a bag.

HANDLES

Prefabricated handles are available in an assortment of material choices, colors, sizes, and styles.

CHAINS

Chains are often used for handles. They are obtainable in an array of sizes, link styles, and materials, and can be used alone or in conjunction with leather straps.

ADJUSTERS

These are used for strap and cord adjustment. Cord release locks are used on sports bags and drawstring bags. Sliders are used for shortening/lengthening flat straps.

GLOSSARY

Frame channel: Gap in the frame where the bag body is crimped in to secure the frame.

Spring-catch fastening: Fastening with a grooved underside to accommodate a lip which inserts into the groove to lock the frame.

Twist-knob fastening: A device made of two knobs that are forced past one another in a twisting action to close the frame.

Roller: Additional tube of metal on a buckle so leather can move freely through the buckle prior to fastening.

▼ **Frames** A selection of frames displaying spring-catch fasteners (top and second), and twist-knob fastenings (third and bottom) in various finishes.

► **Leather handle** A bugatti leather handle component, made with a handle core and attached to a D-ring. It is now ready for connecting to the body of a bag.

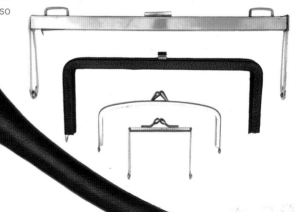

SECTION 2 | HANDBAGS

CONSTRUCTION METHODS FOR BAGS

Objective Gain an understanding of the more commonly used construction methods in designing bags.

Technical knowledge and understanding of construction methods is fundamental to a bag designer. Without this, you run the risk of your bag designs being wrongly interpreted and realized by the manufacturers.

▲ **Multiple construction** A combination of construction methods were used in this bag. The design is a turned-edge T-base with a flap closure. The flap is raw-edged, as is the strap.

MAIN CONSTRUCTION METHODS
There are three main constructions in bag making:
• Turned
• Raw edge
• Butted

These constructions can be used individually or in combination with each other depending on your design. It is also possible to create handbags and other leather goods using a molding method, described on page 105.

THE TURNED CONSTRUCTION
The product is made by sewing the right sides together and then turned inside out. The seams can then be opened and top stitched or glued down. Materials used for this type of construction need to be flexible and relatively supple in order to be turned successfully.

THE RAW-EDGE CONSTRUCTION
This is where the pieces of leather are stitched on the right side and the material is left with raw edges, that is, the bag is not turned inside out after stitching. Vegetan leather is often used with this type of construction, since the edges can be finished in a variety of ways (such as waxing, dyeing, or polishing) before or after construction.

▼ **Completed constructions** Here we can see a range of the methods and styles of construction discussed on these pages, assembled from leather and material.

ONE-PIECE CONSTRUCTIONS

Raw-edge cross construction

Turned W-base construction

Raw-edge T-base construction

Turned T-base construction

TWO-PIECE CONSTRUCTIONS

Turned base two-piece construction

TYPES OF BAG CONSTRUCTION

These illustrations show the three principle types of construction used in bag making: raw edge construction, butted (also called folded edge or faced edge) construction, and turned construction.

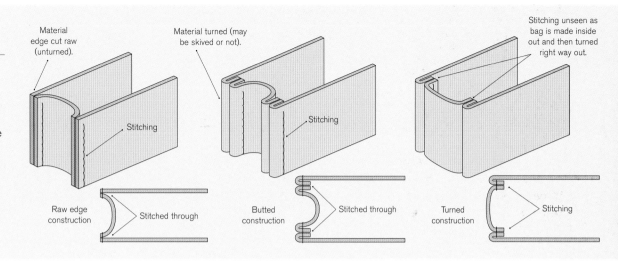

Material edge cut raw (unturned).

Material turned (may be skived or not).

Stitching unseen as bag is made inside out and then turned right way out.

Stitching

Stitching

Raw edge construction — Stitched through

Butted construction — Stitched through

Turned construction — Stitching

THE BUTTED CONSTRUCTION

The butted construction is where the leather/material is turned over on the edge. It could be turned and glued onto a reinforcement or skived and turned onto itself before stitching together.

STYLES OF CONSTRUCTION

Whichever construction method you choose to use, there are a number of styles of construction you can use depending on the style and appearance you want for your final piece. Some of the most common styles of bag construction are described here and illustrated on pages 104–105.

ONE-PIECE STYLES

T-base, W-base, and the cross are all examples of one-piece bags—they are cut from one pattern piece and are stitched together and usually turned. See over the page for examples of these. This construction can be turned, raw edge, or butted.

TWO-PIECE STYLES

A very flat product and the simplest, made from a front and back body sewn together. Volume is limited as there is no means of expansion; however, the bodies can be darted or gathered/pleated to gain volume. This construction can be turned, raw edge, or butted.

MULTIPLE-PIECE CONSTRUCTIONS

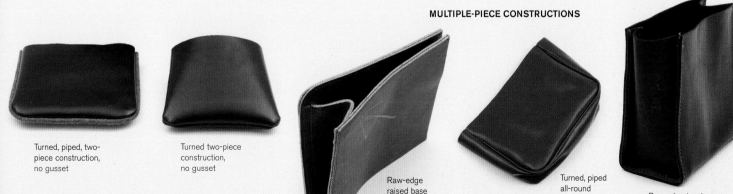

Turned, piped, two-piece construction, no gusset

Turned two-piece construction, no gusset

Raw-edge raised base construction

Turned, piped all-round gusset construction

Raw-edge inset gusset construction

BASE

Essentially another two-piece style, the body of this bag is one component stitched together with the base cut separately. The base could be square, rectangular, circular, oval, or asymmetric. This construction can be turned, raw edge, or used with a collar. This style is not suitable for use with the butted construction method.

ALL-ROUND BODY OR SIDE-INSET GUSSET

This is where the front body and back body are cut in one piece and the side gussets are separate. This construction can be turned, raw edge, or butted.

ALL-ROUND GUSSET

This is the reverse of the all-round body. Here the front and back body are cut separately, and the gusset goes around the edge of the front and back body. This construction can be turned, raw edge, or butted.

HORSESHOE

This is where four identical body pieces are cut—two inner-body pieces and two outer-body pieces. The two inners are then stitched together one-third in from the top edge in a rectangle two-thirds of the length of the body. The two outer-body pieces are then stitched onto the inside panel, one on the front and the other on the back. It forms a flat gusset. A horseshoe can be turned, raw edge, or butted.

RAISED BASE

This is a front and back body, with two side gussets that have a rectangle cut out of the bottom line, leaving the edges of the gusset longer than the central area. When stitched together, the base is raised higher than the body of the bag. This is used with the raw edge or butted construction methods.

CONSTRUCTION STYLES

There are many styles of bag construction which utilize the main construction methods outlined on page 102. Here we look at one-, two-, and mulitple-piece styles.

ONE-PIECE CONSTRUCTIONS

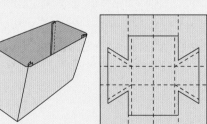

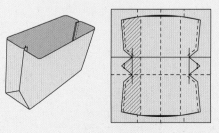

Cross construction

W-base construction

T-base construction

TWO-PIECE CONSTRUCTIONS

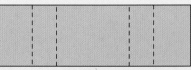

Base construction

MOLDED CONSTRUCTION

This is an advanced method where the leather is stretched over a mold and glued together. Boxes and photo frames are often covered in leather using this method. Handbags can also be made using this construction. Another method is wet molding, where vegetable-tanned leather is soaked in water, stretched, and secured over a mold and left to dry naturally.

EXERCISE: IDENTIFY CONSTRUCTION METHODS ON FINISHED BAGS

Collect a minimum of 40 images of different types of bags from Internet sources or from fashion magazines. Examine each image and determine which construction methods have been used. Make files of each major construction and either stick and paste or cut and copy the bags into the correct construction grouping.

▼ A variety of construction methods
The body of this bag is quilted and demonstrates a turned side-inset gusset construction. The handles are created with a raw-edge construction, and the edges are dyed.

MULTIPLE-PIECE CONSTRUCTIONS

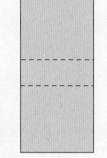

Side-inset gusset construction

All-round gusset construction

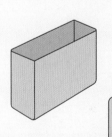

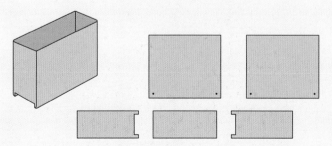

Raised base construction

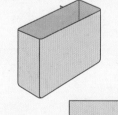

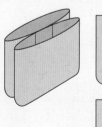

Horseshoe construction

CREATING A MOCK-UP

Objective Learn to create a 3D representation of your design to enable you to analyze the design more fully.

Once your design has been finalized in 2D, the next step is to test it in 3D—we do this by making a mock-up or maquette. Through replicating our design to scale in 3D we can further problem solve and refine designs.

CHECKING THE SCALE OF THE BAG

The scale of the bag will have been one of the elements you explored at the 2D design stage. You should have measurements worked out, but before you decide on material to mock up in and which technique to use, it is useful to review the measurements in relation to the body and how the bag is to be worn.

1. On pattern card, draft out the front body of the bag to the scale. If the body is symmetrical, fold the card in half, the fold line being the center of the front body of the bag. This ensures that you mirror the shape accurately.

2. Cut out with a scalpel or clicking knife with a straight blade. Use a metal ruler for straight edges.

3. Draw on any components/details, such as pocket or handle attachments. If handles are attached to the front body, cut and attach tape, webbing, or rope to approximate this. This gives you the opportunity to review size, scale, position, and proportion as a whole.

4. View yourself in a mirror holding the front body or get a friend or model to hold it for you. If amendments are made at this stage, repeat the exercise until you are happy with the width and depth of the front body. Remember to amend your design sheet if changes are made.

MAKING A 3D MOCK-UP IN CARD

Once you have decided on the size of the front body, analyze the design sheet and consider the depth of the gusset. If you have made any alterations to the original measurements, then change this accordingly. The next stage is to create a mock-up out of card.

1. Draft out each component on pattern card to your measurements, remembering to use the folding technique for symmetrical pattern pieces (see step 1, Checking the Scale of a Bag). Draft the back body, gusset, base, handles/straps, flaps, and components (as your design dictates).

2. Cut out each pattern piece with your knife. Use a metal ruler for straight edges.

3. Add notches at key points to ensure you are placing the patterns together at the correct points.

▲ **3D exploration** The shape of the bag is explored in 3D using card and masking tape. The photographs here and on the opposite page were taken by the designer to record the development of the mock-up. He will evaluate the shape and make any necessary refinements.

ORDER OF ASSEMBLY

Before you stitch anything, you should work out an order of assembly. This will vary slightly depending on the individual components involved in your particular bag, but it needs to be logical and sequential. Generally, for a first sample without a lining, a good sequence to follow is:

1. Assemble component parts first and attach them to the relevant part, e.g., make the handles and then stitch them to the front and back bodies of the bag.

2. Attach the base studs to the bottom of the bag.

3. If the gusset has a zipper, this should also be stitched in before assembling the body of the bag.

4. Gussets are stitched on one side at a time, front or back body.

5. Finally, stitch all the pieces together to form the bag.

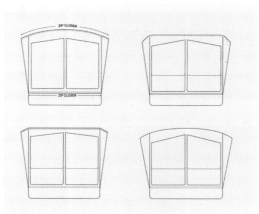

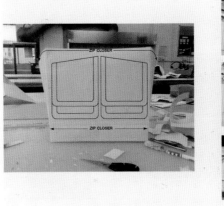

◄ **Further analysis (far left)** The design is refined further in 2D and pocket placement is investigated.

◄ **Refining in 3D** After further 2D development, the selected pocket details are drawn out on the front body prior to assembling the card maquette.

4. Mark with your awl (or a pencil) the location points for handle/strap attachments.

5. Annotate each pattern piece accordingly, e.g., front body, name or number of design, measurement of the piece, date, and your initials.

6. With masking tape, assemble into a 3D form, ensuring your notches match up. Cut a piece of masking tape the same length as the bottom of the front body of the bag. Stick the tape along the front body leaving half the width of the tape over the edge the whole way along. Line up the right-hand corner of the base with the right-hand corner of the front body and use the protruding tape to attach the base to the front body. Tape the opposite side of the base in the same way and attach the back body. Continue this way until the assembly is complete. If handles or straps need to be added, do this now.

7. Review the overall shape and amend where necessary—mark with a pencil if you need to augment the line/curve, change placement of the handle/strap, etc. At this point you can test and adjust where pockets or other details are to be located.

8. Make notes of all the changes and recut the pattern with the changes implemented. You may want to draw all the details on to the pattern pieces at this stage so your second card mock-up gives the complete story of the design.

9. When you are satisfied with the overall form, photograph the mock-up for your records. Disassemble it

carefully because you will be duplicating this pattern and adding seam allowance to create a template for your cutting pattern.

10. Duplicate the pattern and add a seam allowance following the instructions on page 114.

MOCKING UP IN MATERIAL

Once you have duplicated your making patterns and added seam allowances to make your cutting patterns, the next stage is to test your design in material. Throughout your design development you will have tested your material choice, determined the seam types and decided upon the construction method. It is best to mock up in the material from which your bag will be made; you then get a true representation. However, materials are expensive, and some designer-makers use another material to represent the actual material. For example, a medium-weight felt can represent calf skin; calico and canvas are good substitutes for more expensive materials. When choosing a substitute, consider the feel, weight, and performance of the actual material, as well as what other component parts will be used.

1. Prepare the material for mocking up, e.g., iron on reinforcements.

▼ **Testing reinforcements** An all-round gusset design bag with a flap closure is tested to ensure the right level of reinforcement is achieved. This is done by adding a card collar to the top of the bag.

◀ Analyzing the maquette This maquette has been made in canvas and photographed from side and front views. The designer then draws directly onto the photographs which are then used to help visualize the finished product and confirm decisions or explore further designs.

▼ Testing details A corner section of the bag is made up in canvas with closure to test the gusset size in relation to the zipper and the zipper end (which attaches to the gusset with a dura dot). Note that the designer has made comments on the actual sample.

2. Place the pattern pieces carefully on the material. You need to lay your patterns onto the material in a way that uses the material in the most economical way. If you are using leather, you should also avoid any blemishes and thin, stretchy areas, such as belly or offal (see pages 62–63). If you are using fabric, ensure that you lay out and cut on the straight of the grain.

3. Cut out your material. For leather, use a curved blade cutting knife; for fabric, use sharp fabric shears. If you are using leather, remember to skive your seams.

4. Prepare and stitch together your components—handles, straps, and pockets. Double-sided tape is used to hold material together prior to stitching.

5. Stitch your bag together following your order of assembly (see panel on page 106).

6. Inspect and review your bag. Ask another person to wear it and assess it for comfort and ease of use. How does the bag hang and balance? Fill the bag with the type of thing your consumer would put in it—does it adversely affect the shape, or its wearability? Make a note of your analysis and then amendments can be made to the pattern where necessary.

7. Having made your mock-up, you can now decide which is the best method of lining the bag. Will you use a drop-in lining or fixed lining? Note that lining patterns are usually cut 1⁄16 in. (3 mm) bigger than the making patterns and 1⁄4 in. (7 mm) smaller than the cutting patterns.

KEY STAGES

• Review your 2D design and analyze pattern pieces and components.
• Review measurements.
• Draft and cut out the front body and draw on details.
• Review proportion and scale.
• Draft and cut pattern pieces in card. Be sure to label them.
• Assemble and stick together using masking tape.
• Review form and make changes if necessary.
• Redraft and recut pattern then assemble using masking tape.
• Disassemble and duplicate the pattern adding a seam allowance.
• Work out the order of assembly.
• Mock up in material or substitute material.
• Inspect and review.

GLOSSARY

Awl: Spike on a handle used to mark position points on the pattern, leather, or material.

Components: All additional parts of the bag, e.g. external pockets.

Dividers: Tool for pattern cutting, like a double-spiked compass. It ensures accuracy when measuring seam allowance and repeating measurements, and can also be used to mark guidelines for turning and/or stitching.

Draft: Draw out the pattern piece on paper or card.

Drop-in lining: Lining that is stitched into the bag after the main body of the bag is constructed.

Fixed lining: Lining that is stitched in and secured to the inside of the bag during construction.

Notch: Small registration mark on a pattern or cutout pattern piece locating a particular point of note, e.g. marking the point on the front of the body where the strap fitting is to be located.

BASIC PATTERN CUTTING FOR BAGS

Objective Learn about pattern-cutting techniques for bags.

A pattern is the blueprint for the design. Understanding the stages of pattern development and the types of pattern required is essential for a bag designer, especially when dealing with external production of samples.

TYPES OF PATTERN

Pattern cutting for bags is complex and requires precision; it is nothing like pattern cutting for garments. Knives are used to cut the card, and working with leather adds yet another degree of difficulty. Often the material cut from the patterns (leather) cannot be pinned together because holes made by the pins would be left. A wonky seam cannot be unpicked for the same reason. You cannot ease leather, since it does not have a bias/crossway, and it does not come by the yard. It is natural skin that is often flawed so you need to pattern cut around these blemishes. There are five different types of bag pattern that should be prepared:

- The making pattern
- The cutting pattern
- The lining patterns
- The reinforcement patterns
- The master pattern

The making pattern is made first and has no allowances included. It is used to make the maquette or mock-up, which is a 3D representation of the design (see page 106). The design is analyzed at this point and the pattern duly altered if the designer feels further

development/alteration is necessary. This pattern is also often referred to as a net pattern.

Once the card/rough fabric mock-up is made and pattern adjusted, if necessary, the making pattern would then have the seam allowances added. This set of patterns would become the cutting patterns. It is vital that

each pattern is labeled with the correct information: pattern type, pattern piece, allowances, style name, and date.

Another part of the design that needs its own set of patterns is the lining. The lining patterns should be cut in accordance with your design. There are two types of lining: a drop-in lining, where the complete lining is placed inside the made-up exterior and then secured at the top edge so the lining can be pulled out much like a pocket in a garment; and a fixed lining, which is is trapped between the exterior seams as the bag is constructed.

Depending on the type of bag construction and material chosen for your design, your handbag may need a reinforcement pattern. Reinforcements are materials of different thicknesses and stiffnesses used to give the outer material more structure. They can be used to support the weight of fittings or handles and can add strength to the base of bags too. If reinforcements are required, patterns must be cut for these. Depending on the type of reinforcement used and where the extra structuring is required, the pattern would be cut accordingly.

STANDARD INDUSTRY ALLOWANCES FOR BAGS

Turned seam (outside)	¼ in. (6 mm)
Turnover/folding	⅜ in. (1 cm)
Boot seam	⅜ in. (1 cm)
Underlay	⅜ in. (1 cm)
Lining seams	⅜ in. (1 cm)
Topstitching	¹⁄₁₆–⅛ in. (2–3 mm)

ADDING NOTCHES

Notches are reference points on the pattern pieces.

1. On the fold of the pattern piece, cut the corners off the fold line. Place your knife ⅛ in. (3 mm) down the fold line then cut a diagonal, taking away a triangular piece of card. Repeat at both ends of the fold.

2. Open up the pattern piece and match up corner to corner and make a second fold. Repeat the notching along the new fold line. When the pattern piece is unfolded, you will see it is divided into equal quarters, with notches marking the quarter points.

Adding notches can sometimes highlight inaccuracies in your pattern cutting. If your corners do not match when you make the second fold, you have a problem and one of the following is wrong:

- The marking of the measurement.
- The actual measurements or your cutting.

Check these until you find the issue, then carefully recut the pattern to correct your error.

To get an accurate straight line, fold the card and mark in from the card with the awl.

TESTING THE PATTERN

The bag pattern is then tested by producing a first prototype. This would be cut out from a similar or exact material and constructed with reinforcements, if used in the construction.

Analysis of the first prototype would be undertaken, and the designer would make alterations, if needed. If alterations were required, a whole new set of cutting patterns would need to be made. These would then be tested in the same way as the first set of cutting patterns until the designer was happy with the prototype

From the cutting pattern, the master pattern is then made. The master pattern is the one that features all the essential information and dimensions of the finished product. This is in the form of technical annotation and includes the following information:

- Identification of what part of the pattern it is, e.g. front body.
- Information on amount of seam allowances, turnings, and skiving required.
- Details stating how many pieces need cutting, e.g. x 2 gussets.

Registration marks/notches help with alignment of pattern pieces (see page 109), along with information for referencing and cataloging style number/name, season, etc.

BASIC PATTERN CUTTING TECHNIQUES

Outlined here are some of the fundamental pattern-cutting techniques that one should grasp, for cutting a variety of basic shapes that make up the pattern components of most bag styles. Technical knowledge will help inform your design process and add power to your portfolio of skills, making you infinitely more employable.

SQUARING OFF—MAKING A PERFECT 4 IN. X 4 IN. (10 CM X 10 CM) SQUARE

The first fundamental procedure for pattern cutting for handbags is ensuring your pattern piece is symmetrical. This is a process called squaring off, and is done before any pattern cutting begins.

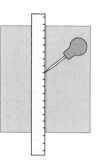

1. Cut a piece of paper or card roughly 6 in. (15 cm) squared. Place a ruler at the center and score top to bottom with an awl.

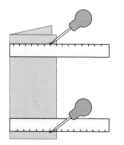

2. Fold the paper in half along the scored line. Measure 2 in. (5 cm) from the folded line approximately ⅜ in. (1 cm) from the top and bottom edges and pierce these points with an awl.

3. Working parallel to the fold, line up the marks with a ruler and cut away the excess card with a knife. When cutting, ensure the knife blade is firmly butted up against the ruler, the ruler is held firmly, and you keep your fingers away from the blade.

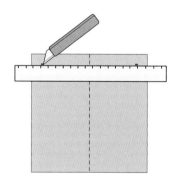

4. Keep the paper folded and lay your ruler perpendicular to the folded edge. Measure ⅛ in. (3 mm) in from the top right corner and pierce with the awl. Press firmly as the awl needs to pierce through two layers of paper.

5. Unfold the paper and there will be a mark on each side of the fold. Line up these marks with a ruler and cut along the width of the paper. When cutting across a fold, always open up the paper otherwise your right angle will be incorrect.

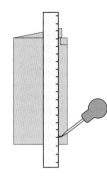

6. Refold your paper. The top right-hand corner is now a perfect 90° angle—it has been squared off. Place the ruler on the squared-off edge, parallel to the fold, measure down 4 in. (10 cm) and pierce through both layers.

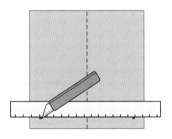

7. Unfold the paper and line up the two marks either side of the fold with a ruler. Cut through the whole width of the paper with a knife.

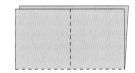

8. To check you have achieved a perfect square, fold in half perpendicular to the scored fold. All corners should match up perfectly. Add notches to your pattern piece (see page 109).

CUTTING A CURVE

To begin, cut a basic rectangular pattern 8 in. x 3¼ in. (20 cm x 8 cm), using the method for squaring off a pattern (left).

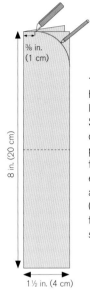

1. Measure and score the halfway point across the length of the pattern piece. Score and fold the paper down the length, then with a pencil, mark ⅜ in. (1 cm) in from the fold on the top edge. With a free hand, draw a curve from the ⅜ in. (1 cm) point. Then cut through the line in one steady movement.

2. Open the pattern up and fold along the width ensuring it is exactly in half.

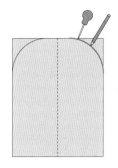

3. Place the awl against the cut curve, drag and score one half of the curved line, transferring the exact curve onto the other end of the pattern underneath. Unfold the pattern piece.

4. Fold the pattern down its length and then cut through the card using the scored awl mark as the guide, in one continuous movement.

5. To complete the pattern piece, fold it in half and add notches (see page 109).

CUTTING AN ELLIPSE

Following the procedure for squaring off a pattern piece, cut a rectangle 8 in. x 3¼ in. (20 cm x 8 cm), adding notches (see page 109).

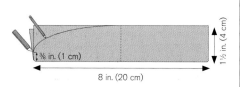

1. Score and fold the card down its length, and from the notch draw a curve freehand in one movement. Cut through the card with the knife in one clean movement.

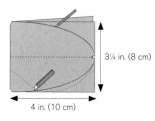

2. Open the card and fold across the width. Place the awl against the cut curve, drag and score one half of the curved line, transferring the exact curve onto the other end of the pattern underneath. Unfold the pattern piece.

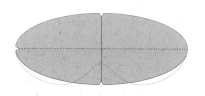

3. Fold the pattern down its length and then cut through the card using the scored awl mark as a guide, in one continuous movement. Open your finished pattern piece.

Note that your sides do not have to be symmetrical—if you wanted to achieve a kidney shape, this could be achieved by folding through the horizontal before marking off your curves. Folding it this way rather than lengthwise allows you the freedom to have asymmetry in your pattern cutting. See the red dotted lines on illustrations 2 and 3 to the left for an example of this.

CUTTING A CIRCLE

1. Using a ruler and awl, score a straight line then fold along the line.

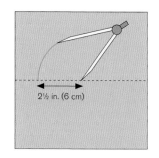

2. Opening the dividers to 2½ in. (6 cm), unfold the card and place the dividers on the center fold line. Push down on the inner arm point and swing the outer divider arm point in an arc, dragging the point across the card to the other side of the center line.

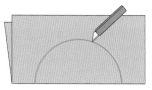

3. Fold the paper along the center line and then cut with a knife, following the scored mark from the center line.

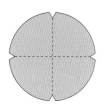

4. Mark and notch your mid-points by folding in half one way and then in half the other way.

CUTTING A TRAPEZIUM

1. Following the same procedure for squaring off a pattern piece, cut a rectangle 6 in. x 4 in. (15 cm x 10 cm). Fold the pattern in half lengthwise and with the ruler measure 1⅜ in. (3.5 cm) along the edge of the top line and mark with a pencil.

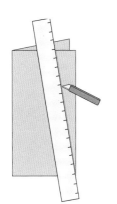

2. With a ruler, line up the pencil mark and the point at the right-hand corner, then cut this line with a knife.

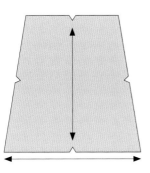

3. Mark and notch your midpoints by folding in half widthways and then by measuring each long side and notching separately at the midpoint.

DUPLICATING THE MASTER PATTERN (MP)

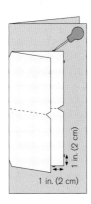

1. Cut a piece of card 1–1½ in. (2–3 cm) bigger than the MP piece, mark the center point, rule and score down the length, and fold. Fold the MP and place it on top of the folded card, folded edge to folded edge. Measure ⅜ in. (1 cm) in from the corners of the MP piece on the horizontal and the vertical. Make registration marks ⅜ in. (1 cm) from the corners with the awl, piercing through the pattern card.

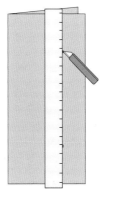

2. Remove the MP piece. With the ruler, line up the two vertical points and then cut through the length of the card.

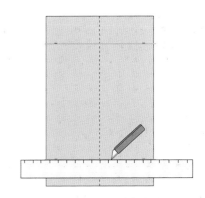

3. Unfold the card and there will be four marks left by the awl. Line up the top set of marks with a ruler and cut across the width. Repeat with the lower marks.

4. Mark and notch your midpoints by folding in half one way and then in half the other way.

PATTERN CUTTING TIPS

ALWAYS open up the card and, with a ruler, line up point to point before cutting.
NEVER be tempted to leave the card folded and cut, since this can lead to inaccuracies. You need to ensure your straight lines are parallel to the perpendicular through the length of the line.

ADDING SEAM ALLOWANCE TO A CUTTING PATTERN (CP) PIECE

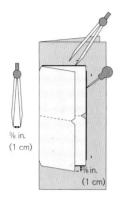

⅜ in.
(1 cm)

⅜ in.
(1 cm)

1. Follow the procedure for duplicating the MP piece. Set your dividers to ⅜ in. (1 cm) and, butting the inner point of the dividers against the making pattern, following the MP edge, drag and score with the dividers. On the outer scored line, measure your corner points at ⅜ in. (1 cm), as in the duplicating procedure above and pierce at this point with an awl.

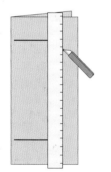

2. With a ruler, line up your registration marks and cut through the length of the card.

3. Open up the pattern, and with a ruler, line up the marks horizontally and cut through the width with a knife. Repeat for the bottom line.

4. Mark and notch your midpoints by folding in half one way and then in half the other way.

DUPLICATING CURVED PATTERN MASTER PATTERN (MP)

1. Cut a piece of card 1–1½ in. (2–3 cm) bigger than the MP piece, mark the center point, and rule, score, and fold down the length. Fold the MP and place it on top of the folded card, folded edge to folded edge. With the awl, score around both curves top and bottom, until you reach the point at which the curve becomes a straight line. At this point measure ⅜ in. (1 cm) toward the center and pierce the card with the awl to make a registration mark. Remove the MP and with the ruler join the awl marks and cut with the knife the length of the card.

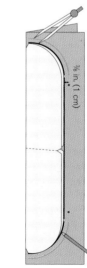

2. Leaving the card folded, cut each curved line following the score line left by the awl. Cut in one clean, swift movement.

3. Mark and notch your midpoints by folding in half one way and then in half the other way.

ADDING SEAM ALLOWANCE TO A CURVED CUTTING PATTERN (CP)

1. For duplicating a curve and adding seam allowance, follow the same procedure but instead of using your awl to score the curve, set the dividers to ⅜ in. (1 cm). Butt up the dividers to the pattern and follow the line of the pattern curve, scoring the allowance by dragging the dividers.

⅜ in. (1 cm)

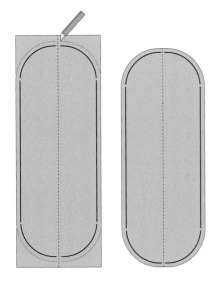

2. Following the scored line, cut all the way around the pattern with a knife.

STEPPING OFF A CURVE

This procedure measures the curve of the pattern, e.g. if you want to make a bag with a curved base and a one- or two-piece body, you need to find the exact measurement of the base. In order to do this, you have to measure the curve accurately.

1. On a piece of pattern card, draw a horizontal straight line with a ruler.

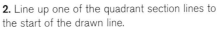

2. Line up one of the quadrant section lines to the start of the drawn line.

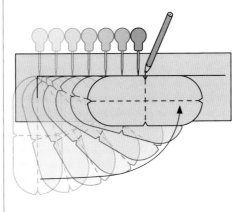

3. Place your awl on the edge of the pattern piece and walk the curve along the drawn line, moving the pattern following the straight line. Slowly and moving the awl a few millimeters each time, you reach the line. Repeat this stepping-off process until your pattern lines up with the straight line you have drawn on the card. At this point, mark with the awl.

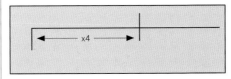

4. Measure the distance between the start of the drawn line and the awl registration point. This measurement is one-quarter of the total measurement, so multiply this by four to give you the total measurement.

SEAM TYPES: BAGS

Objective Learn about seam types in bag construction.

Seam types in bag design have an impact on the overall look, detail, and construction of the bag. How the bag is sewn together has great importance, since it denotes the quality of craftsmanship. It is essential to have a working knowledge of the different seam types in order to fully explore the potential of your designs.

◄ **Butted seams** The handle on this maquette is constructed using butted seams. This was chosen for reasons of aesthetics and strength.

SEAM TYPES FOR BAGS

There are five main seams used in bag construction. Raw edge, butted, turned (which share their names with the three main construction methods, see pages 102–103), boot, and lap seams. The taped seam has also been included here although it is not extensively used.

RAW-EDGE SEAM

The raw-edge seam (also known as a cut-edge seam) is one of the most basic seams used in bag making. The seams are stitched on the right side of the material, and you see the stitch line and the actual edge of the material. The raw-edge seam allows for a variety of treatments and finishes to be applied to the leather edge. This can result in an edge dye coat being applied to highlight or even contrast the leather color. A wax may be applied to give a sheen and a protective seal to the leather edge. It is essential that leather or nonwoven fabrics are used for this seam type otherwise the fabric will fray. Note that if an edge coat or dye of any sort is required, this should be applied after stitching.

BUTTED SEAM

This seam is similar in construction to the raw-edge seam, but instead of the raw edges being on display, the edges are skived and folded in on themselves before being sewn together. The seam shows the turned butted edge with a line of stitches running $\frac{1}{16}$ in. (2 mm) from the edge all the way along the seam.

TURNED SEAM

This seam is where the right sides of the material are placed together, stitched, and turned, so the right side of the material faces outward.

BOOT SEAM

When the turned seam is glued and top-stitched open, it becomes a boot seam.

LAP SEAM

This has the visual appearance of a piece of leather placed on top of another piece. The top layer of leather has a line of stitches running the length of the turnover. Sometimes the overlay is not turned, so it becomes a raw-edge lap seam. This gives the seam a very different appearance and does not have the luxury finish of a traditional lap seam.

BUTTED LAP SEAM

This is a variation on the lap seam, with a double row of topstitching. The top piece of leather or material is turned on itself prior to stitching.

TAPED SEAM

A strip of ribbon or tape $\frac{3}{8}$ in. (1 cm) in width is glued onto the underside of the leather approximately $\frac{3}{16}$ in. (5 mm) from the edge, so that half the width of the ribbon extends beyond the edge of the leather. On the underside of another piece of leather, a line of glue $\frac{3}{16}$ in. (5 mm) wide is applied. When the glue is

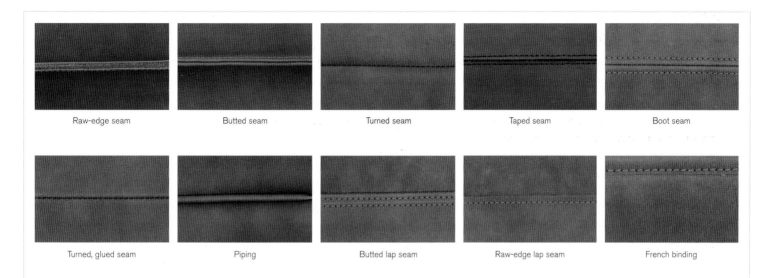

| Raw-edge seam | Butted seam | Turned seam | Taped seam | Boot seam |

| Turned, glued seam | Piping | Butted lap seam | Raw-edge lap seam | French binding |

tacky, this piece of leather is placed on the strip of ribbon protruding from the first piece of leather and the two pieces of leather are butted together, leaving a 1/32 in. (1 mm) gap. When the glue is dry the leather is topstitched on both sides, so the leather is securely attached to the ribbon. This seam can be used on fabric rather than leather as long as the edges are turned prior to taping.

SEAM DETAILS

There are certain details that can be added to seams for both construction purposes and decorative effects.

Piping is often added to a turned seam to give structure to ensure that the shape is retained or to give a slight sporty look to the bag. Color accents and patterns can be added in this way by using an additional or contrasting color. Piping cord/core comes in a variety of thicknesses, material, and weights (see page 99).

Binding can be made from a variety of materials from thin leather to cotton tapes/ribbons. It is used as a decorative detail, adding a design accent with color or shine to highlight a mainly matte leather bag. Binding can be applied to finish a raw edge—the bind is folded evenly in half, wrapped around the edge of the material to be bound, and machine stitched. Some sewing machines have a binding attachment that folds and feeds the leather binding onto the edge prior to stitching.

French binding is also used as a decorative detail. It differs from ordinary binding, in that one edge of the bind is turned and the other is raw.

TYPICAL SEAM ALLOWANCES

Turned seam	1/4 in. (6 mm)
Boot seam	3/8 in. (1 cm)
Butted seam	3/8 in. (1 cm)
Underlay	3/8 in. (1 cm)
Turnover	3/8 in. (1 cm)
Piping	7/8 in. (2.2 cm) width allowance

GLOSSARY

Binding: A strip of material used on a raw-edge construction, to cover the raw edge of material.

Piping: A thin strip of material covering a cord stitched into a seam, for decorative and structuring properties.

Skive: To pare down the outer edge of the leather, to reduce the thickness.

SECTION 2 | HANDBAGS

BAG SPECIFICATION SHEETS

Objective Learn how to create a specification sheet for a bag design.

A specification sheet gives all the vital instructions for the manufacture of a design. It is an essential tool for communication with your factory—the blueprint for your design. A sample will be produced from the information on this sheet—it is therefore absolutely crucial that the details you communicate are accurate, correct, and clear.

VALUE OF SPECIFICATION SHEETS

The specification sheet contains a technical drawing together with all the relevant information needed to produce a first sample. As most manufacturing does not take place in house—often the factory will be located in another country—it is essential that designers communicate clearly, accurately, and concisely. From the details supplied, the factory will cut the pattern and construct the bag from the information supplied. If the specification sheet lacks clarity or information, the factory will fill in the gaps, often resulting in an incorrect sample being produced. The sample will then have to be sent back to the factory with the changes noted for a remake. This incurs a cost in terms of money and time and could impact on next season's selling schedule if production samples are not ready for the new buying season. The better you are at specifying designs, the more valuable you will be to a company.

Specification sheets are constructed using CAD program Adobe Illustrator to produce accurate, sharp technical drawings.

When you regularly work with a factory, you may develop a personal shorthand for your communication with them—be wary of this as pattern cutters, machinists, and production managers change.

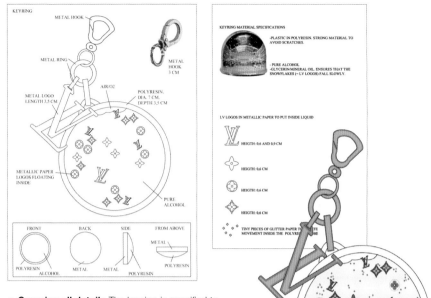

▲ **Covering all details** The keyring is specified to minute detail. The size, scale, and material of the logo is covered in the specification sheet to the right, and the design and main fabrication in the sheet to the left.

▼ **Spec sheet for a foldover bag** Every detail is carefully specified, and nothing is left to chance, from the positioning of the magnet closure to the designer's label.

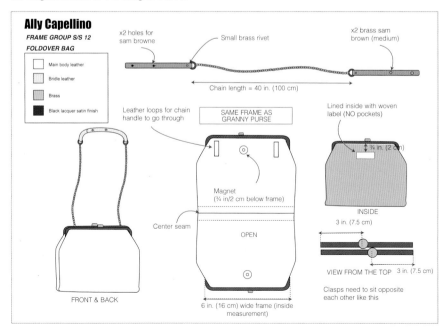

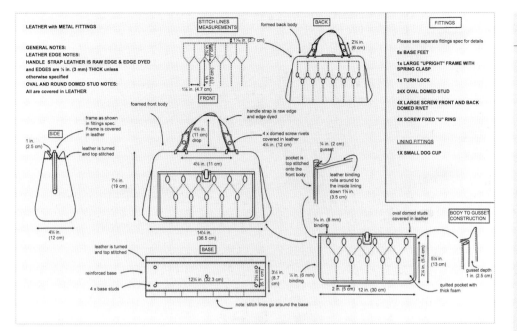

LEATHER with METAL FITTINGS

GENERAL NOTES:
LEATHER EDGE NOTES:
HANDLE STRAP LEATHER IS RAW EDGE & EDGE DYED
and EDGES are ⅛ in. (3 mm) THICK unless
otherwise specified
OVAL AND ROUND DOMED STUD NOTES:
All are covered in LEATHER

STITCH LINES MEASUREMENTS

formed back body

BACK

FITTINGS

Please see separate fittings spec for details

5x BASE FEET

1x LARGE "UPRIGHT" FRAME WITH SPRING CLASP

1x TURN LOCK

24X OVAL DOMED STUD

4X LARGE SCREW FRONT AND BACK DOMED RIVET

4X SCREW FIXED "U" RING

LINING FITTINGS

1X SMALL DOG CUP

foamed front body

frame as shown in fittings spec. Frame is covered in leather

SIDE

leather is turned and top stitched

handle strap is raw edge and edge dyed

4 x domed screw rivets covered in leather

pocket is top stitched onto the front body

leather binding rolls around to the inside lining down 1⅜ in. (3.5 cm)

leather is turned and top stitched

reinforced base

4 x base studs

BASE

note: stitch lines go around the base

oval domed studs covered in leather

BODY TO GUSSET CONSTRUCTION

gusset depth 1 in. (2.5 cm)

quilted pocket with thick foam

▲ **Spec for a quilted-pocket bag** The designer is careful to specify exactly the spacing of the quilted stitches on the front pocket, as such an important design aesthetic would never be left to guesswork.

Base rivets: Rounded studs that are attached to the base of the bag to raise the bag base off the ground and protect the material.

D-rings: D-shaped fitting used for attaching the strap/handle to the body/gusset of the bag.

Spec: Short for specification.

Style number/name: Each product needs to be identified and is given either a unique code number or a name for ease of identification.

EXERCISE: **PRODUCE A SPECIFICATION SHEET FOR AN EXISTING DESIGN**

1. Place a bag on the table in front of you and give it a thorough inspection inside and out.
2. Systematically write down a list of all the elements and components you would need to consider if specifying this design.
3. Following the guidelines on these pages, produce a specification sheet for this bag.
4. If you are doing this in a classroom situation or with another person, swap products and spec sheets and critique one another's work. Have all elements been considered? If not, what is missing?

KEY CONSIDERATIONS

The specification sheet must include:
- A large three-quarter-view technical drawing of the bag design or a large, flat drawing.
- This must convey the bag design, showing all design details in proportion and to scale.
- Technical line drawing of the back view, gusset, top view, interior of the bag, pockets, and base/bottom view.
- Enlarged closeups of small details, fittings, and handles/straps.
- All relevant construction and seam details (see pages 102–105 and 116–117).
- Type and color of threads and stitch length. Note stitch length is usually communicated in stitches to the inch.
- All measurements needed to cut the pattern and make the bag. The measurements should be in inches, centimeters, or millimeters. Use a key to communicate measurements, e.g. "All measurements in cm," then you can just use figures on the drawings.
- Placement/location of fittings and details, e.g. the measurement between the positions of the handles.
- Technical annotation where necessary.
- Materials that the bag is to be made from—supplier's details, color, and code number or name.
- Hardware/fittings to be used—add supplier name and the amount and finish of the fitting, e.g. "⅛ x 1 in. (4 x 26 mm) D-rings, ¼ x ⅜ in. (6 x 8 mm) base rivets in brushed nickel."
- Season the design is for, e.g. "Spring/Summer 2013," and style number/name of the bag.
- Date the specification was produced.
- Number the pages if the spec takes more than one page.

Footwear

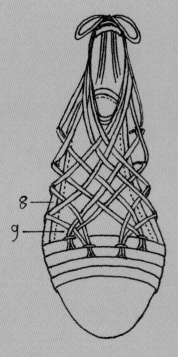

If you are passionate about shoes, footwear is a fascinating area to be involved in. From the master craftsperson in a custom-made business, and the precision engineer producing heel molds, to the conceptual designer whose shoes are not intended for wear but to shock and invite comment, and the technical designer of functional footwear—all are part of the shoe world. The opportunities are endless.

A footwear designer faces a multitude of exciting challenges. Aesthetics are only part of the picture—shoes must be ergonomically sound, fit precisely, protect the foot, and have the capacity to bear the weight of the body. A successful design is both an appealing object and a superb feat of engineering. Most people tend to specialize in one area to develop their knowledge and master the skills involved, developing a network of contacts in other areas.

Design considerations related to footwear will show you how detail and accuracy are all-important. An overview of the types of materials used will help you to understand more about this area. This section also introduces you to the method that is used to produce the majority of footwear: the cemented construction. You will learn the basic principles of pattern cutting, the components involved in shoemaking, and how they fit together.

FOOTWEAR MAKING TOOLS

Objective Learn about the hand shoemaking tools used in the footwear industry.

The pattern-cutting equipment is in common usage worldwide today, with little deviation. Once in industry you will find machinery is used for almost all of the other stages of production. The principles remain the same, and the processes you learn are emulated by the machinery, however sophisticated it is.

Tack knife (1): A tool for removing lasting tacks.

Measuring tape (2): A tape marked in inches and centimeters made from a non-stretch material so that it remains accurate.

Cleaning brush (3): A brush to clean off any dust or dirt.

Awl (4): A pointed tool used for piercing patterns or materials to create location points as a guide for cutting or stitching.

Dividers (5, 15): Measuring tools that can be opened to any required width and used to create a parallel line as a guide for cutting.

Trimming knife (6): Used to remove any irregularities under the shoe after lasting.

Folding hammer (7): Handheld round-ended hammer used to flatten a folded edge.

Pattern knife (8): A tool with a blade on one end and an awl-like point on the other used for pattern cutting.

Curved scissors (9): Used for trimming the lining of the upper and cutting thread.

Clicking knife (10, 20): A cutting knife with a curved blade designed for cutting leather.

Silver marking pen (11): A pen with silver ink used to mark guidelines on upper pieces.

Scalpel (12): A cutting knife with a very sharp blade, used for pattern cutting.

Tacks (13): Small nails used for securing the upper to the insole in the initial stages of lasting. Larger tacks can be used for temporarily attaching the insole to the last.

Paris hammer (14): Also known as a French pattern hammer. Round-ended hammer used to flatten any creases that appear when lasting. The rounded end prevents the surface of the leather from being bruised or damaged.

Sharpening stick (16): A rectangular wooden block with different grades of emery paper on three sides and leather on the fourth, used for sharpening a clicking knife blade.

Bone folder (17): A tool made from plastic or bone used to assist the turning over and pleating of a folded edge.

London hammer (18): Round-ended hammer used to flatten any creases that appear when lasting. The rounded end prevents the leather from being bruised.

Lasting pincers (19, 21): Pincers used to grip the upper and pull it over the insole in the lasting process.

Other tools

Steel rule: A rule made from steel that is strong enough to retain a perfect straight edge, even when used as a guide for cutting with a sharp scalpel (see page 76).

Flexible plastic ruler: A smaller ruler that is flexible enough to curve up the back of a last.

Pencils: 2H, 3H, or 4H pencils are used for technical processes (see page 76). They should be sharpened to a fine point.

Masking tape: 1 in. (2.5 cm) or 1¼ in. (3 cm): An adhesive tape with a slight stretch.

Hole punch: A tool with a range of sizes of round punches used for making round holes in materials (see page 76).

Cutting mat: A self-healing synthetic cutting surface used for pattern cutting.

Clicking board: A board providing a smooth surface on which to hand cut upper pieces. Traditionally clicking boards were made of blocks of wood glued together with the grain vertical, similar to a butcher's block.

Pattern-cutting card: Any very thin, hard card. Good-quality firm cartridge paper can be used as a substitute but will not be as strong.

Adhesive: Rubber solution is used in upper preparation and a stronger synthetic rubber adhesive is used for sole attaching.

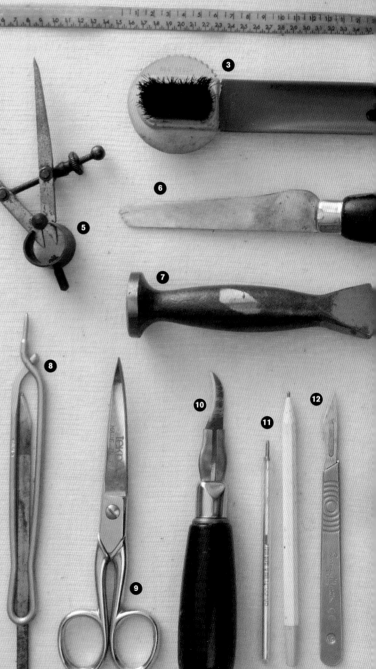

SECTION 3 | FOOTWEAR

FOOTWEAR DESIGNERS AND BRANDS

Objective Learn about key footwear designers and brands.

Shoes can inspire serious lust in both women and men. Women (and men) love what a high heel can do for the length of a woman's leg, and an athletic shoe can suggest athletic prowess. Shoes are essential for comfort, and sometimes most importantly, finishing a look. These designers have been, or are, instrumental in our lust for shoes.

ADIDAS AG
(mid-20th century–contemporary)
GERMAN

The company's name is thought to come from an abridgement of the founder's name: Adolf "Adi" Dassler. The company is based in Herzogenaurach, Germany, along with his brother Rudolf's company (and Adidas's major competitor), Puma. Adidas's popularity was boosted in the United States with the 1986 song "My Adidas" by Run-DMC. Today the company sponsors a wide variety of sports.

Signature style: The trademark three parallel bars, either angled to form a triangle or running along the shoe, have become an easily recognizable symbol of the company.

Iconic piece: The white tennis shoe with the parallel black lines.

ALEXANDER MCQUEEN
(contemporary)
BRITISH

What made Alexander McQueen's work so exceptional was his point of view and his attention to every detail. While his clothing took center stage, the entire presentation was crucial to the realization of maximum impact and effect. The shoes that were created in each collection set trends and challenged conceptions of footwear; they completed McQueen's idea perfectly and created the finished look. Much like his clothing, the shoes that McQueen created for his shows challenged the status quo and inspired countless other designers.

Signature style: Alexander McQueen preferred the stiletto platform and creating high-concept shoes based on traditional Japanese wooden sandals.

Iconic piece: In Spring 2010, Plato's Atlantis, McQueen's last complete collection, saw stunning platform stilettos (right) that defied all concepts of movement or seeming comfort. The collection would not have had the same impact had it not been for these astonishing and unforgettable shoes.

ANDRÉ PERUGIA
(early–mid-20th century)
FRENCH

Perugia began training in his Italian father's shoe shop at the age of 16 in 1909. Already-famous French couturier Paul Poiret discovered a young Perugia and began commissioning work and introducing him to the Parisian jet set. In his career, Perugia worked with designers such as Jacques Fath and Hubert de Givenchy, and other shoe design companies such as Charles Jourdan, as well as having his own clients. During his retirement he wrote his memoirs *From Eve to Rita Hayworth*.

Signature style: Perugia was known for broad and innovative exploration into technique, materials, and silhouette. He was often inspired by other iconic designers and artists such as Picasso, the Surrealists, and Poiret's affection for the *Arabian Nights*.

Iconic piece: With such a long-spanning career in the midst of so many style shifts, Perugia has several iconic styles whose influence is clearly seen in contemporary designers' work. Styles that stand out are his heelless pump shoe and the 1931 fish shoes.

BETH LEVINE
(mid-20th century–contemporary)
AMERICAN

In 1948, Beth Levine started a company with her husband, Herbert Levine, after serving as a model, stylist, and then designer for I. Miller. Beth Levine designed all the shoes, and her husband ran the business. Beth Levine is known

◀ **Extreme footwear** The late Alexander McQueen's extreme platforms figured prominently in his Plato's Atlantis collection, which suggested otherworldly experiences.

Signature style: Spanning most of the 20th century, Charles Jourdan's style has evolved to suit the cultural context and changes within the company.

Iconic piece: The satin stiletto popularized by the 1970s Guy Bourdin advertising campaign cemented the image of the venerable shoe company as sexy and *au courant*.

CHRISTIAN LOUBOUTIN (contemporary)
FRENCH

With no formal training, Louboutin preferred to learn by apprenticing at venerable Charles Jourdan and selling shoe designs to Chanel, Yves Saint Laurent, and Roger Vivier. In the 1990s, Louboutin was one of several designers who brought the stiletto back into popularity. In 1996 and 2008, he received awards from the International Fashion Group, and in 2008, the Fashion Institute of Technology created a major retrospective exhibition of Louboutin's work.

Signature style: One of Louboutin's first jobs was in the Folies Bergère and this has proven to be a major source of inspiration. The titillating anticipation so indicative of the institution can be seen throughout Louboutin's work.

Iconic piece: All of Christian Louboutin's shoes have a signature red lacquered sole calling to mind Louis XIV's practice of wearing a red heel on his shoes in the 17th century. This has unfortunately made Louboutin shoes a target for counterfeiters who use this recognizable signature to sell imitation shoes.

for bringing the mule, boot, and stiletto to the American market in the 1950s and '60s. Levine was a favorite of First Ladies throughout the 1960s and '70s, as well as many celebrity clients.

Signature style: Beth Levine was known for using alternative materials like vinyl, acrylic, and Lurex in humorous and inventive designs such as driving pumps in the shape of a car, slides lined in Astroturf, or stocking boots that extended into a body suit.

Iconic piece: In the 1960s, Beth Levine boots were prominently featured in Nancy Sinatra's publicity shots for the hit song "These Boots Are Made for Walkin'." The demand prompted Saks Fifth Avenue to open Beth's Bootery.

CHARLES JOURDAN (early 20th century–contemporary)
FRENCH

Charles Jourdan opened a workshop in Romans, France, expanding quickly throughout the 1920s from a workshop, to a larger factory, to the launch of his own line. Throughout World War II, like many other shoemakers, Jourdan resorted to using alternative materials to construct his shoes. In the 1930s, Jourdan was one of the first companies to advertise in high-end fashion magazines, cementing his reputation as a widely known and respected name. In 1947, Charles' three sons joined the company and they expanded to become an international brand, as well as manufacturing shoes for Dior and Pierre Cardin.

JIMMY CHOO
(contemporary)
MALAYSIAN

Jimmy Choo came from a family of shoemakers in Penang, and it is a widely quoted fact that he created his first shoe at age 11. After graduating from Cordwainers College and then London College of Fashion in 1989, Choo went on to design for his most famous early client, Princess Diana. In 1996 he formed Jimmy Choo Ltd with British *Vogue* accessories editor Tamara Mellon. In 2001, Choo sold his 50 percent share of the company for £10 million. Today he works on Jimmy Choo couture and occupies himself with charitable endeavors for his native Malaysia. In 2000, he was honored by the Sultan of Pahang in Malaysia, and in 2002 he was awarded the OBE (Officer of the Order of the British Empire).

Signature style: While the company has expanded to other types of shoes and boots, Jimmy Choo shoes are known for the strappy and sexy stiletto.

Iconic piece: The strappy gold pumps that were made for Princess Diana helped launch Choo into superstardom.

JOHN FLUEVOG
(contemporary)
CANADIAN

John Fluevog opened a store called Fox and Fluevog in Vancouver in 1970 with English shoemaker Peter Fox, which catered for the young hip crowd. In 1980, the two went their separate ways, and Fluevog opened an eponymous store in Seattle followed by stores throughout the U.S.A and then the world. In 2002, Fluevog began open-sourcing footwear design, which if chosen, would be manufactured and named after the designer. He has also endeavored to make his shoes,

manufacturing, stores, and studio more environmentally friendly.

Signature style: Fluevog shoes all have substantial squared heels and are geared to be wearable yet innovative, decorative, and stylish.

Iconic piece: Two shoes—the Cox Clog and the Lift-Off—are easily recognizable as Fluevog shoes for the distinctive soles and construction.

JOSEPH AZAGURY
(contemporary)
MOROCCAN–BRITISH

While attending London's Cordwainers College, Joseph Azagury worked in the Rayne shoe department in Harrods to learn everything he could about the shoe business. In 1990, he opened his own store with production based in Italy. Since then Azagury has become established as a designer of simple yet high-end evening and bridal shoes.

Signature style: Joseph Azagury has a consistent, classic, saleable style that incites loyalty in his fans.

Iconic piece: His bridal shoe is never overpowering and always elegant.

KEI KAGAMI
(contemporary)
JAPANESE

Kei Kagami began as an architect in Japan, which seems obvious when you look at his conceptual and artistic shoes and clothing. Kagami gave up architecture to attend Tokyo's Bunka Fashion College, worked at John Galliano in 1989, and then graduated with an MA in Fashion in 1992 from Central Saint Martin's, London. The 1990s saw the launch of his eponymous collection of shoes and clothing that has been in numerous exhibitions and enjoys a small but loyal following. Kagami has been sponsored by YKK zippers and

has used their products in several of his innovative creations.

Signature style: Kagami often uses hardware on his designs, in particular, multiple zippers. The shoes themselves are biomorphic, covering and wrapping the foot in new and unexpected ways with heels to match.

Iconic piece: His heelless shoes seem to defy movement, yet are said to be comfortable and as easy to walk in as platforms, since they have solid steel within the sole for support.

MANOLO BLAHNIK
(contemporary)
SPANISH–CZECH

For someone so well known as a shoe designer, it is interesting that Manolo Blahnik began his early career as a set designer. After an auspicious meeting in 1970 with Diana Vreeland, Blahnik began to study shoe design on her recommendation. In 1971, he moved to London to work with Ossie Clark, and in 1973 opened his first shop. The name of Manolo Blahnik has become synonymous with artful, stunning stilettos as evidenced by his three CFDA awards, three British Fashion Council Awards, his 2007 OBE (Officer of the Order of the British Empire), and the 2001 Honors bestowed by the King of Spain. In 2003, the Design Museum in London featured the design drawings that have been featured in books and magazine editorials.

Signature style: Manolo Blahnik primarily works with stilettos that are richly decorated but always remain elegant and sophisticated. He designs each season with a theme in mind so that the shoes tells a story and lend themselves to romantic interpretations.

Iconic piece: The Ossie that was created for English fashion designer

▶ **Holly-inspired**
From a collection inspired by flora and fauna, this expressive watercolor sketch is by Manolo Blahnik for his holly-leaf-embellished Rogozhin stilettoes.

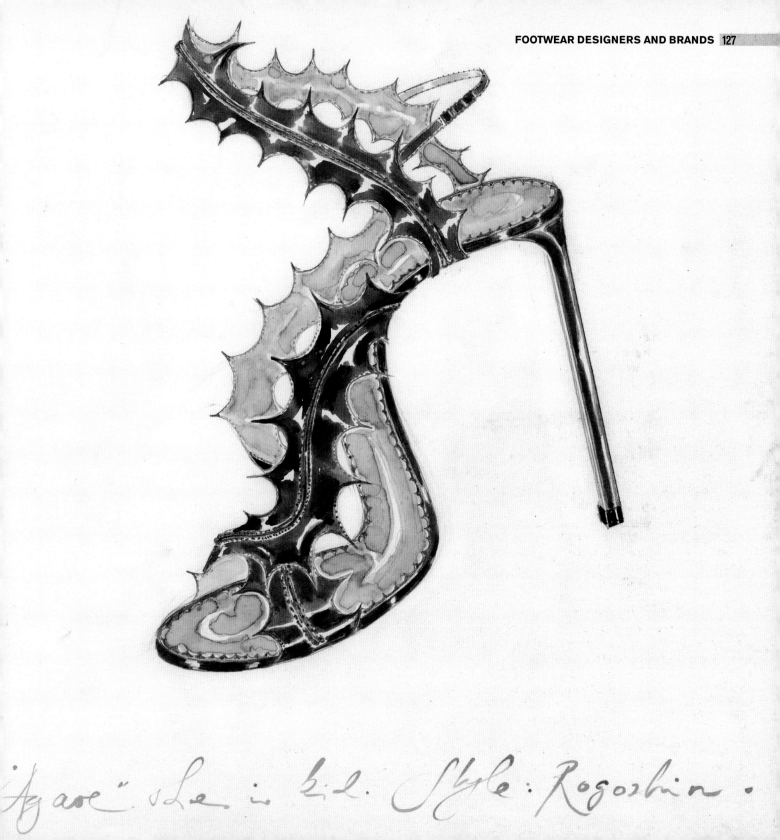

"Agave" shoe in kid. Style: Rogoshin.

▲Snakes on a catwalk
With asps snaking up the catwalk model's legs, Marc Jacobs displays his irreverent humor.

Ossie Clarke in 1972 is a strappy sandal stiletto that has never lost its popularity.

MARC JACOBS
(contemporary)
AMERICAN

Marc Jacobs went to Parsons School of Design and worked for Perry Ellis until 1993. Jacobs and his long-time business partner, Robert Duffy, formed their company in the mid-1980s, and after some initial stops and starts, have created one of the most well-known American brands. The two men have expanded the company to include Marc by Marc Jacobs, Little Marc, and Stinky Rat, and in 1997, Jacobs was appointed creative director at Louis Vuitton.

Signature style: Marc Jacobs balances a sense of fashion-forward style and irreverent humor with references to popular culture and street fashion that make him unique. An example is his juxtaposition of a comfortable wallabee shoe in front and a stiletto in the back, or his series of ballet flats that look like mice or feature a cartoon face.

Iconic piece: In the spring of 2008, Marc Jacobs introduced the Backward Heel. The shoe is styled like a typical pump but the heel is turned around and attached to the instep.

NICHOLAS KIRKWOOD
(contemporary)
GERMAN

Nicholas Kirkwood has sought to create high-concept statement shoes that match design icons like Alexander McQueen, Hussein Chalayan, and his early mentor Philip Treacy. After sporadic encounters with school and work, Kirkwood launched his eponymous collection in 2005. He has been awarded emerging talent awards from Italy, New York, and in 2008 from the British Fashion Awards. He also works with several other designers, in particular, Rodarte, and in 2008 was named accessories designer at Pollini, working with Jonathan Saunders.

Signature style: Nicholas Kirkwood has a geometric and structural style reminiscent of architecture. He is also known for the wide variety of materials from which his shoes are made.

Iconic piece: The platform stiletto with a crescent-shaped front foot has become a recognizable Kirkwood symbol.

NIKE, INC.
(contemporary)
AMERICAN

The company was founded in 1964 as the Blue Ribbon Sports Company by Bill Bowerman and Philip Knight, and only became Nike in 1978. Nike is headquartered in Oregon, outside Portland. The name Nike comes from the Greek goddess of Victory and the company is known for the trademark swoosh and the slogan "Just Do It." In recent years the company has endeavored to improve its image in social and environmental sustainability and continues to lead in technological advancements.

Signature style: The incredible variety of sportswear, shoes, sports equipment, and sports merchandise is instantly recognizable for the trademark "swoosh" that was designed by Carolyn Davidson in 1971.

Iconic piece: The Air Jordan, which gets its name from former NBA basketball player Michael Jordan. The logo called the "jumpman" is a silhouette of Jordan mid-flight on his way to the basket. The Air Jordan cemented Nike as one of the most popular brands of athletic shoe.

PIERRE HARDY
(contemporary)
FRENCH

Pierre Hardy studied fine art and dance in his native Paris, only to find himself drawn to shoe design. Hardy began his shoe designing career at Christian Dior from 1988 to 1990, when he moved to Hermès. In 1999, Hardy launched his own women's collection, quickly followed by a men's line. Besides his successful collections and three boutiques in Paris and New York, Hardy's biggest notoriety has come from working with Nicolas Ghesquière at Balenciaga. Hardy has consistently collaborated with Ghesquière since 2001, helping to define Balenciaga as one of the most fashion-forward houses.

Signature style: Hardy's style is graphic with geometric bold shapes. The shoes simultaneously look heavy and elegant with a wide variety of nontraditional materials such as wood veneer, industrial plastic, and metallic leather.

Iconic piece: For his own collection, Hardy has playfully reinvented the tennis shoe, creating the sneaker stiletto. For Balenciaga, the shoes consistently amaze, from the 2007 stiletto that looks like pieces of sports equipment to the Fall 2010 alligator loafer pumps that had plastic and wood veneer heels.

PRADA/MIU MIU
(early 20th century–contemporary)
ITALIAN

The Prada company has its roots in leather goods from the shop created in 1913 by Mario and Martino Prada. It was not until Mario's granddaughter Miuccia Prada took over the company in 1978 that the brand massively expanded and has become one of the most influential names in fashion. Prada shoes was launched in 1984 and helped to popularize the chunky heel Mary Jane, slingback, and pump in muted colors. In 1993, a diffusion line, Miu Miu, was launched and in that year Prada won Accessory Designer of the Year Award from the CFDA.

Signature style: Miuccia Prada has an abiding sentimental preference for the 1950s and '60s, so often chooses shoes inspired by the time period. Often clunky and with muted colors, they appeal to a different aesthetic, one not of high glam, but of subtle style and intelligence.

Iconic piece: The high-heeled Mary Jane shoe has had a resurgence of popularity thanks to the shoe that is synonymous with Miuccia Prada herself.

ROGER VIVIER
(early 20th century–contemporary)
FRENCH

Roger Vivier studied sculpture at the Ecole des Beaux Arts in Paris, which seems like perfect training for the man who is credited with inventing the stiletto. In 1937, he opened his first atelier and freelanced for several companies, settling at Dior from 1953 to 1963 where he worked for Chistian Dior and then Yves Saint Laurent. In 1953, he designed shoes for Queen Elizabeth's coronation. His work is in the permanent collections of the Metropolitan Museum of Art, Louvre, and the Victoria and Albert Musem.

Signature style: Having worked with so many couture designers, such as Ungaro, Hermès, and Chanel among others, Vivier's style is high glamour with stunning craftsmanship. Roger Vivier introduced the "comma heel," "the ball heel," and the "escargot heel," along with the all-important stiletto.

Iconic piece: Catherine Deneuve starred in the beautiful 1960s classic film *Belle de Jour*, which featured Yves Saint Laurent clothing and Roger Vivier's "Pilgrim Pump," which quickly became a signature shoe.

RUPERT SANDERSON
(contemporary)
BRITISH

Rupert Sanderson began his career in advertising but quickly left to enroll at Cordwainers College, followed by a position first at Sergio Rossi and then Bruno Magli before the companies went corporate. Today Sanderson owns a controlling interest in a shoe factory outside Bologna where all his shoes are produced. In 2008 and '09 he won British Fashion Council's Accessory Designer of the Year and the Elle Style Awards for best accessories. In 2008, Sanderson founded Fashion Fringe Shoes with Colin McDowell to discover new talent.

Signature style: Rupert Sanderson has stated that his design philosophy centers on "less is more" and wants the foot and leg to look as long and graceful as possible.

Iconic piece: Sanderson's pump stiletto that plays with positive and negative space has become a bestseller for its understated grace.

SALVATORE FERRAGAMO
(late 19th century–contemporary)
ITALIAN

In 1919 Salvatore Ferragamo moved from his native Italy to Santa Barbara, California, and then Hollywood with dreams of success. His dreams quickly became reality with many early Hollywood stars as his clients on and off the screen. In 1927 Ferragamo moved back to Florence due to the lack of craftsmen available in the United States. Throughout the rest of his career, Salvatore established a large family firm with his several children filling posts

▲ **Shoe tree** Tracey Neuls gives new meaning to a shoe tree in this colorful collection of day shoes.

in business and creative departments. In the 1960s and '70s after Salvatore's death, his children expanded the brand to include bags, scarves, fragrance, and clothing.

Signature style: Salvatore Ferragamo had an understated style in leathers for most of his career. This all changed during World War II and the material restrictions that went with it. The result was bright, colorful shoes, and the 1938 cork wedge heel that has often been copied.

Iconic piece: In 1938, Salvatore created the suede ballerina with a thin strap for Audrey Hepburn that has become a Ferragamo classic. Additionally the gold-strap, rainbow-colored cork wedge is one of the most often cited shoes for wartime creativity.

SERGIO ROSSI
(mid-20th century–contemporary)
ITALIAN

Sergio Rossi was the son of a shoemaker and began to sell his shoes in the Bologna area in 1966. He met Gianni Versace in the 1970s and worked closely with the fashion designer throughout the decade. During the 1980s, Sergio Rossi became an international brand with quick expansion of stores. In the 1990s, beyond continuing with his own collections, Rossi worked closely with Dolce and Gabbana and Azzedine Alaia. In 1999, Gucci Group bought out Rossi, who subsequently retired in 2005. Today the company is helmed by Francesco Russo.

Signature style: Sergio Rossi effortlessly combined high glamour with a classic Italian aesthetic indicative of the Italian designers with whom he so often worked.

Iconic piece: The sandal called the Opanca, which featured a sole that curved up around the foot, is unique to Sergio Rossi.

SIGERSON MORRISON
(contemporary)
BRITISH–AMERICAN

Miranda Morrison from England and Kari Sigerson from Nebraska met at the Fashion Institute of Technology in New York and in 1991 launched Guts, Glamour, and Elbow Grease, producing everything from their studio in Tribeca. In 1992, Bergdorf Goodman and then other retailers began to carry their shoes, and in 1995 the duo moved production to Italy. In 1997, they won CFDA Accessory Designer of the Year, and have been honored several times for their retail spaces which they began to open in 1995.

Signature style: The two designers often play with multiple straps and ties and combine styles of footwear into one, for example, a boot-sandal high heel.

Iconic piece: In 2003, Morrison introduced a colorful kitten-heel flip-flop, and in two hours they had sold 300 pairs.

TERRY DE HAVILLAND
(mid-20th century–contemporary)
BRITISH

Terry de Havilland took over the family business in 1970 after having lived and worked in Italy. He began making winklepickers (shoes or boots with a long, pointed toe), platforms, and wedges from snakeskin that appealed to the rock 'n' roll and glam-rock crowd. In 1975, de Havilland provided the shoes for Tim Curry in the cult classic *The Rocky Horror Picture Show*. Throughout his career he has changed his product to suit different styles and music genres, earning him the title "rock 'n' roll cobbler." Currently de Havilland has a couture line and a new ready-to-wear collection. He does not make bridal shoes, rather preferring the "honeymoon heel."

Signature style: Terry de Havilland uses leathers and snakeskin with metallic and bright colors to provide a glamorous and sexy look for his fans.

Iconic piece: The platform was popularized by Terry de Havilland, and he was one of the first designers to use it widely.

THEA CADABRA
(late 20th century–contemporary)
BRITISH

Thea Cadabra was influenced by the artistic and wild glam scene in 1970s London and began making her own clothing and eventually shoes. In 1979 she won first prize in a Crafts Council Shoe Show presented by Princess Margaret for her "All Weather Shoe." The shoe was decorated with symbols of different types of weather and became indicative of Cadabra's humor. After traveling and working in Europe and the United States, Cadabra returned to London in 2004 and works with a small artisanal factory in Italy.

Signature style: Thea Cadabra designed shoes to fit into the glam rock scene. They are bright, colorful, and eccentric.

Iconic piece: The Chinese Dragon shoe, the Suspender Shoe, and Rocket Shoe are all typical Cadabra styles. A particularly great shoe is the "Maid Pump" in patent leather, with a white "lace" upper and a white bow at the back ankle. The heels are shaped like women's legs.

TOD'S
(contemporary)
ITALIAN

Dorino Della Valle ran a shoe business out of his basement in Marche, Italy. Things changed when, in the 1970s, his son Diego Della Valle began manufacturing for American department stores. The business quickly expanded to create Tod's then Hogan and Fay, all lifestyle brands. In the 1990s, the company acquired Roger Vivier shoes to broaden its place in the shoe market.

Signature style: Casual, comfortable, soft leather shoes with flat or small heels.

Iconic piece: Undoubtedly the Gommino moccasin driving shoe with the signature 133 rubber pebbles on the sole is instantly recognizable as a Tod's shoe.

TRACEY NEULS
(contemporary)
CANADIAN

In 2000, Tracey Neuls launched her collection TN_29 after graduating from Cordwainers College. She was able to open a boutique in 2005 and subsequently opened an additional line called Homage. Homage, as the name suggests, incorporates time-honored traditions of handcraft with new contemporary ideas. Neuls also cites furniture designer Eileen Grey of the early 20th century as a major influence in her work. She has been the recipient of several awards for her innovative ideas.

Signature style: The interesting-shaped heel is often the first thing noticed on a Tracey Neuls shoe. The heel becomes a decorative element and provides for a comfortable shoe that is eminently wearable.

Iconic piece: Tracey Neuls has a smart, sentimental, and humorous style that experiments with materials and shapes juxtaposed in a new way. As an example, a shoe in the 2011 collection used red fishing line over leather uppers that resemble lace.

STYLE SELECTOR: SHOES

Objective Dozens of shoe and boot styles illustrated and analyzed.

Any aspiring shoe designer should understand the basic footwear styles. The main styles are illustrated and described over these pages. Whatever fashion demands, these traditional shoes and boots will supply most of the answers to your construction needs as a designer. The last shape can be crazy, heels as high or low as you wish, the materials can be extravagant, and the lines extreme, but almost every design will refer to one of these basic styles.

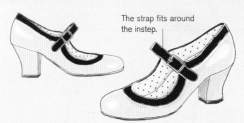

The strap fits around the instep.

Mary Jane

A shoe that is held on the foot by a strap across the instep. It can be fastened with a button or buckle at the side or with a ribbon in the center. Variations on this are twin bar and triple bar.

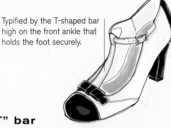

Typified by the T-shaped bar high on the front ankle that holds the foot securely.

"T" bar

A shoe with a strap that rises vertically up the front of the foot, with a loop or slot at the top to hold an instep strap across the foot at right angles, forming the "T" shape that gives this style its name.

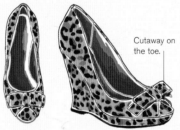

Cutaway on the toe.

Peep toe

A shoe with a small opening at the toe that allows only the big toe to be seen. This feature is often used to create a summer version of a formal shoe but can also be seen in more casual styles, often in fabric.

Strap around the heel.

Sling back

A shoe that is held on to the foot by a strap, which fits around the upper part of the heel at the back, leaving the rest of the heel open. The sling back is a feature of many different types of footwear, formal and informal.

Brogue

Brogue describes the decorative perforations in a ma[ ] shoe, most commonly associated with wingtip laceup[ ] Originally the practice began in Scotland and Ireland fo[ ] outdoor boots that might need draining after wet weat[ ]

Loafer

A traditionally masculine shoe, the loafer has since become a staple of casual, comfortable footwear for either gender. As the name suggests, it is meant to easily slip on and off and has a low heel.

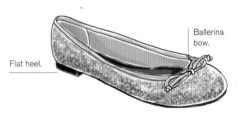

Flat heel.

Ballerina bow.

Ballerina

A flat shoe with a heel height of ⅛–⁵⁄₁₆ in. (3–8 mm), often tied with a small bow at the front reminiscent of a ballet shoe—hence the name.

No straps.

Heeled shoe.

Pump

A slip-on heeled shoe where the topline holds the shoe on the foot without additional straps or lacing.

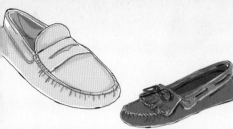

Moccasin

A soft leather shoe originally worn by Native Americans. The sole and side are one leather piece with an additional piece (a vamp) on top. They are decorated with fringe or beading.

Monk

Traditionally a man's shoe that has no lacing and is closed with one or two buckles to the upper side. Women's versions come into fashion occasionally.

Derby/Gibson

A man's shoe in which the lacing eyelets are sewn on top of the vamp. This is also called open lacing. This shoe is more casual than the Oxford.

Knee-high boot

Popularized by Mary Quant in the 1960s during the popularly called Youthquake era, the boot reaches the knee and was a perfect accompaniment to the miniskirt. In the 1960s the boots were usually made from vinyl or leather with a small heel.

Completely backless.

Mule

A mule is a completely backless shoe. It can be open or closed at the toe, and the vamp can consist of one or more pieces or just straps.

Open shoe, usually with strap construction.

Sandal

An open shoe, usually consisting of straps, exposing the toes and often most of the foot, designed to be worn in warmer temperatures. Sandals come in all varieties, eveningwear, beach wear, and casual wear.

A small strap sitting between the big and first toe.

Thong

An open sandal that is held on the foot by a thong that sits between the big toe and the second toe. A very simple style that often consists of just two straps. Styles range from sporty to classy, and pancake flat to high heeled.

Oxford

A lace-up shoe with a toecap lined in two narrow rows of stitching, brogueing along the cap stitching or with a classical wingtip design. The lacing eyelets are sewn underneath the vamp, which is also called closed lacing.

Sneaker/Trainer

A rubber-soled athletic shoe that laces over the instep. The "tennis shoe" is also an early term used to describe an athletic shoe. The British term "trainers" attests to the athletic purpose.

Ghillie

Similar to a ballet shoe, a ghillie is used for Irish and Scottish dance. It is made of soft leather and has crisscrossed laces of ribbon or elastic across the top of the foot and often around the ankle.

Ankle boot

Any boot that ends above the anklebone but does not extend beyond the lower calf.

Espadrille

A shoe that features a raffia or jute sole and a canvas fabric upper. The shoe that was originally a Catalan peasant shoe is now a popular beach shoe. A 1950s style had a canvas strap that wrapped around the ankle.

SECTION 2 | FOOTWEAR

ANATOMY OF A SHOE

Objective Learn about the many different parts that make up a shoe.

If you are passionate about shoes, you will enjoy discovering the hidden parts of a shoe. There is much more to learn than the external appearance of a shoe would suggest. Develop your knowledge to underpin your design skills. For this exercise, the Derby has been chosen, since it is common to men's, women's, and children's footwear from fashion to sportswear.

The unseen, internal parts of a shoe are vital; some create the structure that supports the weight of the body, and others keep the shape of the shoe or support the foot. It is important for every aspiring designer to understand the function of these parts.

The heel, shank, and insole form the structure of the shoe. The heel and shank together create a rigid construction that supports the weight of the wearer's body. Without the shank, the heel and insole would wobble, and the shoe would be impossible to walk in. Flat shoes are the only exception as the insole and sole provide sufficient structure.

The toe puff and heel stiffener are molded to the shape of the last, and maintain the shape of the shoe. The heel stiffener also acts as a support for the heel when walking, keeping the foot in the correct position inside the shoe. Facing reinforcements are used to strengthen the area where the holes are made for the shoe laces so the holes don't stretch and tear the upper material. All shoes that have a fastening, such as straps or buckles, are reinforced in that area. This is essential because the pressure exerted on any fastening is considerable, and the upper material plus lining are not strong enough to support this on their own.

▼ **Constructed Derby shoe**
The shoe has a closed backseam, a folding topline, and a raw-edge tongue. As the lace holes do not have eyelets, an extra-strong reinforcement has been added to the facings.

EXERCISE:
DECONSTRUCT A SHOE

Deconstructing a shoe will help you discover all the parts involved in its construction. Try to find a different type of shoe from the one shown here to expand your knowledge. Keep one shoe as an example of the finished product and deconstruct the other. Photograph each part as you remove it and label it with the correct name. You will need to remove the sock, sole, and heel before you can pull the upper off the insole. Then, to separate the parts of the upper, unpick the stitching carefully using a scalpel.

1 Top piece Fits on the bottom of the heel to provide a strong surface to protect the heel from wear.

2 Heel cover Piece of leather cut to the correct shape and stuck to the heel so it matches the upper.

3 Fiberboard stiffener Inserted between the upper and lining at the back of the shoe to keep the shape of the heel and support the foot when walking.

4 Quarters (two of) Leather parts that are stitched together to form the back section of the upper.

5 Vamp Leather front part of the upper that is marked with a silver pen to create a location line to which the quarters are fitted.

6 Heel Wooden block heel that is strong enough to support the weight of the body without requiring an internal steel structure.

7 Toe puff Reinforcement fitted between the vamp and the vamp lining to strengthen the toe area and maintain the shape of the shoe.

8 Facing reinforcement (two of) Strong reinforcement that is placed between the quarters and the quarter lining to reinforce the area where the holes for the laces will be made.

9 Vamp lining Covers the front part of the inside of the shoe and protects the foot from being rubbed by the rigid toe puff.

10 Sock Inserted at the end of the production process to cover the insole, creating a smooth, comfortable surface for the wearer.

11 Quarter linings (two of) Stitched to the counter lining to create the complete lining for the back of the shoe.

12 Counter lining Stitched to the quarter linings to create the backpart lining. Counter linings are often made from suede to provide extra grip for the heel.

13 Sole Simple synthetic rubber sole with a neatly rounded edge painted black to match the shoe upper.

14 Shank Steel reinforcement that is fixed to the insole to create a bridge between the back of the heel and the joint. This maintains the shape of the shoe and supports the body weight.

15 Insole Central internal structure to which the shank, upper, sole, and heel are attached.

COMPONENTS

The deconstructed shoe in this example is a Derby, sometimes known as a Gibson. The quarters sit on top of the vamp in the finished shoe (left); this is the characteristic that gives the style its name.

SECTION 3 | FOOTWEAR

DESIGN CONSIDERATIONS: FOOTWEAR

Objective Learn the key considerations when designing footwear.

As a designer, it is essential to consider every detail of the product. Once the research stage is over and the direction for the season has been decided, you must use all the information gathered effectively. Adopting the sequential approach described below will enable you to concentrate fully on different aspects of the line at each stage.

THE LAST

The last is the mold that creates the form of the shoe. Last making is a skill in its own right and requires a lengthy apprenticeship to master it. Designers rely on their last maker to create the shapes they need for the season combined with the correct foot-fitting qualities. Almost all lasts of a specific heel height will have a similar shape from the back of the last to the joint, known as the backpart. The major changes in shape take place in front of the joint, known as the forepart. Designers will often alter the forepart of the last to achieve unique toe shapes for their collection, then ask their last maker to create a pair of lasts to each new shape. The backpart should be left untouched—only the last maker has the skill to re-form this area and retain the correct fit. As the last is the foundation of every shoe, it is crucial for a designer to get the shape exactly right to create the look for the season.

Lasts can be altered to fit specific feet, increasing the joint measure for a wide foot or reducing it for a narrow foot. Bespoke shoemakers will change lasts according to the measurements of their client's foot. This is a time-consuming operation and one of the reasons why made-to-measure shoes are so expensive.

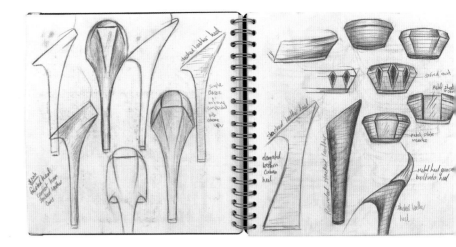

THE HEEL

You will have decided on your heel heights when developing your lasts, since each last is made to a specific heel height. Think about the looks you want to achieve for the season, be they cute, sexy, curvy, or aggressive, and begin to design in 2D. Always draw up your heel ideas on a shoe, not independently. Try out different shapes until you are satisfied, remembering to draw them from all angles—just the side or back is not enough to analyze the shape. If you are planning on using a platform, this must be designed in conjunction with the heel, not only to get the look you desire, but to ensure the heel is correct because the platform increases the height of the shoe. Sometimes the platform and heel will be combined to make a single bottom part for the shoe, known as a unit.

Interestingly you will often find that the heel is the part of a shoe that dates most quickly. Check this out by looking at the shoes in your wardrobe and at last year's fashion magazines. This suggests that heels have a closer relationship to current fashion than other parts of the shoe, and that as a designer, you will be expected to come up with new heel ideas frequently.

PROPORTION AND SCALE

It is important to remember when designing shoes that every millimeter makes a difference. Playing with scale and proportion is part of the creative process. A simple pump with a pointed toe, vertiginous platform, and sky-high heel will look very different from a shoe with the same upper on a soft round toe with a kitten heel.

▲ **Heels** Here the designer is experimenting with heel shapes and levels of detail in a sketchbook. Shading enhances the facets and gives a more 3D effect. To create cohesion in the collection, similar details are used in different ways on high and low heels.

▶ **Edge finishes and treatments** These examples show how the same finish can look quite different depending on the color that shows through the punch holes, the color of the stitching, and the way the edge of the material is treated.

Equally a toe cap one or two millimeters longer or shorter will give a very different look to a shoe. It is good practice to experiment with extremes, then refine your ideas to create wearable products. This will help you to develop an eye for proportion.

MATERIAL, COLOR, AND TEXTURE

Heavily influenced by the season, color adds excitement to a collection and texture adds depth. Material choices will be made carefully with this in mind as well as suitability for the manufacturing process. The mood of a collection will often be determined by the use of materials, color, and texture. For more details on footwear materials, see pages 140–145.

Small details can be added such as punching—these will have another layer of material behind them so that the punched holes are not open. The underneath layer can be in a matching or contrasting color; each will give a different effect.

Don't forget the sole or sole unit—the material, the thickness, the color, and the texture will all make a difference to the finished product:

- A very fine thin edge will create an elegant look; an embossed brand mark on the bottom will enhance this effect even further.
- For a more casual or traditional appearance, you might extend the edge of the sole around the forepart and add an extra thickness such as a narrow strip of leather that could be stitched with a heavy thread.

- A sneaker will have a completely different type of sole unit, usually made from a synthetic compound molded into complicated patterns and shapes.
- The possibilities are endless, and inspiration can be found by looking at every type of shoe in the shops: men's, women's, and children's.

COLOR

The use of color can completely change the look of the shoe. Strong, contrasting colors have a very different appeal from soft tone-on-tone shades. Once you have decided the colors for the season, you should experiment with them to create the best effects for each design, keeping in mind the different needs of your consumers. For instance, a red-and-gold shoe might be perfect for a special occasion but unacceptable in the office. Winter white is a practical choice in some climates but not if the majority of sales are made in a city where snow and rain are the norm in winter. You will always include more shoes in single colors in your line: they sell in greater volume because they can be worn with a wider variety of outfits. To make single-color shoes more interesting, the lining, a small hand stitch, or a sole in a contrast color might be used for visual appeal. Getting the balance right between single-color shoes, subtle tones, and strong contrasts each season takes time.

TEXTURE

Texture also plays its part. A shoe in patent leather will look completely different from the same shoe made in the same color but in suede. Combining textures can add interest where a subtle effect is needed. A single-color shoe made in snake, calf, and suede will be completely different from a shoe made in contrasting colors. Be aware of the different properties of the textures you are using. Suede absorbs water easily and is therefore not the most suitable material for the forepart of a winter shoe or boot, but if fashion dictates that suede is the material of the season, this practical consideration will be secondary.

Try the 2D exercise at right to develop an understanding of materials, color, and texture as a shoe designer.

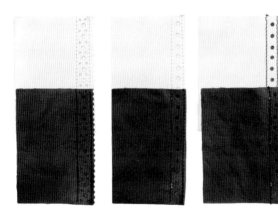

Gimped edge with a two and one punch; often described as brogueing.

Folded edge with a single punch row.

Piped edge with a single punch; two different widths of piping are shown.

2D EXERCISE:
COLOR IN
SHOE DESIGN

1. Take two of your designs and reproduce them each 50 times.
2. Color each one differently:
   - Think about the amount of contrasting color that you might use; try different proportions.
   - Think about using different tones of a single color.
   - Think about how many colors you can use; try one, two, three, etc.
   - Try the different colors in different positions.
3. Analyze the results, and see what works for you.

Repeat this exercise with texture to discover more about the language of design.

▼ **Punch hole pattern** This example, on cream leather, of a pattern created from varying size punch holes is often seen on the toe caps of men's footwear. The contrasting color under the holes draws attention to the detail.

1 Raw edge piped with contrasting leather

2 Raw edge piped with ponyskin

3 Edge bound with ponyskin

4 Seam piped with ponyskin

5 Raw edge with contrasting raw edge leather trim

6 Edge bound with contrasting suede

7 Raw edge piped with contrasting leather

8 Ponyskin bound with contrasting leather

▲▶ **Edge finishes** The designer experiments with all the materials and colors in the line to work out what gives the best effect.

Lap seam: One layer of upper material is placed on top of another, and the two are stitched together with the stitching showing on the overlapping layer. The top layer usually has a raw edge and is therefore not suitable for fabrics.

Run and turned seam: Sometimes known as a blind seam. Two layers of upper material are stitched together face to face. Both seam allowances face the same way, creating a curved edge to the upper layer when the two pieces are opened out and flattened. The stitching does not show, giving a refined, smooth look.

Closed seam: Two pieces of material are positioned face to face and stitched together close to the edge. When opened the seam allowances are spread to either side underneath, creating a flat, neat finish. This seam is almost always used to stitch the back seam of a shoe.

Raised seam: Two pieces of material are stitched together back to back, and when opened out the seam allowances are left standing proud of the upper, creating a casual finish.

CONSTRUCTION TECHNIQUES— SEAMS AND EDGE FINISHES

Small details can make big changes to the look of a shoe. Standard techniques provide a whole range of choices for the designer.

• A closed seam is neat and refined with a subtle indication of the stitching involved.

• A lap seam gives a more casual finish, since all the stitching is visible. To hide all the stitching, a run-and-turned seam can be used.

• A raw edge is the simplest edge finish. This can be finished with a matching color to seal the fibers of the material or a contrast color to add interest to the design. Laser cutting will create a finished edge without the need for further treatment. Raw edges can also be cut with a scalloped edge or gimped (zigzag) edge.

• A bagged edge should be used where the designer does not want any stitching to be visible.

• A folded edge will give a fine, neat finish, and the stitching will be visible.

• A piped edge can be extremely fine or made bolder by adding string internally to increase the volume of the piping. Changing the piping from matching to a contrasting color or material will change the look again.

• Binding an edge creates even more possibilities; the binding can be matching or contrasting in color and material and the width can vary.

Understanding the different techniques and how they can be used will expand your design vocabulary significantly. Pay attention to these small details when you look at shoes in stores and see how others use them.

FITTINGS AND TRIMS

Apart from plain pumps and ballerinas, almost every item of footwear has a form of fastening or adjustment. Consideration must be given to the type of fastening to be used on a shoe or boot. It is your responsibility as a designer to discover what is available and make the right choices for each product. Visiting trade fairs and suppliers will introduce you to the range of products on offer and help you to make the right decisions. See pages 234–236.

• Buckles are produced in a range of sizes, materials, and finishes. Strength is vital as extreme pressure can be put on a buckle if the strap it attaches holds the shoe on the foot.

▼ **Trimmings** Suppliers of ready-made trimmings offer a huge variety to choose from. The lace panel shown can be used on the front of a shoe, the tassel works well on a boot leg, and the "roses" add a feminine detail.

- Velcro is often used for shoes for children or elderly people, since it is easier to fasten than other options. It is crucial that there is a large enough area of Velcro to ensure that the shoe is secure when fastened—this must be considered by the designer.
- Elastic can be used to make a shoe easier to slip on, to gather the top line of a ballerina to hold it on the foot, or to create flexibility in the way a shoe or boot fits. A boot with an elastic gusset will stretch to fit more leg sizes than one without.
- Lace-up shoes and boots require eyelets or ski hooks and shoelaces. Again these come in different sizes, shapes, materials, and finishes.
- Zippers are the most popular form of fastening for boots, but they can also be used at the back of a shoe or sandal to keep the rest of the design free from complication.
- Magnets are now being produced in the right size with sufficient strength to be used as a footwear fastening. Sandwiched between the upper and lining, the magnets are completely hidden, creating yet another option for the designer.
- Trims can be designed and made by the designer or sourced and purchased from a company in the same way as fastenings. Trade fairs and suppliers offer a wealth of ready-made trims in metal, plastic, fabric, Perspex, lace, fur, rubber, and feathers. The materials can also be purchased for designers to create their own trims. Leather or fabric bows, 3D trims, fur bobbles, and sprays of feathers are usually created by the designer in the first instance then produced by the shoe manufacturer. A bow made in grosgrain ribbon will look different from the same bow made in leather. Alter the width of the bow by two millimeters and that will create a new look; have it made in metal and the whole effect will change again. Experimentation is the key to achieving the best solution.
- Metal, plastic, and diamante studs, beads, ribbon, and embroidery are all forms of embellishment frequently used by shoe designers. Create the broadest possible creative vocabulary for yourself by knowing where to source these items and how to use them.

3D EXERCISE: DISCOVER THE IMPORTANCE OF SMALL DETAILS

Cut out some small rectangular samples of material and test the following:
- Stitch along the edge with the smallest stitch length possible with standard thread.
- Stitch along the edge with the longest stitch possible using standard thread.
- Stitch along the edge with a heavy thread.
- Repeat all of these with a double row of stitching.
- Repeat with a triple row of stitching.
- Repeat with a contrast thread.
- Repeat with a different contrasting color.

Think about how you can use this research to inform your designs.

KEY STAGES

What you need to think about when designing shoes:
- Lasts
- Heels
- Proportion and scale
- Material, color, and texture
- Construction techniques
- Fittings and trims

GLOSSARY

Backpart: The part of a last from the back to the joint.

Fittings: Functional parts that relate to the fastening of a shoe.

Forepart: The part of a last from the joint to the end of the toe.

Last: The mold that creates the form of the shoe.

Trims: Decorative parts of a shoe that have no function.

▲ **Shoes** Here are just a few examples of the different looks that can be achieved using the basic principles outlined. Trimmings, unusual material mixes, color, scale, and edge finishes enhance the ladies' shoes; ponyskin, leather, Perspex, and unexpected seam placement give these men's shoes an interesting edge.

MATERIALS AND HARDWARE: FOOTWEAR

Objective Learn about the materials and hardware used in the footwear business.

Becoming familiar with the qualities of materials and hardware is a valuable exercise for any designer. Knowing the potential of every material is an essential design tool. Armed with this knowledge, you will be able to choose the correct material for every shoe you design. It is also important to know how materials perform in the manufacturing process and in wear to achieve the best results. Visiting a trade fair will give you an insight into the whole range of materials and hardware used in footwear (see pages 234–236).

MATERIALS

You only have to think about the different styles of footwear around to begin to understand the extent of the range of materials, trims, and fittings used within the industry. This section gives an overview of the main materials to be aware of as a footwear designer. New materials are being developed all the time and it's important to keep up to date. An interest in future trends, visits to trade fairs, and good communication with suppliers will develop your knowledge and enable you to discover new materials.

LEATHER

Leather is still the most commonly used material in footwear. It has all the qualities to create a shoe that will look good, retain its shape, and last a long time. Every skin comes from a different animal and will vary in size and shape, meaning that each one has to be cut individually in the right way. A skin has less stretch from head to tail than from side to side. It is important to work with this feature when cutting shoes. To aid the lasting process and to ensure the shoe will retain the shape of the last, each part should be cut so that there is less stretch from toe to heel than across the shoe. Industry terminology for this is "tight to toe." Calf, side, and kid are the most common types of leather used for uppers in the footwear industry. These can be finished in many different ways: natural, shiny, patent, suede, etc. Exotics are frequently used in footwear too, from snake to fish skin. Sheepskin and pigskin are commonly used for linings. Care must be taken when selecting pigskin, since in some cultures it is unacceptable to wear this material. The different types of leather and their qualities are outlined on pages 62–67.

TEXTILES

One major advantage of textiles is that they come in a known width and any length can be purchased. As the structure of the material is the same all over, every bit of it can be used, creating less wastage than leather. Textiles can be piled up in multiple layers for cutting so that several pieces are cut at the same time, reducing the cost of this operation.

WOVEN TEXTILES

These can be made from any natural fiber or synthetic compound and they have a regular structure. A loosely woven fabric is not suitable for shoemaking; a close, firm weave is needed. Heavier-weight woven fabrics are used for sneakers, casual shoes, and some sports footwear. These are usually cotton or linen canvas, cotton drill, or similar fabrics woven from synthetic fibers. Fabric fashion shoes can be made from silk, silk satin, cotton, linen, and synthetic fabrics. These are more commonly used for evening and occasion wear and summer footwear.

NONWOVEN TEXTILES

Felt and leather-look synthetic coated materials come into this category. The nonwoven structure where random fibers are sealed together under pressure and sometimes with adhesive added gives these materials some of the characteristics of leather, so that they perform in a similar way in the lasting process. In the case of synthetic materials, a coating of the synthetic compound is spread on top of the nonwoven backer to create the finished material. However, these materials do not retain shape as well as leather. If felt gets very wet, it will lose its shape entirely, and for this reason it is most commonly used for indoor

Lace: Conventionally used for evening and occasion footwear. Requires a backing material to retain shape.

Kid: A fine, strong leather used mainly for women's formal footwear.

Leather embossed to resemble ostrich skin: The embossing process hides any marks on the skin.

Mesh: Used extensively in sports footwear as it is flexible and cool.

footwear. Synthetic-coated materials are now made so that they are breathable like leather, making them more comfortable to wear. Some are available with a knitted structure on the back that is coated with a synthetic top layer. This type of material is often used as a lining and sock to reduce the cost of a shoe. These materials are popular with vegetarian and vegan consumers.

PERFORMANCE MATERIALS

The past 20 years have seen the rising popularity of fashion sneakers and the technological advances have enabled sports footwear designers to create ever more sophisticated performance solutions. Although leather remains the number one choice for footwear, it is now closely followed by performance textiles. Nylon, PU (polyurethane), and PVC (polyvinylchloride)—coated materials were the first to be used in footwear. Because of their lightweight, washable qualities, as well as the range of colors available, they provided the consumer with new choices. Research and development in many industries has since led to a wealth of innovative materials.

Mesh and polypropylene materials such as Polypag, originally developed for the automotive industry, have been adopted by shoe designers. Other new materials are Neoprene from diving suits, Lycra and Spandex from gymnastics, and new technological fabrics developed for astronauts. Polypropylene ropes and webbing—originally used on climbing equipment—are used in lacing systems on climbing boots and running shoes because of their indestructible properties. Pharmaceutical

research has led to silver-impregnated meshes with healing properties being developed. These are now used for lining shoes worn by serious marathon runners. Wicking mesh is used for sailing shoes, breathable mesh for running shoes, and insulating materials for outdoor footwear. From main-street fashion sneakers to high-end performance sports footwear, consumer expectation is high and materials innovation helps to satisfy this.

BACKERS AND REINFORCEMENTS

Woven backers are usually made from finely woven cotton with an iron-on adhesive. They are used to add thickness and control to a material to prevent it from stretching. This type of backer is used on almost all exotic skins and is often used on suede too, since these materials stretch easily.

Nonwoven backers come in different thicknesses and have an iron-on adhesive coating. "Tea bag" backer is lighter in weight and used to add some thickness and control of stretch to materials. Swansdown backer has similar properties but is thicker and used where a material needs extra support. These backers might be used on the quarters of a shoe to prevent the internal stiffener from showing through and to stop the material stretching too much in the lasting process. Most textiles would have a backer of this type to increase the thickness of the fabric, make it strong enough to withstand the manufacturing processes, and prevent it from stretching. For production, the fabric will usually be bought with the backer already attached. Silks, satins, and lighter-weight cottons and linens will require this treatment.

Reinforcements are similar in structure to nonwoven backers but are much stronger. Any vulnerable area will have a reinforcement applied to prevent tearing or stretching. The facings of a tie shoe will have a reinforcement applied before the holes are made to strengthen the area. In some tie shoes, an extrastrong reinforcement might be added so that

eyelets are not needed, leaving the neat holes without metal edging. This is only possible when the upper is made from a nonwoven material such as leather. Reinforcement tapes of different widths are also available. Back seam tape both strengthens the seam and covers it to create a more even surface. Topline tape is a very narrow tape used to strengthen the topline of a shoe and prevent it from stretching. This is particularly important in the construction of ballerinas and pumps where the topline is the only thing that holds the shoe on the foot.

TOE PUFFS AND HEEL STIFFENERS

Toe puffs and heel stiffeners are inserted between the upper and lining and, when set, create a much harder area at the toe and around the heel part of the shoe. They help to retain the shape of the shoe and the heel stiffener provides support for the foot. Toe puffs and heel stiffeners are usually made from thermoplastic materials that are heated to soften them during the lasting process. Once they have been molded to the last shape, they cool and become hard. Some heel stiffeners are made from fiberboard with an adhesive coating. These are preformed and retain their shape for longer, but because they are more difficult to

Silk: Strong but thin and so a backing is applied. Popular for bridalwear.

Synthetics: Utilized to create textures that are not found in natural products.

Exotic materials: Used extensively to add texture and luxury.

Synthetics: Used in fashion and sports footwear.

◄► Swatches At a trade fair, ask for sample swatches of material. Here are two examples of what you might receive. On the left is a swatch card with pieces of one kind of leather. On the right are pieces of fabric held together with a ring. Both show all the colors for the season.

work with, they are only used at the higher end of the market.

INSOLES

The insole is the foundation of the whole shoe. Traditionally insoles were made from leather, and this is still used by anyone making shoes by hand. Fiberboard is the material most commonly used for insoles today. It consists of cellulose fibers bonded together with a synthetic rubber and is produced in different thicknesses and strengths. A single flexible layer of this material is suitable for children's and men's footwear and women's flat shoes. Higher-heeled shoes require more strength, and two different types of fiberboard are blended together to achieve this. The back part will be anything from ⅛ in. (3 mm) for mid-heels to ¼ in. (5 mm) thick for high heels and completely rigid. For the

forepart a 1/16 in. (1.5 mm) flexible board is used. When the insole is cut from the two-part board, care must be taken to place the join in the correct position, just behind the joint.

SHANKS

This narrow reinforcement, used to strengthen the shoe between the back and the joint, is the other structural element that, together with the insole, forms the foundation of a shoe. The higher the heel of the shoe, the stronger the shank must be. A simple wooden or fiberboard shank is adequate for flat and low-heeled shoes to add strength, but high-heeled footwear requires a fluted steel shank to provide absolute rigidity and strength without adding too much thickness.

SOLES

The sole must be made from a strong but

flexible material that can withstand all types of weather and constant wear from walking. Traditionally soles were made from leather, and this is still used for bespoke footwear and at the higher end of the market. Vegetable-tanned leather is used for soles and is much thicker than upper leather because it has to withstand much more wear and tear. The bottom can be finished in many different ways, simply waxed and polished, buffed to create a suede effect, or stained or painted a different color. The edge of the sole can be treated similarly. Rubber is another natural substance used for soling. Natural crepe is one form, and molded rubber is another. Often a rubber sole will be molded directly onto the shoe, creating a waterproof seal. Synthetic rubber and polymer materials also come in a range of colors and textures suitable for soles. Some have a microcellular

◄► Sole materials The same soling material is produced in a range of textures (left). More rugged textures and raised molded sections on the sole unit (right) provide grip in poor weather. This unit is versatile as the extended plain edge enables it to be cut to the right size and shape for any manufacturer.

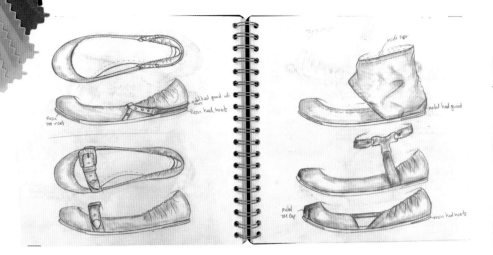

Shoes can be made from any material, even paper, but some materials are more suitable in manufacture and have better wearing qualities. Footwear has to withstand a whole range of weather conditions, protect the foot, and support the weight of the body and the action of walking. Materials need to be strong and flexible, water resistant, and able to be cleaned.

When walking, the impact on the back of the heel as it touches the ground is twice the body weight. This increases to three or four times the body weight when running, which is why the back of the heel wears out before any other part of a shoe. The top piece that protects the heel is removable so that it can be replaced. A molded unit sole does not have this advantage, but the material usually has cushioning properties; it compresses on impact and returns to its original form once the weight of the body is removed from the heel area, giving it a longer life.

The most extreme example of the need for support is the high stiletto heel, which concentrates the body weight on the tiny tip at the end; this force is equivalent to the weight of an elephant.

layer full of tiny air bubbles creating a soft, spongy sole that is very comfortable to wear. Others come with a premolded sole-shaped tread pattern that can be cut to any size.

HEELS

Heels can be made from a variety of materials. Low heels and thick block heels can be made from wood and either covered or stained and varnished. Higher and thinner heels will be molded from nylon or polycarbonate with a steel central core for strength. These can be sprayed with paint or covered with leather or fabric. Heels in men's footwear might be made from layers of leather glued together and sanded to shape. This is a tradi-

tional method of producing a heel and is known as a stacked heel. Heels can also be made from metal, cork, and even Perspex, if the structure is strong enough.

SOLE UNITS

A unit is a combined heel and sole, usually molded, creating one component that is then attached to the bottom of the shoe. It can be manufactured from a range of materials, and the choice will depend on the end use of the shoe.

For sports footwear the units can be simple, rubber one-piece items commonly known as rubber cupsoles, or, more complex multi-sectional units that require fitting together to

▲ **Elastication** The use of elastic in a range of products is examined. The stretch element will mean the shoe stays on the foot even when the vamp is low.

▶ **Stitching** Experimenting with a range of hand-stitching techniques, the designer aims to discover which method and placement to use. The samples are held against the last in various positions to test this visually.

create a performance unit that enhances the wearer's experience when worn for a specific sport. Some rubber cupsoles have an ethyl vinyl acetate (EVA) central layer known as a midsole to provide cushioning for the foot. More complex units for performance footwear may have many pieces fitted together, starting with a thin rubber outsole layer for traction and grip, a midsole possibly made from compressed EVA for flexibility, and a heel insert of a different density of EVA for shock absorption. This type of unit is often used in basketball footwear.

Casual footwear is made for comfort and is heavily influenced by current sports footwear styling. Thermoplastic resin (TPR) and polyurethane (PU) are the synthetic compounds commonly used to produce sole units for this type of footwear. Blown polyurethane is also used frequently. This material is injected with air during the molding process, creating a lightweight sole that has built-in cushioning for comfort.

In fashion footwear, thin synthetic rubber sole units are often seen on flat ballerinas, and some brands use lightly cushioned sole units for their fashion "sport" range.

Sole units have often been used in traditional footwear: wooden soles for clogs to insulate the foot against harsh climates, cork because it's lightweight and cool to wear, and rope units for espadrilles that are still popular for beachwear today.

HARDWARE

Hardware and trimmings are essential in footwear. The majority of shoes have some means of fastening, and the hardware used must be strong enough to be functional and durable. Trimmings are nonfunctional but must be designed to last as long as the shoe they are attached to. The whole area presents the designer with a wealth of opportunities to add interesting details.

EYELETS, SKI HOOKS, AND D-RINGS

Eyelets are metal reinforcements applied to the holes in the facings of a tie shoe to prevent the holes from stretching and tearing. They come in a wide variety of sizes and finishes, both metallic and painted. They can also sometimes be seen on canvas sneakers on the inside near the arch of the foot. In this case they have been applied to create air holes to make the shoes more comfortable in hot weather. Ski hooks, originally used on ski boots, and D-rings are used for the same purpose—to hold the shoelaces in position.

SHOELACES

Shoelaces need to be very strong to withstand the pressure when tying the shoe and when walking. They are available in flat, oval, and round shapes in a wide range of lengths and widths. They are made from cotton, linen, synthetic fibers, or mixed fibers. A huge range of standard colors, textures, and prints is available and any color or mix of colors can be made to order.

ZIPPERS

Zippers are frequently used as closures on boots. They enable the boot to be opened up along the whole length of the leg and down the foot. This make it easy for the boot to be put on and the leg can be cut so that it fits like a second skin once the zipper is done up.

ELASTIC

Elastic is used in gussets to allow the boot or shoe to stretch, making it easier to put on. An elastic gusset in a boot leg will stretch to fit a range of leg sizes, making the product accessible to a wider range of customers.

BUCKLES

Buckles are used to fasten straps on all kinds of shoes and come in a vast range of sizes, shapes, colors, and finishes. Made from metal

Shoe laces: Just a few of the options available. Cotton, leather, and synthetics are most commonly used.

or nylon, it is important to ensure they are strong enough to withstand the pressure exerted on them by walking.

VELCRO

This hook-and-loop fastening is generally used in children's footwear and shoes for elderly people because it is easier to fasten than buckles and laces.

TRIMS

Trims come in every imaginable material, size, and shape. As they are not functional, they do not need to have the same properties as other materials, giving the designer complete freedom to play around with ideas. They range from metal or diamante studs to feathers, flowers, bows, chains, and nonfunctional buckles—anything goes.

Bows: These come in different materials and styles: gathered, casual, or tailored.

Ski hooks and loops: Used for lacing where the laces are either fed through a loop or hooked into the slot in the metal fitting. Available in various sizes and finishes.

Eyelets: Most commonly used on lace-up shoes to reinforce the facings. Can also be used as a decorative trim.

Metal loops/D-rings: The metal loops shown here are used to link straps to each other or to different parts of the shoe, creating a mobile joint. They come in every color and finish imaginable.

Buckles: Essential hardware to fasten straps. Here are just a few examples of some of the sizes, styles, colors, and finishes around.

FOOTWEAR CONSTRUCTION: THE LAST

Objective Learn about the construction of the last.

An understanding of construction is a valuable tool for anyone wishing to work in any area in which an end product is created. If you hope to become a footwear designer, this knowledge will enable you to understand and be understood when working with those involved in production. Your designs will be more thoughtful because you will know what can and can't be achieved by the production units you work with. It should also ensure that your initial prototypes, and later the volume production, will be true to your vision, since you have considered the practicalities of manufacturing from the outset.

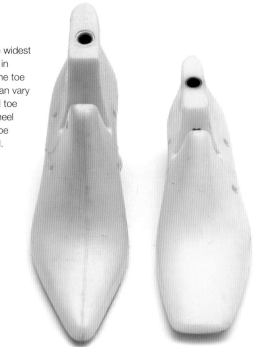

▶ **Women's shoes** The widest range of shapes is seen in women's lasts as both the toe shape and heel height can vary significantly. The pointed toe shown here has a high heel while the wide, square toe takes a much lower heel.

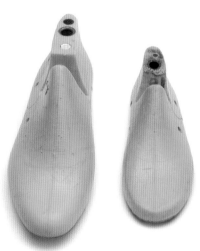

▲ **Children's shoes** Children's lasts conform closely to the shape of the foot, especially in smaller sizes for younger feet. This is to ensure minimal damage to the growing foot that does not mature until adulthood.

▼ **Men's shoes** The wooden last on the left was designed for a casual shoe while the last on the right with a narrower toe is for a formal lace-up.

Once the lasts chosen by the designer have arrived, the construction process can begin. Over the next 10 pages, we look at each stage in this process. One last from each pair will be used for making the patterns while the other will be sent to the insole manufacturer and then to the heel manufacturer to develop the components. The last is taped, a mean form is made and from that a design standard is created (see page 152). An accurate design standard will replicate the designer's lines and form the basic model from which the patterns are cut. The patterns are used to cut the upper pieces from the chosen material which are then stitched together. The lasting process then takes place in which all the components are assembled resulting in a finished shoe.

THE LAST

The foundation of every shoe is the last—the mold on which it is created. A last is made by a specialist last maker working to a design given to him or her by the shoe designer. Traditionally lasts were made of wood, but plastic is most commonly used today. In some parts of the world, metal lasts are used because they can be melted down when they are no longer needed and the materials reused. The last forms the shape of the shoe, which is the most important consideration for the designer. Toe shapes

▶ **Parts of a last** This diagram introduces you to the traditional terminology used for the various parts of a last. It is essential for you to become familiar with the names for the different parts in order to communicate with last makers and with footwear manufacturers.

Top plane

Heel curve

Vent

Backpart

Cone

Hinge

Heel seat

Vamp

Joint

Waist

Toe wall

Toespring

Forepart

The continuous unbroken line all around the last bottom edge is called the "featherline."

change from season to season, and this is the first consideration for a footwear designer at the beginning of a new line. It is also important that shoes fit correctly—however appealing they might be in visual terms, if they don't fit, they won't sell. It is essential to work with a reliable, experienced last maker, since he or she has the knowledge to ensure the last fits well.

The last should be balanced on the joint area where the ball of the foot rests in a finished shoe. When positioned in this way, the toe of the last will not touch the ground; this gap is known as the toe spring. The heel height can also be determined with the last in this position by measuring vertically from the back of the last to the floor. If the correct heel for a last is used, the finished shoe will be comfortable because the body will be supported so that it balances over the ball of the foot.

Lasts vary for different products. A shoe last is carefully shaped to fit closely to the foot in the area of the topline—the top edge of the shoe that is next to the foot. A boot last will be much bigger around the top of the

foot and ankle area to allow the boot to be pulled onto the foot. A very open sandal or flip flop will require a different last again—since there is so little to hold the foot in place, it will spread to its full extent when walking and the bottom of the last needs to be big enough to accommodate this.

KEY STAGES
- Draw the toe shapes you are considering for the season.
- Choose the exact heel heights for the coming season.
- Make an appointment with the last maker to discuss the heel heights and toe shapes.
- If there are any areas of uncertainty, ask to see the last maker's archive for further inspiration.
- Explain what each last will be used for—shoes, boots, sandals, etc.—and discuss any potential fit problems.
- Order sample lasts.
- Make one prototype on each last to check the toe shape is correct, then work can begin on the components.

GLOSSARY

Backpart: The back section of the last.

Cone: The top of the front section of the last.

Forepart: The front section of the last.

Joint: The widest part of the forepart corresponding to the foot joint position.

Last: The mold on which a shoe is made.

Toe wall: The depth of the toe at the front. Often defined by a ridge.

Waist: The central section of the bottom of the last.

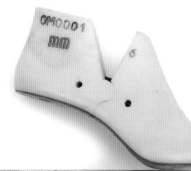

▼ **Measuring heel height** Here the last has been balanced against a straight edge to show the correct toe spring and heel height. With a last positioned in this way, the exact heel height can be measured. When drawing the side view of a last, a designer will often position it in this manner to ensure accuracy.

The gap between the straight edge and the end of the toe is known as the toe spring. This upward sweep assists the walking action in the finished shoe.

FOOTWEAR CONSTRUCTION: COMPONENTS

Objective Learn about heels, insoles, soles, and sole units.

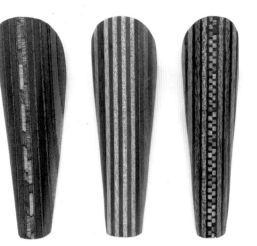

▶ **Heels** The designer has created these heels by layering wood veneer in carefully constructed patterns and shaping them to fit the last.

Understanding the way in which the different components for a shoe are developed is a priority. It will help you realize what instructions you need to prepare to get what you want both aesthetically and technically. When you have agreed a last (see page 146), the next part of the process is to make the other physical components of the shoe: the heel, the insole, and the sole unit. These components are first manufactured as prototypes, using drawings created by the designer. Some components will just require selection while others will require a high level of input from you.

THE HEEL

Once a last has been developed, the heel can be prepared. The designer draws the heel from the side, front, back, and bottom and gives these to the heel maker, together with the last. From these instructions, a wooden model of the heel will be created. If a small variation on a heel from the previous season is required, simple instructions will be given to the heel maker, and the designer will not need to create a set of drawings from all angles. When the sample wooden heel has been approved, more

will be produced to use on the first prototype samples. The heel must fit accurately under the back of the shoe, and as this varies according to the size of the shoe, more than one size of heel will be needed for production. Low and thick block heels can be made from wood for production. The majority of heels are molded from nylon and polymer substances, and, for high heels, a core of steel is inserted to support the body weight. As the molds are expensive to produce, orders for each heel design must be secured before this investment is made.

THE INSOLE

The insole is the next consideration. Although unseen, this is the core of the structure of the shoe to which everything is attached. Insoles for shoes with a heel higher than ¾ in. (2 cm) will normally be made from a two-part fiberboard with a softer, more flexible material in the forepart and harder material at the back. The material at the back will vary in thickness and density according to the height of the heel; the higher the heel, the thicker and denser the back part needs to be, since this will provide the strength needed in wear. Women's low heels, men's footwear, and children's footwear do not require the same strength, and the whole insole can be made of the same material. The

FOOTWEAR PRODUCTION PROCEDURE

A shoe consists of many parts (see page 135). Different skills, knowledge, and equipment are needed to produce each of these parts. Each of the components might be purchased from a different company. Continual communication with suppliers, good project management, and record keeping is required to manage this procedure. If just one component required for the uppers is not available on the day production is scheduled to start, nothing can be produced. Similarly, when the uppers are ready, if insoles, units, soles, or heels have not been delivered, the production comes to a standstill.

▶ **Using metal** In this shoe the fine metal rod acts as a semi-hidden support for the body weight, allowing glimpses of the interior of the heel. The external heel shape, made from two layers of molded leather, is not functional.

insole must be molded accurately to the curve of the bottom of the last. The material is selected, and the last is left with the insole maker, who will produce insoles to fit. Strength is also added in the form of a shank that provides a bridge between the back of the shoe and the joint. This is the part of the shoe where the weight of the body must be supported. A groove will be cut into the insole and the shank fitted into it following the curve of the insole exactly.

THE SOLE AND SOLE UNITS

Standard soles are cut from a skin of leather or a sheet of synthetic resin. The edges are shaped on a machine, rounded, beveled, or grooved, and then painted or dyed to seal the material. In some constructions the sole is stuck to the front of the heel but the heel remains a separate item. This is how a sole differs from a sole unit.

Sole units incorporate the sole and heel and can form the whole of the bottom of the shoe. In some instances a

sole will need to be added to the bottom to create a suitable surface for walking. Most units are created by molding a strong, flexible material that is allowed to set. The process is so sophisticated that two or more colors can be used for a single unit. You only have to look at the range of sneakers available to recognize this. The molds have to be engineered precisely and a range of sizes is needed. This is extremely costly. A company will not invest in a set of molds until they are certain they can make enough sales to justify the outlay. To achieve the required sales, samples must be made and presented to buyers. When wood and cork are in fashion, units are created using wood-turning machinery to achieve the desired shape.

In the past, sample sole units had to be made painstakingly by hand but, with the advent of rapid prototyping, sample sole units can be produced in a very short time. The unit is designed using a CAD system, and the information sent to the rapid prototyping machine that will then print a prototype sample. This technology is being developed all the time. Now machines are available using different-colored materials that can be incorporated in one prototype to create an exact replica of a multicolored sole unit. This method also allows the designer to work at a distance from the prototyping process. The designs can be created in New York, for instance, and the prototype sample in China. A designer might be trained to use the CAD software needed for this process, or in some companies, just produce accurate drawings of the design that would then be passed to an experienced technician. Once the preparation of the heel, sole, and insole is under way, the first patterns for the new range can be cut.

◀ **Sole** Traditional techniques have been used here to create a perfect leather sole and layered leather heel with signature features.

▼ **Insole** This two-part insole consists of a slim flexible forepart and a thicker rigid backpart that, together with the fluted metal shank, will support the weight of the body and maintain the structure of the shoe.

▶ **Wooden sandal** The sandal bottom is carved from a block of wood, the unit is set under the insole and a leather sole has been added to the bottom of the unit. The toe post is made from the same wood as the unit for continuity.

FOOTWEAR CONSTRUCTION: CREATING A DESIGN STANDARD

Objective Learn about the pattern-cutting process in footwear.

Now the last has been designed and the production of the components is under way (see pages 148–149), the next step is to create a design standard from which the pattern can be cut. Although in most instances drawings and specifications will be sent to a manufacturer to create the first prototypes, sometimes there is the opportunity to work directly with the production unit and that is when you need the skills described here. The taping and pattern-cutting process outlined here translates the 3D last shape into 2D shapes that can be cut from flat materials. Learning this process stage by stage will help you to understand the typical way in which footwear uppers are produced and the level of accuracy needed to create a sample that is true to your design. Here, we demonstrate how to create a design standard for a Derby shoe, but the taping method described can also be used to create insole and heel cover patterns.

TAPING THE LAST

The first step is to fully tape the last to create a removable mold of it. Make sure to stick each strip of tape down along the whole length. To get an accurate result, avoid bridging the tape across the curves of the last. Ensure the tape conforms to the contours of the last, and overlap each strip as near to halfway over the previous one as possible. In places you will not be able to attach the tape exactly halfway on top of the previous layer because the curves of the last will affect the way the tape lies. This will not cause problems as long as every layer is overlapping.

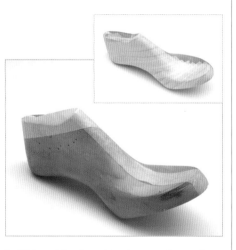

1. Stick a strip of masking tape up the center front and the center back. Starting on the inside, stick one strip of tape across the top, ending just across the center front and center back. Add another layer, overlapping the previous strip halfway. Continue adding layers all the way down the last until you reach the toe. Repeat this on the outside of the last.

2. Next, start from the toe by sticking a strip of tape straight across at right angles to the center line. Continue adding strips overlapping halfway again until you reach the top of the cone.

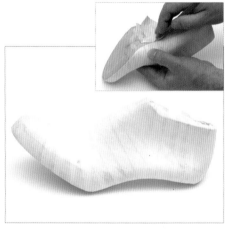

3. Starting from the cone, add strips vertically down the outside of the last and work your way around to the inside until you meet the same place on the cone, overlapping the tape as before. Trim the excess tape away from the underside of the last. You now have a last that is covered with two layers of tape.

CREATING THE FORMS

Designers rarely cut their own patterns as this is a completely different set of skills and a separate career path. Designer-makers will need to take a course that will teach them pattern-cutting skills. Even once the basics have been learned and understood, it requires a lot of practice to become a confident and expert pattern cutter. As a designer, if you are working with the sample production unit, at this stage you would hand over the taped-up last with the design drawn on it to the pattern cutter. All the patterns that would be required to create the Derby shoe constructed in this section are shown to the right. However, it is useful to gain an understanding of the further stages involved in creating a design standard. The steps below describe the process of creating the forms, which are 2D representations of the 3D last from which the patterns will be created.

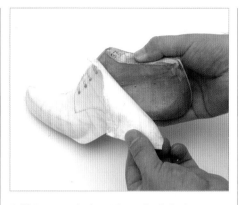

2. Using a scalpel, cut through all the layers of tape down the center-front and center-back lines. Carefully peel the inside section off the last.

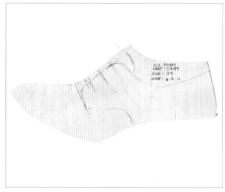

3. Flatten the inside section on a piece of pattern card, and mark it in pencil "inside form." Repeat the process with the outside section, marking it "outside form," and cut them both out.

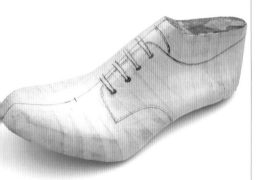

1. Draw a line down the center front and center back of the taped-up last and put two pencil marks across the center line, one at the front and one at the back. Draw the design onto the taped-up last.

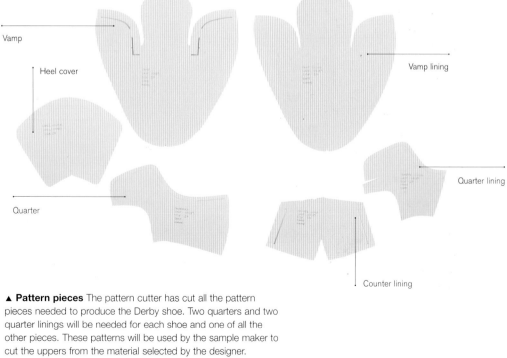

Vamp

Heel cover

Vamp lining

Quarter lining

Quarter

Counter lining

▲ **Pattern pieces** The pattern cutter has cut all the pattern pieces needed to produce the Derby shoe. Two quarters and two quarter linings will be needed for each shoe and one of all the other pieces. These patterns will be used by the sample maker to cut the uppers from the material selected by the designer.

CREATING THE MEAN FORM

The mean form is created to remove any inaccuracies that have occurred during the previous steps by averaging the difference between the two forms. As the 2D representation of the last, it is the basis for the design standard from which the patterns will be cut. Attention to accuracy at this stage is vital as any mistakes will be magnified when the patterns are cut.

MAKING THE DESIGN STANDARD

The design standard is a copy of the mean form with the design lines added and a lasting allowance along the bottom edge. It is used as the master from which all the patterns are cut for an individual design. The design standard is the key stage in the process; if patterns are mislaid they can be recut but if the design standard goes astray the design is lost.

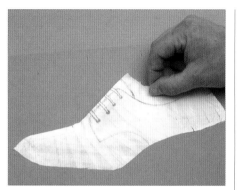

1. Draw around the outside form with a sharp pencil onto a new piece of pattern card. Then lay the inside form on top, matching the location marks at the back and front. Draw around the inside form.

3. Cut through the new "average" line all the way around, except at the bottom of the front, where you should cut around the outside line and then mark the inside line. This is your mean form.

Draw around your mean form onto pattern card. Using your dividers, add an allowance along the bottom edge—¾ in. (20 mm) at the back reducing to ⅝ in. (16 mm) at the front. The two allowances should blend together at the deepest point of the curve along the bottom edge. This is known as the lasting allowance, which is the area that will be pulled over the bottom edge of the last and stuck to the insole. Mark the design lines on and the inside line at the bottom front (see creating the mean form) and then cut this out. Mark the last number and the date—your design standard is now complete. At this stage you would hand the standard over to a pattern cutter who will cut all the pattern pieces required to make your shoe. The pattern pieces for the shoe made in this section are shown on page 151.

2. Draw a line halfway between the two lines all the way around as shown in the diagram.

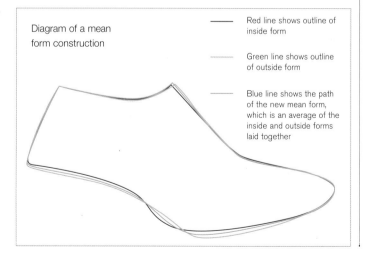

Diagram of a mean form construction

—— Red line shows outline of inside form

—— Green line shows outline of outside form

—— Blue line shows the path of the new mean form, which is an average of the inside and outside forms laid together

KEY STAGES
- Prepare your tools and equipment.
- Cover the last in two layers of tape.
- Create the forms.
- Find the mean form.
- Make the design standard.

SECTION 3 | FOOTWEAR

FOOTWEAR CONSTRUCTION: MAKING

Objective Learn the basic processes involved in cement lasted shoemaking.

Once the patterns have been cut from the design standard (see page 152), the final stage is the actual construction of the shoe. Shoemaking is a complicated process requiring a range of skills and, unless the product is handmade, a significant amount of industrial machinery. It is done by trained professionals. This outline introduces you to the major stages involved in creating a shoe using the design standard created for the Derby shoe in the previous section. Every style of shoe is slightly different and will involve variations in the pattern cutting and construction processes; here we look at a professional shoemaker at work demonstrating a process called cement lasting. This is one of the most common shoemaking processes and involves attaching the upper and the sole with adhesive, which is also known as "cement" in the footwear industry.

MAKING THE UPPER

1. The patterns are used to cut the upper, lining, and reinforcement pieces from the materials selected. Location marks are added to the vamp and counter lining with a silver pen through the slots in the pattern.

2. The toe puff is stuck to the wrong side of the vamp, which is then positioned on the lining with the ¼ in. (5 mm) trimming allowance extending beyond the upper and around the tongue. The raw-edge tongue is stitched to the lining, and the trimming allowance is cut off.

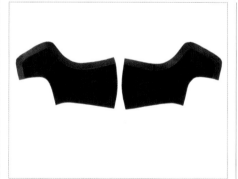

3. In preparation for folding, the quarters are skived along the topline edge to reduce the thickness of the upper material in this area.

4. The quarters are joined together with a closed seam at the back by stitching ¹⁄₁₆ in. (1.5 mm) from the edge with the cut pieces face to face.

5. The seam is flattened and a layer of tape is applied along the seam to strengthen it.

6. A narrow line of tape is applied along the top of the quarters, ¼ in. (5 mm) below the edge which is to be folded (top). This will strengthen the edge and stop the topline from stretching. The top edge is folded over the tape creating a folded edge (bottom).

8. The reinforcement is stuck on to the back of the facings, and the quarters are stitched to the lining along the topline. The trimming allowance is then cut off.

FORMING THE SHOE

1. The insole is temporarily attached to the bottom of the last using two long tacks. These tacks will be removed after the upper is lasted. The upper is warmed to soften the toe puff and stiffener and then positioned on the last. The bottom edge of the upper is pulled onto the insole using lasting pincers and tacks are used to fix the upper in the correct position. The entire edge of the upper is coated with adhesive and stuck onto the insole. The tacks are then removed.

7. This image shows the inside of the shoe where quarter linings have been placed on the marks on the counter lining and stitched in place before the lining is stitched to the quarters.

9. The quarters are positioned on the location marks on the vamp and stitched in place. Holes are punched into the facings and then the upper is ready.

2. To ensure the bottom surface is even, a layer of cork dust suspended in adhesive is spread over the insole. The whole of the bottom area of the shoe and the sole is then covered with a heat-activated adhesive and left to dry.

3. The shoe and the sole are placed in a specially designed oven and heated to activate the adhesive.

5. The shoe is placed in the sole-attaching machine, which exerts pressure on the shoe ensuring a strong sole bond. The shoe is allowed to cool completely, and then the last is removed.

▶ **Derby shoe** After all the steps in the process are completed, you will have a finished pair of shoes and see your design actualized.

4. Once heated, the sole is placed in the correct position on the bottom of the shoe.

6. The shoe and heel are placed on the heel-attaching machine, which drives nails through the insole and into the heel. The final step is to insert the sock into the shoe to cover the insole, clean off any marks, and insert the shoelaces.

SECTION 3 | FOOTWEAR

SPECIFICATION SHEETS: FOOTWEAR

Objective Learn about the importance of specification sheets in footwear design.

A specification sheet is an instruction manual for the preparation of a prototype or sample product. It is essential for a designer or product developer to communicate all the details of the design clearly to the sample room so that they can produce exactly what is required. The more information the sheet contains, the more accurate the finished sample will be. To be understood by everyone, the design and layout of specification sheets must be considered carefully.

CREATING A SPECIFICATION SHEET

A specification sheet or sheets will require different levels of information depending on the individual situation. A designer-maker who is in control of the whole process will not need the same level of information as a factory in China producing samples for a company based in the United States or Europe. Every company will have its own system and layout for specification documents. Whenever you start a new job, you need to become familiar with the specification system as soon as possible. It is important to remember to include everything that goes into the product; this usually requires two or more pages of information.

Footwear is complicated, with each shoe consisting of an upper, an insole, a sole, a heel or unit, and a sock that usually carries the brand label or stamp. The upper almost always requires some form of reinforcement and lining as well as any fastenings or trimmings. Everything to be included in the sample must be recorded. Every specification will have its own code number, and in all instances it should be informative enough to act as a detailed record of the prototype sample. Once a style has been sold, the manufacturer prepares for the volume production. The original specification sheet will provide the information for the

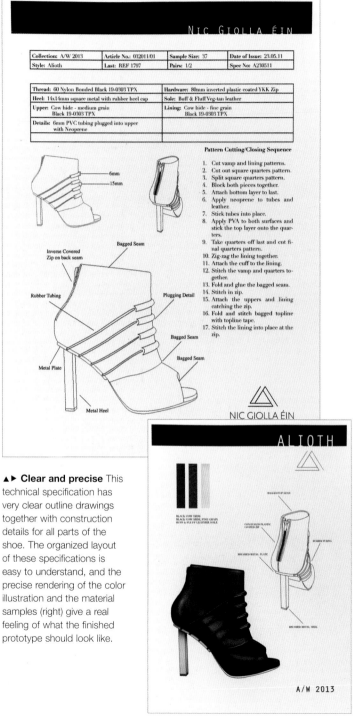

▲▶ **Clear and precise** This technical specification has very clear outline drawings together with construction details for all parts of the shoe. The organized layout of these specifications is easy to understand, and the precise rendering of the color illustration and the material samples (right) give a real feeling of what the finished prototype should look like.

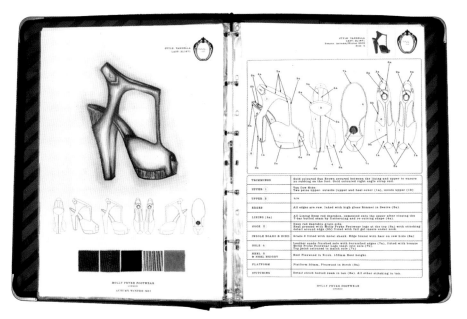

SPECIFICATION PROCESS: DESIGNER-MAKERS

A designer-maker with a simpler type of specification will often include costing details as well as all the details of the product. Keeping all the information in one place simplifies the administrative system. Usually this will be filed under the customer's name, creating a file for each individual client. Problems encountered in the creation of the product will be recorded. This type of business depends mainly on individual clients, some wanting a unique pair of shoes for their wedding or special occasion, and others with extra-large or small feet who cannot find shoes they like in stores. Collaboration with designers needing shoes for their catwalk show is often another aspect of the designer–maker business. As well as being interesting work, this brings valuable press for the owner of a small company. As satisfied clients will often return for more shoes, it is important to maintain records.

instructions for each department in the manufacturing process. In the global market, working with companies that do not share a common language is an everyday occurrence. To overcome language barriers, it is important to find a means of communication that can be understood by everyone. This can be achieved by providing as much visual information as possible supported by code numbers, if available, and a minimal amount of text. Drawing, Illustrator, and Photoshop skills are of vital importance here to achieve the desired outcome.

▲ **Technical drawings**
Below the color illustration is a range of outline drawings showing the design from every possible angle and samples of all the materials to be used. The sheet on the right shows a series of coded technical drawings to ensure that every detail is taken care of.

▶▼ **Naughty set** This specification shows everything visually to communicate with a range of people speaking different languages. The final samples (below) demonstrate the effectiveness of the specification as they are exactly what the designer intended.

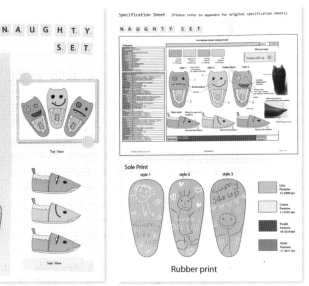

▼ **Complex design** This design is so complicated that the designer has created a series of tables to ensure that every detail is understood by the sample maker. Here we see instructions for the upper construction, laser engraving, and the range of trims to be attached to the upper.

The machine settings required to produce the correct effect are spelled out to the right of the design.

A complete inventory of the range of differently shaped studs used to trim this design.

Here we see the design to be engraved on the sole of the shoe.

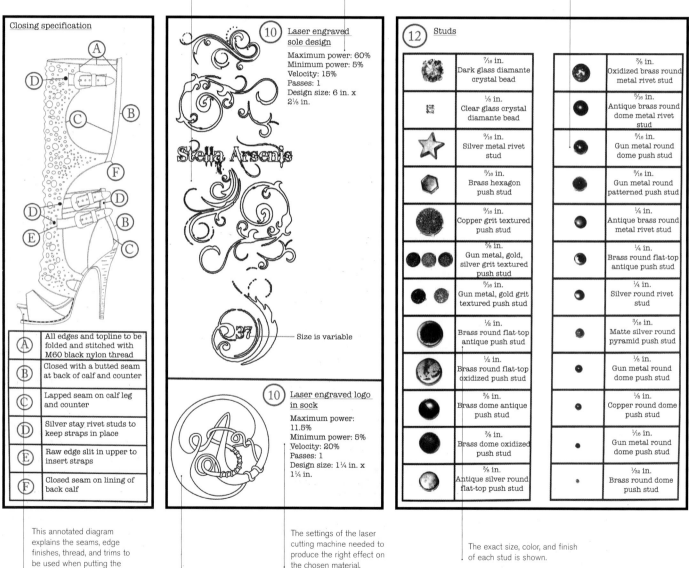

Closing specification

A	All edges and topline to be folded and stitched with M60 black nylon thread
B	Closed with a butted seam at back of calf and counter
C	Lapped seam on calf leg and counter
D	Silver stay rivet studs to keep straps in place
E	Raw edge slit in upper to insert straps
F	Closed seam on lining of back calf

(10) Laser engraved sole design

Maximum power: 60%
Minimum power: 5%
Velocity: 15%
Passes: 1
Design size: 6 in. x 2⅛ in.

Stella Arsenis

37 — Size is variable

(10) Laser engraved logo in sock

Maximum power: 11.5%
Minimum power: 5%
Velocity: 20%
Passes: 1
Design size: 1¼ in. x 1¼ in.

(12) Studs

	⁷⁄₁₆ in. Dark glass diamante crystal bead		⅜ in. Oxidized brass round metal rivet stud	
	⅛ in. Clear glass crystal diamante bead		⁷⁄₁₆ in. Antique brass round dome metal rivet stud	
	⁹⁄₁₆ in. Silver metal rivet stud		⁵⁄₁₆ in. Gun metal round dome push stud	
	⁵⁄₁₆ in. Brass hexagon push stud		⁵⁄₁₆ in. Gun metal round patterned push stud	
	⁹⁄₁₆ in. Copper grit textured push stud		¼ in. Antique brass round metal rivet stud	
	⅜ in. Gun metal, gold, silver grit textured push stud		¼ in. Brass round flat-top antique push stud	
	⁵⁄₁₆ in. Gun metal, gold grit textured push stud		¼ in. Silver round rivet stud	
	½ in. Brass round flat-top antique push stud		³⁄₁₆ in. Matte silver round pyramid push stud	
	½ in. Brass round flat-top oxidized push stud		⅛ in. Gun metal round dome push stud	
	⅜ in. Brass dome antique push stud		⅛ in. Copper round dome push stud	
	⅜ in. Brass dome oxidized push stud		¹⁄₁₆ in. Gun metal round dome push stud	
	⅜ in. Antique silver round flat-top push stud		¹⁄₃₂ in. Brass round dome push stud	

This annotated diagram explains the seams, edge finishes, thread, and trims to be used when putting the upper together.

This illustration shows the design to be laser engraved in the sock.

The settings of the laser cutting machine needed to produce the right effect on the chosen material.

The exact size, color, and finish of each stud is shown.

Spec 1
Chin Strapper

Company: VICE VERSA

Specification number:
AD15052011VICEVERSA1

Size: Mens 9 US

Upper: White nubuck and black patent leather.

Lining: White suede pigskin and black, perforated pigskin.

Sole Unit: Black EVA attached to upper with stitchdown construction.

Sock: White nubuck printed with black color halftone pattern, bound with black patent leather.

Laces: Black rounded leather.

Materials: Leather.

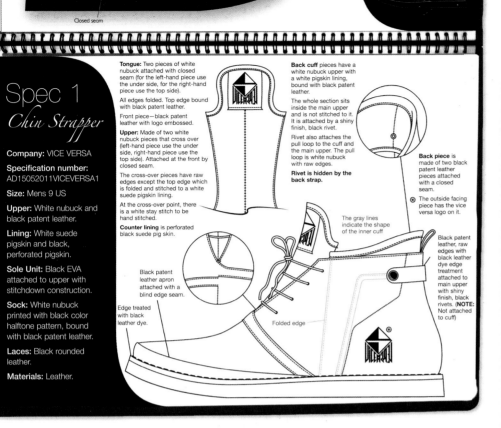

Tongue: Two pieces of white nubuck attached with closed seam (for the left-hand piece use the under side, for the right-hand piece use the top side).

All edges folded. Top edge bound with black patent leather.

Front piece—black patent leather with logo embossed.

Upper: Made of two white nubuck pieces that cross over (left-hand piece use the under side, right-hand piece use the top side). Attached at the front by closed seam.

The cross-over pieces have raw edges except the top edge which is folded and stitched to a white suede pigskin lining.

At the cross-over point, there is a white stay stitch to be hand stitched.

Counter lining is perforated black suede pig skin.

Black patent leather apron attached with a blind edge seam.

Edge treated with black leather dye.

Back cuff pieces have a white nubuck upper with a white pigskin lining, bound with black patent leather.

The whole section sits inside the main upper and is not stitched to it. It is attached by a shiny finish, black rivet.

Rivet also attaches the pull loop to the cuff and the main upper. The pull loop is white nubuck with raw edges.

Rivet is hidden by the back strap.

Back piece is made of two black patent leather pieces attached with a closed seam.

The outside facing piece has the vice versa logo on it.

The gray lines indicate the shape of the inner cuff

Black patent leather, raw edges with black leather dye edge treatment attached to main upper with shiny finish, black rivets. (**NOTE:** Not attached to cuff)

Folded edge

▲ **Text heavy** A clean, clear specification that includes exploded diagrams to explain some of the construction detail. As it is so text heavy, this specification has been designed to communicate with a sample production unit that is accustomed to the use of English.

KEY STAGES

- Insert basic information such as the date, the specification number, and the last name or number.
- Draw the shoe from every angle needed to explain all the details.
- Draw the sole and heel or unit from every angle needed to explain all the details.
- Color the drawings accurately; if you have samples of the materials, scan these in using Photoshop to add the exact color and texture.
- Insert all the drawings into the standard specification sheet supplied by your company.
- Add Pantone color references and number codes for soles, heels, sewing thread, fastenings, and trimmings.

GLOSSARY

Closing specification: Instructions for the production of an upper.

Exploded diagram: Large-scale diagram used to explain a small detail clearly.

Laser engraving: Process that uses lasers to pattern material.

Layout: Design and placement of information on a page.

Sample: Test product or part of a product for a new design or construction.

Specification sheet: A set of instructions for the manufacture of a product.

Text heavy: Containing a lot of written information.

EXERCISE: DESIGN YOUR OWN SPECIFICATION SHEET

From your closet, pick your favorite shoe. Examine it carefully and make notes on how it would be constructed.

- How many pieces are there in the outside and lining of the upper?
- What materials and colors are used for the upper?
- What color is the stitching?
- Are there any unusual stitching, punching, edge finishing, or seam details?
- Are there any fastenings?
- Are there any trimmings?
- How is the bottom of the shoe constructed? Is it simply a sole and heel?
- What materials have been used and what colors are they?
- Does it have a platform or a welt?
- What material has been used and what colors?
- What color is the sock and what is the brand mark used?

Now that you have a list of notes, you must consider how you would relate this information to someone who has never seen your shoe. Do as many drawings as necessary to ensure that all of this information is visualized. Make written notes of any details that cannot be conveyed through drawing, for instance, the materials. Now create a layout and insert all of this information in an organized format that can be easily understood by others. Test this out by showing your finished work to a friend and then show them the actual shoe.

SECTION 4
Millinery

This section of the book delivers an insight into millinery, the art of hat design and construction. You will learn how to position and draw hats on heads, to enable your design ideas to be communicated clearly, and begin to explore how to develop your headpiece designs with the key design considerations firmly at the forefront of your thinking—helping you to evolve and resolve your designs more thoughtfully in response to your brief.

Throughout the section, you will become familiar with correct terminology, equipment, and the tools of the trade. We will introduce you to a range of specialist materials, trims, and techniques used in millinery. You will learn why the bias of the fabric is fundamental in millinery, and you will become conversant with its usage. We look step-by-step at model millinery skills, such as blocking a felt hat and creating a two-piece crown, and learn an array of specialist hand stitches used in the making of model hats.

In the anatomy of a hat section, you will explore the breakdown of the component parts that make up a soft-stitched baker boy cap. You will then learn to draft a series of patterns for stitched hats using a variety of methods.

MILLINERY TOOLS

Objective Learn about the tools used in the millinery industry.

The tools shown on these pages are used universally for model millinery. Specialist tools are increasingly difficult to obtain and may take some tracking down. The processes used in model millinery are emulated by machine in industry. In industry, heated metal pans replace wooden hat blocks, and the hats are blocked using hydraulic presses. Edges are wired, bound, or turned using machines, but the trimming process is still undertaken by hand.

Millinery needles and thread (1, 9): Long, fine needles and thread used for hand stitching.
Thimble (2): Worn on the third finger to aid blocking and hand stitching.
Fabric shears (3): Used for cutting foundations and fabrics.
Small scissors (4): For snipping threads.
Protractor and compass (5, 6): Used in pattern cutting.
Seam ripper (7): For unpicking stitches.
Flat-head pins (8): For blocking and pinning materials/fabric together prior to sewing.
Tailor's chalk (10): Chalk for marking materials prior to cutting.
Tape measure (11): For taking measurements.
Egg irons (12, 13): Heated on gas or electric rings, these irons are used in the hand blocking of felts.
Pliers (14): Used for cutting wire and aiding removal of pins from blocks.

Other tools
Ruler: Used in pattern cutting.
Thumbtacks: Used occasionally for blocking.
Hat blocks: Wooden molds on which hats are shaped.
Hat steamer: Used for steaming felts/foundations/fabrics prior to blocking.
Iron: Used for pressing materials.
Domestic sewing machine: For seaming, hemming, and edge trimming. It is used extensively in millinery for patterned hats.

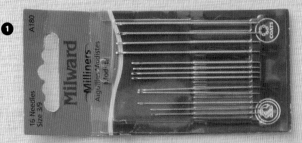

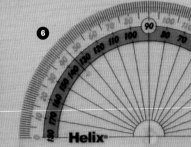

MILLINERY DESIGNERS AND BRANDS

Objective Learn about key millinery designers and brands.

The significance of the art of millinery and the need for hats has always been present, even if the styles shift and change in popularity. These designers span the 20th and 21st century as a testament to how millinery has always been important, even if no longer ubiquitous. Superstar milliners such as Philip Treacy and Stephen Jones have rejuvenated the field, inspiring a new wave of hat designers to create innovative and alluring headpieces that clothing designers need to "finish" the look.

ELSA SCHIAPARELLI (early–mid-20th century)
ITALIAN

Schiaparelli turned to fashion in 1921 after being abandoned by her husband in New York with an infant daughter to raise. She had earlier encouragement from couturier Paul Poiret and returned to Paris to begin an innovative and greatly successful career. Schiaparelli collaborated with several artists and designers, but she was the driving force behind her clothing, hats, and accessories that are instantly recognizable and continue to inspire many contemporary designers from Dolce & Gabbana to Lulu Guinness.

Signature style: Schiaparelli was heavily influenced by Surrealism—the artistic philosophy and the artists themselves. Schiaparelli's work exhibits a type of beauty and elegance re-examined through the lens of a world in chaos, resulting in humor and optimism.

Iconic piece: Without a doubt the F/W 1937/38 Shoe Hat is forever associated with Elsa Schiaparelli. The hat, which was a product of collaboration with Salvador Dali, was wildly popular and spawned several other such looks.

GABRIELLA LIGENZA (contemporary)
ITALIAN

Ligenza trained as an architect and interior designer. While she has a successful millinery store in London, she has never forgotten her love of architecture. In 2010, Ligenza curated a show exploring the intersection of hats and architecture in conjunction with the London Festival of Architecture. Ligenza lives and works in London.

Signature style: Ligenza specializes in using natural materials, specifically light and airy feathers, flowers, or raffia that softly outline the face.

Iconic piece: The hats worn by ladies at the prestigious Royal Ascot horse race meeting in the United Kingdom are often Gabriella Ligenza.

GRAHAM SMITH (contemporary)
BRITISH

After graduating from the Royal College of Art, Smith worked for Lanvin in 1958 for one year, and Michael of Carlos Place from 1960–67 before establishing his own millinery studio. From 1981 through 1991 Graham Smith worked as the design director of Kangol. Smith is also responsible for British Airways flight attendants' hats.

Signature style: Smith created small hats made from traditional materials that were meant to match a lady's dress.

Iconic piece: In 1987, Princess Diana was photographed wearing a white felt Kangol hat that perfectly set off her military-inspired suit.

KAREN HENRIKSEN (contemporary)
BRITISH

Since 2003, Royal College of Art graduate Karen Henriksen has been creating casual, couture, and custom-made hats from her London studio for both her own clients as well as designers such as Ports 1961 and Hussein Chalayan. Henriksen has also authored a millinery book called *Design and Make Fashion Hats*, and worked with interior design firm Pinch to create lampshades.

Signature style: Karen Henriksen has created a style that balances saleable considerations with imaginative explorations in shape and materials. She excels at creating casual hats that have a distinct twist.

Iconic piece: Her 2011 Windswept collection feature the "Dune" visor hats that can easily be rolled up, with a decorative attachment that fastens the roll. This is a perfect example of Henrikson's practicality combined with fashion flair.

LILLY DACHÉ (early–late 20th century)
FRENCH–AMERICAN

Lilly Daché began her career at the age of 15 as an apprentice, which was the custom for working-class girls in the early 20th century. Daché emigrated to the United States sometime in the 1920s and began a successful career creating hats for glamorous women and Hollywood actresses. Since she had so many Hollywood clients, Daché's hats really define the look of 1930s and '40s millinery. In 1946 she wrote an autobiography, *Talking Through My Hats*, and

in 1956, *Lilly Daché's Glamour Book*. Daché had several apprentices that went on to successful careers, most notably fashion designer Halston.

Signature style: Dramatic and graceful, Daché hats always suited the structure of the wearer's face, which is one reason why so many Hollywood actresses wore her hats so loyally.

Iconic piece: Lilly Daché popularized the turban, the brimmed hat molded to the head, and the quintessential 1940s look of the snood.

NOEL STEWART
(contemporary)
BRITISH

Stewart has only been producing his eponymous collection since Fall 2007/8, yet has already attracted press attention and an expanding group of fans. His collections have increasingly become bolder and more experimental, attesting to positive feedback. After receiving his MA from the Royal College of Art in London, he worked with Stephen Jones at Dior. Stewart cites contemporary art and architecture mixed with historical references as the main source of inspiration for his wonderful creations.

Signature style: Thus far in Stewart's burgeoning career, his work consistently uses color and texture in unexpected and experimental ways.

Iconic piece: Stewart's Fall 2011/12 collection MashItUp Strokes featured a black felt fedora with large strokes of brightly colored acrylic paint. This hat indeed exemplifies the inspiration of historical references mixed with contemporary art.

▲ **Fragility encapsulated** Noel Stewart's Coral Bay creation explores balance, movement, and transparency of color.

PATRICIA UNDERWOOD
(mid-20th century–contemporary)
BRITISH–AMERICAN

In 1967, Underwood moved to New York and attended the Fashion Institute of Technology and began working with many American designers who responded to her largely unadorned hats. She has received a COTY, CFDA award, American Accessories Achievement Award, and the Fashion Group International Entrepreneur award. Underwood's hats have appeared in several movies such as *Sabrina* and *Four Weddings and a Funeral*, and are in the collections of major fashion museums.

Signature style: Patricia Underwood has a clean, unadorned style that frames the face in traditional materials.

Iconic piece: The summer widebrimmed hat made of raffia has been rediscovered for its practicality and cool, chic results.

PHILIP TREACY
(late 20th century–contemporary)
IRISH

In 1989, Philip Treacy met and designed a wedding hat for famed style icon Isabella Blow. The meeting spawned a creative and inspirational pairing that pushed Treacy into international fame. Treacy opened his own studio in Blow's basement in 1990 and was asked to work for Chanel in 1991, where he worked for 10 years. In Treacy's career he has won five British Accessory Designer of the Year awards from the British Fashion Council, participated in

◄ A kaleidoscope of butterflies
Philip Treacy's butterfly hat created for Alexander McQueen. Other milliners might have settled for half a dozen butterflies, but Treacy goes the whole nine yards with a swarm of them.

the Florence and Venice Bienniale (with artist Vanessa Beecroft), and was awarded the OBE (Officer of the Order of the British Empire) in 2007. Treacy has worked with several well-known designers, most notably the late Alexander McQueen, to stunning affect.

Signature style: Philip Treacy's hats have astonishing craftsmanship, allowing the materials to seem as if they are defying gravity, effortlessly constructed, and perfectly chosen for the most dramatic outcome.

Iconic piece: It is impossible to narrow the prolific output of Philip Treacy's career, although he excels in the area of fascinators, as seen in his work for Alexander McQueen.

SIMONE MIRMAN
(early–late 20th century)
FRENCH

While living in France with her family, Simone Parmentier worked with Rose Valois and Elsa Schiaparelli. In 1937, she moved to London to elope and Schiaparelli generously gave Simone her English customers' contact information. During World War II, Simone and her new husband, Serge, operated a business out of their tiny apartment. Things began to move quickly, and 1952 found Simone Mirman appointed the Queen's royal milliner. She supplied hats for Queen Elizabeth, Princess Margaret, and the Queen Mother, as well as many other high-profile clients.

Signature style: Simone Mirman was said to have been particularly good at creating hats that suited an individual's face, shifting the silhouette to suit.

Iconic piece: Queen Elizabeth wore Simone Mirman's hat during Prince Charles' investiture. The hat was cream with pearls and looked to be inspired by a 16th-century French or English hood.

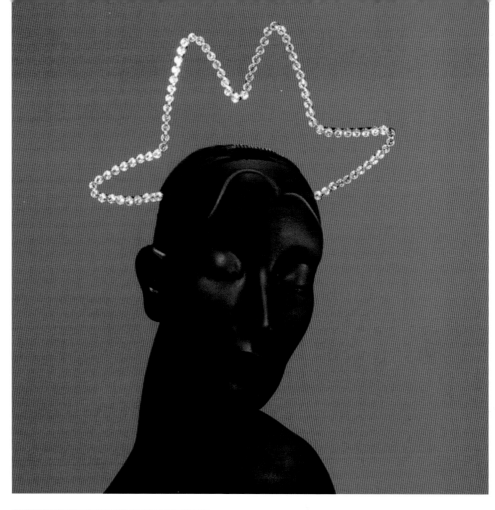

STEPHEN JONES
(late 20th century–contemporary)
BRITISH

The legacy of stunning and imaginative hats began in 1980 when Jones opened his first millinery salon in London. Stephen Jones has worked with many notable designers as well as introducing several different collections each year for a variety of markets under his own name. Stephen Jones is responsible for taking countless up-and-coming and now notable milliners, under his wing, allowing them to apprentice in his studio. His work is in permanent collections in prestigious international fashion museums. Jones most recently co-curated a Victoria and Albert Museum exhibition "Hats: An Anthology by Stephen Jones" that also traveled to New York in 2011. In 2010, Stephen Jones received the OBE (Officer of the Order of the British Empire).

Signature style: Stephen Jones hats often have a quirky sense of humor and reference to British popular culture icons and images. Jones also displays virtuosity with materials and a definitive sense of the dramatic.

Iconic piece: Many Stephen Jones hats may be considered iconic pieces, but the 1987 Vivienne Westwood Royal Crown and the 2009 Union Jack Top Hat are too important to ignore.

▲ **Bugsy Malone**
Named by Stephen Jones, this minimalist item of headwear offers an ironic, two-dimensional take on a gangster hat.

SECTION 4 | MILLINERY

STYLE SELECTOR: MILLINERY

Objective Explore different styles of headware and hats.

Millinery offers a wide variety of confectionery splendor that perfectly frames the face or finishes a look. The hats on these pages often have their foundation in 19th- and 20th-century styles yet are the basis for any contemporary version of millinery. This list of hats contains the fundamentals for future innovative ideas of millinery.

Cloche

A hat that is fit very close to the head with little to no brim, covering the forehead and ears. The cloche, which means "bell" in French, became popular in the 1920s and beautifully matched the bob hairstyle.

Optional decoration at the crown.

Breton

A hat with a soft, round crown and a round upturned brim. Traditionally this was a hat for young girls, wi with a ribbon streaming down th back. In the 1960s they became popular for women when Jacqueline Kennedy was pictured wearing one, and Mia Farrow we one in the movie *Rosemary's Baby*.

Turban

One of the oldest types of head coverings, turbans are worn throughout the Middle East, North Africa, and India, although they are called different names. In fashion, turbans are generally soft fabric sewn together to form a cap to cover the hair with a peaked forehead. The turban is associated with the great couturier Madame Grès, who wore them in the 1930s.

Cartwheel hat

A hat that is derived from the picture hat and was popular throughout the Edwardian era at the turn of the 20th century. The cartwheel had a very large brim and was not decorated, save for a simple ribbon around the crown.

Fascinator

The fascinator refers to an ornament that sits to the front of the head and is attached with a band or comb. Fascinators have their origins in 17th-century fashion, sitting atop ladies' high wigs. They have recently enjoyed a popular resurgence based on the British royal family and the work of famous milliners Philip Treacy and Stephen Jones.

Top hat

Most often associated with 19th-century upper-class n and contemporary formal morning attire. The top hat tall, flat-crowned, broad-brimmed hat. The brim usu curves up at the sides and lower in the front and back

The brim is finished with a tight curl.

Cocktail

Closely linked to a fascinator, a cocktail hat is small and is perched on the side of the head often with a veil. Cocktail hats are formal and can consist of feathers, beads, jewels, or lightweight arranged fabric.

Boater

A boater is a hat made of straw that has a stiff, flat crown, 1 in. (2.5 cm) grosgrain ribbon around the crown, and a stiff, medium brim. The hat gets its name from the habit of 19th- and early 20th-century men of wearing such hats while boating or yachting.

Beret

The beret hat will always be associated with the French and is soft, round, flat crowned, and worn in a variety of ways. The beret is often made from wool or felt and has often been used in military uniforms of a variety of countries.

Pillbox

The American fashion designer Halston is credited with creating a hat consisting of a hat crown with no brim and worn at the back top of the head. Jacqueline Kennedy popularized the hat in America in the 1960s.

Trilby

The Trilby is often confused with a fedora but features a narrower brim that usually has an upturn at the back and a crown that is pinched in the front. The name comes from a stage adaptation of the book *Trilby* by Georges du Maurier.

Newsboy/Flat cap

The hat has a small brim and a soft hat that fits over the forehead and ears. The newsboy is usually made of eight panels so has more of a pouchy look. The flat cap is very similar but is smoother and cannot be individually shaped. It is associated with English country gentlemen.

Optional snap on the top brim.

Fedora

A fedora is a soft felt hat with a crease lengthwise down the crown, or with a C- shaped crown, and a medium to wide brim that can sometimes be tilted down in the front. The fedora was extremely popular as a man's hat in the 1930s through the 1950s.

Baker Boy

The cap is comprised of eight sections, a button on top, and a short brim. The hat references the slouchy look of a beret and the casual look of a newsboy hat. The newsboy and baker boy are often confused.

Eight-piece construction finished with a button on top.

Tuque/Toque

A toque has origins in the fez and cloche. It is a tall brimless hat and is usually made from wool. The toque became popular in the late 1950s and 1960s and matched the hairstyles, simplified boxy collarless jackets, and straight skirts that were popular at the time.

Slouch hat

The women's hat of today has its origins in the Australian and New Zealand military hat that still also carries that name. The men's version is turned up on one side with a chin strap. The women's version can be worn multiple ways.

Picture hat

A hat popular from the later Victorian to the early Edwardian era. The hats were worn on top of the head and heavily decorated with fabric, feathers, imitation flowers, or fruit.

Side Sweep brim

The term refers to any hat that has one side of the brim turned up. The styles are most often seen in picture or wide-brimmed hats and have become common on trilbies for a jaunty look.

Exaggerated asymmetry for visual balance.

Panama

A man's straw hat that originally came from Ecuador and was sold in the Isthmus of Panama, which is where it got the name. The hat looks very similar to the fedora.

Conical hat

The conical hat originated in East and Southeast Asia, and is designed to protect the wearer from the sun or the rain. The hat is kept on with a chin strap and either sits as a conical shape on the top of the crown or has a slight crown on a conical brim.

SECTION 4 | MILLINERY

ANATOMY OF A PATTERNED HAT

Objective Identify the components of a patterned hat and understand the importance of interlinings.

Most fabrics can be used for making pattern hats as long as they are woven fabrics. Hat styles vary greatly, and your creative investigations, exploration of pattern cutting, and knowledge of the individual components required, will enable you to create innovative style variations.

1 Completed hat Six-section baker boy crown with peak.

2 Lining pieces (six of) Identical pieces cut out of polyester.

3 Crown piece interlining (six of) Fusible woven cotton interlining is attached to the underside of the material for the six crown sections prior to cutting to ensure the grain lines of the fabric and interlining match.

4 Crown pieces (six of) Pieces of tweed cut with the interlining attached to form the six-section crown.

5 Peak interlining (two of) The same interlining is also added to the underside and topside of the peak prior to cutting to give it shape.

6 Peak stiffener Sandwiched between the underside and topside of the peak to offer structure and support.

7 Peak (two of) Tweed is cut to form the topside and underside of the hat's peak.

8 Grosgrain ribbon Acts as the head fitting for the baker boy hat.

INTERLININGS

Most patterned hats need some sort of structure to support the fabric and help the hat to keep its shape. Interlinings give structure to the hat and enable a diverse variety of fabrics to be used. All interlinings (with the exception of peak stiffeners) need to be woven. Interlinings vary in terms of fiber content and density of weave, which will in turn affect the weight. The easiest to use are fusible interlinings, which have an adhesive coating that is heat-activated by an iron or heat press.

Some of the most commonly used interlinings are listed here:

Woven fusibles: Muslin (very lightweight); batiste (fine, soft, and lightweight); sheer, fine polyester (lightweight and opaque), cotton, and polycotton (available in a variety of weights); domette (light/medium-weight with a fleecy surface); canvas (variety of medium- and lightweights available).

Woven non-fusibles: Crin (light/medium-weight and opaque); French canvas (medium-weight); tailoring canvas (available in a variety of medium and heavy weights).

Nonwoven interlinings: Extra-heavy sew-in interfacing and polypropylene sheets are both used for creating peaks.

EXERCISE: **EXPLORE A HAT**

Visit a thrift store and purchase a fabric patterned hat.

1. From observations, draw what you expect each pattern piece to be. This does not have to be to scale.
2. With a seam ripper, carefully rip the seams of the head fitting and lining so the seams are exposed. Label and photograph the pattern pieces as you go.
3. Remove the peak or brim (if it has one), and work your way through the rest of the hat opening seams and revealing the interlining (if present).
4. Lay out all the component parts and photograph.
5. Copy all the pattern pieces onto card for future use. Remember to label each pattern piece: grain lines, interlining required, seam allowance, style name, and center front/center back are important to note.

COMPONENTS

To demonstrate all the component parts of a patterned hat, here we look at a peaked baker boy cap with a six-section crown. The interlining is attached to the crown and peak fabric prior to pattern-cutting so would not be individual pieces at this stage but the underside of the crown pieces and peak. Here, we have shown three of the crown sections from the underside, to show the attached interlining, and three from the right side. We have shown the peak in the same way.

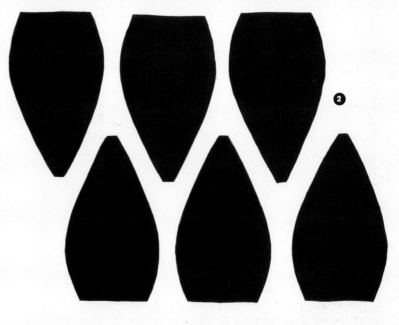

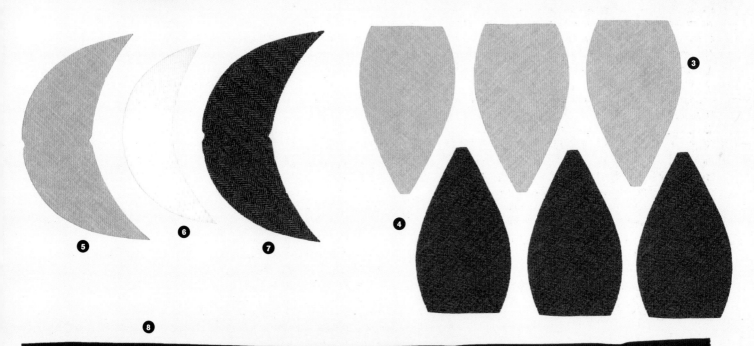

SECTION 4 | MILLINERY

DESIGN CONSIDERATIONS: HATS

Objective Understand key design considerations when designing hats and headpieces.

Designing hats is a diverse and varied discipline. It can be a very creative, complex task that has more in common with sculpture than fashion. It can be considered a careful assemblage of component parts, a single category within a larger range of accessories, or it can be an adjunct to the main collection of a fashion brand/label. As an accessory designer, whether you focus on hat design or not, it is useful to have an insight into this area of fashion design.

THE PARAMETERS OF THE BRIEF

The start of any design project is the brief (see page 14). This will outline the constraints and opportunities of the project. The planning stage of the project is key, and careful consideration at this stage is essential.

Research is your creative trigger in the generation of ideas and is at the very heart of the design process. This, however, needs to be balanced with evaluation of the needs of your target consumers, their wants and desires, brand signature if designing for a brand/label, mood of the season, market level you are designing for, and price points you need to hit, along with the technical considerations relating to manufacture and production methods linked to sales predictions and price. Having established the key considerations (see pages 36–47), the most important factors in the design of a hat/headpiece are discussed below.

SHAPE

The hat design often starts with the mold, wooden block or aluminum pan—the blueprint for the shape. Blocks can be bought in a range of shapes and sizes for both crowns and brims. As a designer, you will build up a collection of these. If your design is very specific, for instance if the hat has a uniquely shaped crown, you

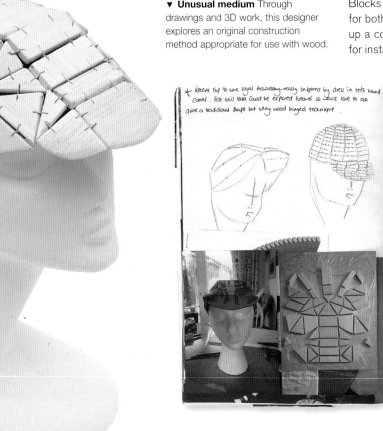

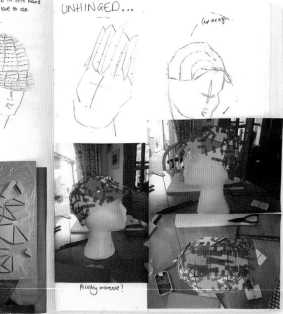

▼ **Unusual medium** Through drawings and 3D work, this designer explores an original construction method appropriate for use with wood.

GLOSSARY

Block: A wooden/aluminum form used as a mold to shape a hat on.

Lead times: The precise time materials will take to be delivered from ordering.

Minimum quantity: Smallest amount a supplier will sell of a particular material/fabric or fitting.

Swatches: Small sample pieces of material.

DESIGN COMMUNICATION

Expressing your designs in an engaging way that can be understood clearly by others is a crucial skill for a designer. Visual accuracy is important for clear design communication. Without this ability, your designs may not be communicating what you intend and could be open to misinterpretation. The following pages will help you gain this clarity.

◄ Scale and proportion
Here the designer plays with proportion and scale by oversizing the trimming. Balance and wearability have been resolved through careful 3D development.

may need to make your own block, alter an existing one, or get it made by a specialist block maker. If you are working with a factory, a visit to view their library of hat shapes (aluminum pans) is essential prior to the design stage, as the cost of having a set of aluminum pans cast could be prohibitive. At the start, it is essential to know what the options available to you are.

STYLE
The choice of styles is wide and ever-expanding, at the couture end (see pages 168–169). You need to consider whether your design is to be made up of a:
Crown and brim: Such as a picture hat, Breton, or cloche. More masculine examples of these are Stetson, fedora, trilby, and cap.
Brimless crown: As in a pillbox, turban, cocktail, or toque.
Fascinator: A whimsical decoration that perches effortlessly on the head.

Soft pattern hat: Such as a baker boy, sailor, sun hat, or baseball cap.

PROPORTION AND SCALE
These considerations are key and need to be explored through your early design stage and refined at development stage. Proportion and scale of the crown in relation to brim, and trim in relation to the scale of the hat, are very important and can affect the design's overall line and balance and, therefore, the aesthetic of the design. A tall bulbous-shaped crown with a small upturned brim could look very odd and out of proportion, but reducing the height and width of the crown or increasing the scale of the brim may help adjust the proportion. However, quirky proportions can work very successfully, but you need an attuned eye to see the possibilities. Sketching out, revising, developing, and refining your crown, brim, and trim proportion will help you identify the more successful designs.

► Finding balance
Balance, weight, and fit have been carefully considered here as the hat sits low on the forehead. The wire head band will disappear into the wearer's hair so the hat will appear to float upon the head.

BALANCE AND LINE

To achieve a balanced design is essential in millinery. Hats need to sit on the head comfortably, easily, and securely. Designs that are too one-sided or top heavy can be affected by gravity and will slip off, at worst, or simply look incongruous. Asymmetry in hat design is often very flattering, and can produce an interesting line, but it can be incredibly difficult to get just the right degree of balance of line with the design; a tool to consider in achieving balance is the design of the trim. Size, volume, and position of the trim can help give the hat/headpiece the balance it needs. Never underestimate the importance of trim in cases like this. Make sure you design trims alongside the hat: they should never be an afterthought but be fully integrated. Draw out temporary balance lines: a vertical and horizontal that cross at 90 degrees just above the eyebrows will help when considering balance in your design.

MATERIALS AND FABRICS

For which season are you designing and what are you designing with? Materials/fabrics need to be researched at the start of the project and decisions made early. Materials are very important and link inextricably to methods of production, so decisions you make here will affect the process used to construct the hat. Research to establish lead times, minimum quantity, and price need to be conducted and sample swatches ordered before decisions can be made. Seasonal favorites are felt, fur, faux fur, leather, wool, and heavier-weight fabrics for winter, straw and lighter fabric for summer. Hats made from self-supporting materials, such as felt and straw, are often quicker and therefore cheaper to produce because there are fewer construction processes.

COLOR PALETTE

What are the trend colors for the season? In spring, light neutrals and pastels are favored; strong brights and nautical colors are staples for summer; warm earthy colors are often present in fall collections; and dark, somber colors prevail during the winter season, often with the addition of a winter white. An accessories designer will always be working toward a particular season or a specific line, e.g. Cruise Line, and the color palette will be influenced by this, but color can have a dramatic effect on hats, and although there are seasonal favorites, color needs to be explored.

TRIMMINGS

Fabrication? Color contrast or self? Bows, feathers, stripped quills, lace flowers, leaves, pompoms. The list is endless. Experiment with the scale of trim to discover the best solution. Try two or three options before making the final choice.

TEXTURE AND SURFACE

Flat, woven, draped, pleated, quilted, embroidered, or beaded? Textures can have an impact and are worth exploring. Weight can be an issue, as well as buckling crowns and denting brims, so thought is needed when designing, and testing/sampling is essential.

CONSTRUCTION

How will these hats be realized/made and in what quantity? Price points will have an impact on these

▼ **Dramatic looks** In this sketchbook the designer explores the line to achieve the right degree of drama for the runway.

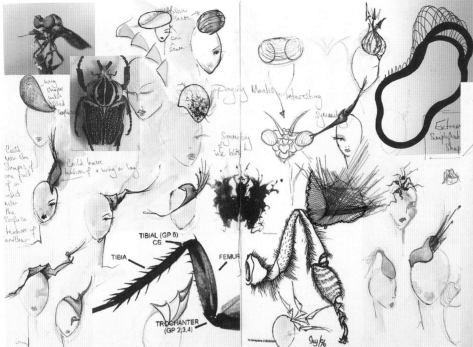

decisions. The more handwork the hat requires in production, obviously the more expensive it will be. Designs of a limited run will also command a relatively high price. The cheapest hats to produce are the soft pattern hats, which are constructed in the cut and sew method.

Blocks: Mass-produced or limited run? Will a block need to be made/ordered?

Seams: Will they work with the material selected?

Stitching: Will you use matching thread or contrasting as a feature? Is the stitching just for practical purposes or for decoration? Are you using standard thread or a heavier, decorative one?

Edge finishes: Will they work with the material? If you are using binding or piping, what size will this be, and what will it be made of? Will it be a matching or contrasting color or texture?

FUNCTION

Always consider the purpose of the hat—where and when would your consumer be wearing it? Should it be casual or more formal? Is it for regular wear, or is it strictly occasional wear?

▲ **Exploring lines** Line, form, and balance are explored in this sketchbook. Exciting sculptural design ideas are derived from a study of insects.

WEIGHT AND WEARABILITY

This links directly to shape, form, material usage, and construction method so it needs to be considered at the start of the design process. Extensive use of wire and interlinings can add weight that may make the hat impractical or uncomfortable to wear. Balance can also be affected by weight. Explore methods of construction and consider the implications of the choices you have made before you embark on production.

The hat needs to fit on the head and be easy and secure to wear. Methods of attaching the headpiece or hat to the head are extremely important. Prongs, feet, combs, wire, Alice bands, and elastic are all ways of securing hats to the head. How and where to attach these fittings is very much dependent on the design. You will need to carefully consider gravity, weight, and counterbalance.

▲ **3D considerations** This series of 3D experimentations examines balance, line, and silhouette. This is an important part of the process. Millinery is a sculptural art and much of the design development is undertaken in a 3D way.

SECTION 4 | MILLINERY

DESIGNING HATS: HEAD PROPORTIONS

Objective Learn how to draw hats on heads.

Communicating the design of hats in 2D is quite a complex procedure and certainly has its challenges. Many experienced milliners work in a more 3D-oriented way, but sketching out initial ideas is always essential, whether you are communicating with your clients or a member of your team. Hats/headpieces need to be drawn on the head to have real meaning. Without the head and facial details, it is hard to understand the drama created by a downward-sweeping brim or the coquettish nature of a jauntily perched pillbox.

▼ Hidden features This model tilts her head slightly downward to emphasize the line and upward sweep of this sinamay hat. Hats often conceal the face, so proportion lines are really useful when drawing and designing.

Getting the hat to appear to sit on the head is often difficult for the beginner, as well as establishing where the hat should sit and what views you need, to communicate the 3D nature of the design. So, here we will look at the proportions of the head and correct position of facial features. We will also consider the hat views you should consider when designing.

DRAWING THE HEAD

Most of us start drawing a head by sketching out an oval shape. It is very important to think about the head and the dome of the head, the width and length of the head, and not focus solely on the facial area. Hats need to sit and fit on the head. Once you have established a good head shape, you should then add the facial features or suggestion of the features.

To ensure you have the features positioned correctly, the general proportional rule is: The eyes should be halfway down the head. The nose should be halfway between the eyes and the bottom of the chin. The mouth is located one-third of the distance from the nose to the chin, and the ear tips are on the same level as the eyes.

Once you have drawn the head and face, you may find it useful at first to draw a light balance line, indicating the horizontal and the vertical line. This is useful when positioning hats that are worn at an angle, or communicating an asymmetric brim line or crown.

DRAWING THE HAT

Before you draw the design of the hat, think about where the hat would sit on the head. Visualize wearing it, and then consider how deep the crown would be. Will the tip of the crown touch the top of the head or not? At what point would it sit on the head? Is the brim symmetrical or not? Does it turn up or down? Is it the same width all the way round?

Draw with a sharp pencil to start with so you can erase mistakes, and always leave the dome of the head drawn in pencil so you can erase it once you are happy with the position of the crown on the head.

Remember when drawing that the hat fits the head snugly because of the use of the bias or head fitting.

DRAWING TYPES

Once you have mastered your views, explore different types of visual communication.

- Thumbnails for initial design ideas.
- Working drawings for development of ideas.
- Design development drawings.
- Illustration drawings for presentation.

- Illustrative styles.
- Pen and ink for flowing line illustration.
- Pantone/markers for color and vibrancy of line.
- Scanning and image manipulation using CAD programs, such as Illustrator and Photoshop.
- Combine collage and drawing.

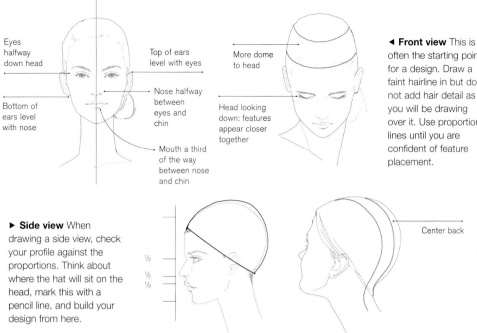

Eyes halfway down head

Bottom of ears level with nose

Top of ears level with eyes

Nose halfway between eyes and chin

Mouth a third of the way between nose and chin

More dome to head

Head looking down: features appear closer together

◀ **Front view** This is often the starting point for a design. Draw a faint hairline in but do not add hair detail as you will be drawing over it. Use proportion lines until you are confident of feature placement.

▶ **Side view** When drawing a side view, check your profile against the proportions. Think about where the hat will sit on the head, mark this with a pencil line, and build your design from here.

½
½
⅓

Center back

A hat should not sit away from the head but where the crown or head fitting touches the head it should be finished with a rounded edge, not a sharp line, to suggest this. The hat is a 3D object, and you will need to consider perspective and foreshortening when drawing hats and headpieces.

▲ **Three-quarter view** Remember a hat is a 3D form, and you need to consider all angles. Hats rarely have the same look or dimensions at the front and back. Establishing the center back point is essential for drawing an accurate back view.

KEY STAGES
• Eyes halfway down the head.
• Nose halfway between the eyes and the bottom of the chin.
• Mouth one-third of the distance from nose to chin.
• Ears (tips) are on the same level as the eyes.
• Draw the neck and shoulder line.

◀ **Hat position** These three profiles show different options for how a hat can sit on the wearer's head, depending on style.

FOUNDATION MATERIALS

Objective Learn about the essential foundation materials used in hat making.

Black French canvas: A medium-/lightweight, unsized foundation fabric.

Lightweight sinamay: A self-supporting straw used in layers.

Traditional straw esparterie: Used for shape-making and for the foundations of fabric hats.

In order for a hat to retain its shape, it is necessary to use a material that will hold its form. All fabric hats require a foundation of some sort in order to maintain their shape. Materials that are used for foundation shape-making must be pliable when steamed or damped, but when blocked and dry, they must be able to hold the desired shape. They act as a support for whatever fabric covers them and must be cut and shaped on the bias (see page 180). Using the correct foundation for the design is essential. Here we look at some of the foundation materials most commonly used in millinery.

Fur-felt cones: These are available in a huge spectrum of colors and finishes.

ESPARTERIE

Esparterie is the most traditional material for shape-making. It is a double-layered material, being made of a coarse straw with an open weave and a top layer of fine muslin. When dry, esparterie is hard and brittle and if folded it will crack, but when damp it is pliable and can be eased and blocked into almost any shape. However, being a woven material, it does have limitations; the bias will only allow so much fullnes to be pulled out before the fibers start to overlap, creating gathers and folds so sections will occasionally need to be added. When dry, it holds the shape and design of the block. Esparterie is used as a foundation for many fabrics and can support heavier fabrics such as velvet and satin. The

muslin-covered layer gives a smooth surface under the fabric, so there is no need for an interlining. It is also used for making handmade blocks, which is an extremely advanced millinery skill.

BLOCKING NET

This is a heavily sized cotton net with a large mesh—it is a lightweight foundation and because of this it is sometimes doubled for extra strength. Unlike other foundation materials, this does not need to be cut and shaped on the bias. It is incredibly sticky to work with, but once damp it blocks very easily and rarely needs to be seamed or sectioned. It is often used to develop and refine designs in 3D, prior to finalizing the design and making. Blocking net can support most light- and medium-weight fabrics and is often used for lace hats as white net can be spray-dyed to a certain extent. There used to be many weights and textures of nets available but these are increasingly difficult to find.

ELASTIC CANVAS

Elastic canvas is a sized, open-weave cotton fabric, used as a foundation for blocked, fabric hats. As it's a woven fabric, it does have limitations and will need to be seamed otherwise it will start to gather over on anything more than a very shallow crown. It can be blocked by using steam or a damp cloth. It makes a firm foundation and retains its shape well. Elastic canvas is good for supporting medium- to heavy-weight fabrics but will need an interlining as its texture will show through most fabrics.

Capelines: A variety of straw capelines in parisisal and rough wheat straws.

Blocking net: A foundation material used with lightweight fabrics.

Tarlatan: Lightweight interlining fabric for smoothing out the surface and seams of the foundation.

Millinery wire: Available in various thicknesses, covered in black or white thread.

Strip straw: Usually coiled onto blocks and sewed.

FRENCH CANVAS

A linen-cotton canvas of medium weight, French canvas is not sized but it can be stiffened with the application of felt stiffener prior to its removal from the block. Often used for supporting drapes and making head-fittings for turbans, French canvas can also be used as an interlining for patterned hats.

MILLINERY BUCKRAM

A loosely woven, sized, cotton fabric, available in both single- and double-ply. Traditionally, it was used to make hats for the theater, as it is relatively cheap and strong. It may be blocked or sewn and is also sometimes used to make handmade blocks, for limited use. Note that it is very different from bookbinding buckram, which is made out of jute.

TARLATAN AND LENO

These are both loosely woven, sized, lightweight, cotton-muslin fabrics; leno is slightly heavier than tarlatan. They are more commonly used for interlinings and binding wire edges. Historically leno was used doubled to create blocked foundations for fabrics such as lightweight jersey.

SINAMAY

Sinamay is made from banana plant fiber. It is available in a rainbow of colors and a variety of weaves and finishes. It is available woven with Lurex, in two-tone colors, woven in a basket weave or waffle pattern, matted together in a tangle, printed, and embroidered. It is wonderfully versatile for trimming hats—it comes by the yard, 3-feet (90-cm) wide, but it is also available woven into bias ribbon in a variety of widths. Types of trims that can be made from sinamay include flowers, bows, looped rosettes, draped swirls, draped head ribbons, and edge finishes for brims. The only issue with sinamay is that the edges will fray when cut, so they need finishing either by turning or rolling. See pages 200–203 for more on trims.

ROUGH STRAWS

This is the generic name given to any straw other than sisals and parisisals. "Rough" usually denotes a larger fiber, hence a more noticeable weave. These straw capelines/cones are woven in a variety of fancy patterns and can be woven from a number of natural fibers derived from plant matter as well as synthetic fibers, including: xian, coconut, wheat, twisted sisal, wheat, banana, paper, and raffia. These straw bodies can be brittle and will not last usually more than a few summer seasons.

STRAW BRAID

This is the generic term given to strip straw, available in many fiber types both natural and synthetic, and purchasable in a variety of widths and weaves. Braid can be used to make hat bodies—the braid is spiraled outward and stitched by hand or by machine.

Brim reed: A plastic wire that is used mainly in fabric patterned hats.

CAPELINES AND CONES

These can be made of felt or straw and are the basic shape around which a blocked hat is formed. A capeline is the rough shape of a hat and is used to make a hat with a crown and a flat brim, ready to be blocked into your chosen shape (see pages 194–199). A cone is a conically shaped hood that is used for blocking small hat shapes or crowns.

Panama straw: Traditional straw used for both men's and women's hats.

Millinery buckram: Often used in place of esparterie as it is cheaper and more readily available.

Paper esparterie: Synthetic esparterie lacks the strength of straw esparterie.

Black twisted xian: A fun, summer straw.

Wheat straw: A fragile straw used often for sun hats.

Knitted sisal: An example of a decorative finish to a traditional fiber.

USE OF WOVEN FABRICS IN MILLINERY

Objective Understanding how to use woven fabrics correctly.

Whether making patterned hats, creating a blocked foundation, blocking fabric to cover the foundation, or creating a bow for a trimming or fascinator, the rule of thumb is all woven fabrics must be cut on the bias/cross grain. The bias of the fabric has stretch, and we use this to mold the flat piece of fabric to fit the head.

FINDING THE BIAS

1. Woven fabric is made up of vertical and horizontal thread. The horizontal thread is passed over and under alternative vertical threads, building up the fabric layer by layer. The vertical threads are called the warp, and the horizontal threads the weft.

2. Fold your fabric from the selvage edge, lining up the warp of the folded edge with the weft of the fabric underneath it at a 45-degree angle, thus creating a triangle. The diagonal formed is the bias. Put a row of basting stitches along this fold to secure the bias.

3. Lengths or strips of material cut on the bias are needed for many purposes: wide ones for side bands of crowns, trimmings, draping, etc.; and narrow strips used for bindings, rouleaux, and for smaller trimmings. For cutting bias strips, use the method described above, then measure off the width of the strip required, mark with tailor's chalk or baste line, and repeat. When all the strips have been marked, cut along the chalk or baste lines.

4. When fabric is pulled on the bias, a natural distortion occurs. This movement is created by the spaces in between the threads of the warp and weft. The looser the weave of the fabric, the greater the movement, which can occur in both directions.

◀ **Working on the bias** The crown foundation and covering fabrics for this cocktail hat have all been worked on the bias. All the fullness of the fabric is pulled out through the bias so the fabric can mold, crease-free, to the hat block.

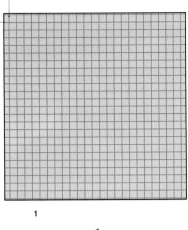

Warp

Weft

1

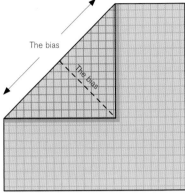

The bias

The bias

2

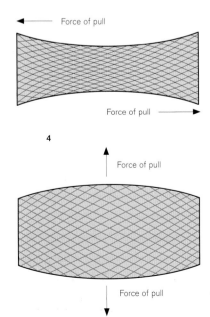

Force of pull

Force of pull

4

Force of pull

Force of pull

▶ **Cutting on the bias** Here the milliner cuts a bias strip in preparation for trimming the draped crown shown in the top left corner.

JOINING BIAS STRIPS

1. Joining bias strips is best done on the straight of the grain and the selvage grain, especially if the fabric is patterned, striped, or checked. Place the two ends to be sewn together, right-side facing inward. The edges need to meet exactly and the bias-cut edges of the strip should be at right angles to each other, with the sharp points projecting beyond the edge.

2. Pin and stitch by machine or with backstitch (see page 183) along the straight of grain and between the two right-angle corners.

3. With a pair of scissors, trim the points of the seam allowance that protrude from the horizontal of the bias strip.

4. Press the seam open with an iron.

5. Now you have your finished joined bias strip.

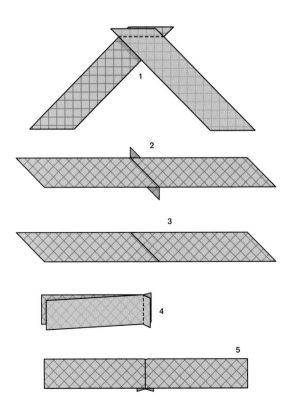

EXERCISE: **MAKING A HEADBAND**

A headband is used in a similar way to a head wire—to support the hat, especially the brim, during making.

1. Cut a bias strip out of elastic canvas or buckram, 1½ in. (4 cm) in width by approximately 25 in. (63 cm) in length. Using wire stitch, wire the band all the way around, ensuring you overlap the wire by 1½ in. (4 cm) where it joins.
2. Cut a bias strip of tarlatan 1½ in. (4 cm) wide, then pull it taut, working your way along its length. Fold the tarlatan in half lengthwise, and then cover the wire using a millinery backstitch. You will probably need more than one strip of tarlatan in order to bind the headband. When finished, press the band with an iron.

GLOSSARY

Bias: 45-degree diagonal line going across the grain of the fabric.

Crown: The portion of a hat that covers the top of the head.

Drape: A loose fold.

Fullness: Gathers, created by a square of fabric over the crown, prior to blocking.

Press: To iron.

Rouleau: A bias strip of fabric sewn together and turned out.

Sized: Impregnated with starch to add stiffness to a fabric.

Warp: Vertical threads in a woven fabric.

Weft: Horizontal threads in a woven fabric.

SECTION 4 | MILLINERY

MILLINERY STITCHES

Objective Learn stitches used in model millinery.

Model millinery relies heavily on hand-stitching techniques. There are not too many stitches to learn, and you may already be familiar with some, since they are similar to those used in needlework. Some of the stitches are used for a particular process only, but practicing and learning these stitches will give work a more professional edge. Hats and headpieces by the best milliners have a blown-together look, in which the stitches are imperceptible. This is the finish you should aim for.

WIRE STITCH

This stitch is used to attach wire to hat brims primarily, but it's also used when making a headband and occasionally trimmings. It is a very important stitch, since the wire needs to be stitched securely to give support and structure. Always use double thread when wiring and knot the ends together. Place the wire on the edge of the brim and over-sew the wire four times or so. Then, stitching toward yourself, make a stitch exiting just below the wire. Do not pull the thread through—ensure you leave a

loop. Then put your needle through the back of the loop toward you and pull tightly—this forms a little knot on the top edge of the wire. Repeat the process, leaving a gap of approximately ⅝ in. (1.5 cm) between each stitch. Do not be tempted to pass the needle through the front of the loop, since this will not form a knot and the wire will be loose.

JOINING WIRE TOGETHER

Finishing off a wire is as important as the stitching, and if not joined correctly, can eradicate all the hard work you have

done wiring the brim. When measuring the amount of wire required, always add an extra 2½ in. (6 cm) to the required length—this is used as an overlap. Wiring a brim always starts from the center back. Start 1¼ in. (3 cm) over the center back mark, and once you have stitched all the way around, continue by placing the wire inside the existing wire you have already stitched on. At each wire-end point, ensure you have made extra wrapping stitches to secure the ends.

WIRE IN A FOLD

This stitch is used when the brim is to be finished with a turned edge (hemmed).

Measure the wire required including the 2½ in. (6 cm) overlap, preshape the wire, and bind the ends together, placing the join at the center back. Place the wire to the brim, approximately ⅜–⅝ in. (1–1.5 cm) in from the point at which you will turn your edge, and secure at four points—front, back, right side, and

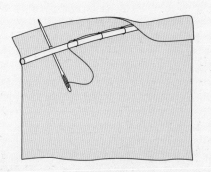

Wire stitch   Wire in a fold   Backstitch

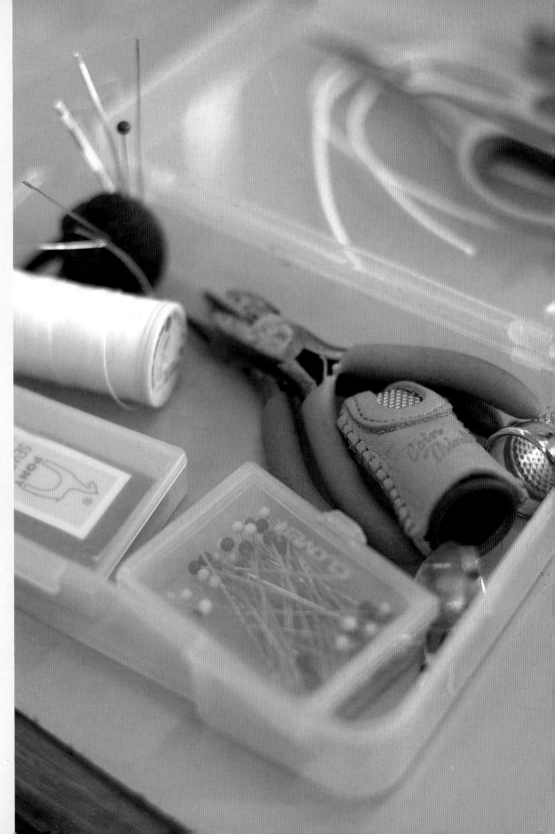

left side—with a diagonal stitch. Then starting at the center back, follow the above instructions for the wire stitch, but instead of passing your needle straight through the brim on the edge, catch the brim and, before pulling the stitch through, pass the needle through the back of the loop to the front and then pull the knot tight. Repeat the stitch approximately ⅝ in. (1.5 cm) along.

BACKSTITCH

Backstitch is the strongest stitch; it resembles a machine stitch on the upper side. To make this stitch, knot your thread then take a stitch of about ⅜ in. (1 cm) in length, bring your needle back out just before the end of the stitch you made and repeat the process. This stitch is used for stitching crowns to brims.

BASTING STITCH

This is usually a temporary stitch used for holding layers of fabric together prior

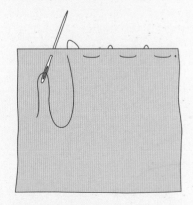

Basting stitch

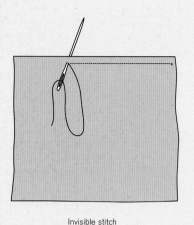

Invisible stitch

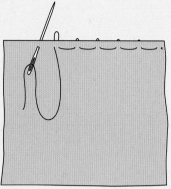

Stab stitch

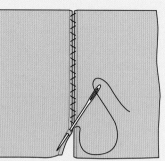

Darning

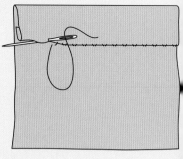

Slipstitch

STITCHING TIPS

Always use a thimble when stitching. This protects the middle finger, which pushes the needle through the layers.

Prior to stitching with wire, it is essential that the wire be straightened—since wire is bought coiled, it needs to be straightened to take out the excess spring. This is done by carefully and slowly running the wire between your thumb and forefinger while applying pressure to the wire against the curve of the wire.

to machining, or for marking the material. To start the stitch, make a knot and pass your needle through to the top side and make a stitch of about ⅝ in. (1.5 cm). Make a smaller stitch on the underside of about ¼ in. (0.5 cm), pass the needle through the top layer, and continue in this manner. Some people prefer to make the stitches the same length each side of the fabric. This stitch is also used for gathering fabrics—to do so, stitch the area to be gathered as above and then simply pull the thread to get the desired effect.

INVISIBLE STITCH

This is used mainly for hemming edges and binding edges with grosgrain ribbon. The stitches need to be very discreet and unnoticeable. Knot the threads, then make a small stitch to bury the knot inside the hem, pass the needle through the edge of the hem, and then pass the needle through to the other side vertically, just catching the brim. Pass the needle back through diagonally, making a tiny stitch catching a fiber/thread or two. Ensuring the stitch is secure but invisible, repeat this process. If stitching grosgrain ribbon, you will need to do the

vertical stitch on both sides but angling the needle.

STAB STITCH

Stab stitch is used for various processes: holding trims in position, block making, stitching folds/drapes, and many other uses. The stitch is made by passing the needle through the hat to the other side, usually making a small horizontal stitch on the inside and a larger horizontal stitch hidden on the outside. The stitch length can vary depending on the job in hand.

DARNING

Darning is used for making an invisible edge-to-edge join in felt. Place the edges of the felt together and stitch diagonally through the thickness of the right-hand edge, catching the fibers in the middle of the felt. Moving diagonally by ⅛ in. (3 mm), stitch the left-hand side of the felt and repeat until you have reached the end of the brim. End the stitch with a few secure backstitches.

SLIPSTITCH

This stitch is used to invisibly join two folded (turned) edges. It is used for

Whipstitch

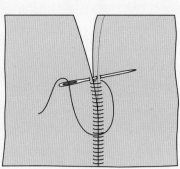

Grafting

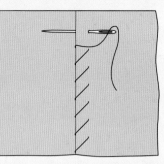

Diagonal basting

hemming, finishing edges, attaching lining, and facing. Knot your thread and secure on the inside of one of the folded edges, pass your needle through to the outer edge of the fold, then make a stitch directly opposite in the other folded edge. Make a stitch of ¼ in. (0.5 cm) hidden in the folded edge and repeat, passing your needle through one folded edge directly to the opposite folded edge, ensuring the catching stitch does not show by positioning it in the fold of the edge.

WHIPSTITCH

This is used for joining felt together where the join will not be seen, for example, on the inside or the underside. Hold the edges right-side together, and make even, horizontal stitches along the length of the seam, whipping the edges together. The needle should pass through the edges of the felt the thread, drawing the edges together tightly. Press the seam flat after finishing.

GRAFTING

Grafting is performed in the same way as the whipstitch, but the edges are sewn butted up to each other edge to edge. The stitches pass through the underside to the central core of the felt and so only show on the wrong side of the felt.

DIAGONAL BASTING

This stitch is used for securing fabric to foundations and for stitching tips and sidebands together while on the block. Stitch horizontally ⅜ in. (0.5 cm), leaving the knot in between the edges to be joined, then make a diagonal stitch about ½ in. (1 cm), passing the needle through the topside, catching the underneath side, and back out. Repeat the process. Shorter horizontal stitches appear on the inside while larger slanted stitches show on the outer side.

▲ **Stitching wire** Here we see wire being stitched into the edge of a buckram foundation.

GLOSSARY

Grosgrain ribbon: A corded ribbon used for trimming hats.

Straws: Long, strong millinery sewing needles. They can be passed through numerous layers of fabric easily.

SECTION 4 | MILLINERY

DRAFTING A SECTIONAL CROWN PATTERN

Objective Learn one method of drafting a sectional crown.

Sectional crowns are used widely in millinery, particularly where woven fabrics are chosen, as opposed to capelines and cones of either felt or straw. This method can be used to draft many patterns. Each head size will need a new pattern, as will crowns of differing heights and numbers of sections. With slight alterations to reference points, sectional berets, tams, or baker boy caps can also be drafted using this method (see Variations).

◄ **Baker boy** This baker boy cap has been made with top-stitch detail. See Variations on the opposite page for instructions on how to achieve this crown pattern.

First, you need to decide on the number of sections required, and work out the required head measurement and how deep you want the crown to be.

1. Divide the head measurement by the number of sections and draw line A–B of the resulting length, e.g. 22 in. (55.8 cm) / 6 = 3.6 in. (9.3 cm). Find the center point of A–B and mark that point C.

2. Taking a ruler, with a pencil, draw a perpendicular line from point C to the required length (depth of the crown) and mark point D. Draw a horizontal line approximately 1½ in. (4 cm) centered on point D. Then place a protractor 90 degrees on line C–D. Measure off 60 degrees for a six-section crown. Mark 30 degrees each side of line C–D. These points will be X and Y.

DRAFTING THE PATTERN

The center point is where all the sections join to form a circle. A circle is made up of 360 degrees, so if your crown requires six sections, the angle of each peg section must be measured precisely at 60 degrees. If you have too much fabric, the center of the crown sections will not fit smoothly together or sit snugly; too little and you will end up with a pointed crown.

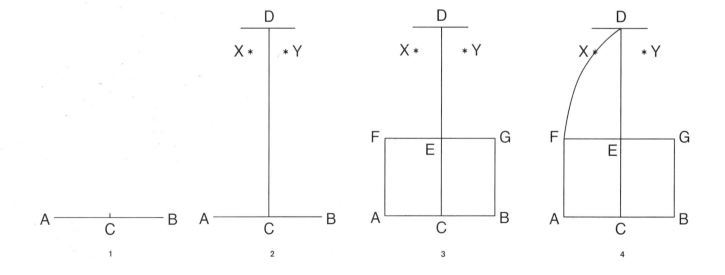

3. Measure one-third up line C–D and mark point E (this is where width is added to the crown) for a tight-fitting crown at point E. Repeat the A–C–B base line measurement ensuring the line is parallel. Label these end points F and G. Then with a ruler, join A to F and B to G, forming a rectangle.

4. Freehand join point D through X to F in a smooth curve.

5. Fold the paper accurately along the middle line C–E–D and cut precisely along the line you drew connecting D–X–F–A and along A–C. As you folded your paper, you will also be cutting along the undrawn lines D–Y–G–B and B–C at the same time, giving you a symmetrical pattern piece. This is your "making pattern." Mark it as such, including the number of sections, head size, and line of grain.

6. Place this pattern on to a larger piece of card and make point holes with your dividers where line C–E–D was on the making pattern.

7. Then set dividers at ⅜ in. (1 cm) and score up around the whole making pattern. At the base (headfitting line), set the dividers to ¾ in. (2 cm) and score the card. This additional ⅜ in. (1 cm) will give you enough of an excess to turn if required. Remove the making pattern. Then with a ruler, join the center pinpoints C–E–D and fold carefully along this center line. Cut precisely following the score marks. This is then your cutting pattern. Name it and add the same details as the making pattern, adding the amount of seam allowance.

GLOSSARY

Capeline: A straw or felt shape used to make a hat with crown and flat brim.

Cone: Conically shaped hood of felt or straw used for blocking small hat shapes or crowns.

Grain line: A line that indicates how the pattern piece should be laid on the fabric for cutting.

Head measurement: Circumference measurement around the head, ultimately where the hat will sit on to the head.

EXERCISE: **PRACTICE DRAFTING SECTIONAL CROWN PATTERNS**

Following the method detailed, make a five-section, and an eight-section, fitted crown pattern for differing head sizes. Then exploring and altering measurements and line, make four other patterns of varying height and shape.

Repeat this exercise with texture to discover more about the language of design.

VARIATIONS

Adding extra height in the crown along line C–E–D and width across line F–E–G will result in a floppy, flat crown. This could take a peak and would result in a baker boy hat. Adding a narrow strip/side band stitched on the head fitting and a pompom would make a tam or a sectional beret.

◄ **Sectional crown** This hat has been constructed in sections. The crown has been made from a bias strip that is joined at the center back. The top edge has been gathered, drawn together, and then stitched onto a narrower, stiffened headband, peaked, and trimmed.

SECTION 4 | MILLINERY

CONSTRUCTING A SECTIONAL CROWN

Objective Having drafted your sectional crown pattern (see page 186), learn how to construct the crown.

The sectional crown pattern method can be used for many style adaptations—it is even used for the baseball cap. Conventional methods vary slightly, since some milliners prefer to construct the crown in two halves and then complete the last seam in a continuous line, stitching the two halves together from one side to the other across the top. Purists prefer the pairs method (whereby the peg components are joined together in pairs prior to stitching) and never stitch over the top center point. Both methods are described here.

◄ **Many variations** Here we see the same style of sectional cap made using a variety of fabrics. Note how the material and color usage changes the appearance of the cap.

The fabric choice is that of the designer. If the fabric is patterned, striped, or checked, you need to consider how you will join the patterns—as the sections are cut on the bias you may want to use the interesting effects created by the diagonal. If however, the fabric is flimsy, you may need to add an interlining, such as Stayflex, which is a woven iron-on fabric. Never use a nonwoven iron-on, since this will prevent the fabric's natural ease in the warp and weft. This will result in an ill-fitting hat, as the fabric will not hug the head. Other interlinings can be used, such as a lightweight foam, canvas, or tarlatan. Patterned hats are often top stitched with lines of machine stitching to give extra stiffening and body.

CONSTRUCTING A SIX-SECTION CROWN (THE PAIRS METHOD)

If you are prestiffening your fabric with an iron-on interlining, do this first, ensuring you are lining up the grains on each fabric.

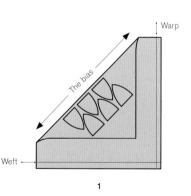

1. Find the true bias of the fabric as described on page 180. Lay your cutting pattern (see page 187) on the bias of the fabric—use the grain lines marked on your pattern to ensure the match with the warp and weft. Lay out your cutting pattern piece on the reverse of the fabric and mark around the pattern with tailor's chalk, marking the center point at the base line. Then take your making pattern and line it up with the center mark, ensuring you have an even seam allowance all the way around and then mark up with chalk. This is the line you will stitch to. Repeat for the number of sections of the crown and carefully cut out with scissors. Then number the sections 1–6 (if there are six sections) on the reverse of the fabric.

2. Pin the sections together in twos down one side 1–2, 3–4, and 5–6. If you pin horizontally across the fabric section bisecting the chalk stitch line, you will be able to sew over the pins. Always pin from the tip to the head line. Machine stitch these together taking care to start at the tip by inserting your machine needle into the apex of the chalk line but never over it. Leave long enough thread ends to tie off—do not use the reverse stitch on the machine because this would cause unnecessary bulk. Once stitched, press the seams open. You will have three sets of twos if making a six-section crown.

3. Pin section 2–3 and machine as before, pulling threads through and tying off, then press open the seams. Repeat this process, pinning, stitching, and pressing open section 4–5. The last seam to be joined is 1–6. This is the most difficult and requires tacking prior to machining to ensure you do not end up with a hole or oversew on to another section. Press this last seam open.

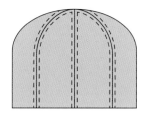

4 Side view

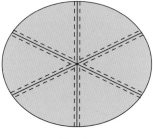

4 Top view

4. Finally, top stitch all the seams on both sides, continually accentuating the star at the top of the crown.

The crown is then ready to be stitched onto a brim (see pages 190–193) or have a peak added (see page 193).

DESIGN CONSIDERATIONS

- The adjustable or elasticated strap at the back. If adjustable, will you use a buckle, a slider, Velcro, snaps, or buttons?
- Shape and size of the peak.
- Color of thread for stitching and top stitching
- Lining fabric.
- Trimmings. Will there be a pompom, covered button, or other trim in the center of the crown?
- If you are attaching to a brim, how will this be trimmed?

CONSTRUCTING A TWO-SECTION CROWN

This is also known as a tip-and-side-band crown. A dome hat block is the easiest to start with.

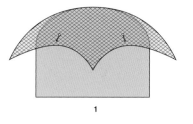

1

1. Cut a square of elastic canvas or buckram, enough to cover the curved tip of the crown. Place the canvas on the tip of the crown block with the bias at the center front.

2. Steam the canvas or spray lightly with water to dampen. Pin the opposite straight of the grain to the block (as you cannot pull any fullness through these parts as there is no give), then pull and pin all the fullness to the bias points. Remember to hold the fabric under tension as you pin it to the block. Working at opposite sides of the block, manipulate the bias until all the fullness has been reduced. Leave to dry. When dry, mark and trim the tip to ensure a good even shape, mark the center front with a vertical baste stitch, press, and remove from the block.

3. For the side band, cut a bias strip, leaving a generous seam allowance. Wrap the side band around the crown block, secure the overlap at the center back with pins, then using your elastic band or hat string, secure the base, pinning just above the elastic/string. Steam or damp the side band and pull upward, pin the back, front, left side, and right side and then in between these points until the edge is blocked and the fabric wraps the block tightly. Leave to dry.

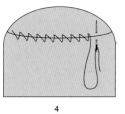

4

4. When dry, press lightly and mark the center front. Trim the overlap back seam ½ in. (1 cm), mark the overlap with tailor's chalk, and slip the side band off over the top of the block. Stitch the seam using a backstitch. Then slip back on the block (tip down so you don't open out the gentle curve of the side band).

5. Place the tip back on to the block, lining up your center front marks. Where the tip overlaps the side band, press with a polishing motion (small circular strokes pressing firmly against the block). Then using a diagonal basting stitch (see page 185), sew the tip to the side band, while still on the block. Once stitched press firmly again.

6. To finish and obtain smooth seams, cut a bias strip of tarlatan. Pull it to soften the fabric, then damp lightly, stretch, and pin over the seams. Press the tarlatan onto the seams using the polishing motion and press firmly against the block. The crown is now ready to be covered.

GLOSSARY

Fullness: Where fabric does not sit flat on the hat block without gathering.

Grain line: A line that indicates how the pattern piece should be laid on the fabric for cutting.

Peak: A partial brim, usually extending out at the front of a hat or cap.

Straight of the grain: Following the line of the weave of fibers.

SECTION 4 | MILLINERY

DRAFTING A BRIM PATTERN

Objective Learn two methods of drafting a brim pattern.

There are many methods for drafting brim patterns which result in contrasting finished designs. Two are described in this section: the cone method and the darted pattern method.

◄ **Working with tweed** This rakish hat in tweed features a turned-up brim. Note the clever use of the tweed grain on the sectioned crown.

THE CONE METHOD

The cone method is a quick, reliable, and easy method. It also allows for variation of design: upturned, downward, and side sweep, symmetrical or asymmetric. This method can also be adapted and used for making a beret or toque pattern too.

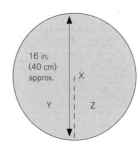

1. Using lightweight pattern card, draw a circle with a minimum diameter of 16 in. (40 cm). Cut the circle out with care and find the center point. Mark this X. Draw a straight line from the center to the edge and cut along this line. Mark one side of the line Y and one side Z.

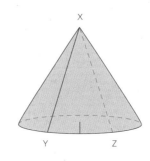

2. Overlap the two sides of the line you have just cut, by moving Y over Z to give the desired angle. The more acute the angle of the cone, the narrower the brim will be. It will also have the propensity to hold an upsweep or turn-up. When you have decided on the angle required, draw up the edge of the overlap and mark the edge of the back seam. Stick securely with sticky tape. This will become the position of the center-back seam.

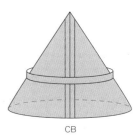

CB

3. Shape and pin your headband to the desired head measurement. Then having decided what type of brim shape you require (symmetrical or asymmetrical), place the headband onto the cone. Line up the center back of your headband with the center-back seam you have just created (CB). If you require a symmetrical brim, you will need to measure down from the bottom of the headband to the edge of the brim (you will need someone to assist you here by lightly holding and moving the headband as instructed). When you are happy with the headband, draw a line around the bottom of the headband with a sharp pencil.

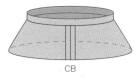

CB

4. Remove the headband, peel back the sticky tape, and spread the cone out flat. Cut away the excess card from the overlap as indicated by the pencil mark. Set your dividers to 1 in. (2.5 cm) and follow the headband pencil mark around, scoring the card lightly as you follow the line. Then cut away the excess from the middle.

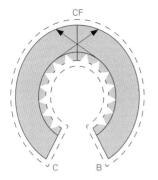

5. Fold your pattern exactly in half to find the center front and mark with a cross. Then, starting approximately 1¼ in. (3 cm) from the back seam, snip out small triangles from the top of the head-fitting line to the bottom original head-fitting pencil line.

6. Add annotation to the pattern—grain lines (usually indicated with an arrow showing the direction of the grain) at the center front to indicate it needs to be cut on the bias, and head measurement and style number or name of the hat for future reference. Mark with "x 2," to indicate two patterns need to be cut (for accuracy, always turn the pattern and cut one from the top side and one from the underside). You should also indicate the pattern has no seam allowance, only head fitting. This is the making pattern.

7. Place the making pattern on to another piece of card. Pierce through the card at the center-front point. Set your dividers to ⅜ in. (1 cm) and score around the pattern from one center-back inside edge to the other. Do not add seam allowance to the head fitting. With a pencil or the divider, mark around the crimped head fitting, then cut out. This is your cutting pattern, which you should mark up as per the making pattern.

RESIZING BRIM PATTERNS

As a rule, drafting a brim pattern always starts with the head-fitting measurement. The head fitting is oval for most hats. For a 22 in. (55.8 cm) head measurement, draft an oval 7½ in. (19 cm) in length by 6½ in. (17 cm) in width. To increase or reduce the head size by ⅜ in. (1 cm), draw a line ⅛ in. (3 mm) on the inside of the 22 in. (55.8 cm) head-fitting oval to reduce the size, and on the outside to increase the size. For example, for a 22½ in. (57 cm) head measurement, you need an oval 7⅝ in. (19.3 cm) in length by 6⅝ in. (17.3 cm) in width.

BERET AND TOQUE PATTERNS

For a beret pattern, follow the instruction for the cone method. Having completed step 3:

1. Place the cone on another piece of pattern card and draw around its circumference, add ⅜ in. (1 cm) seam allowance with dividers, and cut the circle out. This will become the tip of the beret.

2. Instead of adding 1 in. (2.5 cm) to the head-fitting line, add only ⅝ in. (1.5 cm).

3. Cut a bias strip of 3¼ in. (8 cm) wide x the head measurement, adding ¾ in. (2 cm) for seam allowance.

4. Only one beret pattern needs to be cut, unlike the brim, which requires an under side and a top side.

For a toque, follow the method for the beret but ensure your cone is at a very acute angle, therefore making the circumference of your tip much smaller. If you envisage illustration 4 on the opposite page upside down, this will give you an idea of what a pattern for a beret or toque will look like.

▶ **Simple, timeless, stylish** This style of soft, wool beret with a side band can be created by following the adaptation of the cone method shown above.

▶ **Contrasting materials** A narrow back-flipped brim using tweed and leather to great effect. When using two different materials such as this, you must ensure that they are of a similar substance. Iron-on interlining can be used to create this.

THE DARTED METHOD

Similarly to the cone method on the previous page, with the darted method you begin with a circle. The circle is cut into and closed, or folded at points around the circle to create darts which will give the shape to the brim.

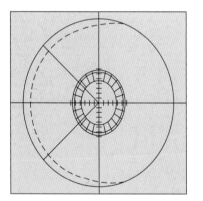

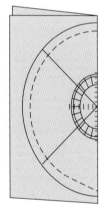

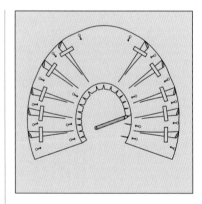

1. Once the head fitting is established, draw an oval head measurement onto the pattern paper/card, allowing enough width for the widest part of the brim. Then fold the paper to give the center-front, back, and both side points on the head fitting—these crease marks act as a reference point when drafting the outer edge of the brim. Mark between these points so your paper is now divided up in eight equal parts.

2. If your brim is symmetrical, fold in half along the vertical line and cut accurately through both sides of the paper along the dotted line as shown here.

3. Measure in 1 in. (2.5 cm) from the headline with your divider to create the brim stand. Then snip in ½ in. (1 cm) intervals around the brim stand to the head fitting. Using the radial lines as a guide, draw out the desired brim shape, as per your design, then cut away the surplus paper. Pin the brim stand to the headband. Used as it is presently, this pattern would give you a completely flat brim.

Bias: Cross grain of any woven fabric.

Brim: Projecting edge of a hat usually protruding from the crown. It can sweep upwards or turn down; it can be symmetrical or asymmetrical.

Brim stand: The part of the brim which fits inside the crown and on to which the crown is attached.

Head fitting: The point at which the hat sits on to the head. It usually has a grosgrain ribbon to enhance the fit and add comfort.

Headband: Wired canvas bias strip used as a tool to support the brim of a hat while the hat/pattern is being made.

Peak stand: The part of the peak that fits inside the crown. The stand allows the peak to be attached to the crown.

3D EXERCISE: DRAFTING A PEAK/VISOR PATTERN

1. Lay your headband on a piece of pattern paper/card.
2. Draw around the front portion of the headband, marking the center front, then add 1 1/4 in. (3 cm) to the head fitting line for the peak stand.
3. Draw a straight line with a ruler of the length of the peak required. For a symmetrical peak, fold along the center line and draft out half the peak, ensuring you bring the line back to meet the head fitting pencil line. Then cut from the fold to your head fitting and peak stand, following the line drawn. While still folded, snip the peak stand down to the head fitting.
4. To test the shape of the peak, pin the paper pattern carefully onto the headband and adjust if necessary. For a more slanting peak, dart the paper to the required angle first before following this method.

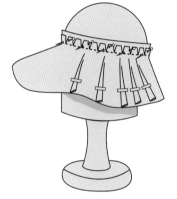

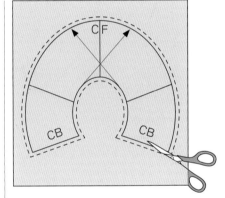

▶ **Adding a peak**
Here we see the same cap shown with peaks in three contrasting materials, plastic, tweed, and leather, to create various looks.

4. To shape the brim, darts are needed. Darts must taper out before the head fitting line so you do not reduce the head size as you dart. To make a dart, simply fold the paper up toward the head fitting and sticky tape the dart closed. If darts are applied to the eight radial points, the resulting shape would be a fairly deep cloche with an even slant all around. To get a more asymmetrical slant, more darts need to be placed on the downward sloping side.

5. Once you are happy with the shape and line you have achieved, remove the headband and cut through the center back line. Place on another piece of paper/card with the darts still taped up. Mark around the edge and brim stand carefully. Before you cut out, add seam allowance around the brim edge and center-back seam. Cut out and then pin this new pattern back to the headband to check you are happy with the shape.

6. Mark up the pattern with all relevant annotation—head size, description, and style name or number.

SECTION 4 | MILLINERY

BLOCKING A HAT

Objective Learn how to shape a felt capeline by blocking.

Blocking is a technical process in which a hat shape is molded. The material is either steamed or damped to render it pliable. It is then stretched and secured to the block, dividing the fullness up equally and eradicating all gathers and folds.

HOW TO BLOCK AND ASSEMBLE A HAT

Felt and straw are the only two materials in millinery that can be shaped into a dome without the need for seams. Felt is a nonwoven material made when loose fibers are matted together under pressure in the presence of steam. There are many kinds of felts: wool felt, fur felt, melusine, mouflon, peachbloom, and velour. All felts become malleable and can be stretched in any direction when steamed. When dry, they retain their shape. Here we look at how to block a felt hat and assemble a hat consisting of a simple crown and brim. The method and principles are the same for making a more complex shape—preparing the blocks, stiffening the felt, blocking, steaming and stretching, drying, wiring, joining, and trimming.

PREPARATION
1. Cover blocks in plastic wrap.

SHAPING CROWN
2. Using a Jiffy hat steamer, steam the felt capeline/cone all over to dampen the area, but concentrate on the crown section.

6. Ensure you pin all the way around, below the spring, string, or elastic (if you are using). With a nail brush, gently knock out the pile. If brushing, use circular clockwise motions, working your way down from the center of the crown. Do not use thumbtacks, since these can rust and ruin the felt. They also leave big holes in the felt, and, more damagingly, the block.

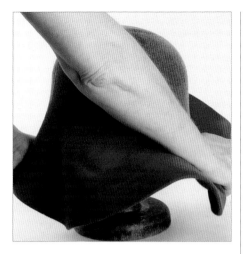

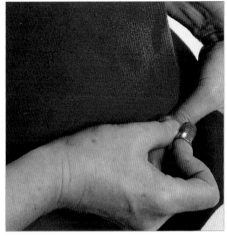

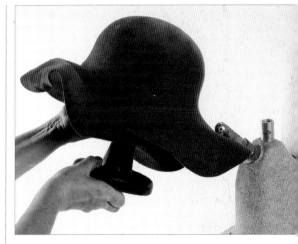

3. When the crown area is becoming hot and malleable, remove from the steam and, holding the back and front of the brim, pull down firmly and sharply over the crown block.

4. With blocking pins, pin the felt to the block—this is done by holding the pin between your thumb and fourth finger and pushing with your thimbled third finger. Keep the felt under tension as you pin.

5. You can then slip your blocking spring, string, or elastic down over the brim (if you are using). Keep the felt pliable with repeated steaming while working around, dividing and pulling out any fullness between the front, back, and two sides. The felt crown should shape easily if you are using a dome crown block.

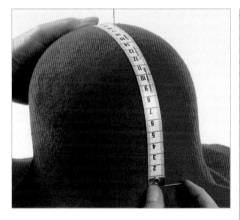

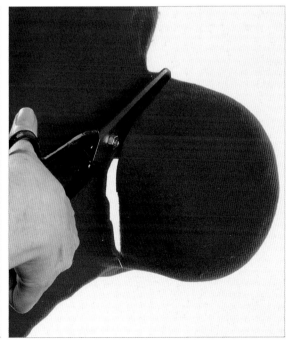

7. When the felt is completely dry, remove the blocking spring, string, or elastic and also the pins (you may want to use pliers for this). Measure and mark the depth of the crown required with tailor's chalk or pins. Tack a line to mark the front of the crown.

8. Carefully cut the brim off, making the initial cut with a scalpel or clicking knife. You need to end up with a ring of felt. Take care not to stretch out the headfitting when doing this.

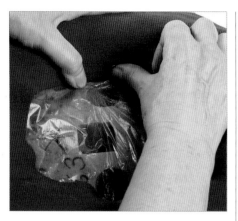

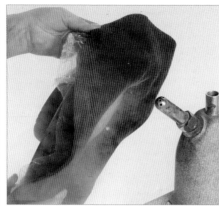

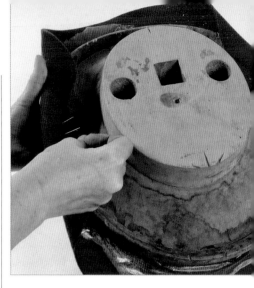

9. Depending on the size of the headfitting you require, you may need to shrink the center of the felt ring. To do this, steam the area around the hole and pull horizontally toward the center hole, working your way around the hole, steaming, pulling, and shrinking away the surplus felt.

10. This brim has an inverted headfitting so ensuring you have the right side of felt facing you, divide the headfitting in equal parts, and pin the headfitting down to the brim block.

11. Continue to steam and pin. Once the headfitting has been pinned all the way round and there are no puckers or gathers, steam and pull the felt to the edge of the block, securing the back, front, left, and right side with pins.

◄ **15.** If the brim is to be bound with ribbon, you should wire the edge to ensure it retains its shape (see pages 182–183). Straighten the wire prior to use. Start your wire 1 in. (2.5 cm) from the center back and place it right on the cut edge of the felt. If you are doing a turned felt edge, ideally you will have blocked your brim down past the edge of the block, so you can use the groove left by the edge of the brim to sit the wire in, and the edge to assist with turning the hem over. If doing a turned felt edge, follow the instructions for wire in a fold on page 182.

CREATING A TURNED FELT EDGE

For a turned felt edge, once you have wired your fold, turn your felt edge over the wire pinning front, back, left, and right sides, then pin in between—pin vertically toward the outside edge of the brim and press gently with a lightly damped cloth. Then, using a slipstitch (see page 184), hem the turn or tack the turning over the wire and then machine stitch the edge.

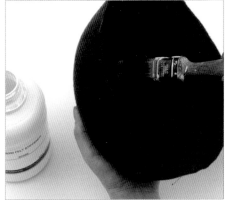

12. Divide up any fullness, then steam and pull all fullness out, and secure at the edge with pins. The felt should fit snugly to the block without any gathers, pleats, or folds. Steam and brush or knock the felt and leave to dry.

13. Felt stiffener can be applied prior to or after blocking. This is applied to the wrong side of the felt with an almost dry brush. Starting at the front, mark and paint onto the felt and work your way around. Care needs to be taken if applying after the blocking because the hat can quite easily become misshapen.

14. Remove the pins, and mark the center-front with a vertical tack stitch. When the brim is dry, trim it to the required width.

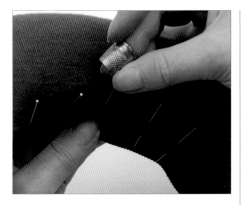

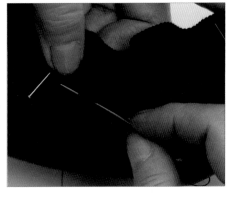

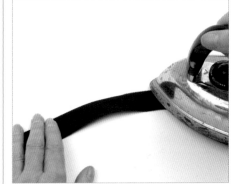

ATTACHING THE HEADFITTING
16. Cut a grosgrain ribbon the head size required plus 1¼ in. (3 cm), turn one end over by ⅝ in. (1.5 cm), pin on top of the other end, overlapping by ⅝ in. (1.5 cm), and stitch these together invisibly at the bottom. Turn your brim upside down, line up the center-fronts of the brim and grosgrain, and vertically pin your headfitting ribbon front, back, left, and right sides, divide any fullness equally, and continue to pin in between.

17. The edge of the grosgrain should not hang down below the brim when turned the right way around. Using a slip stitch, sew the bottom edge of the grosgrain to the bottom of the felt brim stand.

18. To bind your wired brim with grosgrain ribbon, fold the grosgrain in half, pressing firmly along the fold with your nail. Carefully press with an iron in a curved motion with the fold facing the outside—this will pre-shape the ribbon, ensuring you do not have any fullness or gathers in the ribbon.

19. Start by pinning the ribbon to the brim center-back, leaving an excess of ⅜ in. (1 cm). Stab the pins through the ribbon and through the felt into the ribbon on the underside of the brim. Where the grosgrain meets edge-to-edge, fold back the remaining end on its self.

20. Undo the pins from the back to the sides, leaving the pins in the front section, and turn both ends of the grosgrain toward you so the wrong side is facing you. Then using a whipstitch (see page 185), stitch up the back.

21. Once this is done, miter the edges of the ribbon by snipping a triangle off each seam at each edge of the ribbon. Re-pin the ribbon to the brim, which should fit tightly.

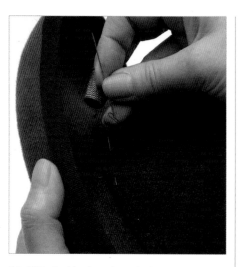

24. With double thread, stitch the crown on the brim stand using a back stitch. Take care not to stitch through the grosgrain headfitting.

25. The hat is now ready for trimming (see pages 200–203).

22. Stitch on using an invisible stitch, or tack the ribbon and then machine stitch it on.

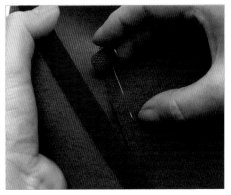

REATTACHING CROWN AND BRIM
23. Line up the center-front marks on the crown and the brim. Pin the crown over the brim at the front, back, left, and right sides. In case there is any fullness, ease or stretch out, before pinning in between.

Blocking: The process of molding a hat shape. The material is either steamed or damped to render it pliable. It is then stretched and secured to the block, dividing the fullness up equally, and eradicating all folds.

Blocking spring, string, or elastic: Tools used to hold fabric straw or felt to a block.

Brim stand: The part of the brim that fits inside the crown, the bottom of which often forms the headfitting.

Fur felt: Made using the fibers of fur-coated animals—rabbit is most commonly used.

Melusine: Felts that have a flat, silky pile, which varies in length. A short pile gives a satinlike surface while longer piles can be brushed up to resemble exotic furs. These felts are made from a mix of fur fibers.

Mouflon: Similar to the long-piled melusine, but because it is made of wool from the mouflon sheep, it is not silky in appearance. These are delicate felts and care is needed when blocking, since excessive steaming can damage them.

Peachbloom/velour: A felt that has a velvet finish to it.

Wool felt: Usually made from sheep's wool, the best being made from merino wool. Sometimes synthetic fibers are added to cheaper-quality felt.

BLOCKING A STRAW HAT

Blocking a straw hat is a very similar process to that of a felt with three main differences to note:
- Straw is usually damped with a damp cloth rather than steamed.
- Straw is stiffened after it is blocked but while still pinned to the block.
- Straw behaves very differently to felt when blocked. As straw is woven, it has a limited amount of malleability and stretch, and this very much depends on the type of weave and the type of straw fiber used to weave the capeline. As a rule of thumb, the tighter the weave of the straw, the less malleable it will be.

▶ **Bold and beautiful** This hat, with upturned brim and classic dome crown in red sisal straw, is trimmed in a dramatic manner using fabrics and feathers. The edge of the brim is wired and turned giving a clean finish so the eye is drawn to the detail of the trimming.

SECTION 4 | MILLINERY

TRIMMINGS FOR HATS

Objective Learn about the various trimmings that can be used to decorate hats.

Ostrich feather pad

Burnt peacock feather

Peacock sword feather

The trimming is an integral part of the design of a hat. Trimmings are always considered at the design stage. The trimming is used to balance the design of a hat, add drama, and make a statement, drawing the eye of the viewer to a focal point. The trim can make the design; in fact, the trim sometimes is the design, as is the case with fascinators.

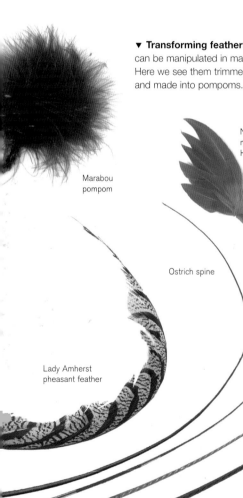

▼ **Transforming feathers** Feathers can be manipulated in many ways. Here we see them trimmed, stripped, and made into pompoms.

Marabou pompom

Novelty feather butterfly made from trimmed Hackle feathers

Ostrich spine

Decorative ostrich spines (all 4)

Lady Amherst pheasant feather

Golden pheasant feather

TYPES OF TRIM

The trimming is where the designer can really let his or her creativity shine—hats can be completely altered by the choice of type and color of trim. Carefully designed trimmings can balance the hat, adding harmony to the overall line of the silhouette. Hat block shapes are often carried through from season to season but the trimming and application dramatically change. A somber hat with a small tailored bow can become something much more exotic when a plume of coiffured feathers is added.

Edging of the brims and hat bands are also part of the trim—how you finish these is equally important. Bound edges and hat bands often coordinate, and a variety of ribbons, braids, and fabrics can be used. An important factor is the bias or how you can eliminate fullness in the ribbon or braid for trims—if using fabric, it needs to be cut on the bias.

- Grosgrain ribbon is often used because it can be ironed and shaped, eradicating fullness. It comes in many widths— no. 3 and no. 5 are most often used for edging brims.
- Hat bands can be gathered at each end, drawing away any fullness from the ribbon around the crown. Pre-prepared bias binding is also available and used effectively for brim edges.

FEATHERS

Feathers are a by-product of the meat industry, and they can also be harvested when the bird sheds its feathers, usually during the summer months. There are many types of feather available on the market—they vary greatly in terms of length, texture, aesthetic, and finish. Feathers are very versatile and can be used in a great many ways. They offer a great wealth of trim ideas and solutions.

Feathers that are used for trimming come from a variety of birds, such as

Burnt
ostrich
feather

Trimmed
ostrich
plume

Turkey coquille
feather pad

Flocked
polyester
pansies

Sprig of Lily-
type flowers

Partridge
feathers
stitched onto
a ribbon and
sold by
the yard

Saddle Hackle
feather fringe,
sold by the yard

Orchid
spray

White silk
camelia
stem

Handmade rose
in organza

Black silk
rose

▲ **Versatile trimmings** You can use feathers in their original colors or dye them, keep them in their original form or burn them, or transform them into pads or fringes.

pheasant, ostrich, peacock, goose, turkey, guinea fowl, and partridge. Feathers offer a wide variety of types, from the very soft, downy, fluffy feathers to the strong flight feathers. Some feathers have distinctive natural patterning and colors. Feathers are sold in their natural colors, but more often they are dyed.

Single quills can be trimmed into arrowheads, spears, or petal shapes, decorated with diamantes, or burnt so only a few filaments remain. Feather quills can also be curled or stripped bare so that only the spines remain—the spines can then be decorated and patterned to great effect.

Feathers can also be purchased sewn onto ribbon by the yard, wired together as plumes, made into pompoms, or even fashioned into flowers. Smaller feathers are purchased by weight while larger feathers are often sold separately or by the dozen. Feather pads are small feathers that are glued onto a canvas backer. These can be used singly or en masse to completely cover the hat and create a dramatic look.

Care must be taken when using and handling feathers—they are fragile and over-handling can cause feathers to separate. From the central quill, filaments called barbs extend outward to form the vane. Each barb has a series of hooklets and barbules that lock together to give strength to the feather. When the hooklets and barbules become separated, this causes a gap in the feather.

FLOWERS
Artificial flowers can be bought or made, and many types are available. Flowers for millinery were originally made from silk—now most are made in polyester or rayon. Size and type also vary greatly, from huge tuba roses to the tiniest spray of cherry blossom. Cheaper flowers have plastic stems—these are not ideal because they are hard to sew through. However, you can find flowers made from many materials: feathers, sinamay, organdie and organza, crin, straw, ribbon, strip straw, and felt to mention a few.

Flowers are used extensively on summer hats and headpieces, since they are

▶ **Fashioning flowers** These flower trims have been made from a variety of fabrics in order to mimic a huge range of different flower species.

light in weight and add a freshness of spring or summer blooms. They add a splash of color and variety of texture.

The more realistic ones require specialist tools that are now very difficult to find, and the process is very labor-intensive and therefore costly. There are very few handmade flowers nowadays.

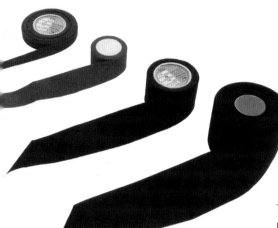

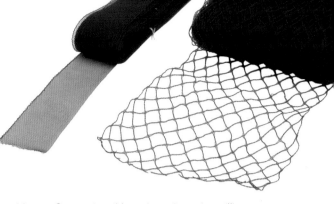

◄► **Function and frippery** Grosgrain ribbon (left) is used extensively for trimmings and headfittings. Crin (right) and veiling (far right) are used to add a sense of drama to a hat.

BOWS

Bows are a common trimming that have been used in millinery throughout the ages to dramatic and whimsical effect. There are many types of bows, such as a flat bow, tie bow, tailored bow, butterfly bow, double bow, triple bow, quadruple loop bow, vertical loop bow, and many others. Components of the bow can differ greatly and these can have an impact on the overall design of the bow.

The components of a bow are:

• A loop
• A tie over across the center of
  the loop
• Two ends/tails

The loops can be flat or gathered/pleated in the center. Ends can be short, long, symmetrical or asymmetric, cut at an angle, cut with a fork, blunt-ended, or frayed. Bows can be made from a diverse range of fabrics and materials, from traditional grosgrain, satin, and veiling to Perspex, or even wood.

RIBBONS

Ribbons are very versatile and have many uses in millinery. The diversity and choice is incredible: Ribbons can be patent, satin, wired edge, velvet, grosgrain, sinamay, flat braids, bias bindings, lace trimmed, etc. Ribbons can be used alone or with other materials to form any number and variety of trims. They can be plaited, braided, pleated, or interwoven. Your creativity can really shine through when exploring the possibilities.

Grosgrain ribbon is unique in millinery—it is both functional and decorative. In women's hats, it is always used as the headband in a hat or headpiece. The headband has two purposes—it helps secure the hat to the wearer's head and it protects the hat from the wearer's sweat and hair oil/products. Grosgrain has a woven-in flexibility—when damped it will shrink; when ironed, it will hold a curve; and it also pleats well.

VEILING

Veiling is a decorative net that is usually made in a diamond repeating pattern but can also be made in a (honeycomb) octagonal repeating pattern. It always adds a sense of drama to any hat or headpiece and is often used as part of the trim of a hat—it is not usually used on its own. The rise in popularity of

APPLICATION METHODS FOR VEILING

Veiling can be draped around the hat or onto a brim around a crown, and it can be draped around the edge of a brim so the veiling falls across the face of the wearer—soft silk veiling is used for this purpose. Veiling can be:

• Steamed and blocked to hold the veiling away from the face on a cocktail hat—this is called a cage veil.
• Softly gathered from the base of the crown, coming down across the brim, and falling straight down over the edge of the brim.
• Scrunched into ruffles or folded and twisted into rosettes.

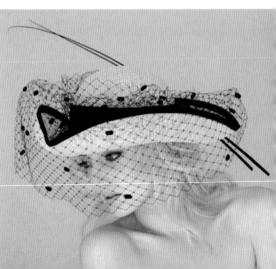

► **Veiling** Merry widow veiling is gathered and stitched onto the crown, spilling over the brim, before the hat ribbon is stitched in place.

Metallic fabric leaves

Strip straw discs

Chains for decorative headbands

Decorative quill end piece

Metal snaffels

Decorative metal fixtures

Bugle beads

Braided and chain tassels

Large brass dome buttons

▲ **Extensive choice** The choice of trimmings for hats is staggering, from buttons to beads, chains, tassels, and flowers, so you can add your design signature to any style.

Flower stamens

EXERCISE: MAKING BOW TRIMS

1. Source the following materials:
- 3 ft. (1 m.) of crin.
- 20 in. (50 cm) of sinamay (remember to cut on the bias) or sinamay ribbon (ensure that it is bias ribbon).
- 30 in. (75 cm) of fabric (remember to cut on the bias).
- 3 ft. (1 m.) of grosgrain in any width.
- 3 ft. (1 m.) velvet ribbon.

2. Using the information in this section, make six different types of bow trims.

fascinators has seen a resurgence in the use of veiling.

Historically, many different types of veiling were available, but now the most common is Russian veiling, which is available in various gauges and a selection of finishes. It is made from fine nylon and silk, and metallic veiling is made from polyester.

Veiling is sold by the yard and is available in a variety of widths—9 in. (23 cm), 12 in. (30 cm), and 18 in. (46 cm) are the more common widths. It is categorized by size of the diamonds in the fabric—$\frac{3}{16}$ in. (5 mm) or $\frac{3}{8}$ in. (1 cm) is all that is manufactured now, but in the past there were finer and more coarse veils. Decorative finishes can be added to the veiling to create different effects, such as diamantes/rhinestones, pearls, and chenille bobbles.

CRIN

Crin (horsehair) is made from polyester filaments woven into material that can be either tubular or flat. It comes in a variety of widths, colors, and weights. It is woven on the bias, and with this come its unique characteristics. It is incredibly strong and has a memory so it will bounce back to its original shape. The selvage edge that runs at the top of the edge of the fabric has a dense thread running through the weave. This thread is used to draw and gather in through the length of the fabric, enabling circles and curves to be achieved without visible gathers. Crin looks very modern and it has a semi-transparent, lustrous gauze. Crin is most often used as a trimming material, but it is possible for a skilled milliner to make a hat entirely out of crin.

Types of trims that can be made from crin include circular veils/visors, bows, looped rosettes, scrunched ruffles, and flowers. It can also be used to stiffen fabric bows.

BEADS, DIAMANTES, TASSELS, BUCKLES, AND MORE...

These and much more can be used in myriad ways to ornament and embellish the hat or headpiece—the options are limited only by your creativity.

GLOSSARY

Crin/horsehair: Made from polyester filaments that are woven into material. It can be either tubular of flat.

Lignes: The French unit of measurement for width of ribbons.

Sinamay: Made from banana plant fiber, this is available in a rainbow of colors and a variety of weaves and finishes.

Small leather goods

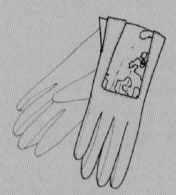

In this section we enter the world of small leather goods. You will learn exactly what the term refers to and why SLGs, belts, and gloves are vital for brand recognition and sales, and also understand how and why SLGs, belts, and gloves are often included as an integral part of a fashion line.

You will build on the design considerations and criteria learned in the Creative Process section, focusing on the key criteria for SLGs: function, practicality, and form. We also take a look at the specific criteria relating to belts and gloves, in the manufacture of which material choice is an overriding factor. The issue of sizing, as it relates to gloves and belts, is also covered in this section.

The construction methods and seam types for bags apply to SLGs and belts to a great extent, so methods learned in the Handbags section can be applied to these products. Here, we focus on glove construction and specialist terminology, using the anatomy of a glove to show an exploded view of the component pieces that make up the product. You will learn about the specialist materials used for belts and gloves. SLGs will usually be designed using the same materials as the main bag line, which have previously been covered.

MATERIALS AND HARDWARE: SMALL LEATHER GOODS

Objective Learn about the specialist materials and hardware for small leather goods, gloves, and belts.

Imitation leather: grain patterns are embossed onto replica crocodile skin.

Understanding material usage is imperative as a designer. Knowing what to ask for when researching and sourcing is an essential skill to possess. It will save you time and money because ordering unsuitable materials is a costly mistake to make. A great many small leather goods are designed specifically to use the surplus leather created after a line of bags has been designed and made. So to this end, appropriate leather and materials have been covered in the Handbags section of this book (see pages 96–99). In this section we will concentrate on gloves and belts, both of which require very specific and often specialist materials.

GLOVE LEATHER

Gloving leather is a specialty, and quality gloves cannot be made from just any type of leather. The tanners of glove leather have to ensure suppleness; finesse, softness, and elasticity are tanned into the skin. The raw materials are extremely important, since certain types of leather have characteristics that are more suitable for tanners to turn into glove leather. Leathers that are strong and with a fine, even grain are the most suitable for glove design.

Cabretta: Hair sheep leather that is soft, fine, and even grained. It is a strong and supple leather, and it feels like a second skin, offering great comfort to the wearer. It has a smooth, regular, and refined surface, and cabretta leather can be finished in a variety of ways: glace, nubuck, suede, metallic, or lacquered.

Goat skin: Available in a variety of colors and finishes. Note the pebbled grain finish.

Kid skin: Velvet-soft leather that is hardwearing and finer in grain than goat skin.

Deer skin: Very soft and supple but has incredible strength and elasticity. The surface of the grain is more pronounced than the hair sheep.

Peccary: Peccary skin is from a wild pig found in the Amazon jungle. Peccary is easily recognizable as being from the hog family because it has the characteristic cluster of three dots over the surface of the skin. It is the absolute best leather, unequalled for comfort. Its main characteristics are its strength and softness.

Slink lambskin: The skin of a premature lamb/still born, it is incredibly soft and supple and very expensive. The best slink comes from New Zealand.

Slink calfskin: Leather made from the skin of stillborn calves, it is expensive because it is only harvested from cows that die when in

Kid skin: Here, perforated, plain, and with a machine stitch applied to replicate quilting detail.

calf or stillborn calves. This leather is particularly soft and is highly valued in the craft of glove making.

Shearling/sheepskin: Used mainly for casual winter gloves and mittens, it has the benefit of its own furry lining.

Goatskin: Used for lesser-quality gloves, it is hard wearing and coarse, but lacks the handle and stretch needed for quality dress gloves.

Cowhide: Too thick and bulky for dress gloves, cowhide is often used for more casual, cheaper gloves.

Exotic skins: Used for their unique aesthetic qualities, such as ostrich, crocodile, python, or lizard, as well as mink, fox, and other furs from farm-bred animals. Often used for design details and cuff trims rather than the body of the gloves.

GLOVE FABRIC

Stretch fabrics: Fabrics that can be used for gloves have expanded with the addition of Lycra and elastane too, adding a vital stretch to the fabric weaves. These include Lycra mixes of silk, velvet, and nylon, which are popular choices for formal evening gloves.

▼ **Lining fabric** Have fun with contrasting color linings in your designs.

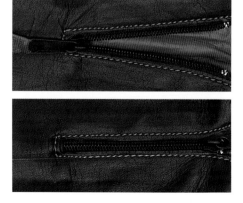

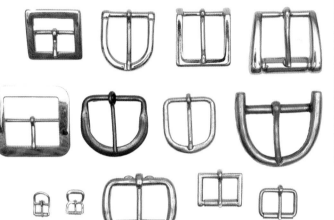

▼ **All colors...** For buckles, colors include chromed, silver, gold, rose gold, nickel, gun metal, antique bronze, pewter, or enameled, brushed, antiqued, or high-shine.

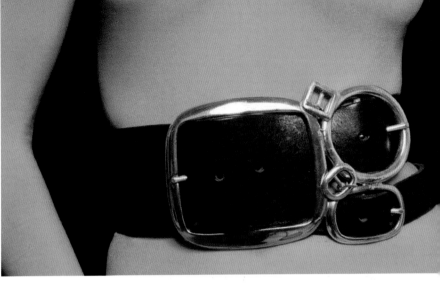

▲ **...All shapes** Buckles can be rounded, square, oval, rectangular, or novelty.

Other fabrics used are:
• Stretch PVC
• Stretch duchess satin
• Stretch satin
• Stretch cottons
• Stretch net
• Stretch lace net
• Stretch crochet net
• Stretch embroidered net

Knitted fabrics: Wool and acrylic are widely used for casual winter gloves, wrist warmers, and fingerless gloves and mittens.

Sports gloves: Polyester fleece, nylon nets, vinyl, cowhide, and Goretex- and Teflon-coated fabrics are all used.

Lining fabrics: These need to be incredibly thin so they do not add any bulk materials. Fabrics used include silk, polyester, finely knitted acrylic, wool, and cashmere.

GLOVE FITTINGS

Fittings used for gloves include snap fasteners, buckles, eyelets and hooks, buttons, roller bars, Velcro, and zippers.

BELTS

Belts can be made from a wide range of materials and leathers. The choice of material has a huge impact on the design, e.g. a raw-edge belt can only be made successfully if a bridle leather is used. For a raw-edge belt, the best leather is cowhide that has been vegetable tanned, and the best part of the hide to use is the butt. The leather from the butt is strong and even in grain and substance.

Belting leather: Full-grain cowhide that has a firm feel, a smooth finish, and is vegetable tanned with a grease grain finish. It is usually ⁵⁄₃₂ in. (3.5–4 mm) in thickness.

English bridle leather: A natural-textured, full-grain leather analine or semi-aniline dyed and finished with a coat of wax or oil. It is often sold by weight equivalent to thickness.

Belting and bridle leather: Sold in butt, half butt (which is a bend), shoulders, half shoulders, half side, and full hide. You can specify your required thickness when ordering.

Goat and lamb skin: Usually need to be backed/reinforced and the edges turned.

Exotic leathers: These include snake, lizard, crocodile/alligator, ostrich, stingray, and shark skin. They are often backed onto leather to give substance to the belt.

Backers: Nonwoven backers are often used for belts, as are composite leather backers. The backers need to be flexible but retain their shape and should not stretch. Backers can be self-adhesive or not.

Fastenings: If a particular fastening method or mechanism is used on the bags in the line, can this be used for the belt?

Sam Browne/mushroom fittings, zippers, rivets, studs, diamante, and chains are just a few types of fittings we often see used on belts. Research others and investigate how these could be used, as decoration and also for practical purposes.

SECTION 5 | SMALL LEATHER GOODS

DESIGN AND CONSTRUCTION

Objective Understand the importance of small leather goods in relation to the product line and the specialist nature of some of the criteria used in their design.

◄▼ **Desirability and functionality** The term "small leather goods" embraces everything from luxury stationery items like this croc-skin notepad to key fobs.

The term "small leather goods" includes a wide range of products from purses to writing folders and smartphone covers. Fashion accessory brands have realized that there is much to gain from introducing aspirational consumers to lower-priced products, so these are often included within a line of accessories. As small leather goods form part of a line of products, the design details will already have been determined by the key handbag pieces in the line. Scale of detail needs to be considered as small leather goods are designed to fulfill a specific function and are often small in size.

DESIGN CRITERIA

Each particular accessory has its own unique design challenges and considerations that need to be addressed when embarking upon a design project. In this section, gloves and belts are discussed separately; all other small leather goods (purses, wallets, key fobs, and so on) will be dealt with under the small leather goods heading. There will inevitably be a crossover of criteria, but the relationship to the product area and how they affect the individual design is often quite different. Construction methods and seam types are unique to gloves, but—broadly—the same for handbags, belts, and small leather goods.

Designing within the fashion accessory genre, there are some criteria that remain constant no matter what type of accessory you are designing:

• **Brief** A set of instructions, outlining what you are being asked to do.
• **Season** This will have been determined by your brief usually, but does need to be considered throughout your design process. The season will affect color palette, material choice, and also appropriateness of motif, if relevant.

• **Consumer** The consumer needs to be a focal point in design, as ultimately products need to be desirable and saleable. The aim is to create and fulfill a desire, or a perceived need, within your target group.
• **Color** Your color palette will be established through your research, and seasonal trend colors may well have an impact on your choice, but how you apply and position your color and accent colors needs experimentation and investigation. Always try a variety of options before deciding upon the colorway.
• **Materials** Need to be researched, sourced, and determined before the design process begins. Often small leather goods are designed to use surplus materials from the main bag production— but this is not always the case. You should always investigate and ponder the mix of materials, outers, linings, and trims. Material choice is extremely important and can add to the success or ultimate failure of any product.

▲ **Playful and practical** Small leather goods may be practical, but they are also an opportunity for a designer to have fun.

DESIGN CONSIDERATIONS FOR SMALL LEATHER GOODS

Small leather goods are small products that may be carried in the hand, bag, or pocket. Many handbag companies diversify into this product area to increase brand awareness, extend their offer to the consumer, and to use surplus leather waste pieces profitably. Without exception, small leather goods have an end use and are practical. So in order to design small leather goods effectively, it's necessary to define their purpose and understand how the consumer uses the product.

FUNCTION, PRACTICALITY, AND FORM

As small leather goods are almost all practical products by their very nature, the Bauhaus theory of form following function should be applied to a greater extent. Small leather goods are often designed to carry something, for example, a phone case, coin purse, spectacles case, or credit card holder. It is key to research the dimensions of the products the goods are to carry/protect. Draw a scaled-down version of the product that is designed to be carried/protected, then explore the shape that could contain this—just because credit cards are rectangular does not mean the card case needs to follow the shape exactly; however, it does need to function effectively.

PROPORTION, BALANCE, AND LINE

Proportion, balance, and line and silhouette are all key ingredients to consider when designing. It is essential to consider how the key design elements from your handbag line can inform the design of the small leather goods. Proportion, balance, and line need to be explored in relation to the small leather goods type and relate to the product being carried or protected.

MATERIALS

Often exclusively made of leather surplus, the leather properties and characteristics need to be suitable for the product and the construction methods. Strong, thin leathers are best suited for wallets and purses with bank card inserts, since bulk is always going to be an issue with the many folded edges, overlaps, and seams. Cowhide is used in the majority of small leather goods, but exotics such as ostrich, snake, reptile, stingray, and fish skins are often used for their decorative qualities. Lining materials need to be hardwearing and thin—polyester, silk, cotton, and cotton mixes are common.

CONSTRUCTIONS

Techniques follow bag construction and seam types already discussed in the Handbags section (see pages 102–105 and 116–117).

Raw-edge construction is one of the most basic seams used. The seams are stitched on the right side of the material. The stitch line and the actual edge of the material are on view. The raw-edge seam allows for a variety of treatments and finishes to be applied to the leather edge. (Please note that if fabric is used it will fray.)

▲ **Novelty items** An unusual arrowhead buckle gives this belt an element of humor.

◀ **Small leather goods** An opportunity for anyone to own a little bit of designer heaven.

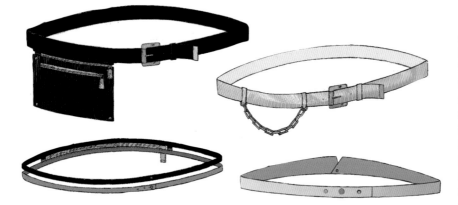

▲ **Belts** Early sketches for a collection of belts with added embellishments, such as a zippered pouch, a chain, and studs.

Butted construction is where the material is turned over on the edge. It could be turned and stuck on to a reinforcement or onto itself before stitching together.

Molded construction is where the leather is stretched over a mold and glued together. A box or photograph frame covered in leather is a good example of this.

Turned construction is where the product is sewn right sides together and then turned the right way around after stitching.

These constructions can be used individually or in combination, depending on your design. Closely aligned to construction methods are seam types, which can be found in the Handbags section (see pages 116–117); seam types include butted seam, turned seam, boot seam, lap seam, jeans seam, and taped seam.

As well as seam types, there are certain details that can be added to seams for both construction purposes and decorative effects (see page 117), such as piping, binding, and French binding.

FITTINGS AND HARDWARE

Fittings and hardware need to be explored in relation to the particular small leather goods you are designing. Small leather goods often form part of a line of products, so design details may already have been determined by the key handbag pieces in the collection. Scale of detail needs to be considered because small leather goods are usually small in size. Can hardware/trims be sourced in a variety of sizes? Is a closure required—zipper, snap, magnetic lock, or tie? How secure does the closure need to be? Explore by sketching a variety of methods before choosing, and investigate placement of, amount of, and scale of details and trims before decisions are made.

DESIGN CONSIDERATIONS FOR BELTS

At their most basic, belts are single leather straps that are available in a variety of lengths, colors, and widths, with buckles as the fastening mechanism. Belts are often designed and made by specialist belt companies whose product focus is solely on belts; however, they are also often included in an accessory line, extending the brand and offering entry-price-point accessories to the consumer. Belts can be both functional and decorative, and trends are driven by the clothing trends for the season, e.g. low-slung hipsters require a very different style and size of belt than a high-waisted pencil skirt, so trends need to be observed and taken on board when designing belts.

MATERIALS

Belts can be made from a wide range of materials and leathers. The choice of material has a huge impact on the design, e.g. a raw-edge belt can only be made successfully if bridle leather is used (see page 207). For a raw-edge belt, the best leather is cowhide that has been vegetable tanned, and the best part of the hide to use is the butt. The leather from the butt is strong and even in grain and substance.

Goat and lamb skin are also used, but usually need to be backed/reinforced and the edges turned. Exotic leathers are often used, and these include snakeskin, lizard, crocodile/alligator, ostrich, stingray, and shark. These are often backed to give substance to the belt.

BELT SIZES

Size	Women's	Men's
Small	22–24 in. (56–61 cm)	30–32 in. (76–81 cm)
Medium	26–28 in. (66–71 cm)	34–36 in. (86–91 cm)
Large	30–32 in. (76–81 cm)	38–40 in. (96–101 cm)
Extra large	34–36 in. (86–91 cm)	42–44 in. (106–111 cm)

HARDWARE AND CONSTRUCTION

Belts need to be fastened and the most common fastening is a buckle. Most buckles are made out of some form of metal—common metals and alloys that are used for buckle manufacture are nickel, brass, and zinc alloy (for more on fittings, see pages 100–101).

Construction methods for belts are the same as for small leather goods and bags (see pages 102–103). Edge options include turned, raw edge, butted, and molded.

Consideration needs to be given to materials in relation to construction methods, and, in addition, different types of leather may need to be sourced. Descriptions of these can be found above with the small leather goods and fuller details can be found in the bag section (see pages 74–119).

SIZES

Sizes usually correspond to the waist measurement and span the more common size ranges for men and women (see panel, left); however, sizes are often classified as small, medium, large, and extra large. Belts are often adjustable and can span 4 in. (10 cm).

DESIGN CONSIDERATIONS FOR GLOVES

Gloves are unlike any other accessory, in that the success of the glove design is heavily reliant upon the materials chosen by the designer. The fit of the glove is determined by the quality and stretch of the material and the skill of the cutter who stretches out the leather in preparation for cutting. It takes three years to master the cutting trade. Gloves are cut with the stretch going around the hand—if they were cut with the stretch running down the length of the hand and fingers, each time we pulled the fingers to remove the gloves we would be stretching them.

The pattern and construction is a key indicator of the quality and value of the glove. The most expensive gloves are constructed with a double fourchette and quirk—the fourchette is the gusset that fits inside two adjacent fingers, and the quirk is the piece that connects the fingers at the base of the fingers. The quirk allows for extra comfort, added movement, and a more contoured fit. Standard patterns are often adapted for a design, and each size of glove will have its own set of patterns.

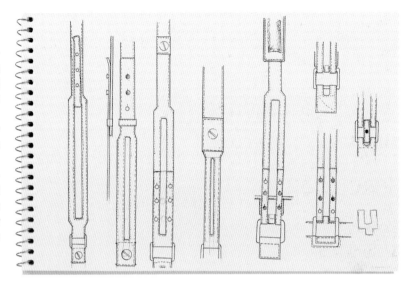

▲ It's in the detail
With all small leather goods, it's important to pay attention to detail. This sketch pad explores lots of options on the same theme.

▶ Prototypes
Prototypes are tried out in leather before design adjustments are made.

MATERIALS

Whatever product you are making, your materials and leathers need to be selected carefully and with knowledge of how the leather/materials will perform (see page 206). When sourcing, it is advisable to seek advice from your manufacturer. Note that quality gloves must be made from specialist gloving leather to ensure elasticity and suppleness (see page 206 for more information on gloving leather).

FUNCTION AND PRACTICALITY

Identifying the consumer helps to determine where the consumer will be wearing the gloves and for what purpose. Gloves are seasonally biased and are only included in Fall/Winter collections. Most gloves are considered practical, but some are more about making a fashion statement, so you need to establish the level of practicality that is required for your design project. Recently there has been a trend for gloves that have the first finger or part of the first finger exposed and fingerless gloves that just cover the lower knuckles

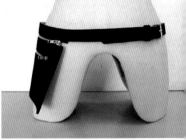

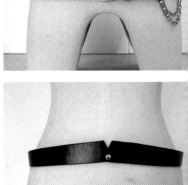

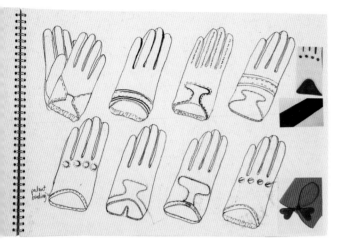

◄ **Sketch pad** (far left) Here the designer explores different styles of glove opening. Even a simple, functional object like a glove can lend itself to myriad design options.

into construction methods is essential, and direction from the manufacturer is advised here.

Seams can be raw edge or turned. Whether the seams are hand stitched or machined is often determined by price point.

One of the most important things that must be considered at the design stage is the passage of the hand in and out of the glove—the palm of the hand is much wider than the wrist so the opening presents us with a design issue that needs to be resolved

FORM

The form of a glove is to an extent prescribed by the shape of the hand and fingers, but there is scope for creativity: extended cuffs, cutouts, and so on.

PROPORTION, BALANCE, AND LINE

Of all accessories, gloves are under perhaps our closest scrutiny because they are often close to the face and in our line of eye. Proportion can be distorted through the use of fur. Fingers can appear shortened if overly decorated. Balance of detail across the pair, whether matched or intentionally mismatched, is something to explore through your development of ideas.

DETAILS

Details mainly focus on the trank of the glove, which is the main part of the glove, particularly across the back of the hand. Points (back lines) are often seen, which are three lines of stitching that point to the apex at the base of the fingers. Fancy stitch detailing and ridged tucks are also used on the points. Further areas for design detail can include the wrist area—exploring entrance and exit of the hand—and opening and closure details. Gauntlet/cuff length type and shape can be investigated, and so can fingers, details up or around the fingers, and whether the gloves are full fingered or fingerless. Edge trims, bound edges, and decoratively stitched edges should all be areas of exploration and investigation at the design stage.

FITTINGS

Fittings can be both decorative and practical. They are often used for closures—buttons, eyelets, hooks/ribbons, zippers, snaps, and buckles are often seen, but

on the hand. This is in part due to the increased use of smartphones with touch-sensitive screens. You may need to consider this and design in features for your gloves that accommodate this relatively new technological phenomenon.

STYLE

What style is suitable or appropriate? This very much depends on the target consumer, your brief, and the design aesthetic of the line.

FIT

Leather gloves need to have a tight, smooth fit, so offering a range of sizes is very important. You need to consider this during collection planning. Leather gloves mold and shape to the hand with wear. To correctly measure a hand to establish the size required, wrap the tape measure around the back of the hand over the knuckles and around the palm—do not include the thumb. Close the fingers to make a fist and read off the measurement.

Top-quality gloves are sized in French inches—a Charlemagne foot is 11 in. (28 cm), unlike the imperial measurement, which is 12 in. (30 cm) to the foot. Less expensive gloves are often more generically sized.

CONSTRUCTION

Construction needs to be decided upon at the design stage, since this will impact on the overall appearance and also impact on the cost of manufacture. Research

▲▼ **Mittens rock** In these rough sketches for design prototypes, the designer has been mindful of how the glove should slip on and off the hand. Here, the focus is on lacing.

researching other options is always recommended. These need to be explored for both aesthetic and practical purposes, and sometimes adjustments made to compromise one for the other.

KEY STAGES

What to consider when designing small leather goods, belts, and gloves:

- Brief
- Season
- Consumer
- Color
- Materials
- Function and practicality
- Style
- Fit
- Constructions
- Form
- Proportion, balance, and line
- Details
- Fittings
- Hardware

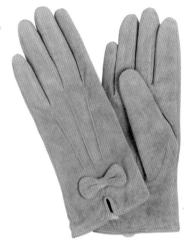

COMPONENTS

1 Trank The main part of the glove that consists of the front, back, and fingers.

2 Fourchette The gusset that runs between each finger of the glove to give shape and aid movement. A double fourchette is the gusset that fits inside two adjacent fingers. This is used in conjunction with a quirk—there are three per glove.

3 Thumb piece This folds in half and is inserted into 4.

4 Thumb opening Shaped insertion point for thumb piece.

Quirk: (not shown) A small, usually diamond-shaped, gusset used in conjunction with the double fourchette. The quirk is fitted to the base of the adjoining fingers at the inside of the glove. The quirk allows for extra comfort/flexibility and a better fit.

▲ **Points** Three decorative lines of stitching, called points, run down the back of the trank from just below the base of the first, second, and third fingers. The middle trank is always slightly longer than the others. Traditionally the average lengths of these are 2–3 in. (6–7 cm).

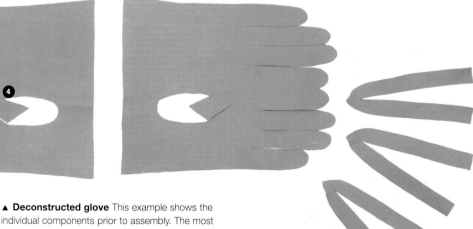

▲ **Deconstructed glove** This example shows the individual components prior to assembly. The most important consideration, apart from the beauty of the leather, is fit. This is owed to the skill of the master cutter, and a different pattern is required for each individual size.

Resources and professional practice

A successful career in any field depends on many things, and one of the most important factors is that you love what you do. We all enjoy doing what we do well, and the sense of achievement from being good at something gives us confidence. Some people are fortunate in that they know from an early age exactly what they want to do. Others, even when they know where their talents lie, have to investigate all the options to find a career that inspires them.

This final section will offer some practical advice and skills, and suggest routes to help you find a direction that's right for you and help you on your chosen path. From applying to college programs to preparing your résumé and learning about trade fairs, it is all covered here.

5 STEPS TO SUCCESS

Objective Working in the industry is sometimes difficult, always interesting, and in a successful season a real joy; if you are passionate about accessories, this is the career for you. You will require a lot of patience, passion, and hard work. Here we pinpoint five steps to get you on the right path to a successful career.

BE PROFESSIONAL

It is never too early to start working toward your future. In any situation, there are certain qualities that are necessary whatever the role, and you can start to develop these at an early age. Punctuality, reliability, good time management, and the motivation to work hard are essential. Having good manners, working well within a team, and being able to communicate with people will make you more effective in anything you undertake. Personal presentation should be considered too: a well-groomed appearance will not go unnoticed.

Similarly, some basic skills are required whatever your career aspirations. A good level of numeracy and written and oral skills in your native language are vital. Knowledge of the English language, too, is essential if you plan to study or work in the United States, U.K., and many other parts of the world. Computer skills are also key in our global society. At a minimum you should be able to produce well-presented, word-processed written work and communicate clearly via e-mail. The ability to create tables and charts is also very useful.

LEARN ABOUT THE INDUSTRY

Once you have decided that a career in the accessories industry is the right choice, you can start to develop your understanding of the area. A good way to do this is to get a Saturday or vacation job as a sales assistant in a store that sells the type of accessories you like. Through this you will learn about the products on offer and the needs of the customers that you serve. Your confidence in communicating with people will develop both in your role as an employee and in serving the public. This experience will also demonstrate your serious interest in accessories when applying for acceptance to a college.

RESEARCH PROGRAMS

You should investigate the different programs offered and find out the entry requirements for those you are interested in. Ensure your studies at school cover the required areas and work hard to achieve the results you need. Develop your drawing skills, and start to prepare your portfolio. Choosing exactly the right program, and the right school/college is the next step. Draw up a shortlist and try to go to the open days of all the schools/colleges you have selected. You will not only get more information through doing this but also the chance to speak to current students and sense the atmosphere. It is a good idea to apply for several programs to stand the best chance of being accepted. Once you have decided, put your application in on time and get your portfolio ready for interviews.

WHILE YOU ARE STUDYING

When you have started on your program, take every opportunity to learn. Students who prepare for and attend every class, practice what they are taught, are curious and ask questions, and hand in every assignment on time are more successful than those who don't. Many colleges offer extra support for some areas of study; take advantage of everything available to help you improve.

During your program do one or more internships or part-time jobs to gain experience and an understanding of the language and culture of the commercial world. In this environment you will start to make contacts and develop a professional network. This will add to the quality of your résumé and give you confidence when being interviewed.

As you near graduation, you need to start working toward getting a job. Prepare your résumé and a mini portfolio—send this to every company you would like to work for and invite them to your final show. Register with recruitment agencies, and apply for any jobs that are advertised. Some students are lucky and are offered jobs at their final show or by a company they have interned with; others have to work much harder to secure their first job. Make sure you and your portfolio are ready for interview. For many students this is a difficult time, since they find themselves up against the competitive world outside and no longer sheltered by the academic environment. This is when self-motivation, determination, and self-belief are vital; keep trying—there will be something out there for you.

THE WORLD OF EMPLOYMENT

Once you start your first job, you will find that you still have a lot to learn. The expectations of your company will help you to develop into an experienced professional. You will have to work at a fast pace using the company systems, have a good memory, and be accurate in everything you do. Loyalty to the company and discretion will be taken for granted. During the season you will be expected to work long hours without extra pay and often your job will involve travel or representing your department at events in the evening. At busy times your personal life will be nonexistent, since you will have to respond to whatever is required, often at short notice.

As you gain experience, you will take on more responsibility, move into more senior roles, and probably move from company to company. If things go well, eventually you will realize you have reached the position you envied when you started out in your first job.

KEY STAGES

- Develop basic qualities and skills.
- Get a part-time job that involves working with accessories.
- Investigate programs.
- Take the right classes for entry to college and prepare your portfolio.
- Apply and prepare for interview.
- Work hard throughout your program to develop your knowledge and skills.
- Do as many internships and part-time or vacation jobs as possible to get a range of experience.
- Prepare your résumé and a mini portfolio prior to graduation.
- Send your details out to every company you would like to work for and apply for any positions that are advertised.
- Register with agencies that deal with graduate positions.
- Never give up: you will get that crucial first job if you keep trying.

PORTFOLIO PRESENTATION

Objective Construct a portfolio that showcases your talent.

Your portfolio is crucial to your success. It is a visual celebration of your design aesthetic, demonstrating your skills and knowledge. The optimum number of projects in a portfolio is six. Through these you should highlight your strengths and avoid displaying your weaknesses. Different jobs require different approaches to design and particular sets of skills. You should have 10 projects available from which you will choose the six most appropriate for the interview in question.

When you put your portfolio together, it is a good idea to use the convention of reverse chronological order; the most recent work at the front and the oldest work at the back. The advantage of this is that a prospective employer can see the progression of your skills through the portfolio. If this results in similar projects following each other, you should consider revising the order to create more interest.

For a specific job interview it is often necessary to reorganize your portfolio, to ensure the projects that demonstrate the skills required by the employer are at the front, followed by work that shows the full range of skills you have to offer. If your work varies in quality, make sure the first project is fantastic to get the interview panel involved, and equally the last piece of work should leave your audience with a good impression. The most important thing is that the work is exciting enough to make the audience want to keep turning the pages.

PLAN THE FORMAT

Choose a strong portfolio that will protect your work, travel well, and last a long time. Look at portfolios in art and graphic supplies stores; you can't make an informed choice if you don't know what is available. The standard size is 11 in. x 14 in (28 cm x 35 cm). Buy the best-quality plastic sleeves that you can afford—the clearer and finer they are, the better your work will look.

It is important to decide on the orientation of your portfolio: landscape or portrait. There is nothing more irritating than having to turn a portfolio around to see the contents properly. You need to make your portfolio as user-friendly as possible so that the focus is on the content.

▲ Keep the audience interested Subtle use of color, and an interesting mix of inspirational imagery convey the mood of the project in this portfolio. It draws you in immediately and makes you want to turn the page to see what comes next.

◄ Plan Although the content varies heavily between these two pages, together they tell a story and show a range of skills. Experimentation and the influence of the inspiration is clearly visible in the final product line.

Consider the skills that are required in the workplace and your strengths. Then, if you are applying for a specific job, highlight the skills outlined in the job description. This should help you to put your portfolio together in a way that will emphasize your strengths and address the needs of a prospective employer.

PLAN THE CONTENT

Once you have analyzed the skills you wish to display, you need to decide on the content for each project in your portfolio. You should vary the content so that your portfolio does not appear formulaic while making sure that within the projects you have examples of all the different aspects of your work. Always have sketchbooks available. They should be tucked into the pocket of your portfolio or arranged at the back in consecutive order so that you can present them with ease as you start talking through each project.

Finally you should decide on the presentation style in detail. You should have used the same paper throughout each individual project, but the paper could vary from one project to another. If you feel that it is wrong to have different papers in your portfolio, you could reprint or color photocopy the projects that are on a different background to create a unified look. Always use the best-quality paper you can find. The title pages might be in the same paper as the project they are introducing or you could use the same paper and style for each title page for continuity. Always opt for the most visually appealing result.

Always check that your portfolio is clean and free from dust or crumbs before attending an interview. It is unprofessional to present anything that is less than immaculate. Many people make this mistake; don't let it be you.

The time spent preparing your portfolio is a good investment. The result should be professional, provide a focus for discussion, and above all, be exciting. Being enthusiastic about your portfolio will allow you to relax and perform confidently in an interview situation, giving you the best possible chance of landing the job you desire.

▼ **Focus on content** When putting together her portfolio, this designer has taken care to orientate everything in portrait format, enabling the viewer to concentrate on the content. A professional finish is achieved by using the same paper throughout.

KEY ELEMENTS TO PRESENT IN YOUR PORTFOLIO

Skills
- Research
- Hand drawing
- Design
- Illustration
- Use of color
- Use of materials—attach swatches of real materials/samples of techniques where possible
- Technical drawing
- Technical knowledge
- Product development knowledge
- Market awareness
- Marketing knowledge
- IT

Content
- Mood/concept/consumer/details board
- Customer profile
- Trend forecast
- Line plan
- Design development sheets including technical details
- Photographs of finished products/prototypes
- Specification sheet
- Product development processes
- Point-of-sale/marketing material
- Sketchbooks—keep them in the pocket of your portfolio or tucked in safely at the back

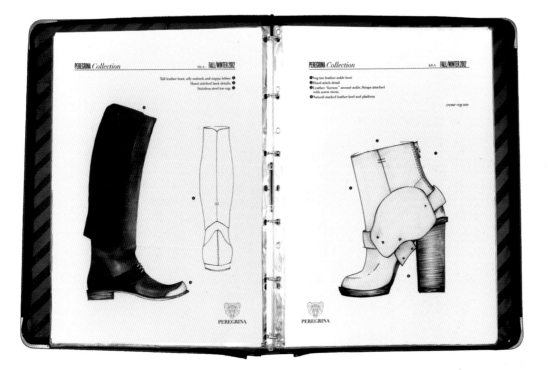

CREATING YOUR RÉSUMÉ

Objective Learn how to create an effective résumé.

Your résumé—a document outlining your personal details, education, skills, and experience—is a crucial professional tool used to target your industry and the job you desire. It is your initial introduction to a company and your future success will depend on it.

RÉSUMÉ APPROACHES

If you are interested in a specific job or in working for a particular company, you can be sure that many others will be too. Every day hundreds of résumés are thrown in the garbage because they don't address the specific situation, they are too wordy, they contain mistakes, or they are just badly constructed. Do not let that happen to you.

The information that goes into a résumé should tell a prospective employer what you are potentially capable of in relation to that company. It should reflect your personality and your strengths, fit the industry you are aiming at, and show that you have the skills needed for the job.

You should prepare a standard résumé with all the relevant information, but every time you approach a company or apply for a specific job, you should tailor your résumé to match the needs of the situation. Check the job description to identify what is important within the role or check the Web site to find out as much as possible about the company and what career opportunities are available. Target the requirements outlined by the employer by addressing them in the content of your résumé. It is useful to change the order of the information you provide to match the order of the skills and experience listed in the job description. This makes it much clearer and easier for the recipient to react to and demonstrates your analytical ability.

Use your design skills to advantage by demonstrating that you can create an informative and visually impressive document that will attract attention from an employer. Keep it clear, clean, and simple; your audience needs to see the information at a glance. Choose the font and layout carefully; you need to highlight the areas that are of importance in the job you are applying for through your presentation style. Use different sizes of font, bold, and italic to draw attention to specific things. A dense, overcrowded page will put the recipient off; space is a very important part of the presentation.

THE CONTENT

The content should be organized in a logical order and cover the following areas, with a title for each section.

PERSONAL DETAILS:
Name, address, e-mail address, and telephone number.

PERSONAL OBJECTIVES:
A short introductory statement describing what sort of person you are, what you want to do, and why you think you have what it takes. This should be expressed succinctly using businesslike terminology. For example: "Creative accessories design graduate, experienced in working with a team to a client's brief and delivering relevant solutions on time."

THINGS TO AVOID

- Do not use imagery behind text.
- Do not use your résumé to show your drawing skills.
- Do not have an unprofessional e-mail address (for example, "shoequeen@...").
- Do not overwhelm your reader with a dense, text-heavy résumé.
- Do not tell your life history.
- Do not send the same résumé out to everyone but research each company you apply to, then modify your résumé to suit. If you are applying for a position that has been advertised, examine the job description carefully and tailor your résumé information to enhance the areas where you match the description.

POINTS TO REMEMBER

- Keep your résumé to one page if possible, never more than two—it should be succinct.
- Use a heading for each section.
- Use good-quality paper if presenting a hard copy.
- If sending by e-mail, make sure it is readable on screen.
- Organize information in a logical sequence.
- Always start with current information, then work backward in reverse chronological order.
- Use the present tense when referring to your current situation and the past tense for previous experiences.
- Ask someone to proofread your résumé to ensure the information is correct and that there are no spelling mistakes or grammatical errors.

EMPLOYMENT:

Start with your current job and work backward. State the start and finish dates for each job, the company name, your position, and the key aspects of your role. Highlight the experience that is relevant to the position you are applying for.

EDUCATION AND TRAINING:

Start with the most recent and work backward in reverse chronological order. Do not go back further than high school. Include any relevant training courses you have done since leaving school. Even a first aid course could be useful, since every company needs people trained in this area.

COMPETITIONS, AWARDS, AND EXHIBITIONS:

Start with the latest and work backward chronologically. List any competitions or awards you have won or been shortlisted for and any exhibitions of your work.

SKILLS PROFILE:

List your skills in the order they appear within the job description. If you are not applying for a specific job, then list your skills in order of proficiency within each category.

In this section you should outline:

- IT and CAD skills, listing all relevant applications and level of expertise.
- Technical skills, relevant to the job you are applying for.
- Language skills, stating the level, i.e. fluent or conversational.
- Management skills: Creative thinking, time and project management, communication, team working, self-motivation, problem solving, etc.
- Driver's license.

RELEVANT INTERESTS:

Anything that demonstrates skills or qualities such as organization, leadership, motivation, teamwork, or charity work should be included. For example "running" is not informative, but "Completed the New York marathon in 2011 and raised $2,000 for breast cancer awareness" gives a sense of you as a person.

REFERENCES:

Always state "References available on request." You may have several options of references, and will want to use the most appropriate people. It is polite to contact your chosen references each time you wish to use them.

SAMUEL SHEPHERD SHOE DESIGNER

Here the candidate gives an idea of who he is and what influences his design signature.

List work experience starting with your current job and working backward. Avoid appearing over-qualified if you're applying for entry-level positions.

Contact Information
Tel: 215-555-1234
Email: samuel@emailaddress.com
Address: 14 Example Street, New York, 10001, NY
Online portfolio: www.yourwebsitehere.com
Full Driver's License

Personal Statement
Fresh, passionate individual with an innovative eye for footwear design and a growing interest and understanding of the fashion footwear industry and of today's consumer. A love for craftsmanship and his signature quirky individual styling, which both challenges and pushes boundaries in design and construction.

Professional Experience/Employment

07/2009–05/2010 Jonathan Kelsey Ltd
- Working as Jonathan's intern, supporting all areas of his own line business and freelance for Mulberry, Matthew Williamson, Hunter and Richard Nicoll.
- Researching and designing winter and summer lines. Attending Lineapelle in Italy with Jonathan and factory visit.
- Supporting press office with sample requests and publication communications.
- General office management including liaising with factories and clients, office administration such as customer invoices and line sheets.

11/2009–08/2010 Kurt Geiger Ltd
- Men's design intern working with designers and contributing to designing lines.
- Attending trend meetings, outlining the future lines.
- Store reports and competitor analysis, undertaken practically on main street.
- Footwear designed features in the F/W 10 and S/S11 ranges for KG and French Connection men's.

08/2010–10/2010 Yellowdoor
- Worked alongside the Art Directors in the studio with advertising campaigns, window displays and event design. Design work for large mall.
- Supported Mary Portas with a new project that included working alongside Clarks and visiting their head office.
- Worked with the team on a photographic shoot for Clarks Originals, which included artistic visuals, model and photographer sourcing, and going on location to photograph the campaign.

Education

2010–2011 Savannah College of Art and Design
School of Fashion Accessory Design
MFA in Accessory Design

2006–2010 Parson The New School for Design
BFA in Fashion Design

2002–2006 Example High School

Using reverse chronological order all relevant education is listed.

Achievements
- Awarded Cordwainers Scholarship award in 2009 for my second year final major project.
- Designs selected to be presented to Kangaroo in a recent collaboration with the College.
- Course representative for the College committee

Skills
Creative
- Excellent all-round skills with not just an awareness of design, but business.
- Market, customer, and brand always explored in depth in all design work with an overall intention to provide a line for the target customer.
- Design work demonstrates designs sheets, line plans, specification sheets, store reports, cost and supply.
- Electives have been taken in surface enhancement for leather and buying and merchandise.
- Attended Lineapelle from 2008 to 2010 sourcing materials and gaining industry contacts.

The level, breadth, and range of creative skills are outlined here.

Technical
- Confident and expanding understanding of pattern cutting and construction including stitching, laser engraving, and leather properties all of which recorded in a technical file.
- Can apply and understand the shoe making process from heel construction, lasting, sole units and insoles with the appropriate technical terminology.

The range of understanding and the potential application of knowledge and essential skills are shown.

IT
- Confident user of Photoshop, Illustrator, InDesign all Office packages and Romans CAD.

Interests
- Fashion, art, reading—particularly on fashion culture and business.
- Tennis at a competitive level including several doubles tournament wins. Swimming and skiing. Interest in stand-up comedy and completed a "Stand up and Deliver" course in May 2010.

References available on request.

SECTION 6 | RESOURCES AND
PROFESSIONAL PRACTICE

CREATING YOUR COVER LETTER

Objective Create a letter outlining the position you are applying for and what you can do for the company based on your company research.

A cover letter outlines to a prospective employer the position you are interested in and why you would be a suitable candidate. Together with your résumé, your cover letter is your first impression on the company to which you are applying.

COVER LETTER CONTENT

A cover letter should be concise and to the point. Every cover letter should be customized to fit the company you are contacting. Consider the content very carefully; this should not be a repeat of the information on your résumé. This is your opportunity to sell yourself and show something of your personality. Before you begin the letter, you should do some research to find out as much as possible about the company you are writing to. It is good practice to check out the career opportunities on the company Web site, and find out the name of the person you should write to, particularly if you are applying speculatively.

If you are applying for a specific job, start by stating the job you are applying for and where you saw it advertised. If you are approaching the company to inquire about opportunities, you should explain the type of job or internship you are looking for.

Next, outline what you are doing at present, in detail, whether you are in employment or a student. Outline the skills you have that relate to the job advertised and state where and how you gained each of these skills—part-time work, education, internship, your current job, etc. If you are approaching the company speculatively, you should outline all the skills you have that apply to the particular area you wish to work in and explain where and how these skills were acquired.

Then explain what you know about the company and outline what in particular attracts you to it. This is your opportunity to show that you have been proactive in researching the company.

End with a short statement saying how you would appreciate the chance to discuss the job or future opportunities in person. You could add your availability for interview if you are approaching the company without responding to an advertisement.

COVER LETTER FORMAT

- The letter should be type written and only one page in length.
- The style of the letter should be similar to that of your résumé to create a unified look.
- The standard format is to put your address at the top right-hand side, then the name and address of the person you are writing to on the left-hand side, and the date on the right-hand side. As a designer, you might want to offer something more creative than the traditional format. It is important to retain clarity of communication if you choose a different style.
- Either start with "Dear Mrs. Smith" and end with "Yours sincerely" OR start with "Dear Sir/Madam" and end with "Yours faithfully."
- If a hard copy is required, use good-quality paper.
- When your letter is finished, make sure you get someone to proofread it for you and correct any errors. Something as simple as a spelling mistake or grammatical error can result in rejection.

CURRENT PRACTICE

It is now more usual for résumés and cover letters to be sent by e-mail and for a company to request a mini-portfolio of work to be attached. This consists of four or five pages of images of your work that give a flavor of your strengths as a researcher, designer, and collection builder. There is also something to be said for mailing a hard copy of your résumé with examples of your work as it will make your work stand out more than a generic e-mail. Make sure you always have your mini-portfolio available and updated. This also applies to your résumé. As soon as you have acquired a new skill or won a competition, etc., you should add it to your résumé. Once you have a track record within your chosen field of design, this must be managed carefully so that your résumé is not overloaded with information. Select your key successes and highlight those, removing lower-level achievements.

POINTS TO CONSIDER

Use professional, empowering language in relation to your skills and experience to enhance your cover letter:
Achieved. Attended. Coordinated. Created. Designed. Developed. Established. Negotiated. Organized. Planned. Supported.

Use professional terminology when commenting on transferable skills; this is particularly important if you are highlighting a skill that you obtained through experience in a different industry:
Adaptable. Communication. Determination. Initiative. Leadership. Organization. Self-motivation. Teamwork. Time management.

David Wilson
Any Design Group
1 Design Avenue
London
SW1 4EG

ALISON SMITH
a.smith@example.com
123 Example Lane
Chicago IL
312-555-4321

May 7, 2011

Dear Mr Wilson,

I am currently studying for an honors degree in Footwear Design at Cordwainers @ London College of Fashion, University of the Arts, London, from which I graduated in July 2011.

Since seeing your collection at Première Classe in Paris I have been inspired by your work and followed your progress in the press. I found the recent profile of your company in Wallpaper really interesting as it revealed more of the personality of your business.

My degree course has given me the opportunity to be creative within a marketing framework; designing for a purpose. As you can see from my résumé I am adept at CAD as well as freehand drawing and 3D development. My time management and team working skills developed significantly during my internship through being made responsible for the successful organization, delivery, and quality of sample production for the design team.

From your web site I see that you are launching a graduate program for young designers. I would very much like to show you my portfolio with a view to being considered for this program. It would be an excellent opportunity to learn more about all aspects of design in the commercial world. I believe the skills and knowledge I have would, in return, add value to your team.

I look forward to hearing from you.

Yours sincerely,

Alison Smith

Example: The same letter shown in a traditional format and a more creative presentation.

ALISON SMITH
a.smith@example.com 312-555-4321
123 Example Lane Chicago IL

Dear Mr Wilson,   May 7, 2011

I am currently studying for an honors degree in Footwear Design at Cordwainers @ London College of Fashion, University of the Arts, London, from which I graduated in July 2011.

Since seeing your collection at Première Classe in Paris I have been inspired by your work and followed your progress in the press. I found the recent profile of your company in Wallpaper really interesting as it revealed more of the personality of your business.

My degree course has given me the opportunity to be creative within a marketing framework; designing for a purpose. As you can see from my résumé I am adept at CAD as well as freehand drawing and 3D development. My time management and team working skills developed significantly during my internship through being made responsible for the successful organization, delivery, and quality of sample production for the design team.

From your web site I see that you are launching a graduate program for young designers. I would very much like to show you my portfolio with a view to being considered for this program. It would be an excellent opportunity to learn more about all aspects of design in the commercial world. I believe the skills and knowledge I have would, in return, add value to your team.

I look forward to hearing from you.

Yours sincerely,

Alison Smith

DAVID WILSON
Any Design Group
1 Design Avenue London SW1 4EG

SECTION 6 | RESOURCES AND
PROFESSIONAL PRACTICE

INTERVIEW

Objective Guidelines on
how to prepare for and
perform at interview.

Your résumé and cover letter have impressed the company you applied to, and you have been invited to an interview. Reply politely accepting the appointment and saying how much you are looking forward to meeting the person conducting the interview.

PLAN AHEAD

Find out exactly where the interview is being held, work out your journey in advance, and estimate the time it will take. Plan to arrive 10 minutes early, allow extra time for delays, and set your departure time accordingly. Take the letter confirming your appointment with you so that you have the contact details available should anything go wrong.

Prepare your portfolio carefully. Make sure everything is in pristine condition. Think about what is required in the job you are being interviewed for. Your portfolio should display all of the skills you have that relate to the job. Select the most appropriate projects for an interview and put them in order to highlight particular skills.

You might be nervous in an interview situation and need to appear professional and knowledgeable. Practice presenting your portfolio before an interview; get to know the content and what you want to say about it. Talk positively and enthusiastically about your work. The title pages will help you; they act as a reminder when your attention has been diverted by questions from an interview panel. Offer your sketchbook to the panel before talking through a project; it provides another focus if there is more than one person interviewing and shows off your research skills and breadth of ideas.

Research the company to ensure that you come across as knowledgeable at interview and to avoid asking irrelevant questions. Make sure you know about all the ranges and visit retail outlets to find out exactly what the products look like and how they are marketed. If you have been provided with a job description, go over it and analyze exactly what is required by the company. Think about how you can prove that you have the skills, knowledge, and personal qualities needed to perform in the role. This is your opportunity to display your personal qualities as well as your portfolio to the interview panel. Do not be tempted to pretend you can do things that you can't; be straightforward about gaps in your knowledge.

Think about the type of questions you might be asked. The interviewer will want to know why you are interested in the role, what attracts you to the company, and what skills you can offer. More importantly they will want to know about you as a person. Be prepared to talk about your strengths and weaknesses. You might

UNCOMMON INTERVIEW QUESTIONS
(THAT YOU MAY STILL GET ASKED!)

- What color was the door to this office?
- What makes you laugh?
- Who would you invite to your fantasy dinner party, and why?
- What else have you applied for?
- When did you last get angry/cry?
- Tell me a joke.

be asked to describe a difficult situation you encountered and how you solved the problem. You could be asked what you consider to be your greatest achievement. You will be asked about your aspirations; describe your dream job and where you see yourself in five years. Make sure you are aware of developments and new designers in your field and that you can talk about them. Standard questions are: Whose work do you admire? Which magazines do you read? Don't go for the obvious; make your answer interesting, proving you have a passionate interest in your specialist area.

Prepare a list of questions in advance that focus on the company and the job. Remember what you want to ask if the information is not made clear during the interview. It is inappropriate to ask about the salary at a first interview. If you were offered the position, this would be negotiated before you signed a contract with the company. It is more important to ask questions about the size of the team you would be working with, how many people you would report to, or what you would be responsible for to come across as serious and professional.

Think about what you are going to wear and prepare your outfit. You should present yourself with as much care as your portfolio. Dress in an appropriate manner for the company you are being interviewed by. Whatever your style, you must pay attention to your hair and nails—they should be immaculate. Make sure your outfit is clean and pressed and that your accessories are spotless. Avoid wearing jewelry that makes a noise; a bracelet that rattles as you go through your portfolio can be distracting.

THE INTERVIEW

Arrive at the venue, present yourself to reception, and ask for the person you have the appointment with, explaining you are there for an interview. Consider your body language, walk tall, sit up straight, and relax. Greet people with a handshake, a smile, and make eye contact. This will give an air of confidence. Do not cross your legs, play with your hair, or look down at the table or desk. Don't feel the need to fill silences with endless chatter. You need to be seen to be calm and in control. Your résumé has demonstrated that you are qualified for the job; the interview will now gauge how well you would fit into the existing team, as well as giving you the opportunity to elaborate on your résumé and cover letter. Before going into the actual interview, take three deep breaths to relax your body.

At the end of the interview, thank the panel for their time and the opportunity to meet them.

CREATE A GOOD IMPRESSION

- Dress appropriately
- Arrive 10 minutes early
- Greet people with a handshake and a smile
- Make eye contact
- Speak clearly and confidently
- Answer questions honestly
- Be relaxed and enthusiastic
- Ask thoughtful questions

And remember...

The outcome of most interviews is decided in the first two minutes. First impressions really count.

POTENTIAL CAREERS

Objective Learn about careers in the accessories industry.

A whole range of potential careers exists in the accessories industry. From design to delivery, every detail must be taken care of in the right way. To achieve this, it is essential that people with the appropriate skills and knowledge are employed at every stage of the process. Different companies will divide responsibilities in different ways. Everything is interconnected, and each area of development feeds into the next, allowing scope for flexibility where one role dovetails with the next. There are core responsibilities for each career path, but the peripheral duties will differ. In a small company, each member of staff will be expected to cover a wider range of duties while a large company will have clearly defined job specifications for every position. To be successful it is important to understand the whole picture as well as keeping up with developments in your own area of expertise.

BUYER/MERCHANDISER

Although two different jobs, these roles cross over in so many ways that every individual company will have its own remit for each role. A small company might even expect one person to cover both of these areas. Each company will divide up the role and responsibilities in a way that works for its organization.

The buyer has the more creative role in selecting the collection for the season that is right for the target consumer. The merchandiser will have an administrative function in providing figures and financial forecasts to maximize profitability. Once the season budget is set, the categories of product required will be defined and the number of products at each price point in each category. This creates the structure for the collection.

The buyer needs to have an eye for a product that will appeal to the consumer at the price they are prepared to pay and the desired quality level; a balance between understanding figures and being creative are the skills required. Good relationships with suppliers are essential and achieved through clear communication, negotiation, and organization.

The merchandiser decides how the merchandise is allocated to the various retail outlets then analyzes sales and profit constantly. He or she will also organize repeat orders where an item is so popular it is going to sell out before the season is over. Once sales start to drop, the merchandiser will decide which products will be put on sale and what the reduction should be.

Numeracy skills, and the ability to read and understand figures and budgets, together with the relevant computer skills are the most important attributes for this career path. Communication and the ability to organize are important too.

COPYIST

This role is unusual in that it is unique to the millinery business. A copyist will be given a hat together with a card outlining details such as the block number, the size of the ribbon to be used, and the trimming. Working to the measurements of the original hat, the copyist produces an exact replica of the model. Once the copy is finished, it will be presented to the head designer, together with the original, for checking. This is a valuable way to learn more about the millinery business, understand quality standards, and gain experience in making.

DESIGNER

Opportunities for designers exist worldwide at every market level. A designer's responsibilities will vary significantly depending on the size and type of company. A large corporate company may provide a clearly defined job description limiting your role to a specific area that dovetails into the roles of others to create a well-managed whole. A smaller company will probably expect you to perform a much wider range of tasks, be involved in the daily running of the organization, and more flexible in your attitude. Every organization is different, and the way to succeed as a designer is to develop the full range of skills that might be required. There are also many opportunities to work as a freelance designer in the accessories industry; this is a good direction for those who prefer to manage their own work, have a more varied working life, or perhaps work part time. Hand-illustration and CAD skills are of primary importance. Research into trends, the market, the consumer, and finding inspiration are necessary, although in some companies these areas might be covered by other departments. Knowledge and understanding of the technical aspects of the product are of value when creating specification sheets and if visiting manufacturing units to check that samples are being produced in the correct way to achieve the required look. Good communication and time-management skills are also essential for any designer.

DESIGNER-MAKER

A designer-maker needs to have a high level of technical as well as design skills and knowledge of suppliers. The cost of setting up a workshop is the first consideration. Even with the most basic equipment, this will be much more expensive for footwear than accessories. A cooperative venture or renting space in someone else's workshop would reduce your setup costs. If you plan to make everything yourself, your output will be low, and you must be aware of how long everything takes to price your work effectively. To make a living, you will need to target a clientele that can afford one-off, high-cost products. This requires PR in the right place at the right time; you may need to employ someone to do this. You will also need accounting and marketing skills. Striking a balance between what you do and what you pay others to do is crucial to the success of this type of business. Developing a good reputation takes time but will lead to success.

ILLUSTRATOR

Illustrators usually work on a freelance basis for the press, publishers, and advertising agencies. Each job is unique and will have its own, specific brief outlining exactly what is to be illustrated. To add to the mood of the article or publication, illustrators will be chosen for their particular style. A designer who is also a good illustrator can extend his or her freelance opportunities by seeking work in this area. Strong drawing, rendering, and CAD skills are required to be a successful illustrator, together with good communication, negotiation, and time-management skills.

PR (PUBLIC RELATIONS)

This is an ideal career for someone who enjoys being involved in the fashion world and working with people. Small companies will employ a PR agency that works for a range of clientele, often specializing in a particular area such as fashion. Larger companies will have their own PR department. Marketing and organizational skills are essential to promote the designer or company the agency has been commissioned by. In this wide-ranging job, you might be arranging a launch party one day, sending samples out to the press the next, and organizing printing of promotional material the following day. The range of contacts and services required to support the performance of these tasks is vast, and it is vital to manage this database and develop the network continually. A firm but friendly personality and a calm manner are essential qualities for success in PR.

PRODUCT DEVELOPER

The product developer is the link between the designer and production. At the start of the season, the product developer will often be responsible for getting the prototype samples delivered on time to the designer's specification in preparation for line selection. Once a design has been approved, it must be tested for quality and durability. Changes will be made to ensure the final product will perform to the brand and the consumer's requirements and go through the manufacturing process smoothly without losing the essence of the original design. A high level of technical knowledge is needed for this job, together with an eye for detail. Good computer and communication skills are essential too because the product developer must ensure that every detail of the development is recorded and that the final version of the product is approved and specified exactly.

PRODUCTION MANAGER

The production manager oversees all aspects of the production, from beginning to end. This involves estimating quantities of material and ordering it along with all trims and hardware, and ensuring that accessories are made on time and to the required standards, and that they are shipped correctly.

The production process works to the same annual cycle as fashion design. The time frames for those working in production will vary tremendously depending on what kinds of accessories they are producing and for whom, but on average the process starts around a year in advance. The client would start with a design brief, giving an overview as to what they are looking for this season and the kinds of trends they want to see. The production manager would then work with a team to put a strategy together to present to the client. The production team would respond to the client's brief but try to build on it and offer something extra. They would research the market themselves, using information gleaned from shopping trips and other clients, and in their strategy would offer a whole range of options that the client could choose from.

If the client likes what they see, then the factory can go straight into sample production, but the client may well be hearing strategies from a few production companies, so the production managers might end up in a competitive negotiation, with the client playing one factory against the other to get the best ideas for the best prices. Once given the go-ahead, the production manager would send a product brief to the factory to get some samples produced to the specifications that have been set.

The production manager works with the packaging design team to decide what kind of packaging to use and to write the words that would go on the labels (this might sometimes be outsourced to a packaging company).

When the samples come back from the factories, the production manager would present them to the client, and the client might make some changes and then make a final decision about whether to start production. If the order goes ahead, the production manager commissions the factory to make a dozen or so bags, say, which are then sent out to testers—a group of people who use the products and feed back on fit, comfort, and so on—and if that stage all goes to plan, the production manager and technical director would set up a contract seal meeting with the client and get mass production in motion.

Many manufacturers and retailers who design their own product have a whole production team. Production managers there function in much the same way as factory production managers, analyzing and pricing accessories, but they negotiate with factory managers to find the best placement for the specific bags or shoes. They work closely with the designers, merchandisers, and buyers on the details and the embellishments of the accessories and with the production managers in the factories to make sure that the spec packages are followed exactly.

SALES ASSOCIATE
The job of a sales associate is not thought of as glamorous, it's not particularly well paid, and it's certainly not the ultimate goal

---

SARAH KEELING INTERVIEW
PRODUCT DEVELOPMENT ASSISTANT
FRED PERRY

1. How would you describe your company?
Fred Perry is strongly driven by its heritage. Starting as a sportswear brand in 1952, it has developed one of the most enduring and affectionate relationships between youth culture and sportswear. Known mainly for menswear, the company has successfully grown into footwear, accessories, womenswear, and most recently childrenswear. Despite being a popular global brand, Fred Perry strives to maintain its status as a niche brand that lets the product absorb the wearer's individual personality.

2. What are the responsibilities of a product developer?
The main part of my job is to communicate our design team's ideas to our factories in order to produce a line every season that we present to all our markets. This includes day-to-day communication to monitor fabric development, samples, and components. Each season we develop a series of prototype samples that will illustrate any new ideas the design team may have. From these prototypes a 280-piece line is designed, which is communicated to our factories through detailed specification sheets and technical drawings. This two-week period is an intense time for us—there is a lot to do, and we cannot slip on the deadline, since this will affect every deadline in the timeline. Once we have sent all our specs out, factory visits are made to view the samples and make any changes. This is a great time as it's the first time we see a complete sample, and we can make face-to-face decisions with our factories. In addition to developing our seasonal lines, I work on comparison reports to assess our competitors' lines and prices. I work with the rest of the team to negotiate prices with our factories and build our pricing structure for each season.

3. What methods of communication do you use to contact your suppliers?
We find it easier to communicate through e-mail, since this gives us a record of everything that is being said. Often when we need an answer urgently we talk over the phone; however, this can be difficult for our factories as there can be a language barrier.

4. Does your job involve travel?
Yes, I get to travel to our Portuguese factory twice a year for our development trip to view the samples. We spend a lot of time with our suppliers during these trips because it helps to build relationships and understand as much as we can about the current dealings of the factories. I also travel to various trade shows, looking for

for many aspiring fashionistas. However, it is the bedrock of the entire industry.

You need to look after the stock, making sure that everything is in the right place and the floor is well stocked, neat, tidy, and attractive. A really good knowledge of the stock is very helpful, as you can find your customers exactly what they want and make helpful suggestions about alternatives. Some customers will want you to help them to pick out accessories—you must get the balance right between giving the customers all the help they need, and not making them feel pressured or closely watched. If you like interacting with people you haven't met before, you are likely to do well.

For some this is a job with enough variety and stimulation to keep them satisfied for years, but for others it can be a really useful stepping-stone toward another goal within the industry, or a part-time or vacation job while you are studying. Experience on the sales floor will stand you in good stead if you are interested in buying, merchandising, and designing and is essential if you are interested in store management.

SAMPLE ROOM MANAGER

A sample room manger is responsible for organizing the sample room, planning the manufacturing of the samples, overseeing the staff, meeting clients' demands, and maintaining quality. Strong organizational and managerial skills are required, as well as a high level of technical knowledge and the ability to supervise people. The manager also needs to maintain good relationships and negotiate prices with suppliers of materials, components, and fittings to ensure that whatever is needed for a sample is available at the right time at the right price. Knowledge of developments in technology is important too, to ensure the sample room is equipped with the correct up-to-date machinery to remain competitive by being as efficient as possible.

new suppliers and materials inspiration for our design team.

5. Did your BA course give you the skills needed for your job?

My degree gave me a great foundation to pursue all the areas of the footwear industry I was interested in. I was always more of a sample maker than a designer and the degree supported this by giving us time to work with technicians on our practical work and build our individual skills. Also, working through the whole development process with my own designs to a finished sample meant that I understand what information needs to be communicated at each stage to our factory. For my final project, I had to manage each stage of the product development as I was making my own samples. This was great practice for how I communicate to suppliers and manage my time in my job.

❝The development trips are always exciting because you see lots of samples together and it helps to visualize the line as a whole.❞

6. What is the most rewarding feature of your job?

The beginning stages of development are always the most fun. You're working with the factories and fabric suppliers to give you something new and fresh. It's the first time we see something solid and not just a CAD. The development trips are always exciting because you see lots of samples together, and it helps to visualize the line as a whole.

7. What do you like least about your job?

Having to deal with different time zones becomes quite frustrating sometimes. Our Far East factories are 7–8 hours ahead so have pretty much done a full day's work when we arrive in the office at 9 a.m. We have to make the first few hours of our day count and sort out any problems before the factories go home. You can waste a day waiting for a reply sometimes, but it just means you have to be on the ball every morning to make sure you get all the answers you need. Unfortunately, time zones are a factor we have to accept and we adjust the way we work to prevent any problems.

Sarah Keeling
Footwear Product
Development Assistant
Fred Perry

STORE MANAGER

Your job as the manager of a store, department store, or concession in a department store is to manage the stock, people, and processes to maximize sales and minimize costs.

As a store manager, you will spend a surprising amount of time managing people, and that is often both the stimulation and the challenge of the job. Your staff team is likely to be made up of a real mix of people and dealing with this range of people, and trying to make sure that everyone knows what they are doing, has the skills and knowledge to do it well, and is motivated, is a daily challenge. You will be drawing up schedules, training, and monitoring staff (there is usually a high turnover of staff in retail sales, so training new staff is often a big part of the job), and making sure that someone is on the cash registers, someone has put the stock on the shelves, and someone is available to speak to the customers, while ensuring that all staff are well-supported.

The stock is your responsibility: you need to manage deliveries, making sure that the right items are on the sales floor, and do regular stock inventory to monitor loss and theft. You will be involved in floor reorganization, making space for stock, and highlighting particular lines.

As a rule, the more senior you are within store management the less contact you would have with customers on a daily basis, but you would tend to get involved in customer complaints so your good judgment, negotiation skills, and customer service are important. Department stores and other larger stores can sometimes be more sociable and have perks such as a staff lounge,

KATHRIN LODES INTERVIEW
ACCESSORIES DESIGNER
VIVIENNE WESTWOOD

1. When did you first become interested in bags and accessories?

I can't actually pin it down to an exact date. I did an apprenticeship in tailoring prior to studying accessories design. After this degree I studied pattern cutting and engineering for the clothing industry for one year. When I was doing my apprenticeship I ended up doing a lot of bags in my spare time. My boyfriend at the time was a sculptor and inspired me a lot. For me, a bag is a fashion item, but because it's not directly related to the shape of the body like garments, in a way it is a sculpture. So, a bag gives you more freedom and it just suits every kind of body shape.

2. How long have you worked at Vivienne Westwood?

Ten years ago I started as an intern, working as a tailor and pattern-cutter—I worked on the couture pieces as well as the other collections. During my studies I worked freelance at Vivienne Westwood, where I worked either for the Gold Label collection or helped with the bags. Shortly after my graduation in 2006 they offered me this job. On the accessories team, we have a design manager, a product manager, two design assistants, and a senior designer (me).

3. How important is technical knowledge in your role as designer?

Technical knowledge is vital. If you understand the technical side it is easier to work within your given parameters.

4. How does your season start?

Our season starts with a line plan, which states the size of the collection and price points for each line. Then we do research and once we have decided what ideas we want to go ahead with, we start drawing down ideas or experimenting three-dimensionally.

5. How do you conduct your research? Are you given concepts to explore?

We set a theme and explore this. We do our research in the library, vintage clothes stores, and exhibitions. Of course things that cross your way every day inspire you as well. And I shall not forget to mention our archive, which is always a great place to research.

6. How important is it to know your consumer?

To know your consumer is vital. You need to understand their needs, likes, and dislikes if you want to make sure you develop a viable collection. As we have customers all over the world, our collection needs to offer a variety of different lines.

7. What is your design cycle for the year?

In late April we start with the research for the new collection. In July we start but you would have more responsibility working for a small independent store—you are expected to behave as though it were your own business and make a wider range of decisions.

TREND FORECASTER

Dissemination of forward thinking and discovering new developments through research is the primary aim of trend forecasting. The communication and presentation of these discoveries is of paramount importance, whether through handmade books or a Web site; everything must be perfect. In this global industry, trend forecasting must take into account everything that is happening worldwide but tailor the way the information is collated, categorized, and communicated to relate to different markets and cultures.

The trend forecaster needs to maintain knowledge of movement in the mainstream areas by visiting fashion shows and shopping areas, but more importantly to search out the new. It is essential to discover up-and-coming areas in every major city worldwide—stores, galleries, bars, restaurants, music venues, etc. Exhibitions of student work and off-schedule fashion shows often reveal exciting new directions. Attention to cultural, social, political, and economic trends is critical, since all of these areas influence people's needs, opportunities, and desires significantly. Talking to people wherever you go will help you to catch the mood and understand it. A genuine desire to discover the new, and the discernment to know what will be influential, is vital.

submitting designs until the end of September. The development process will be finished by the end of October and the sample collection production can start.

8. Do you visit material/fabric fairs? Which do you favor?

We go to Antiprima in Milan and Lineapelle in Bologna twice a year. Additionally to that we go to St. Croce, Italy and visit tanneries directly. Lineapelle is great and has lots to offer. It is unfortunately quite late in the season so we instead use it as a starting point for the next season or finish things with suppliers we have started working with earlier in the season.

9. What are the highs and lows of your job?

I really enjoy so many things that my job entails—from research up to presentation of the final product, and I must say I have really, really great colleagues to work with. It is challenging to make the collection work taking into consideration all your given parameters, but I find it very satisfying that I can work on a product

> **"Consumers are less interested in quick fashion; they want good-quality items and are willing to pay for them."**

from the initial idea to a final product, which allows you to control the final outcome. If there is such a thing as a low, maybe it's the fact that sometimes you sacrifice a lot of your private time and there are certain personal things you have to put aside.

10. What is the toughest lesson you've learned?

From the experience I've had, it's really important that you discuss problems as soon as they arise.

11. What is the next big movement?

The movement is already here. I think people want to know more about their products, so ethical/sustainable fashion will get stronger and stronger. Consumers are less interested in quick fashion; they

want good-quality items and are willing to pay for them.

12. What advice would you give to a young designer?

You have to love what you do! And you have to be prepared to work hard.

Kathrin Lodes
Accessories Designer
Vivienne Westwood

COMPETITIONS, INTERNSHIPS, GRADUATE TRAINING PROGRAMS

Objective Ways to stand out from the competition.

Entering design competitions, doing an internship, or signing up for a graduate training program are all approaches that will help to distinguish your résumé from everyone else's.

▶ **Sculpture or shoe?** Part of an MA student's final collection, this piece combines wood, steel, and Perspex in a sculptural form that is a wearable shoe. A key element is the attention to the finish of all the materials.

COMPETITIONS

Competitions are run by design groups, retail companies, and education programs to encourage new talent among fashion students. Entry is usually confined to students enrolled on particular programs, such as fashion design, fashion merchandising, or fashion management programs.

DEBUT ACCESSORY
www.fashionexposed.com

Fashion Exposed is part of the Australian fashion/footwear/bags and accessories trade fairs. This competition is for graduates and new designers from Australia or New Zealand who are ready to go into business. Candidates must have a finished collection, look book, Web site, and production in place. The prize is a fully fitted stand in the Fashion Exposed trade fair.

DRAPERS STUDENT FOOTWEAR DESIGNER OF THE YEAR
www.drapersonline.com

An annual competition open to all U.K. students. *Drapers* provide a brief and entrants must submit a complete project including a prototype product. Finalists are invited to the glamorous Drapers Awards Ceremony, where the winner is announced and the award is presented. The winner and the runners-up are interviewed and appear in the next issue of *Drapers*.

DESIGN A BAG ONLINE. FASHION ACCESS
www.designaccess-fa.com

This competition, aimed at designers and students, began in 2006 and by 2010 it was attracting entrants from more than 20 countries worldwide. Designs are submitted online and the judges award marks for: originality of design, fashion trend awareness, and wearability. There are three categories each offering a cash prize. The overall winner receives a cash prize and a four-week pattern making course at the Ars Sutoria school in Milan, Italy to enable the winner to realize his or her prototype bag. The completed bag is then exhibited during the Fashion Access trade fair in Hong Kong.

INDEPENDENT HANDBAG DESIGNER AWARDS
www.hbd101.com

This is currently the only international design competition of its kind. It is designed to promote up-and-coming handbag designers in the United States and around the world. The competition is held annually and a finished product must be submitted. Prizes are awarded at a gala evening in New York. There are several categories every year including one aimed at students—Best Student-Made Handbag. Other awards include Most Innovative Handbag, Best Handbag—overall style and design—Best "Green" Handbag, Best Handmade Handbag, and Best Use of Crystallized Swarovski Elements.

ITS INTERNATIONAL TALENT SUPPORT
www.itsweb.org

This competition was created to offer a bridge between schools and the industry, giving young designers exposure and the opportunity of job offers. It is held annually and is open to students in their final year of study and recent graduates worldwide. Candidates submit visuals of their collection electronically, and from this a shortlist of finalists is drawn up. The Accessories category includes footwear, headwear, softwear, bodywear, jewelry, bags, and related small accessories. Finalists are invited to the awards weekend in Trieste, Italy, where the accessories students display their collections. A catwalk show is held in the evening to show the work of the apparel finalists and the winners of all sections are announced. There are three prizes for the Accessories section: Accessories Collection of the Year, YKK award, and Modamont award. Every winner receives a cash prize.

SALVATORE FERRAGAMO
www.museoferragamo.it

From time to time, Salvatore Ferragamo runs footwear design competitions open to students currently attending college. As these are not held on a regular basis, it is essential to check the Web site for information.

FASHION FRINGE ACCESSORIES
www.fashionfringe.co.uk

This competition is aimed at graduates and young designers who are almost ready to set up their own business and have really thought about what it means to be a luxury designer. Entrants submit a small portfolio of 2D work and a personal statement in which they should preferably be able to demonstrate that some of their work has been used commercially. Four finalists are selected for interview by a panel of judges. The winner is chosen on the day and receives a six-month paid internship with a luxury footwear brand.

FOOTWEAR NEWS/FIT
www.fnshoestar.com

Students at the Fashion Institute of Technology in New York can compete in the Shoe Star competition organized by *Footwear News* and sponsored by the industry. Contestants present work created during the fall semester, and from that, finalists are selected. They take part in a series of five design challenges during the spring semester. This work is judged, and the winner selected.

INTERNSHIPS

Internships can be anything from a day's work experience with a company to a whole year working as part of a team. Some undergraduate degrees have an optional year where students have a year-long internship and earn an extra qualification in industrial studies. Other courses offer a one-semester placement opportunity where students gain credits toward their degree. In several European countries, students are expected to complete their degree course and then do an internship known as a "stage," usually lasting six to nine months.

Some internships are paid at the normal rate for a junior, some at the minimum wage, others offer expenses only, and some offer no financial reward. In fashion, the more prestigious the label, the less likely that payment will be offered—the experience gained by the lucky few who succeed in getting an internship is considered reward enough. At the mid- and lower-market levels, more paid internships are available. Every company has its own way of rewarding interns.

One thing is certain: The experience of working in the commercial fashion world at whatever level is invaluable. Not only do you learn about the whole cycle of events during a season and the pressures of each job, you also develop time management, communication, and team-working skills—essential for anyone to be successful in his or her chosen career.

GRADUATE TRAINING PROGRAMS

The majority of large corporate companies run graduate training programs. For graduates of design courses, these can take the form of an "ideas lab" where commercial restrictions are not imposed. Other training programs introduce graduates to different departments to discover where they can contribute most effectively. Some simply employ the graduate in the type of work they are interested in at a junior level. Adidas, Camper, Nike, and Pentland Industries plc are just a few examples of major brands who offer opportunities to graduates.

SECTION 6 | RESOURCES AND PROFESSIONAL PRACTICE

ACQUIRING KNOWLEDGE

Objective Learn as much as you can about the business you want to be in.

Add to your fund of knowledge by attending trade fairs, visiting museums, and surfing the Internet.

TRADE FAIRS

Trade fairs are held every season and are useful for those involved in a particular industry. A wealth of suppliers gathered in one place makes it easier to compare what is on offer in terms of style, variety, price, and quality. Anyone looking for a new source of supply will find it a real advantage to attend the appropriate trade fair. The focus on a specific industry also provides a unique networking opportunity for everyone who attends.

Trade fair dates vary from year to year and sometimes the venue changes. You should always check out the Web site before planning a visit to any trade fair.

There are two types of trade fair for the accessories industries—design and manufacturing requirements fairs and finished products fairs.

DESIGN AND MANUFACTURING REQUIREMENTS

Everything involved in creating accessories products is on show. Designers, technicians, and manufacturers seek out the latest trends and materials, technological advances, and new developments in machinery and processes. Until you have visited one of these trade fairs, you cannot imagine the wealth of products and suppliers available to support whatever area of the industry you wish to work in.

North America
United States
The NE and NW Materials Shows
(NE is in Danvers, Massachusetts;
NW is in Portland, Oregon)
www.americanevents.com
The same show travels to both venues twice a year. Leather, synthetics, textiles, components, and trims are shown, and trend and color information is available too.

Europe
France
Première Vision, Paris, France
www.premierevision.com
Divided into sections, this is the major materials fair held in Europe for the fashion industries. Held twice a year, exhibitors come from all parts of the world to show their goods. All types of textiles can be found as well as leather, trimmings, and fabric treatments. Textile designers also show their work here and there is a small trends section for each specific division.

Le Cuir is the leather area, which is of major importance to those involved in the accessories industries. Alternative materials suitable for the production of accessories can be found in other divisions—canvas, linen, cotton, and synthetics. Student groups are allowed to visit this trade fair on one specified day; a valuable experience to see what is on offer within the industry and how materials are sourced. Responding to the needs of the global fashion industry, Première Vision also holds previews in New York, São Paulo, Japan, Shanghai, Beijing, and Moscow.

Italy
Lineapelle, Bologna, Italy
www.lineapelle-fair.it
This fair focuses on everything required to create accessories: machinery, tools and equipment, CAD/CAM software, leather, tanning, textiles of all types, components, fittings, and trims. There is also an impressive trend and color section that is highly regarded by the industry. In Milan, London, and New York, Anteprima is held twice a year prior to the Lineapelle fair. This is a pre-season trend show organized by the Lineapelle team to inform trend forecasters, materials manufacturers, and designers of early ideas for the season. A new offshoot is Lineapelle Asia that has become part of the China Import and Export Fair in Guangzhou (Canton).

Asia
China
All China Leather Exhibition
Shanghai, China
www.acle.aplf.com
Held at the same time as the China International Footwear fair, this show concentrates on the manufacturer's

needs. Machinery, tools, leather, materials, components, and fittings are available. This show also travels to Hong Kong and New Delhi to support the industry needs of those countries.

China Shoe Tec, Dongguan, China
www.chinashoesexpo.com
Exhibitors at this fair are middle- to high-end footwear manufacturers almost exclusively from the local area, which has the biggest shoe production in the world.

Vietnam
The International Exhibition of Shoes and Leather, Ho Chi Minh City, Vietnam
www.shoeleather-vietnam.com
This fair concentrates on machinery and tools, components and fittings, and leather and materials for the accessories and upholstery industries, mainly focusing on local production. Some sports and canvas footwear is sometimes shown.

FINISHED PRODUCTS
Product fairs show the current season's product offer for buyers to select their lines from. Searching for new and exciting designs from existing and new suppliers and developing new contacts is one aspect of the buyer's work at a fair. Comparing prices and the quality offered by several manufacturers of the more basic styles planned into their line enables buyers to check the competitiveness of their current supplier. Any aspiring accessories designer should visit one of these fairs to see the enormous range of choice available at every market level.

North America
United States
Chicago Shoe Expo, Chicago, Illinois
www.chicagoshoeexpo.com
The Footwear Event, Chicago, Illinois
www.thefootwearevent.com
A range of footwear and accessories is shown at the Chicago Shoe Expo, and the Footwear Event concentrates more on sports and casual products.

WSA World Shoes and Accessories, Las Vegas, Nevada
www.wsashow.com
Magic, Las Vegas, Nevada
www.fnplatform.magiconline.com
These events are held twice a year and cover all categories and price levels of footwear and accessories. Magic concentrates more on new and emerging brands.

Transit, Los Angeles, California
www.californiamarketcenter.com
Focus, Los Angeles, California
www.californiamarketcenter.com
Transit showcases footwear, and Focus concentrates on apparel, accessories, and lifestyle products. Both fairs show a mix of new and established labels.

FFANY, New York, New York
ffany.org
Fashion Footwear Association of New York organizes fairs four times a year for the American Apparel and Footwear Association.

Central America
SAPICA, Léon, Mexico
www.sapica.com
Footwear and leather goods show held twice a year.

Europe

UK

Pure, London, UK
www.purelondon.com
London Fashion Week
www.londonfashionweek.co.uk
Pure and London Fashion Week show a mixture of apparel, accessories, and footwear. New designers are promoted in addition to the many well-known fashion labels.

Moda Footwear, Birmingham, UK
www.moda-uk.co.uk
Moda Accessories, Birmingham, UK
www.moda-uk.co.uk
These events are held twice a year at the same time showing a broad range of product categories, mainly in the mid-market level.

France

Premiere Classe and Who's Next, Paris, France
www.premiere-classe.com
This fair is held twice a year. In addition to the main venues, several small exhibition spaces are used across the city with products of a similar market level on show—each of these is given a different name. All types of accessories are on show. Every exhibitor is vetted, and there is serious competition to obtain an exhibition space at this prestigious event.

Germany

Bread and Butter, Berlin, Germany
www.breadandbutter.com
This is the show that concentrates on casual, street, and sports footwear twice a year.

GDS, Dusseldorf, Germany
www.gds-online.com
This trade fair is held twice a year, and

although only footwear is shown, the vast range of products exhibited covers all categories and market levels from manufacturers worldwide.

Italy

Micam, Milan, Italy
www.micamonline.com
Mipel, Milan, Italy
www.mipel.it
Held simultaneously twice a year, Micam is purely footwear, and Mipel covers all other leather-based accessories.

Spain

Modacalzado, Madrid, Spain
www.ifema.es
More than 600 leather footwear and accessory brands take part in this annual event—all of them are leaders within their respective market segments.

Iberpiel, Madrid, Spain
www.ifema.es
Held twice a year, Iberpiel specializes in leather-related products—garments, gloves, bags, belts, and footwear. Unusually, machinery, tools, leather, and textiles are shown here too.

Asia

China

China International Footwear Fair, Shanghai, China
www.ciff.aplf.com
Footwear and leather goods fair exhibiting products mainly manufactured in the Far East. It is held twice a year at the same time as the All China Leather Exhibition.

Australia and New Zealand

Australian Shoe Fair
www.australiashoefair.com

Bags and Accessories
www.bagsandaccessories.com.au
Both fairs are held simultaneously once a year in Melbourne and once a year in Sydney.

MUSEUMS

Virtual Shoe Museum
www.virtualshoemuseum.com

North America

Canada

Bata Shoe Museum, Toronto, Canada
www.batashoemuseum.ca

United States

The Costume Institute, Metropolitan Museum of Art, New York, New York
www.metmuseum.org

FIDM, Fashion Institute of Design and Merchandising, Museum and Galleries, Los Angeles, California
www.fidmmuseum.org

The Museum at FIT
New York, New York
www.fitnyc.edu

Europe

Northampton Shoe Museum
Northampton, UK

V&A Costume Court
Victoria and Albert Museum
London, UK
www.vam.ac.uk

Fashion Museum, Bath, UK
www.museumofcostume.co.uk

Dents Factory Museum, Warminster, UK
www.dents.co.uk

Walsall Leather Museum, Walsall, UK
www.walsall.gov.uk/leathermuseum

Musée Internationale de la Chaussure
Romans, France
www.ville-romans.com

Offenbach Leather Museum Offenbach
Frankfurt, Germany
www.ledermuseum.de

Ferragamo Museum, Florence, Italy
www.ferragamo.com

Museo della Calzatura
Sant' Elpidio a Mare, Italy
www.santelpidioamare.it

Bertolini International Shoe Museum
Vigevano, Italy

Museum del Calcat, Barcelona, Spain

National Shoe Museum
Izegem, Belgium

Netherland Leather and Shoe Museum
Waalwijk, Netherlands
www.info@schoenenmuseum.nl

Tassenmuseum Hendrikje Museum
(bags and purses), Amsterdam,
Netherlands
www.info@tassenmuseum.nl

Musée de la Chaussure Bally
Schonenwerd, Switzerland

Asia
Marikine Shoe Museum, Manila,
Philippines

INTERNET RESOURCES
Conducting Web-based research allows for efficient and diverse exposure, and can provide a solid foundation before advancing to other means of research, such as printed material and museums. Researching designer runway shows, historical garments, global trends, and museum artifacts, the variety of sites can provide you with plenty of useful material.

www.firstview.com
One of the best sites for browsing a seemingly limitless amount of designer runway shows, most free of charge, some for cost. This site also sells videos of runway shows, books, and photos, and provides a calendar for forthcoming fashion events.

www.style.com
"The online home of *Vogue*" lets you view selected runway collections and runway videos online, free of charge. Information is also provided via blogging, trends and shopping, menswear coverage, and more.

www.vintagefashionguild.org
A rich resource for those interested in vintage fashion. Read about fashion history, view book reviews, learn how to date vintage finds, and use the blog with other aficionados.

www.hintmag.com
View collection highlights, read show reviews, keep up-to-date on fashion news and events, and stay connected to the "industry at large."

www.wgsn.com
A seemingly endless amount of information is offered about fashion around the world and the trends that shape the industry.

www.wwd.com
Through membership, Women's Wear Daily (WWD) offers daily and thorough coverage of the fashion industry around the globe. One of the best news resources for staying up-to-date.

www.fashion-era.com
The site for researching period fashion, offering extensive illustrations and text to contextualize each period.

www.fashion.about.com
From learning about style basics, reading blogs during fashion week, skimming Hollywood's "best dressed lists," shopping for fashion, and obtaining links for historical research, this site has it covered.

▲ **Fashion is art**
These incredible molded shoes are on display at the Victoria and Albert Museum in London.

RECRUITMENT AGENCIES

Recruitment agencies provide a valuable service in bringing together employers and employees. All agencies keep a bank of talented people on record, so that when an employer contacts the agency outlining an opportunity in its organization, the agent can respond immediately with suggestions of suitable employees. They will also organize interviews and negotiate on behalf of their clients. Almost all agencies cover the whole of the world even if their office is based in only one country. Traditionally the company seeking to fill a position will pay the agency for finding the right person, not the person who is looking for work.

The key fashion agencies are highly proactive, and many of them are privately owned companies where personal attention is paramount to maintain their reputation. Their extensive network in the fashion business is constantly developed and nurtured. They also visit as many graduating shows as possible to discover new talent and make a note of "ones to watch." Although some only deal with employment for experienced staff or high-level executive positions, it is worth contacting them and introducing yourself once your portfolio is ready. If they like what they see, they will keep you in mind and ask you to return when you have the requisite experience. This can be daunting for a graduate, since you obviously need a job to gain experience.

In recent years more recruitment agencies have started working with opportunities for graduates, creating a more positive situation for students leaving college. One new agency, Arts Thread, was set up to create opportunities for design graduates and is proving to be extremely successful.

New types of networking have opened up, allowing job seekers the chance to post their résumés and portfolios, and employers to advertise their vacancies. These are Web sites where everyone involved pays a small fee to have a presence and can then see what is available. None of the services of the traditional agency are offered, such as setting up introductions, interviews, and talent spotting.

RENOWNED RECRUITMENT AGENCIES

24 SEVEN TALENT
24seventalent.com
Nine offices across the U.S. and one in London.

ANNETTE COVE ASSOCIATES
annette@annettecove.com
Specializes in footwear and accessories.

DENZA
denza.co.uk
Vanessa Denza.
3rd floor, 33 Glasshouse Street, Westminster, London W1 5DG

ELITE ASSOCIATES
eliteassociates.co.uk
Elite Associates Europe Ltd.
3rd Floor, 102–108 Clerkenwell Road, London EC1M 5SA

FASHION THERAPY
fashiontherapy.com
Contact Fiona Abrahams. Based in London and New York.
1 Lyric Square, Hammersmith, London W6 0NB
New York contact: stateside@fashiontherapy.com

FLORIANE DE SAINT PIERRE & ASSOCIES
FSPSA.COM
Based in Paris and Milan.
52 Boulevard Malesherbes, 75008 Paris, France
Via San Pietro All'Orto 17, 20100 Milan, Italy

FOUR SEASONS RECRUITMENT
frsl.co.uk
Landmark House, Hammersmith Bridge Road, London W6 9EJ

▶**Milliner at work** Milliner Edwina Ibbotson adjusts a hat in the run-up to the Royal Ascot races in England.

FOURTH FLOOR
fourthfloorfashion.com
Based in New York and Los Angeles.
1212 Avenue of the Americas, 17th Floor,
New York, NY 10036
10100 Santa Monica Boulevard, Suite 900,
Los Angeles, CA 90067

INDESIGN
indesignrecruitment.co.uk
Joanna Neicho and Julius Schofield.
1 Ashland Place, London W1U 4AQ

SMITH AND PYE
smithandpye.com
Alice Smith and Cressida Pye.
17 Willow Street, London EC2A 4BH

SOLOMON PAGE GROUP
solomonpage.com
260 Madison Avenue, New York, NY 10016

TAYLOR HODSON
taylorhodsonfashion.com
133 West 19th Street, 2nd Floor, New York, NY10011

GRADUATE WEB SITE
ARTS THREAD
artsthread.com
Alex Browning and Katie Dominy. Global creative
Web site giving graduates an opportunity to showcase
their work.

OTHER WEB SITES OF INTEREST
stylecareers.com
thefashionspot.com

❝*When we set up Arts Thread in 2009, we knew we were creating something very special as no one globally had created a Web site, magazine, and recruitment consultancy solely for the benefit of design graduates worldwide. The speed of growth has certainly surprised us! It has become apparent that Arts Thread is bridging the gap between education and creative industry.*❞ *Co-owner of Arts Thread, Alex Browning*

WHERE TO STUDY

This is not an exhaustive list of places to study accessory design and construction. All the internationally renowned schools are mentioned, together with many highly praised smaller schools, run by professional designers and makers who also specialize in short programs taught in small groups. The larger schools also run short programs and summer schools. Check their Web sites to see what is currently on offer. Almost all of the schools mentioned teach in English.

The Web site shoemakingbook.com provides a comprehensive list of small shoemaking schools worldwide. Most of these are taught in the language of the country in question.

USA
LOS ANGELES
FIDM fidm.edu

Fashion Institute of Design and Merchandising
Los Angeles Campus, 919 South Grand Avenue, Los Angeles, California 90015–1421
• Associate of Arts Advanced study program: Footwear Design (9-month program).

NEW YORK
FIT fitnyc.edu

Fashion Institute of Technology
Seventh Avenue at 27th Street, New York, NY 10001-5992
• BFA in Accessories Design and Fabrication.
• AFA in Applied Sciences.

PARSONS newschool.edu

Parsons The New School for Design
66 Fifth Avenue, New York, NY 10011
• BFA in Fashion Design.

SAVANNAH
SCAD scad.edu

Savannah College of Art and Design
School of Fashion Accessory Design
Admission Welcome Center, 342 Bull Street, Savannah, Georgia, USA
• BFA in Accessory Design.
• MFA and MA programs in Accessory Design.

Short programs
NEW YORK
Carreducker carreducker.com

Deborah Carre and James Ducker
• Intensive hand shoemaking programs by Carreducker of London who travels to New York every year to teach.

SAN FRANCISCO
Prescott and Mackay School of Fashion and Accessory Design prescottandmackay.co.uk

Fourth Street Studios, 1717D 4th Street, Berkeley, CA 94710
• Shoemaking and footwear design programs. Tutors from the Prescott and Mackay School travel to San Francisco to teach short programs.

UK
COVENTRY
Coventry School of Art and Design coventry.ac.uk

Department of Design and Visual Arts, Coventry University, Priory Street, Coventry CV1 5FB
• BA Hons Fashion Accessories.

LEICESTER
De Montfort University dmu.ac.uk

Faculty of Art and Design, De Montfort University, The Gateway, Leicester LE1 9BH
• FdA Footwear (2-year program).
• BA Hons Footwear Design (3-year program).

LONDON
Central Saint Martins csm.arts.ac.uk

University of the Arts London
Central Saint Martins, Granary Building, 1 Granary Square, London N1C 4AA
• MA Fashion Accessories (program lasts for 1 year and 2 terms).

London College of Fashion fashion.arts.ac.uk

University of the Arts London
20 John Princes Street, London W1G 0BJ
• FdA Cordwainers Footwear Design and FdA Cordwainers Fashion Accessory Design (2-year programs).
• BA Hons Cordwainers Footwear Design and Product Development (3- or 4-year options).
• BA Hons Fashion Jewelry and Accessories (3-year program).
• MA Fashion Artefact and MA Fashion Footwear (15-month program).

Kensington and Chelsea College kcc.ac.uk

Hortensia Center, Hortensia Road, London SW10 0QS
• BTEC Millinery (12-week and 24-week programs).
• HNC Millinery (1-year program).

Royal College of Art rca.ac.uk

School of Material, Royal College of Arts, Kensington Gore, London SW7 2EU
• MA Fashion Womenswear or Menswear Footwear and MA Fashion Womenswear or Menswear Accessories and MA Fashion Millinery (2-year programs).

NORTHAMPTON
University of Northampton northampton.ac.uk

Avenue Campus, St. Georges Avenue, Northampton, Northamptonshire NN2 6JD
• BA Hons Fashion-Footwear and Accessories (3-year program).

NOTTINGHAM
Nottingham Trent University
nottingham.ac.uk
School of Art and Design, Nottingham
Trent University, Burton Street, Nottingham
NG1 4BU
• BA Hons Fashion Accessory Design
  (3-year program).

Short programs
LONDON
Carreducker carreducker.com
Deborah Carre and James Ducker, Cockpit
Arts Studio E2G, Cockpit Arts, Cockpit Yard,
Northington Street, Bloomsbury, London
WC1N 2NP
• Intensive hand shoemaking programs.

Paul Thomas Shoes
paulthomasshoes.com
Paul Thomas Shoes, Bethnal Green, London
• Intensive hand shoemaking programs,
  taught in small groups.

Prescott and Mackay
prescottandmackay.co.uk
The Teaching Studio, Prescott and Mackay
School of Fashion and Accessory Design,
c/o Black Truffle, 52 Warren Street, London
W1T 5NJ
• Footwear, bags, belts, and millinery—design
  and production.

Leatherwork programs
leathercourses.co.uk
Valerie Michael and Neil McGregor, 37 Silver
Street, Tetbury, Gloucestershire GL8 8DL
• Bags and small leather goods production
  and leather carving.

Anthony Vrahimis–Accessories Leather
Goods anthonyvr.com
13 Tollington Way, London N7 6RG
• Pattern-cutting and construction for bags
  and SLGs.

FRANCE
CHOLET
Institut Colbert cnam-paysdelaloire.fr/
styliste-modeliste-chaussures
Institut Colbert, Cholet, France
• Diploma programs in Footwear Design and
  Construction.

GERMANY
PIRMASENS
German College of Footwear
Design and Technology (Deutsche
Schuhfachschule) isc-pirmasens.de
Marie-Curie Strasse 20, 66953 Pirmasens,
Germany
• Seminars and short programs for
  professionals.

ITALY
MILAN
Ars Sutoria arsarpel@arsarpel.it
International Technical Institute of Art of
Footwear and Leather Goods
Via I Nievo 33, 20145 Milan, Italy
• Short intensive technical programs.

Domus domusacademy.com
Via G Watt 27, 20143 Milan, Italy
• 1-year Masters program in Accessory
  Design in partnership with Ars Sutoria.

Istituto Marangoni istitutomarngoni.
com
Via Pietro Verri 4, 20121 Milan, Italy
• 1-year Masters program in Fashion
  Accessories.

FLORENCE
Accademia Riaci accademiariaci.info
Via De' Conti 4, 50123 Florence, Italy
• 1-year/semester program in Leather
  Design and Construction.
• 1-year Masters program in Leather Art.

Polimoda polimoda.com
Via Pisana 77, 50143 Florence, Italy
• BA Footwear and Accessory Design
  (3-year program).
• MA Advanced Fashion Footwear and Bags
  Design (1-year program).

JAPAN
TOKYO
Bunka Fashion College bunka-fc.ac.jp
Fashion Accessories and Textiles
Department
3–22–1 Yoyogi, Shibuya-Ku, Tokyo
151- 8522, Japan
• 3-year advanced diploma = BA.

Short programs
TOKYO
Bench Made benchmade.jp/workshop
Yukiko Bassett Okawa
Shiba BLD. 3rd floor, 6-7-7 Seijo, Setagaya-
Ku, Tokyo 157-0066, Japan
• Hand shoemaking programs.

AUSTRALIA
ADELAIDE
TAFE South Australia International
tafesa.edu.au/international
Level 2, Currie Street, Adelaide 5000
• Certificate 3 in Footwear Production and
  Certificate 4 in Custom-Made Footwear.

Short programs
ADELAIDE
TAFE South Australia International
Details above.

MELBOURNE
Prescott and Mackay School of
Fashion and Accessory Design
prescottandmackay.co.uk
Workshop of Bespoke Shoemaker Brendan
Dwyer, Room 7, 3rd Floor Nicholas Building,
cnr Swanston Street and Finders Lane,
Melbourne, Australia
• Shoemaking programs. Tutors from the
  Prescott and Mackay School teach short
  programs in Melbourne.

ACCESSORIES

TECHNICAL

Aldrich, W. (2007)
Fabric, Form and Flat Pattern Cutting.
London: Blackwell Science.

Double, W. C. (1960)
*Design and Construction of
Handbags.* London: OUP.

Goldstein-Lynch, E. et al. (2004)
Making Leather Handbags.
Hove: Apple Press.

Henriksen, K. (2009) *Fashion Hats
(Design and Make)* London: A&C
Black.

Hobson, S. (1975) *Belts for All
Occasions.* London: Mills and Boon.

Lingwood, R. (1980)
Leather in Three Dimensions. New
York, London: Van Nostrand Reinhold.

Michael, V. (1994)
The Leatherworking Handbook.
London: Cassell.

Salaman R. A. (1996)
*Dictionary of Leather-Working Tools
c. 1700–1950 and the Tools of Allied
Trades.* USA: Astragal Press.

DESIGN

Anlezark, M. (1990) *Hats on Heads.*
Australia: Kangaroo Press.

Cummings, V. (1982) *Gloves.*
London: Batsford Press.

Gerval, O. (2009) *Fashion
Accessories.* London: A&C Black.

Huey, S. and Draffan, S. (2009) *Bag.*
London: Laurence King.

Jones, S. et al. (2009) *Hats: An
Anthology.* London: V&A Publishing.

Leurquin, A. (2004) *A World of Belts:
Africa, Asia, Oceania, America from
the Ghysels Collection.* Milano: Skira.

Smith, D. (2005) *Handbag Chic: 200
Years of Designer Fashion.* Atglen, PA:
Schiffer Publishing.

Steele, V. & Borrelli, L. (2005) *Bags:
A Lexicon of Style.* London: Scriptum.

Wilcox, C. (1998) *A Century of Bags:
Icons of Style in the 20th Century.*
London: Apple.

Wilcox, C. (1999) *Bags.*
London: V&A Publishing.

Worthington, C. (1996) *Accessories.*
London: Thames and Hudson.

FOOTWEAR

TECHNICAL

Garley, A. M. (2006) *Concise Shoe
Making Dictionary.* 2nd ed. Rutland:
Garley.

Jones, F. G. (2008) *Pattern Cutting:
Step-by-Step Patterns for Footwear:
A Handbook on Producing Patterns
for Making Boots or Shoes.*
Rawtenstall: Noble Footwear.

Sharp, Michael H. (1994) *The
Pattern Cutter's Handbook: A Step-
by-Step Guide to Producing Patterns
for Footwear Production.* 2nd ed.
Lancashire: Footwear Open Tech Unit.

Spryke, Tim (2006) *Bespoke
Shoemaking: Learn to Make Shoes
by Hand.* Australia: Artzend
Publications.

Thornton, J. H. (1970) *Textbook of
Footwear Manufacture.* 3rd ed.
Heywood Books: Butterworth and Co.

Vass, Lasz et al. (2006) *Handmade
Shoes for Men.* Germany: Konemann
Verlagsgesellschaft Mbh.

DESIGN

Blanchard, Tamsin (2000) *The Shoe:
Best Foot Forward.* London: Carlton.

Choklat, A. and Jones, R. (2009)
Shoe Design. Cologne: Daab
Publishing.

Cox, Caroline (2004) *Stiletto.* London:
Carlton.

Huey, S. and Proctor, R. (2007) *New Shoes*. London: Laurence King.

Peacock, J. (2005) *Shoes: The Complete Sourcebook*. London: Thames and Hudson.

Riello, G. and McNeil, P. (2006) *Shoes: A History From Sandals to Sneakers*. Oxford: Berg.

RESEARCH, BRANDING, DESIGN, MATERIALS, AND MARKETING

Bell, Judith (2005) *Doing Your Research Project*. 4th ed. Maidenhead: Open University Press.

Borrelli, L. (2000) *Fashion Illustration Now*. London: Thames and Hudson.

Burke, S. (2006) *Fashion Computing: Design Techniques and CAD*. Burke Publishing.

Colussy, K. (2005) *Rendering Fashion, Fabric, and Prints with Adobe Photoshop*. Upper Saddle River, [N.J]: Pearson Prentice Hall.

Eissen, K. and Steur, R. (2007) *Sketching: Drawing Techniques for Product Designers*. Amsterdam: BIS Publishers.

Frings, G. S. (2005) *Fashion From Concept to Consumer*. 8th ed. London: Prentice Hall.

Hines, T. and Bruce, M. (2001) *Fashion Marketing: Contemporary Issues*. Oxford: Butterworth-Heinemann.

Jackson, T. and Shaw, D. (2006) *The Fashion Handbook*. London: Routledge.

Manlow, V. (2009) *Designing Clothes: Culture and Organization of the Fashion Industry*. New Brunswick, [N.J.]: Transaction Pub.

Morris, R. (2009) *The Fundamentals of Product Design*. Lausanne, Switzerland: AVA.

Nicholas, D. (1994) Fashion Illustration Today. London: Batsford.

O'Mahoney, M. (2002) *Sportstech: Revolutionary Fabrics, Fashion, and Design*. London: Thames and Hudson.

Randall, G (1997) *Branding*. 1st ed. London: Kogan Page.

Seivewright, S. (2007) *Research and Design*. Lausanne, Switzerland: AVA Publishing.

Shibukawa, I. and Takahashi, Y. (1990) *Designer's Guide to Color*. San Francisco, California: Angus and Robertson.

Webb in Jackson T & Shaw D (Ed) *The UK Fashion Handbook* – Ch. 6. Routledge.

PERIODICALS
TECHNICAL/INDUSTRY
The Hat Magazine
Footwear Today
Out On A Limb
Drapers
Footwear News (United States)
Satra Bulletin International

DESIGN/FASHION
Accessori Collezioni
Impuls
Obbietivo Moda
Moda Pelle Styling
Vogue Pelle
Ars Sutoria

WEB SITES AND BLOGS
www.biomechanica.com
www.bryanboy.com
www.catwalking.com
www.caci.co.uk
www.centuryinshoes.com
designaddict.com
facehunter.blogspot.com
www.ganttchart.com
nymag.com/fashion
www.satra.co.uk
www.selvedge.org
www.shoeinfonet.com
showstudio.com
streetpeeper.com
stylebubble.typepad.com
stylelikeu.com
surveymonkey.com
thecuriouseye.blogspot.com
www.thesartorialist.com
www.trendtablet.com
www.trendwatching.com

GLOSSARY: HANDBAGS

Across-the-body bag: A small bag with a long adjustable shoulder strap worn over one shoulder and across the body. Also known as a swing pack.

Awl: A spiked tool used to mark position points on the pattern, leather, or material.

Back: This is one piece of leather that includes the butt and shoulder areas, but not the belly. The best leather is near the spine at the butt end.

Back body: The back part of the bag/product.

Barrel bag: A small shoulder bag or purse with circular gussets that give the body a cylindrical shape.

Base: The bottom of the bag/product.

Belly: Leather from this area is a stretchy, softer leather of varying thickness.

Belting leather: Full-grain, vegetable-tanned cowhide that has a firm feel and a smooth finish.

Binding: A strip of material used on a raw-edge construction, to cover the raw edge of material.

Bone folder: More commonly made out of plastic, a bone folder has a rounded, curved end and a more flattened, pointed curved end. It is mainly used for boning down seams and turning edges, but it can also be used as a pusher to push out turned corners.

Bowling bag: This bag has the body shape of half an oval, usually constructed as an all-round gusset with turned, and often piped, seams. Handles are attached to the front and back body, and it has a zippered closure. Was originally designed as a sports bag for carrying bowling balls, hence the name.

Bucket bag: A two-piece base construction with turned or often raw-edge seams. The body of the bag is sometimes wider at the top edge, tapering to the base, which gives it a bucket shape. It is often closed by the drawstring method.

Bugatti handle: A bugatti handle has a rounded rope, paper, or plastic core running through it. The leather strap is cut with

shield shapes called chapes at each end. The strap is wrapped around the core and stitched with a raw-edge seam, stopping just before the chapes. The chapes are then stitched onto the front and back body of the bag.

Bum bag: See fanny pack.

Butt: The thickest, strongest part of the hide and considered the best leather cut for firmer items, such as belts.

Butted construction: Where the material is turned over on the edge—it could be turned and stuck onto a reinforcement or onto itself before stitching together.

Chapes: The bottom ends of a bugatti strap—the parts that are stitched to the body of the bag.

Clicking knife: A wooden knife handle to which curved and straight blades can be attached.

Closure: The method used for fastening a bag closed.

Clutch bag: A bag that does not have a handle or strap—it is held in the hand or clasped to the body under the arm.

Collar: An often reinforced strip of leather/fabric that is stitched onto the inside top edge of the body of the bag.

Colorway: One of several different color combinations offered.

Components: All additional parts of the bag, e.g. external pockets.

Construction: The method by which the bag is put together.

Contact adhesive: Glue that needs to be applied to both surfaces.

Corrected grain: Leather that has part of the grain surface lightly abraded with an emery wheel or sandpaper to even out the surface and eliminate scarring.

Crew punch: A tool used for cutting a slot of a given size in leather.

Cross construction: Made from one piece of material shaped like a cross.

Cutting mat: A self-healing synthetic cutting

surface used for pattern cutting.

Cutting patterns: All seam and turning allowances are added to the making patterns in order to get the cutting patterns.

D-ring: A fitting in the shape of the letter "D," usually made from metal and used for attaching a strap or handle on to the body/gusset of a bag.

Doctor's bag: See Gladstone bag.

Dog clip: A trigger clip used for detachable straps.

Double-sided tape: Adhesive tape often used to hold work in place prior to stitching.

Dividers: A tool for pattern cutting that looks like a double-spiked compass. It ensures accuracy when measuring seam allowance, repeating measurements, and it can also be used to mark guidelines for turning and/or stitching.

Draft: Drawing out the pattern piece on paper or card.

Drop-in lining: A type of lining that is stitched into the bag after the main body of the bag is constructed.

Duffel bag: Round base with an all-round body. The closure is by the drawstring method, which is also the carrying shoulder strap.

Eyelet: A metal fitting that reinforces a punched hole, used for decorative and functional purposes.

Fanny pack: Essentially a belt with a bag stitched to it. The bag area is three-dimensional, and it can be worn low slung around the hips or tight around the waist. Also known as a bum bag.

Fittings: Refers to any hardware added to the bag.

Fixed lining: A type of lining that is stitched in and secured to the inside of the bag during construction.

Flap: A piece of material attached along one edge and covering the opening of a bag/wallet or purse.

Folded edge or butted construction: Where the leather/material is turned over on

the edge. It can be turned and glued on to a reinforcement or skived and turned onto itself before stitching together.

Folding hammer: A small leatherworking hammer used for folding seams and edges. One end has a rounded head and the other is chisel-shaped.

Frame bag: Has a closure that is a solid frame. Frames can be made for plastic, fiberboard/card, or wood, but most commonly metal.

French binding: A decorative detail used to cover a raw-edge seam. It differs from ordinary binding in that one edge of the bind is turned and the other is raw.

Front body: The front-facing side of the bag/product.

Full-grain leather: Having the original grain surface of the skin.

Gladstone bag: Named for British prime minister William Gladstone, a Gladstone bag is a small suitcase that separates into two equal sections. It is built over a rigid frame and is typically made of stiff leather. Also known as a doctor's bag.

Glue brush: A brush used for applying glue.

Glue knife: A spatula-type knife used for accurate glue application, especially for turnovers.

Gusset: A component of a bag usually used to hold the back and the front body together and add depth/volume.

Handle: A means of carrying a bag, usually hand held.

Hardware: Refers to any fittings used on the bag: buckle, D-ring, base stud, closure, lock, etc.

Hobo: A slouchy bag that is worn over the shoulder, often with a curved base.

Holdall: A large, soft bag usually turned and piped, such as a gym bag.

Hole punches: A tool used to cut round holes through material. They are available in a variety of sizes.

Horseshoe construction: Where four identical body pieces are cut—two inner-body pieces and two outer-body pieces. The two inners are then stitched together to form a flat gusset.

Kelly bag: An iconic handbag by Hermès made famous by Grace Kelly, used to hide her pregnancy.

Magnetic dot: A method of fastening where the closure system is a magnetic clasp—a male piece fits into a female piece.

Making patterns: These are the patterns that are made first and have no allowances included.

Maquette/mock-up: An initial 3D version of your design that helps to clarify shape, proportion, and size.

Masking tape: Used for taping pattern pieces together when mocking up.

Master pattern: Pattern that has all the essential information and dimensions of the finished product.

Messenger bag: Adapted from a style originally worn by cycle couriers. This rectangular bag has a long front flap and often a turned construction. It is worn on the shoulder and is a popular men's work bag.

Metal ruler: Used to ensure a straight edge when cutting both leather and paper/card.

Mock-up: See maquette.

Molded construction: Where the leather is stretched over a mold and glued together. A box or photo frame covered in leather is the easiest way to describe this.

Neoprene glue: A very strong contact adhesive used in molded constructions.

Net pattern: A general term for patterns that represent the finished size, i.e. without allowances.

Notch: A small V-shaped registration mark on a pattern or cutout pattern piece, locating a particular point of note, e.g. marking the point on the front of the body where the strap fitting is to be located.

Patterns: Paper or card pieces with instructions intended as a guide for making a product.

Paring knife: Used for paring down and hand skiving (thinning the substance of leather).

Piping: A thin strip of material covering a cord stitched into a seam, for decorative and structuring properties.

PVA glue: A water-soluble glue used as a permanent bond.

Raised base: A front and back body, and two side gussets that have a rectangle cut out of the bottom edge, leaving the edges of the gusset longer than the central area. When stitched together, the base is raised higher than the body of the bag.

Raw edge: A cut edge of leather or material usually finished with edge dye or wax.

Raw-edge construction: Where the leather is stitched together on the right side and the leather is left with raw edges.

Registration marks: Used for accurately locating components when constructing the bag and for reference when pattern cutting—usually a nick or point mark made by the awl.

Reinforcement patterns: Pattern pieces for the areas that need to be strengthened. These are unique to each bag and depend on the material used, fittings, and style of bag.

Reinforcements: Materials of a different thickness and stiffness used to give the outer material more structure or add support to fittings or components.

Rivet: A two-part device consisting of a post and cap that is often used to replace stitching or used alongside stitching to add strength to joins, e.g. straps to bags.

Rotary hole punch: A hand tool with a variety of sized heads that revolve with a variety of sized punches that cut round holes in material.

Rubber solution: A high-tack, low-strength, natural rubber adhesive used prior to stitching.

Rucksack: Derived from the classic knapsack.

Sam Browne: A mushroom-shaped fitting that is used instead of a buckle. It is riveted to a piece of material, and the fitting is forced through a slotted cut forming a closure. Also known as a mushroom or post.

Satchel: Derived from the classic school satchel.

Scalpel: A sharp knife used for pattern cutting with a changeable blade.

Score: To cut partially but not all the way through for ease of folding and accuracy.

Seam allowance: The additional material needed when sewing seams. The actual amount of seam allowance is dependent on the seam type.

Sharpening stone: A stone to sharpen your blades on—oil and whetstones are available.

Shopper: Derived from the classic grocery bag, this is a very simple open-topped bag without any closure, usually hand held, but longer handles have been added to accommodate wearing over the shoulder.

Shoulder: This is a softer area of the hide, often used for making bags.

Shoulder bag: A small- to medium-sized bag worn on the shoulder by means of a strap.

Side: The hide cut in half down the middle, including the belly areas.

Skive: To pare down the outer edge of the leather, to reduce the thickness.

Strap cutter: A specialist adjustable tool that cuts leather straps.

Stepping off: The process used to measure the curve of a pattern piece.

T-base: A one-piece pattern construction, taking its name from the inverted T-shape on the side gussets when constructed.

Toaster: A small handheld bag resembling the shape of a toaster. It has a three-quarter zippered gusset, and it is usually a turned, piped construction.

Tote bag: Similar to a shopper but has a closure and often external features such as pockets.

GLOSSARY: FOOTWEAR

Turned construction: The product is sewn together inside out and then turned the right way around.

Turning allowance: Additional allowance added to a making pattern to allow material to be turned prior to construction.

W-base: A one-piece construction that takes its name from the W-shape on the side gussets when constructed.

Weekender: A large, soft holdall with handles, often with a detachable shoulder strap, and a zippered or flap closure.

Adhesive: Chemical compound that will stick two materials together.

Awl: A pointed tool used for piercing patterns or materials to create location points as a guide for cutting or stitching.

Backers and reinforcements: Internal strengthening materials to maintain shape and prevent tearing.

Backpart: The part of a last or a shoe from the back to the joint.

Back seam: The seam at the back of the shoe that joins the two quarters together.

Backstrap: A strip of material stitched on to cover the back seam for extra strength.

Blind seam: A seam where one upper piece is laid on top of another, face to face, and stitched along the edge of the top layer. The piece on top is then folded over to hide the stitching.

Blown PU: Polyurethane that has been injected with minute air bubbles to create a more lightweight and flexible material.

Bone folder: A tool made from bone or plastic used to assist the turning over and pleating of a folded edge.

Bound edge: An edge treatment where a strip of material is stitched to the outside edge, face to face, then folded over to the inside and stuck down (often known as French binding).

Buckle: An adjustable fastener that holds a strap in place.

Cemented construction: The upper is lasted on to the insole and held in place by adhesive. The sole is then attached to the bottom with adhesive. In this construction the word "cement" refers to the adhesive used.

Cleaning brush: A brush to clean off any dust or dirt.

Clicking: Cutting leather or any other material used for uppers.

Clicking board: A board providing a smooth surface on which to hand cut upper pieces.

Clicking knife: A cutting knife with a curved blade designed for cutting leather.

Closed seam: A seam that joins two upper pieces together by stitching close to the edge 1/16 in. (1.5 mm) with the pieces held face to face.

Closing: Preparing and stitching the upper part of the shoe.

Components: The parts of a product.

Construction: The way the parts of a shoe are assembled.

Counter lining: The lining at the back of the shoe around the heel area.

Cutting mat: A synthetic cutting surface used for pattern cutting.

Dividers: Measuring tools that can be opened to any required width and used to create a parallel line along an edge as a guide for cutting.

Dog tail: A curved piece at the top of the outside quarter that overlaps the inside quarter and is stitched to it. This creates a stronger join.

Edge treatment: The way the edge of a piece of an upper is finished.

Emery paper: Strong paper coated with

particles of emery, a mineral, and used to smooth surfaces and reduce substance. Similar to an emery board used for filing nails.

EVA: Ethylene vinyl acetate is a synthetic material used for soles.

Eyelet: A metal reinforcement for a lace hole.

Fiberboard: A material created from fibers (usually cellulose), bonded together with adhesives in sheet form.

Fittings/hardware: Functional parts that relate to the fastening of a shoe.

Flexible plastic rule: A smaller rule that is flexible enough to curve up the back of a last.

Folded edge: The edge of a cut piece that is folded over and stuck.

Folding hammer: A small, handheld, round-ended hammer used to flatten a folded edge.

Forepart: The part of a last or a shoe from the joint to the end of the toe.

Form: The 2D representation of the inside and the outside of a last.

Gimped edge: A raw-edge cut in a zigzag shape.

Heel: The component at the back of the shoe that sits under the heel of the foot.

Heel height: The vertical height from the bottom of the shoe upper at the center-back to the ground.

Hole punch: A tool with a range of sizes of round punches used for making round holes in materials.

Insole: The internal section that the upper is attached to then covered by the sole.

Lap seam: A seam that joins two upper pieces by overlapping one on top of the other and stitching along the edge of the piece on top. The piece on top is known as the overlay. The part of the underneath piece that is overlapped is the underlay.

Last: The mold on which the shoe is made.

Lasting: Stretching the upper over the last and attaching it to the insole.

Lasting pincers: Pincers used to grip the upper and pull it over the insole in the lasting process.

Lining: The inside layer of the upper that is in contact with the foot.

Location marks: Marks to indicate the positions pieces should be placed in to join them together correctly.

London hammer: A round-ended hammer used to flatten any creases that appear when lasting. The rounded end prevents the surface of the leather from being bruised or damaged.

Masking tape: An adhesive tape with slight stretch.

Mean form: The average between the outside and inside forms.

Measuring tape: A tape marked in inches made from a non-stretch material so that it remains accurate.

Midsole: A layer that sits between the upper and the sole of a shoe. In sports footwear, the midsole is usually molded together with the sole.

Paris hammer: Sometimes known as a French pattern hammer, a round-ended hammer used to flatten any creases that appear when lasting. The rounded end prevents the surface of the leather from being bruised or damaged.

Pattern: The 2D card shapes used to cut the upper pieces in material which, when stitched together, form the shoe upper.

Pattern-cutting card: Any very thin, hard card.

Piped edge: A raw edge with a piece of piping stuck behind it and stitched in place.

Prototype/sample: A 3D test of a design idea or component.

PU Polyurethane: A synthetic material used for soling and sometimes as a coating for synthetic upper materials.

Quarters: The parts of the shoe that cover the back of the foot at either side.

Raw edge: A clean, cut edge.

Scalloped edge: A raw-edge cut in a scalloped shape.

Scalpel: A cutting knife with a very fine, sharp blade used for pattern cutting.

Shank: The internal structure that sits under the insole, acting as a bridge between the heel and the joint, to create the strength to carry the weight of the body.

Sharpening stick: A rectangular wooden block covered with emery paper used for sharpening a clicking knife.

Silver marking pen: A pen with silver ink that is used to mark guidelines on upper pieces.

Ski hook: A hook for holding shoelaces in place, originally used on ski boots.

Skive: Reducing the thickness of a material along an edge to a predetermined width. Usually used in upper construction in preparation for an edge treatment or seam.

Sock: The lining that covers the insole and which the foot sits on.

Socking: Inserting the lining that covers the insole inside the shoe.

Standard: The mean form with the design lines and allowances for lasting added, from which the patterns for the shoe upper can be cut.

Steel rule: A rule made from steel that is strong enough to retain a perfect straight edge, even when used as a guide for cutting with a sharp scalpel.

Stiffener: The internal molded structure that keeps the heel part of the shoe firm.

Tack: A small nail used for securing the upper to the insole in the initial stages of lasting. Larger tacks can be used for temporarily attaching the insole to the last.

Tack knife: A tool for removing lasting tacks.

Toe cap: A piece of material covering the toe area of a shoe.

Toe puff: The internal molded material that retains the shape of the toe.

Toe shape: The shape of the toe of a shoe

viewed from above and from the side.

Toe spring: The vertical distance between the toe end of the last from a horizontal surface when the last is held in the correct position for the heel height.

Topline: The edge of the upper part of the shoe where it meets the foot.

TPR (thermoplastic rubber): A synthetic rubber that always softens with heat and hardens when cool.

Trims: Decorative parts of a shoe that have no function.

Upper: The part of the shoe that covers the top and sides of the foot

Vamp: The part of the upper that covers the front of the foot.

GLOSSARY: MILLINERY

Baker boy cap: An eight-piece sectional crown with a small peak, the crown of which is not fitted to the skull.

Bandeau: A headband of material, structured or unstructured.

Basting: Also known as tacking, a temporary stitch to hold fabric pieces together or for making temporary reference marks.

Beret: A cap made from felt, felted jersey, or fabric with a soft, wide, circular crown.

Bias: The cross grain of any woven fabric.

Bicorne: Hat of the late 18th and early 19th century—wide brims were folded up to form two points.

Block: A wooden form used as a mold to shape, by hand, a brim or crown.

Blocking: The term used to describe the action of molding a hat shape. The material is steamed or damped to render it pliable. It is then stretched and secured to the block, dividing the fullness up equally, eradicating all gathers and folds.

Blocking net: Heavily sized cotton net with a large mesh—a lightweight foundation and is sometimes used double layered.

Blocking spring, string, or elastic: A tool used to hold fabric straw or felt to a block.

Block stand: A turned wooden support on which blocks are positioned while being worked on, to elevate them and allow them to be spun around for ease of work.

Boater: A flat-topped hat with a small flat brim. Traditionally, made of stiffened straw braid.

Bowler: An oval hat with a round rigid crown and a small curved brim. Also known as a Derby, because the style was made popular by the Earl of Derby in the 19th century.

Breton: A women's hat with a domed crown and brim turned up all around.

Brim: The projecting edge of a hat, usually protruding from the crown. It can sweep upward or downward, and it can be symmetrical or asymmetrical.

Brim reed: A flexible clear plastic available in a variety of thicknesses from 0.85–2 mm that is used to strengthen brims of regular shape—mainly for fabric hats.

Brim stand: The part of the brim that fits inside the crown, the bottom of which often forms the head fitting.

Buckram: Stiff, woven cotton fabric, used to make hats. May be blocked or sewn. Sometimes used by milliners to make blocks for limited use.

Cap: A hat with a small peak/visor at the front.

Capeline: A straw or felt shape—the rough shape of a hat—used to make a hat with crown and flat brim, ready to be blocked into your chosen hat shape.

Cartwheel: Large brimmed hat with a small tight-fitted crown.

Cloche: Women's hats, popular in the 1920s, with a close-fitting round crown, with no brim or a small flare at the brim edge.

Cockade: An ornamental rosette of ribbon or cloth, worn on a hat as a decorative trim.

Cocktail hat: A small, often frivolous hat for women, usually worn forward on the head.

Cone: Conically shaped hood of felt or straw used for blocking small hat shapes or crowns.

Copyist: A milliner who makes a number of copies of the original model/design.

Cowboy hat: Hat with a high crown and wide brim, originally worn by cowhands. Usually made of felt or leather.

Crown: The top part of a hat that sits on the head.

Cutting patterns: All seam and turning allowances are added to the making patterns (see pages 109–115) in order to get the cutting patterns.

Dolly: A linen and card representation of the head that is easy to pin into. Also known as poupée.

Domette: An interlining fabric that has the appearance of flannel. It is loosely woven and has a fluffy surface.

Elastic canvas: An open-woven cotton sized fabric used as a foundation for blocked fabric hats. It can be shaped when steamed or damped, and holds its shape when dry.

Esparterie: A woven and sized material made of esparto grass and cotton muslin, sold by the sheet used as a stiffening in the construction of hats. It is also the material more traditionally used for the making of blocks for limited use. Also known as spartre and willow.

Fascinator: A whimsy or decorative trim worn on the head or in the hair, often dramatic in appearance.

Fedora: A soft, small-brimmed felt hat with a tapered crown that is dented lengthways. It is sometimes called a Homburg.

Felt: Cloth made from wool, fur, or hair, compacted (felted) by rolling and pressing in the presence of heat and moisture.

Fez: Brimless, conical, flat-topped cap traditionally worn by men in some Islamic cultures, made of red felt with a tassel attached at the top center.

Foundation fabric: Fabrics used to make the basic hat shapes, usually sized with a stiffening agent. These fabrics are pliable when damp and hold their shape when dry.

French canvas: A medium-weight cotton/linen canvas, lightly sized and extremely pliable. Used as a foundation fabric.

Fur felt: Any hood or capeline made using the fibers of fur bearing animals—rabbit is more commonly used.

Fusible interlining: Woven fabric with an adhesive on the backside activated by heat also known as iron-on backer.

Grosgrain ribbon: A corded ribbon used for trimming hats. It is often used on the headband (inside the crown) and also for binding edges of both straw and felt brims because it curves when ironed and comes in a variety of widths.

Hat: An item worn on the head, originating from the Saxon word meaning "hood."

Hat elastic: Thin, rounded cord elastic, used

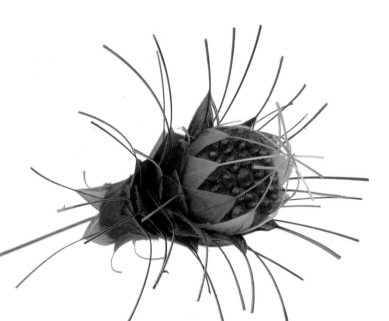

to help secure the hat to the head, sewn in underneath the headband and worn at the back of the head under the hair so it cannot be seen.

Hat steamer: An electrical device that produces a steady source of steam.

Head fitting: The point at which the hat sits on to the head. It usually has a grosgrain ribbon to enhance the fit and add comfort.

Headband: Wired canvas bias strip used as a tool to support the brim of a hat while the hat/pattern is being made.

Homburg: A man's felt hat, with a narrow upturned brim, and a depression in the crown, trimmed with a band and small bow. Allegedly it originated in Homburg in western Germany. Also called a fedora.

Hood: Cone or capeline of felt or straw for making hats.

Interlining fabric: These are used to cover the hat foundation—they add body and can give a soft slightly padded appearance. They can conceal the texture of the foundation fabric and also protect fine fabrics from the coarse foundation and possible snagging on the hat wire. Domette and tarlatan are examples of these.

Juliet cap, calcotte: A round close-fitting skull cap, first seen in the Renaissance.

Jute hood: Cone or capeline made of jute fiber.

Making patterns: These are the patterns that are made first and have no allowances included.

Melusine: A felt that has a flat silky pile. The pile varies in length—a short pile gives a satinlike surface while longer piles can be brushed up to resemble exotic furs. These felts are made from a mix of fur fibers.

Milliner: Artisan who designs and makes hats.

Millinery: The art of making hats.

Millinery wire: Wire covered in cotton thread used for supporting edges of brims and also used in block making. It is available in a variety of thicknesses.

Model hat: A hat made by hand—usually by one person—and not mass produced.

Mouflon: Is similar to the long-piled melusine but as it is made of wool from the mouflon sheep, it is not silky in appearance. These are delicate felts, and care is needed when blocking because excessive steaming can damage them.

Nap or pile: Short fibers, extending above the surface of cloth, fabric, or felt, creating a soft, downy effect such as on velvet.

Newsboy cap: A soft hat with a small brim and a pouchy appearance. Usually made of eight panels.

Pagoda hat: A shallow conical straw hat with a large brim to protect the wearer from the sun.

Panama: The name given to straw woven in Ecuador, Peru, and Colombia.

Panama hat: Straw hat made with Panama straw.

Parasisal: A 2 x 2 weave of sisal fiber used to make cones and capelines. It is available in a variety of grades, depending on the fineness of the fiber.

Peak: A partial brim, usually extending out at the front of a hat or cap. Also known as a visor.

Peak stand: The part of the peak that fits inside the crown. The stand allows the peak to be attached to the crown.

Picture hat: A hat with a very wide brim.

Pillbox: A small brimless crown with a flat tip and vertical sides. This hat was made by the designer Halston and popularized by Jackie Kennedy. Pillboxes can be made in most types of fabric.

Pompom: A fluffy or woolen ball, tuft, or tassel.

Quill: A large stiff feather from a bird, usually the wing or tail—sometimes striped of its plume and/or burnt.

Raffia: A natural straw from Madagascar, the Raffia palm or its leaf is woven into cones, capelines, and braids.

Royal Ascot: The world-famous horse race

meeting at Ascot, famed for Ladies' Day, a unique occasion where women wear fantastic hats and headpieces.

St. Catherine: Patron saint of milliners in France, celebrated on November 25.

Sectional crown: A crown made in sections—it can be anything from three sections to ten sections.

Side band: The vertical part of the crown that is attached to the tip.

Sinamay: Banana plant fiber woven into lengths sold by the meter and available in a variety of colors.

Sisal: Comes from the fiber of the abacá and is used to make cones, capelines, and woven fabric.

Sisal hood: Cone or capeline of sisal fiber made with a 1 x 1 weave.

Sized: Impregnated with starch to add stiffness to a fabric.

Skull cap: A small, close-fitting cap made of fabric.

Slouch hat: A soft hat with a high crown and drooping flexible brim. Also called a Garbo hat, for the name of the actress who wore this style in many films.

Smoking cap: Men's pillbox-shaped cap, worn during the 19th century to prevent the hair from smelling of tobacco.

Snood: A band for the hair that has a hairnet supporting the back of the hair.

Sombrero: A Mexican hat with a high, conical crown and very wide brim. Usually made from straw or felt.

Spartalac: A white plasterlike coating that is painted on to stiffen esparterie hat blocks.

Stetson hat: The original cowboy hat, with a high crown and a wide brim made of beaver fur felt, which rendered it waterproof. Crowns and brims were often customized, with brims rolled slightly and crowns with central indents and pinch dents at the front.

Stiffening: Originally shellac or gelatine was used, but these have now been superseded by cellulose or PVA-based chemicals. It is applied by hand or dipped, to stiffen felt or straw.

Stovepipe hat: A tall 19th-century top hat, made popular by U.S. President Abraham Lincoln.

Straight of the grain: Where the weft threads cross the warp threads at a 90° angle.

Strip straw: Flat straw braid sold by the hank.

Suede felt: Fur felt hood or capeline with short nap. The surface texture resembles suede, and it is also known as a peachbloom.

Tam o'shanter: Beret of Scottish origin with a close-fitting headband, usually trimmed with a pompon.

Thimble: Worn on the middle finger to protect the fingertip from being punctured by either the needle when sewing or pins when blocking.

Thinners: Solvent used to thin down felt and straw stiffeners, and clean the brushes.

Tip: The top part of the crown.

Top hat: A man's tall cylindrical hat with a narrow brim, made of silk plush. The original top hats were made of beaver felt. Also called a "Plug Hat" in the United States.

Toque: A small, close-fitting brimless or nearly brimless hat for a woman.

Tricorne: Originated from the 18th-century men's hat—wide brims were folded up to form three points. A popular style for women in the 1980s.

Trilby: A soft felt hat, usually made of fur felt (rabbit). It has a dented crown and flexible brim and usually has a small feather trimming.

Trimming: Finishing decorative element—bows, flowers, and feathers are all popular trims.

Turban: Worn originally by Muslim and Sikh men, women's draped turbans can be structured and unstructured.

Veil: A covering of fine fabric or net for the head and/or face.

Velour felt: Fur felt hood or capeline with uniform nap and velvetlike surface texture.

Visor: A partial brim, usually extending out at the front of a hat or cap. Also known as a peak, it is used as a shade against the sun.

Wheat straw single or double: A stiff coarse straw, usually left its natural golden brown color. Single wheat is 1 x 1 weave, and double wheat is 2 x 2 weave.

Wool felt: A felt usually made from sheep's wool, the best being made from merino wool. Occasionally synthetic fibers are added to cheaper quality felt.

Xian: Capeline made of an Oriental straw.

GLOSSARY: SMALL LEATHER GOODS

GLOVES

Binding: Edge trim at the upper edge of the cuff that is both decorative and functional.

Button length: A unit of measure referring to the length of the glove from the base of the thumb at the wrist to the hem. The measurement is expressed in "buttons," where one button equals about 1 in. (2.5 cm), e.g. a three-button glove measures 3 in. (7.5 cm) from the base of the thumb to its hem.

Cabretta leather: Leather from the skin of hair sheep.

Clute cut pattern: A full glove pattern, palm shape, and fingers cut together in one piece.

Cuff: The piece of fabric that extends beyond the palm of the hand. It can be flared in the case of gauntlets or close fitting.

Davey tip: A turned leather welt sewn on to the outseam to strengthen and protect the stitches.

Double fourchette: The gusset that fits inside two adjacent fingers—there are three per glove. This is used in conjunction with a quirk (see below).

English thumb: The pattern for the thumb is cut with the trank, which allows for better maneuverability of the thumb (also known as the Bolton thumb).

Fourchette: The single-piece gusset that runs between each finger of the glove to give shape and aid movement.

Glace (glazed) kid: Chrome-tanned goatskin and kidskin leather, in black or color that has a glazed finish.

Gore: An insert in the cuff that causes it to flare, usually triangular in shape.

Half prix/prick/pique seam: The seams on the glove back are sewn using this method, while seams on the glove front use a less expensive one.

Inseam: Where the gloves are stitched inside out, then turned through on completion. No stitches can be seen, and the seams are inside the glove.

Lining: Fabric added for added warmth, comfort, or ease of wear, and that should be attached to the fingertips.

Musquetaire: The opening on the inside of the wrist, which means that the hand can be removed from the glove while leaving the sleeve in place.

Outseam: With the seam on the outside of the finger.

Points: One or three decorative lines of stitching that run down the back of the trank from just below the base of the first, second, and third finger. The middle trank is always slightly longer than the others. Traditionally, the average lengths of these are 2½–3 in. (6–7 cm).

Prix/prick/pique seam: Where the right side of the material is facing outward and the edges are sewn together leaving a line of stitches and the raw edge visible. This type of seam is often used for heavier-weight leathers.

Quirk: Small, usually diamond-shaped gusset used in conjunction with the double fourchette. The quirk is fitted to the base of the adjoining fingers at the inside of the glove. The quirk allows for extra comfort/flexibility and better fit.

Quirk thumb: A separate thumb piece and quirk pattern are cut, assembled, and then sewn into the hole in the trank (also known as a French thumb).

Set-in thumb: Cut from a separate pattern piece that is sewn into the hole cut in the trank.

Single fourchette: The gusset used in value gloves can restrict movement and add bulk—six per glove.

Stays: Reinforced sections on the palm of the glove, often seen in sports gloves (also known as Hearts).

Thumb: This piece of the glove is cut separately from the trank.

Trank: This is the main part of the glove that consists of the front back and fingers.

Welt: A thin strip of leather sewn into the seam to strengthen it. A welt is sometimes used in the seam at the crotch of the thumb and the base of the finger.

BELTS

Aniline finish: A clear finish with little or no pigmentation.

Bandolier: A belt that is worn over one shoulder and across the body.

Belting butt: A double back with the tail cut off at the butt line.

Belting butt bend: A double bend with the tail cut off at the butt line.

Bend: A back with the shoulder cut off at right angles to the backbone line at the break of the fore flank.

Bridle leather: A harness-finished strap leather.

Cartridge: A decorative belt that features looped cylinders around the girth of the belt, inspired by a belt that originally held ammunition.

Chain belt: A belt made out of chain, often linked together by larger metal rings or loops of leather. They can be single, double, triple, or more stranded.

Cinch: A wide, tight belt worn around the waist, giving the impression of a narrow waist, also called a waspie.

Corset: A belt that mimics a corset—laced or buckled tightly to enhance the waist and give it the look of an hourglass silhouette.

Crew punch: A punch that cuts a slot in the leather through which the buckle prong passes.

Cummerbund: A pleated belt worn over the waistband of the trousers, originally menswear and worn with an evening suit/tuxedo. It fastens at the back and is often made from satin.

Double ring: An adjustable belt that is fastened by pulling the end of the belt through two rings. Often made in leather but can be a woven braid.

Edge beveler tool: A hand tool used for finishing the edges of vegetable-tanned or

bridle leather. There are many designs of edge beveler available that leave a range of different finishes to the edge.

Figure of eight: A very long belt that wraps twice around the body before being secured by a buckle.

Flat braided: A raw-edge flat braided leather belt, often made of vegetable-tanned leather.

Full grain: Having the original grain surface of the skin.

Harness leather: A self-explanatory term that sometimes includes collar and saddlery leathers. Harness leather, including these related items, is practically all made of vegetable-tanned cattle hides.

Iron: Term used for measuring thickness or sole leather; 1 iron equals $\frac{1}{48}$ in (0.5 mm).

Obi: A soft, supple, wide leather belt that wraps around the waist and the ends pass through the belt and tie either in the front or at the back. Inspired by the formal Japanese sash worn around a kimono.

Reversible: A dual-colored belt, one color on one side and a different color on the other with a buckle that twists, to allow choice.

Sam Browne: A thick leather belt with a thinner strap attached that is worn over one shoulder. Named after a British army general who lost an arm and couldn't draw his sword without the aid of this belt.

Sash: A belt that is often fabric or very soft napa leather. It has strands of thronging or braided leather and can be tied loosely, knotted, or tied in a bow.

Skinny: A very narrow belt less than ⅝ in. (1.5 cm) in width.

Slouch: Sits loosely on the hips, it contours by being curved, with the widest curve sitting on the hips.

Strap cutter: A hand tool used for cutting strips of leather (also known as a draw gauge).

Studded: A leather belt, heavily decorated with metal studs across the surface.

Top grain: The grain split of a hide from which nothing has been removed except the hair and associated epidermis.

Vegetable tannage: A generic term to cover the process of making leather by the use of tannins obtained from barks, woods, or other parts of plants and trees.

INDEX

CREDITS

Quarto would like to thank the following designers, agencies, and students for supplying images for inclusion in this book:

Accessorize 213
Adelaide Tam 54bl, 218bl
Alex Dowson 159
Ally Capellino 9bmr, 74, 89l/r, 118b, 204
Andreia Chaves 246
Andrew Meredith 40
Annemaj Modalal 46, 94bl
Anya Hindmarch 34ml, 78
Areti Phinkaridou 12
Barbara Aranguiz 4
Betty Bondo 23tr, 118t
Bora Kim 29
Borba Margo 9bml, 207, 209, 245
Caroline Morgan 208t/m
Catherine Vernon-Smith 59
Chau Har Lee 8bmr, 73tl, 232, 247
David Dooley 73
Diego Oliveira Reis 143
Emma Hancock 149
Eting Liu 69, 105tr,119tr
Felicity Thompson 26tl
Forever 21 34r
French Connection 34mr
Georgina Wray 23
Getty Images 32b, 34l, 79, 83, 124, 224, 239
Graham Thompson 212m
Harvey Santos 30bl
Holly Gaman 4br
Hugo Boss 94b
James Nisbet 19
Janice Rosenberg 58
Jee Hyun Jun 56, 157
Jeffrey Campbell 2, 9bl, 120
Jessica Hearnshaw 59tr, 90
Judy Bentinck 202
Julia Crew 27br, 28ml, 29tr, 48bl
Karen Henriksen Millinery 173, 188, 190bl, 192, 193
Keely Hunter 49, 172
Laura Amstein 8bml
Laura Apsit Livens 249
Laura Kirsikka Simberg 219

Leana Munroe 72, 251
Lucy Burke 102tl
Lucy Rowland 60
Lydia Tung 5tl, 51tr, 54tl, 88
Manolo Blahnik 33tl, 127
Marc Jacobs 33r, 128
Maria Del Mar Anotoli 28bl, 31, 55, 92tl, 93, 94bl
Min Kyung Song 149
Molly Pryke 10, 16, 27, 44, 52, 148, 157
Natalie Smith 43, 45tr/tl, 73, 75, 94tm, 95br
Noel Stewart 165, 176, 187, 199
Pantone 39t
Rachel Drener 175tr
Rex Features 82, 166
Rizvi Millinery 8br, 160, 248
Rob Goodwin 9br
Samira Shan 205br, 218tl
Samuel Shepherd 57t, 221
Sandra McClean 22, 156
Sarah Bailey for Aquascutum 4tr, p.94t, 205tr, 210tl, 211br, 212tl
Sonia Fullerton 61, 121.
Sophia Webster 139
Sophie Beale 11, 53, 56, 161, 173, 175tl, 180
Stella Arsenis 136, 143, 158
Stephen Jones 167
Tanya Chancellor 15, 48tl, 50, 92bl, 95tr, 211tr
Tariq Mahmoud 139, 148
Tracey Neuls Design 1, 130, 139 (white pair)
Photo courtesy of UAL 242
Vatinika Patmasingh 106, 107, 108tl
Victoria Spruce 72
Photo courtesy of WSA 235
Yegie Kim pages 12, 21, 70
Zara Gorman Ltd 174

All step-by-step and other images are the copyright of Quarto Publishing plc. While every effort has been made to credit contributors, Quarto would like to apologize should there have been any omissions or errors—and would be pleased to make the appropriate correction for future editions of the book.

We would also like to say a special thanks to Noel Palomo-Lovinski for contributing the style selector, and designers and brands sections; and to Christina Brodie for the deconstructed glove on page 213.

With thanks to Julia Crew, Sarah Day, Ian Goff, Tracey Kench, Pui Tsoi, and Tony Vrahimis at the London College of Fashion; Kirsten Scott and the millinery students at the Kensington and Chelsea College; and Sarah Keeling, Kathrin Lodes, and Shoko Yamaguchi for their contributions. Our thanks also to the designers who have offered us their support: Ally Capellino, Zara Gorman, Caroline Morgan, Yasmin Rizvi, and Noel Stewart.

Jane's thanks go to her husband Dave for his love and support.